49.50

DATE DUE

D1224222

CAREER OPPORTUNITIES in REAL ESTATE

CAREER OPPORTUNITIES in REAL ESTATE

THOMAS FITCH

Foreword by
DAVID J. NETTINA
Former President, Chief Financial Officer, and Chief Real Estate Officer
American Financial Realty Trust

Ferguson

An imprint of Infobase Publishing

Career Opportunities in Real Estate

Copyright © 2009 by Thomas Fitch

Ferguson
An imprint of Infobase Publishing
132 West 31st Street
New York NY 10001

Library of Congress Cataloging-in-Publication Data

Fitch, Thomas P.
  Career opportunities in real estate / Thomas Fitch ; foreword by David J. Nettina.
    p. cm. — (Career opportunities)
  Includes bibliographical references and index.
  ISBN-13: 978-0-8160-7186-9 (hbk. : alk. paper)
  ISBN-10: 0-8160-7186-1 (hbk. : alk. paper)
 1. Real estate business—Vocational guidance. I. Title.
  HD1375.F58 2009
  333.33023'73—dc22   2008018313

Ferguson books are available at special discounts when purchased in bulk quantities for businesses, associations, institutions, or sales promotions. Please call our Special Sales Department in New York at (212) 967-8800 or (800) 322-8755.

You can find Ferguson on the World Wide Web at http://www.ferguson.infobasepublishing.com

Cover design by Takeshi Takahashi

Printed in the United States of America

Bang Hermitage 10 9 8 7 6 5 4 3 2 1

This book is printed on acid-free paper.

CONTENTS

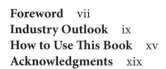

FOREWORD

by David J. Nettina

The breadth and scope of the real estate professional opportunities presented by this guidebook reflect an industry that is more exciting and dynamic than ever before in its history. Indeed, macro-market forces resulting from globalization, technical innovation, and the diversity and sophistication of the capital markets have resulted in revolutionary change. In turn, they have created an unprecedented demand for highly skilled professionals in traditional and emerging fields of real estate, as well as talent well versed in both the public and private sectors and the financial skill sets required by both. And, while a sole practitioner will still undertake the core, traditional activities of real estate acquisition, financing, and management, he or she will need at least a general understanding of many of the varied fields outlined within this book to operate both independently and successfully.

A good way to begin to organize and evaluate the numerous real estate career options you will read about here is to categorize them by your personal interests or personality type. For instance, someone who eschews the thought of cold-calling and negotiating would not likely be comfortable as a commercial leasing representative. But, if you have a keen interest in the environment, you might, in the alternative, find yourself a great career as an environmental scientist managing groundwater issues on a development project. So, simple though it may seem, knowing yourself is of huge value in prioritizing opportunities.

A second approach, let's call it the "bundled approach," is to look to your longer-term career objective—your end-game, if you will. Will you be a real estate entrepreneur? A public company CEO? A legal or financial professional? Then, envisage which broader-skill types of roles you would be prepared to take on that might serve as the building blocks toward that larger goal. For instance, it is common for real estate attorneys to move from the practice of law to the fields of development or leasing or investment banking. So too, accountants become corporate treasury or financing executives or investment bankers.

Unfortunately or fortunately, there is no one way—no one can tell you for sure what specific experience you will need in order to obtain your goal. In my career, I have found that over the course of several years the bundled approach has made it possible for me to develop a large-scale shopping mall, serve as the chief financial officer of private and public companies (having vastly different skill sets) and serve as a chief operating officer in multiple settings. There really is no one set winning model to identify and reach your long-term objective. But knowing yourself and determining your end-game are still a good idea. Start right here:

Creator/Entrepreneur: The maximum risk-taker in our industry is the developer or founder of the firm. This also is to whom the greatest financial rewards generally flow. The founder/entrepreneur takes the initial financial risk, either alone or in partnership with other investors to acquire or develop real estate. This is where the initial vision to develop, re-develop, or acquire a portfolio of real estate assets becomes reality. This entrepreneur needs not only a broad base of real estate knowledge, but must also have the courage to take risks. Founders come with many skill sets, but the key to their success are strong financial skills, complemented by construction or deal-making or other core skills.

If you are an entrepreneur, but have an inclination for one of the supporting fields in real estate, you may satisfy this need by being the founder of a supporting enterprise, such as one related to construction, real estate brokerage, and the like. You don't have to be the "all in" developer type to find entrepreneurial opportunity in the industry.

Manager/Operator: The scaling of real estate firms, as well as the growing dynamic of public ownership has led to the institutionalization of professional management. Leadership roles in these enterprises, whether President/CEO or other "C" level rank, require technical skills, as well as a general background in a number of supporting skill sets.

Contributor/Provider: These are the careers that can be entry level as well as highly specialized. For instance you may begin your career as a real estate attorney and become the real estate practice head. The financial rewards of the contributor/provider are substantive and the work can be as varied as your client base.

Ironically, while this book can familiarize you with the varied career opportunities in our industry and the likely pre-requisites to develop the necessary skills, there are intangibles that are keys to becoming successful. In fact, if you ask 20 people in our industry what they think makes for a successful real estate person you will likely get 20 different answers. And, don't discount luck and happenstance.

But, if I were asked to pick one trait or characteristic of the successful real estate person, it would be *persistence*. While working in the banking sector, I took advantage of a sudden opportunity to move to a large, rapidly growing private development firm. Outside the door of the company founder's office was a plaque engraved with the words "*press on*," which I came to understand to be the hallmark of our business. The regional mall development business is a complex and challenging real estate enterprise. Over the course of my tenure at this firm I would be responsible for modernizing its property management company, financing its new development activity, leading the development of a large regional mall, and engineering a financial turnaround during one of the worst real estate recessions in history. In all, but no less in the last role, I learned the value of the word *persistence*.

With a willingness to take on unrelated opportunities and the risks associated with them, I acquired many of the skills outlined in numerous career fields. This enabled me to move on and take on additional challenges, including leading a private company through a public offering and transition to the standards required to be a public company. Having acquired skills as a chief financial officer and chief operating officer in the public markets, I have been able to address many difficult issues, while instilling confidence in our people and investors that we would achieve our objectives.

Even having acquired the skill sets of several different career fields with relevant application to real estate, I found that *persistence* carried the day over the constant obstacles. Developing a large-scale real estate project has many roadblocks, which usually start with the challenge of convincing a local population that your project will not negatively impact the community, drain resources, or hurt local business. Government agencies must approve environmental and infrastructure impacts, a process than can move on a schedule much slower than yours. Key tenants have to be attracted. And, of course, the lifeblood of real estate, money (financing), must be secured. You will find yourself doing all of these things with a healthy amount of opposition, changing economic climates and other challenges. The only characteristic that will help you to prevail is *persistence*.

I have held a number of other high-level real estate positions since those days and have dealt with a host of other challenges. The one thing I could always count on was my early lesson when I first started out. So let me leave you with what Calvin Coolidge is credited with saying about *persistence*:

> Nothing in the world can take the place of persistence. Talent will not: nothing is more common than unsuccessful men with talent. Genius will not: the world is full of educated derelicts. Persistence and determination are omnipotent. The slogan *press on* has solved and always will solve the problems of the human race.

This is a great industry with dynamic and rewarding career opportunities. Those rewards are both financial and creative. Think expansively, keep your options open and be adaptive. The road ahead will be exciting.

—David J. Nettina
Former President, Chief Financial Officer, and
Chief Real Estate Officer
American Financial Realty Trust

INDUSTRY OUTLOOK

More than 5 million people in the United States make their living in real estate. At its pared down essence, the real estate industry is about selling, leasing, managing, and improving land. The range of occupations in real estate is as extensive as the types of property on the market today—covering everything from commercial, residential, and industrial properties to mixed-use properties developed for urban markets. People employed in real estate occupations provide the services necessary to support all these activities.

Sales and leasing of real estate is probably the largest occupational grouping. Most property offered for sale is sold with the help of an intermediary, a real estate broker. Residential real estate brokers account for eight out of every 10 jobs in real estate sales. Real estate is more than sales. Supporting the sales activities are people in related occupations, such as appraising, financing, and title searching. Beyond selling real estate there are careers in planning, developing, and managing properties. Expansion of financing activities to the secondary mortgage market, a trend developing over the past 20 to 30 years, has added a new series of occupations—real estate securities analysis and securities underwriting. Bundling commercial property loans into securities to be sold to insurance companies and other investors is a common practice in today's real estate market. The popularity of real estate investment trusts (REITs) as a financing tool is another factor influencing the industry's future.

The evolving picture of real estate finance raises an important question: How is real estate holding up compared to other sectors of the U.S. economy? The Yale School of Management, in an industry review, says real estate as an industry has been doing quite well across the country. Residential real estate, buoyed by a record-setting surge in home values and affordable financing from 2002-05, has led the industry, but other real estate sectors are holding their own in most regions of the country.

While real estate has gone through some dramatic changes, as noted above, the industry itself is slow to change. The industry is dominated by a large number of very small firms and a relative handful of very large companies. Many of today's largest real estate developers are also property owners and managers. At the opposite end of the scale are thousands of independently owned and managed real estate brokerage, appraisal, and real estate service firms.

Real estate is a cyclical industry, rising or falling in step with the overall economy. Employment prospects through 2014 are expected to keep pace with growth in real estate development across the country. The nation's continuing need to develop new housing units, shopping centers, and mixed-use properties will determine the employment picture in real estate. In the near term, looking out over the next two to three years, much is riding on the housing market's ability to engineer a turnaround from the collapse in house prices following several years of double-digit growth in home values. Looking beyond that, the employment picture in real estate remains relatively bright.

Real Estate as an Asset Class

Over the past decade, the real estate industry has become more global in scope. What was once a very fragmented business dominated by private equity firms, independent real estate entrepreneurs, has shifted to become a mixture of small private equity firms and very large investor-owed development and management companies. These large companies operate much like any other capital-intensive industry group. This transformation has also fostered significant changes in methods of capital formation by public and private equity real estate companies, real estate investment trusts, and real estate funds catering to the needs of institutional investors. For owners and users of corporate real estate, real estate has emerged as a strategic asset. Real estate owners have attempted to centralize their cost management to bring greater efficiencies to the core business. There has also been a trend toward outsourcing of back office support functions such as accounting, tax management, and record keeping.

The capital structure of the industry, that is, the way real estate projects are financed, has also seen dramatic changes in recent years. Real estate investment trusts have become major sources of capital for both acquisition and development. The total market capitalization of public REITs has grown from $10 billion in 1991 to more than $312 billion in 150 plus REITs as of December 31, 2007.

Accompanying this shift in financing is a slow whittling away of the old-boy network and back room deals for which real estate was famous. With public ownership through REITs and other financing vehicles came greater market transparency—information about real estate financing suddenly was more easily obtained. The entry of REITs and deal financing by Wall Street investment banks had a stabilizing effect on the industry and gave developers an alternative to commercial bank financing.

REITs have also played a prominent role in the globalization of real estate. According to Ernst & Young's 2007 Global REIT Report, the world outside North America has for the first time overtaken Canada and the United States as measured by the total number of REITs in operation. As of June 30, 2007, there were 253 REITs operating in Germany, the United Kingdom, Japan, Hong Kong, and other nations, versus 195 in North America. Only one year earlier, North American REITs numbered 253 compared to 198 around the rest of the world.

Structure of the Industry

Real Estate Sales and Leasing: Real estate sales and leasing covers one of the largest employment sectors in the industry. Included here is everything from residential real estate sales to commercial and industrial property leasing. This sector has two very large categories of real estate professionals: real estate sales agents and real estate brokers. Generally speaking, sales agents work directly with consumers, and brokers supervise agents. Real estate brokers can also handle property sales, but they have more broadly defined responsibilities and must pass a different set of licensing exams.

In a typical residential property sale, the sales agent solicits property listings from homeowners to sell their homes and shows the property to buyers interested in buying the listed property. Real estate brokers assist agents by providing branding, advertising, and other services that help sales agents complete transactions. The broker may create his or her own brand or affiliate with a national (or regional) franchisor that offers marketing support through a recognized brand name such as Century 21, Prudential, or Re/Max. While franchised brokers often receive help in training sales staff and running their offices, they bear the ultimate responsibility for the success or failure of their firms. Some real estate brokers work exclusively with home buyers; they typically try to find housing from the available listed properties, provide buyers with information about comparable home sales, and may also help buyers in becoming pre-qualified up to a certain level of financing. These brokers are known as "buyer's brokers" or "cooperating brokers."

Real estate brokers and sales agents held about 564,000 jobs in 2006, according to the U.S. Bureau of Labor Statistics. Sales agents held approximately 77 percent of these jobs.

Most real estate brokerage firms are small, independently owned and managed companies, according to the National Association of Realtors (NAR). Seventy-three percent of real estate firms report their full-time sales licensees are independent contractors, according to NAR's 2006 Profile of Real Estate Firms. Many are part-time sales agents, combining their real estate activities with other careers.

Independent contractors also dominate in commercial real estate sales. Sixty-one percent of commercial brokerage firms say that all of their full-time and part-time sales licensees are independent, self-employed contractors. Commercial real estate brokerage firms work for landlords, tenants, and buyers or sellers of commercial real estate. They assist clients by locating properties matching their requirements, negotiating the best terms on behalf of their clients, and managing the sales or leases to ensure that the agreed-upon terms are enforced at contract signing. Typically, commercial real estate brokerage is a 100 percent commission-only business, so it is a high risk, high reward career.

Real Estate Management: Real estate management is the administration, operation, marketing, and maintenance of real property to achieve the goals of the property owner. These goals typically include such things as maintaining occupancy rates, achieving a specific return on investment, and maintaining property values through scheduled maintenance and repairs. Specific jobs generally fall into three categories: site manager or facility manager, property manager, and real estate asset management.

Site managers work with residential properties such as apartments, cooperatives, or condominiums. If they live on-site they are known as "resident managers." Site managers oversee the day-to-day operations of a property, handling technical operations such as electrical or mechanical systems and relations with current and potential tenants. The site manager plays a central role in collection of rents, marketing to prospective tenants, income and expense recordkeeping, and financial reporting to the property owners.

Property managers are a middleman, or liaison, between the actual property owner and the on-site manager. They maintain close contact with the site managers and oversee day-to-day operations of the site managers and other employees doing work contracted by the property management firm. The property manager follows a management plan approved by the property owner; this plan covers all aspects of the physical plant, financial operations, tenant relations, market positioning, and community image building. Of all the segments in real estate, property management has been hardest hit by the wave of mergers and acquisitions sweeping the industry over the past 10 years. For job seekers, this means fewer opportunities with locally owned and managed property management firms. Best opportunities may be found with the very large property management firms active in one or more

industry sectors, such as office buildings or apartment complexes.

Real estate asset managers deal with real estate as a financial asset. Some people refer to asset management as a numbers game. Asset managers focus their attention on managing a property (or a portfolio of properties) as an investment. They look for activities that will add value to each property under management, with an eye toward long-term capital appreciation as well as short-term cash flow, according to the National Association of Industrial and Office Properties, an industry trade group. Typically, financial performance goals are laid out by the asset manager and then carried out by the property manager.

Asset management is an emerging field in real estate. Specific job responsibilities of an asset manager can vary tremendously, depending on the property owner and the type of real estate owned. But generally, asset managers are involved in all phases of a property's life cycle, from property acquisition or purchase and day-to-day operations management all the way to eventual sale to another owner or investor. Asset managers have to pay close attention to changing market opportunities, demographic or economic factors, and any financial market activity potentially impacting borrowing costs and financial performance.

Real estate managers are employed by any of the following: property management firms, sometimes referred to as fee managers because they collect a fee for management services; full-service real estate companies, firms that offer a side range of professional services; real estate development firms, which have a property management staff for company-owned properties; commercial banks, which often function as equity partners in addition to providing mortgage financing; real estate investment trusts, which employ asset managers to evaluate portfolio acquisitions; or public or private corporations, which often have substantial real estate holdings. Government agencies, insurance companies, colleges, and universities employ property managers and site managers to oversee their directly owned properties.

Real Estate Development: Real estate developers work in one of the most challenging areas in real estate—taking a property idea and making it a reality. This is a high risk, high reward occupation.

This is a very complex process, involving a large number of professionals: architects, engineers, zoning officials, builders, commercial lenders, and prospective tenants. The development process involves managing labor, managing money, and overseeing construction crews. Development is quite possibly the most competitive—and most volatile—part of the real estate industry.

When financing is cheap and readily available, developers rush to bring their projects to market. When the credit supply begins to dry up, as occurred in the early 1990s after several years of commercial sector over-building and again in the credit crunch of 2007-08 when lenders began tightening credit terms following a collapse in the subprime mortgage market, developers reacted by scaling back on new projects. In the 1990s, commercial real estate prices crashed, and developers ventured into other areas of real estate. Many of the largest real estate developers today are also property owners and managers.

Commercial property developers, aside from the very large publicly owned companies, are typically privately owned companies. These firms often bring in outside equity partners to finance the project. People entering real estate development generally start out as analysts doing market research and feasibility studies. After learning how to analyze projects, they typically are assigned to work on a specific project where they have frequent contact with investors, attorneys, and the project design team during the design and construction phase of a development project.

On the residential side of the market, home builders create and develop residential communities. This is another very entrepreneurial business where the risks and rewards are high. Constructing homes is a multi-disciplinary business by nature, involving a high degree of cooperation by various professionals. Home builders work closely with design consultants, local planning and zoning officers, community members, and bank lenders supplying project financing. The home building industry is also highly regulated. Home builders must file for approvals for environmental impacts, growth management, or meeting other statutory requirements. Home builders can be locally managed developers who acquire land and gain approval to sub-divide into smaller building lots, or at the other extreme,

large publicly owned companies which acquire land, construct, and sell the homes.

Real Estate Acquisition and Analysis: The emergence of real estate as a legitimate asset class (in addition to common stocks, cash, and bonds) has created a whole new series of occupational titles. Any investing in real estate requires a thorough understanding of how to analyze the value of a property, zoning laws, environmental impact studies, and any other regulations standing in the way of buying and developing a piece of property. Real estate professionals who develop and manage real estate investment trusts and other real estate investments are highly skilled financial types, who typically have an advanced degree—an M.B.A., a master's degree in real estate, or a combination of post-graduate education and on-the-job experience.

Included in this category are real estate investment bankers. The investment bankers stand at the intersection between the real estate markets (Main Street) and the capital markets (Wall Street). They provide corporate finance services and strategic advice to other real estate professionals. Publicly traded REITs and real estate operating companies provide a sizable portion of the client base, which also includes large privately owned real estate companies and financial investors (pension funds, for instance) in real estate opportunity funds. Typical transactions include commercial mortgage-backed securities (CMBS) financings, corporate bond offerings, public equity offerings (including initial public offerings or IPOs), equity private placements, and advising clients on the purchase or sale of real estate companies or portfolios.

These financings are often very complex. Investment banks typically have real estate finance divisions that employ mortgage loan originators and underwriters who originate loans the bank intends to sell to capital market investors, as well as investment bankers who manage the securitization process. In a CMBS financing, for instance, the bankers managing the process typically take between 100 and 200 loans, package them together in a public offering of securities, and then sell the bonds to various investors. The bonds are assigned a credit rating by a bond rating agency. Entry level positions include working in loan originations, and project management. More senior level investment bankers oversee the securitization process and work closely with both the origination staff and the sales desk, which has responsibility for distributing the bonds to investors.

Some Notable Trends

Real estate, much like other industries, is influenced by political and environmental forces—one of these being the rise of "green" building and construction. Higher energy costs and concerns about the impact of global warming have led developers and property managers to become more energy efficient. This trend is noticeable in both residential and commercial construction. The National Association of Home Builders (NAHB) announced in 2008 a national green building program designed to give builders an incentive to build environmentally friendly homes. Builders can achieve certifications they can advertise to the public. The NAHB says green building can add up to $38 billion in home sales by 2010, accounting for 10 percent of U.S. housing starts by 2010, up from a 2 percent market share in 2007. Homeowners trade higher up-front costs, as much as 3–5 percent of the total cost of a home construction, for higher energy savings.

Major home builders are going green for the first time or are expanding existing programs. Previously, environmentally friendly home building was limited to a niche market of smaller builders. Selling homes with Energy Star rated energy efficient appliances, better insulation, and solar panels is becoming a big business—a bigger part of the home construction industry. The U.S. Green Building Council promotes energy efficient design and construction through its Leadership in Energy and Environmental Design (LEED) program. The program assigns various ratings such as Gold LEED certification or Platinum certification, its highest rating, to building projects utilizing solar photovoltaic panels for generating electric power, on-site water conservation, or other recommended guidelines for energy consumption.

General Employment Trends

Professional occupations and service-related occupations account for an increasing share of the U.S. economy. As real estate is largely a service industry, an increase in overall employment means additional hiring in real estate occupations. Professional and related occupations and service occupations—two occupational groups on opposite ends of the educational and earnings ranges—are projected to account for more than six out of 10 jobs created over the 2006-16 period, according to the U.S. Bureau of Labor Statistics. The Bureau projects total employment will increase by 15.6 million jobs during this decade, slightly less than the 15.9 million jobs created in the previous decade. As Baby Boomer generation workers enter their retirement years, a sizable number of job openings will occur as employers replace people retiring or voluntarily leaving the work force.

The industry's approach to recruitment and hiring has changed very little in recent years, despite the introduction of Internet job boards and search engines. Employers tend to hire through informal networks and do very little recruiting through college campus tours, so having the right connections is very important. Real estate is very much a "who you know" world.

Looking at the broader employment picture, career opportunities in most real estate occupations are expected to maintain pace with employment growth in other industries, according to the U.S. Bureau of Labor Statistics (BLS). Real estate professionals often say their industry is built from the ground up; their attention is always focused on local markets when it comes to development.

The emphasis on education will continue. While the economy will generate jobs at all educational levels, employment opportunities will be greatest in occupations in which an associate's degree or higher is required. Individuals with a four-year degree or higher or a four-year degree with related work experience will, according to BLS data, have the greatest number of job opportunities to choose from in a job search. People with post-graduate degrees in real estate can often have their pick of employment opportunities, and at higher salaries. Job candidates with a master's degree in real estate, for instance, are reportedly commanding salaries 20 percent higher than M.B.A. graduates.

Real estate is one industry in which a portfolio of skills, both technical and interpersonal, can pay big dividends. This is particularly true in occupations where there is a high level of personal contact with clients and prospects, such as real estate development or property management. While a college education is becoming the entry level for most of the positions profiled in this book, there is a general caveat: skills that are specific to one real estate market aren't necessarily transferable to other markets.

The real estate industry's continuing need for people with the financial skills to evaluate development deals or potential acquisitions has created something of a talent shortage in many areas. U.S.-based property management and development firms are extending their reach globally, a trend evident since 2000 but more recently accelerating, straining their front line resources. Some of the largest global services companies are attempting to meet the challenge by creating in-house talent and employee development services.

This talent gap is particularly severe in emerging markets such as China and India, and also in parts of the European Union. Recruiting and retaining talented workers is a front-burner issue in North America as well. The Real Estate Roundtable, an industry group of senior executives from America's top publicly and privately owned real estate entities, reports that finding, hiring, and retaining qualified employees is a major issue for real estate development and property management firms.

Summary of Opportunities

Career opportunities across the spectrum of the real estate industry are expected to increase moderately over the next five to 10 years. Some of the best opportunities for college graduates are in commercial real estate, where there is a growing talent shortage for experienced facility managers and project managers. Corporate real estate operators are reporting strong hiring of asset managers—people who can control expenses and efficiently manage a group of properties. Also in demand are financial analysts who have a firm understanding of real estate fundamentals and are also fluent in financial reporting.

As real estate has emerged as an asset class in its own right, big investors like corporate pension funds want to interact with people who can easily communicate their bottom line results in the language understood by professional investors. Job candidates with advanced degrees in business or finance are getting a priority look. There are many niche markets in commercial real estate, all with a growing need for talented professionals. Regardless of the specific needs of any position, people entering the market today need a blended set of skills—a combination of professional expertise and "soft skills" or people skills to be competitive in the market.

On the residential real estate front, there will always be opportunities for enterprising individuals who want to build a career in real estate sales—regardless of the outcome of the credit crunch of 2007-08 and the collapse of the housing market bubble. The same can be said for the independent real estate entrepreneur adept at sniffing out underpriced properties and patient enough to hold on for the long term. In sum, there are probably more opportunities in real estate today than at any time in recent memory. A sampling of these opportunities is profiled in the pages that follow.

HOW TO USE THIS BOOK

The job descriptions in this book provide an overview and discussion of 74 positions in real estate development, finance, property management, and sales. They are divided into eight categories: Accounting and Finance, Administration, Construction, Development, Lending-Underwriting, Property Management, Sales and Marketing, and Other Careers Related to Real Estate.

Employers often have different job descriptions for the same position, so there can be wide differences in position responsibilities from one employer to another. A company's size, organizational structure, management style, and other factors determine specific job requirements—the duties an employee is expected to perform. The position descriptions on the following pages are intended as generic descriptions, based on publicly available information and interviews with industry experts. Each entry is organized as follows.

Career Profile

The entry begins with a section that briefly summarizes key aspects of the position—its essential purpose, including duties performed, salary range, employment and advancement opportunities, experience, skills, and personality traits. If state licensing or industry certification is an entry requirement, these special requirements are also noted. The Career Profile presents a precise summary of the major facts in the full text. This up-front summary includes the following:

- *Duties:* A brief synopsis of the major responsibilities of the position profiled

- *Alternate Title(s):* Commonly used additional titles for the position. These alternate titles are often used interchangeably.
- *Employment Prospects* and *Advancement Prospects*: This is a rating of the overall opportunities for entry or advancement. The ratings—Excellent, Good, Fair, or Poor—indicate the chances for employment or advancement in terms of job competition, supply and demand, relative turnover, and the total number of available jobs. These ratings may be interpreted as follows: *Excellent*: demand greater than supply or high job turnover, indicative of positions or job specialties with highest market demand; *Good*: demand somewhat greater than supply, opportunities likely to grow faster than opportunities in all industries; *Fair*: demand and supply balance out, about average employment opportunities; *Poor*: supply greater than demand or low job turnover, may indicate a need for specialized skills. The ratings are a subjective evaluation by the author, based on published industry research, interviews with professionals in the occupation, or the viewpoints of industry observers.
- *Prerequisites:* A listing of four sets of criteria for job entry, including Education—minimum education for entry or preferred education; Experience—length of service or type of work generally required for entry; Special Skills and Personality Traits—major attributes or personality traits often useful for obtaining the job; and Special Requirements—state licensing requirements or professional certifications required to perform the job.

Career Ladder

This indicates the location of a position within a typical career path. In most career profiles the position described is the middle one, sandwiched between a more junior position and an advanced position. The positions listed in the Career Ladder indicate the most common or direct routes to employment. There are many variables to a career path and the positions listed in the Career Ladder are not the only ones. The jobs in the lower rung of the career ladder are usually referred to in the Employment Prospects or Experience/Skills sections of the career profile. Positions in the upper rung of the ladder are usually discussed in the section on Advancement Prospects. Note that not all positions in the career path are discussed separately in the book.

Position Description

This is the longest part of the position profile and it describes the nature of the work. It presents an overview of the position's major responsibilities, the typical workplace environment, the reporting line, and the range of activities performed. Individuals usually perform many, though not all, of the position functions listed in the Position Description. Actual duties performed will vary according to employer, industry sector, and the exact requirements for the position. Bulleted lists are often used to summarize important tasks or concentrations.

Salary Range

This is an approximate indication of what an individual may expect to earn in this position. In most position profiles the lower figure is the midpoint salary, the salary earned by approximately 50 percent of individuals in that position, while the higher figure is the salary earned by those in the 75 percent quartile. Highly experienced individuals or highly compensated individuals often earn considerably more. The salary range is best used as an indication of the relative value of the position compared to other positions profiled. Actual starting salaries are determined by academic training, years of experience, industry credentials, employer size and location, and also by the number of qualified applicants for any position. When salaries are dependent on

achieving specific education goals, such as continuing education to maintain job skills, that information is also included. Fringe benefits, commissions, and performance bonuses are included when that information is relevant or helpful.

Salary information comes from the U.S. Bureau of Labor Statistics or from salary surveys performed by professional associations, compensation consulting firms, executive search firms, or other organizations.

Employment Prospects

The entry rating in the Career Profile is expanded here. Opportunities for employment are reviewed in terms of the estimated number of positions available nationally, employment turnover, and demand for special skills. This section describes the job outlook today—the probability of being hired—as well as the outlook in the future. If a position has above average employment growth over the next several years, the employment opportunities are highlighted in this section. This section usually states whether individuals are recruited directly from high school or college or from other industry positions. Entry routes and probabilities of getting a job are discussed at length. Employment outlook information comes from the U.S. Bureau of Labor Statistics or from various industry sources.

Advancement Prospects

This section describes the opportunities to move up the career ladder from the position profiled. The typical advancement paths, such as advancing into management or to alternative career paths, are discussed here. The possibilities for advancement are discussed in terms of turnover at the next level, special skills, or experience requirements in more senior positions, as well as other career tracks available to an individual.

Education and Training

This section covers the level of education or training likely to be required by prospective employers, such as high school graduate, two-year college (associate degree), four-year college (B.A. or B.S. degree), or graduate degree (for example, a master's degree in real estate, or an M.B.A. degree). The minimum education or training requirements are noted, as well as employer-provided training after the date of hire. Required courses, certifications, and recommended degrees are included where appropriate or recommended. Complementing the Education Section, Appendix I contains a list of colleges and universities offering relevant degree and non-degree programs, training courses, and seminars.

Most of the positions described in the book require at least a high school education. Some positions do not require any formal education beyond high school, such as real estate sales agent or real estate entrepreneur. However, many real estate agents and brokers have taken college-level courses or have two-year or four-year college degrees. Many of the more specialized positions, such as real estate financial analyst, portfolio manager, project manager, or asset manager, do require a four-year degree or an advanced degree. The more training or education an individual acquires, the easier it is to obtain a position in one of these challenging but fast growing occupations in real estate.

Experience, Skills, and Personality Traits

Experience, job skills, and personality traits are often as important to a career in real estate as formal education. This section summarizes the intangible abilities and social skills that are most important for success in the position profiled. If prior employment in a related position or internship is helpful, this information is included. There is also some indication of the kind of personality most suited for the work; this should be taken as only a suggestion, not a recommendation.

Special Requirements

This section describes any state licenses an individual is normally expected to attain in order to qualify for the position, or licensing an individual is expected to achieve within a specified time period after being hired.

Unions and Associations

Many people involved in real estate advance their careers and enhance their professional growth through membership in professional associations. The associations or professional groups most often associated with the position profiled are mentioned here. More information about these trade associations, including phone and fax numbers and Web sites, can be found in Appendix II—Professional Associations and Organizations.

Tips for Entry

This final section gives a series of suggestions that can help an individual prepare for entry into the position. The first suggestions are geared to high school or college students who are still choosing courses, internships, or work-study opportunities. Later suggestions give pointers for gaining work experience for the résumé, and, eventually, entry level positions.

Other Resources in This Book

The appendixes that follow the job descriptions contain additional resources that can help in selecting a college or university offering courses of study in real estate, land plans and urban planning, or construction management; obtaining a real estate license; contacting professional associations; or conducting a job search.

Appendix I lists colleges and universities offering two-year, four-year and graduate degree programs and non-degree certificate programs.
Appendix II contains a list of professional associations and organizations.
Appendix III contains a list of professional certifications.
Appendix IV contains a list of professional real estate periodicals.
Appendix V contains a list of major real estate management firms.
Appendix VI contains a list of state real estate brokerage and sales agent licensing agencies.
Appendix VII contains a list of real estate research organizations.
Appendix VIII has information on planning your career in real estate.

ACKNOWLEDGMENTS

The author wishes to recognize professional associations and organizations that provided research materials, salary information, job descriptions, employment surveys, and other documents for the preparation of this book. The contributions of the following are gratefully acknowledged: American Escrow Association; American Institute of Architects; American Institute of Certified Public Accountants; American Institute of Constructors; American Institute of Professional Bookkeepers; American Institute of Real Estate Appraisers; American Land Title Association; American Planning Association; American Securitization Forum; American Society of Home Inspectors; American Society of Landscape Architects; Appraisal Foundation; The Appraisal Institute; Association of Real Estate License Law Officials; Building Owners and Managers Institute; California Escrow Association; CCIM Institute; CEL & Associates, Inc.; Commercial Mortgage Securities Association; Community Associations Institute; Construction Management Association; CoreNet Global; The Counselors of Real Estate; Institute of Management Accounting; Institute of Real Estate Management; International Association for Advancement of Cost Engineering; International Association of Assessor Officers; International Association of Shopping Centers; International Facility Management Association; International Maintenance Institute; The International Relocation Association; International Right of Way Association; Mortgage Bankers Association of America; National Affordable Housing Management Association; National Apartment Association; National Association of Certified Home Inspectors; National Association of Exclusive Buyers Agents; National Association of Home Builders; National Association of Home Inspectors; National Association of Housing and Redevelopment Officials; National Association of Industrial and Office Property Managers; National Association of Legal Assistants; National Association of Mortgage Brokers; National Association of Professional Surveyors; National Association of Real Estate Investment Managers; National Association of Real Estate Managers; National Association of Real Estate Professionals; National Association of Realtors; National Association of State Boards of Accountancy; National Center for Housing Management; National Federation of Paralegal Associations; National Investor Relations Institute; Pension Real Estate Association; Public Housing Authority Directors Association; Risk and Insurance Management Society; Society of Cost Estimating and Analysis; Society of Industrial and Office Realtors; Society of Real Estate Appraisers; Specialty Consultants, Inc.; TOTAL LLC; U.S. Bureau of Labor Statistics; Urban Land Institute; Worldwide ERC.

Thanks also to David Nettina, who offered numerous suggestions and improvements to the job profiles on the pages that follow. Thanks also to my editor, Sarah Fogarty, and the staff at Facts On File for their tireless efforts in guiding this book from concept to publication.

ACCOUNTING AND FINANCE

COMMERCIAL REAL ESTATE CREDIT ANALYST

CAREER PROFILE

Duties: Develops and analyzes financial and accounting information relating to borrowers' financial condition; prepares and maintains credit standings of current borrowers; furnishes information in response to credit inquiries

Alternate Title(s): Commercial Real Estate Analyst, Real Estate Finance Credit Analyst

Salary Range: $45,000 to $60,000 and up

Employment Prospects: Good

Advancement Prospects: Good

Prerequisites:

    Education or Training—Four-year degree with concentration in accounting, business, or finance

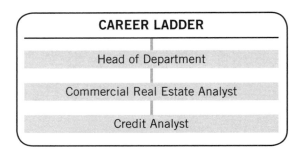

    Experience—Two to five years' experience in commercial real estate

    Special Skills and Personality Traits—Working knowledge of commercial real estate underwriting

Position Description

Commercial Real Estate Credit Analysts evaluate credit quality of mortgages, commercial loans, and consumer loans and assign risk ratings. They perform in-depth credit analysis of new and existing real estate financings. They evaluate the credit risk associated with office buildings and other commercial properties. They develop and analyze financial and accounting information relating to borrowers' financial condition, prepare and maintain credit standing reports of current borrowers, and respond to credit inquiries from banks or real estate investors. They work with the real estate transaction team from the initial bid, or loan request, to loan closing and approval by the loan committee. They assist other members of the lender's credit department and loan officers.

Credit analysts also examine loan portfolios for compliance with internal or external credit and risk management guidelines. They work in the audit department or credit department of financial institutions and commercial finance companies. They perform due diligence financial analysis of borrower-submitted information to determine how much the bank can reasonably lend, based on the borrower's credit history, collateral, and ability to repay. They prepare executive summaries for presentation to the loan underwriting team or to the loan committee.

Credit analysts identify problem loans, such as past-due loans and loans with insufficient collateral. They write up a summary of their analysis if loan repayment becomes doubtful and report these findings to the bank's asset-liability committee, senior loan committee, and board of directors. They may also act as senior credit analysts and coordinate credit reviews of commercial loans. Banks rely on the data gathered by the loan review analyst in calculating their loan loss reserves (funds set aside to cover possible loan losses) as required by federal banking regulations.

Commercial Real Estate Credit Analysts may do any or all of the following:

- review preliminary financing packages, perform cash flow analysis, and structure financing
- participate in property inspections with the underwriting team, assisting in evaluating a specific property, its competition and the overall market
- assist the underwriter in drafting a narrative describing the asset, location, market, financial performance, and borrower's business plan
- evaluate third-party reports on property condition, environment, and property appraisal to identify potential issues or areas requiring further investigation
- perform ad hoc analysis and other reports as requested by the loan underwriting team
- provide analytical support for deal origination and new business development

Commercial credit analysts work in an office setting and typically work long hours. A 40- to 50-hour work-week is typical. Occasional travel may be required to inspect a borrower's property or examine loan collateral.

Salaries

Salaries of Commercial Real Estate Credit Analysts usually range from $45,000 a year for individuals starting their career to $60,000 or more. Analysts employed in the larger banks, which typically approve the multi-million dollar loans to real estate developers, can earn $100,000 or more. They may also earn a performance bonus tied to the success of the department or the lender's overall performance and return on assets in a particular year.

Employment Prospects

Employment opportunities will grow as the economy expands, increasing the demand for workers with financial expertise. There are ample employment opportunities for individuals with some experience in a credit analysis, commercial lending, or loan collection and loan workout. Some financial institutions hire recent college graduates as trainees for entry-level positions in loan analysis or loan review departments.

However, the job market for credit analysts is very competitive. The number of job openings is expected to be less than the number of applicants. Candidates with expertise in accounting and finance, particularly those with a master's degree, should enjoy the best job prospects.

The real estate market is very cyclical, tending to expand or contract in step with the overall economy. This economic linkage may cut into employment opportunities for credit analysts, as happened during the 2007–08 "credit crunch"—a period when banks curtailed their lending activity to limit their potential write-offs stemming from overbuilding in the residential housing market.

Advancement Prospects

Commercial loan analysts can advance to management positions, such as manager of the loan review department. Other advancement options might be moving to positions of increased responsibility, such as loan workout manager or manager of the credit and collections department. Advancement to more senior positions may require upgrading job skills to stay current with industry trends and changes in banking regulation. Credit analysts can improve their advancement prospects by taking continuing education courses or getting an advanced degree. Many firms pay all or part of the costs for employees who successfully complete a post-graduate academic program. Although experience, ability, and leadership are emphasized for promotion, advancement can be accelerated by having an advanced degree. Some higher level positions may require a master's degree in finance, risk management, or a related area.

Education and Training

A bachelor's degree in finance, accounting, or a related field of study is the foundation academic preparation for a career as a credit analyst. Recently, however, employers increasingly seek graduates with a master's degree in business administration, economics, finance, or risk management. These academic programs develop analytical skills and provide knowledge of the latest financial analysis methods and technology.

Continuing education is vital for financial managers, who must cope with changes in federal and state laws and regulations and new financial instruments. Firms often provide opportunities for workers to broaden their knowledge and skills by encouraging employees to take graduate courses at colleges and universities or attend conferences related to their specialty. Some colleges and universities offer distance learning, or online, graduate degree programs, which may be an option for those who want to upgrade their skills while holding down a full-time job.

Experience, Skills, and Personality Traits

Individuals should have at least one year's experience in commercial underwriting, depending on the specific position requirements, or related work experience. Good decision-making skills and problem-solving skills are essential in this position. Some prior experience as a loan officer or loan workout officer working on delinquent or past-due loans is a good stepping stone to a career as a credit analyst. Some experience in multifamily or federally insured residential loans, hotel, and mixed-use development can be very useful background.

Credit analysts need to have excellent written and verbal communication skills, as they often are required to make presentations to a loan committee comprised of senior loan officers.

Analysts should be detail-oriented, with in-depth analytical aptitude and strong knowledge of Excel spreadsheet program and ARGUS real estate database software.

Unions and Associations

Commercial credit analysts can become members of several professional associations, including CoreNet

Global and banking associations such as the American Bankers Association for networking and career advancement opportunities.

Tips for Entry

1. Get some on-the-job experience in banking by working part-time in a branch office or loan department while attending college.
2. Take courses in accounting, business administration, or finance or courses to improve your computer skills working with spreadsheet accounting programs.
3. Check out job opportunities on the Internet by visiting the Bank Administration Institute's career center (http://www.BankJobSearch.com) or the American Bankers Association's career website (http://aba.careersite.com).

FINANCE DIRECTOR

Duties: Responsible for fund-raising and capital market activities, banking relationships, financial engineering and deal structuring; may participate in start-up of investment funds

Alternate Title(s): Financial Officer, Real Estate Financial Manager

Salary Range: $131,000 to $190,000

Employment Prospects: Good

Advancement Prospects: Good

Prerequisites:

    Education or Training—Four-year degree in accounting, finance, or a related field of study

    Experience—Five to seven years' commercial real estate or public accounting experience

    Special Skills and Personality Traits—Strong financial modeling and communication skills;

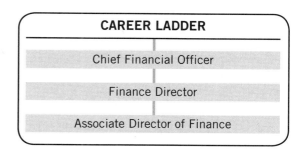

strong knowledge of financial analysis and general accounting principles; excellent supervisory skills

    Special Requirements—Professional certification, such as Certified Public Accountant, recommended or required

Position Description

The Finance Director is an advisor to senior management on many fronts: fund-raising and capital market activities, banking relationships, financial engineering, and deal structuring. These officers also play a key role by assisting in structuring investment funds. The Finance Director reviews the investment portfolio and analyzes the best ways to raise money to buy more properties.

The role of the Finance Director is changing in response to technological advances that have significantly reduced the amount of time it takes to produce financial reports. They perform more data analysis and use it to offer senior managers ideas on how to maximize profits. Finance Directors play an important role in mergers and consolidations, global expansion, and related financing. These areas require extensive, specialized knowledge to reduce risks and maximize profit.

Their primary duties include planning activities in support of a company's strategic growth plan and forecasted profitability or loss. These managers provide financial insight and analysis to identify business issues, risks, and profitability opportunities. They give analytical support for new business initiatives, offer recommendations to solve problems, and perform cost/benefit analyses on proposed ventures or acquisitions. Finance Directors and their associates are responsible for due diligence on new acquisitions, accounting reviews, and

accounting reports to senior management and financial regulatory agencies.

In performing their duties, Finance Directors will:

- analyze and identify new investment opportunities
- create financial models in Excel
- work closely with borrowers, real estate brokers, and financial partners
- prepare and analyze market surveys
- conduct property visits and market tours
- provide analytical support for special projects
- perform due diligence reviews as required by senior management
- prepare investment memorandums for senior management and the board of directors

Finance Directors work long hours in an office environment, typically 50 to 60 hours a week. Financial managers are on the road regularly, visiting affiliated companies, business partners, and customers. They are frequent participants in industry conferences and educational seminars.

Salaries

Finance Directors are well compensated for their long hours. Finance Directors earned base salaries of $131,000 to $190,000 in 2006, according to a salary survey by CEL & Associates, Inc., a real estate consulting firm specializing in compensation. This is well above the median salary of financial managers in all occupations. In addition to salary, Finance Directors typically receive an annual incentive bonus or performance bonus averaging one-third of their base salary. Finance Directors also receive a standard benefit package of company-funded health insurance, life insurance, paid vacations, and employee retirement plan.

Employment Prospects

Demand for Finance Directors with commercial real estate experience or public accounting experience will remain strong over the next several years. The long-run prospects are very favorable because more people will be needed to handle financial transactions and manage complex investment structures, which are fairly common in real estate. Some companies hire financial managers on a temporary basis, to see the organization through a short-term crisis or to offer suggestions for boosting profits. Other companies may contract out all accounting and financial operations.

Job seekers will face a competitive market as the number of job openings may be fewer than the number of applicants. Candidates with expertise in public accounting and finance, notably people who have a master's degree and or a professional certification, will have the best job prospects.

Advancement Prospects

Advancement is generally to a senior management position, such as managing partner, chief executive officer, or chief financial officer. Experienced financial managers who display a strong grasp of the operations of various departments within their organization are prime candidates for promotion to top management positions. Some financial managers transfer to closely related positions in other companies in real estate or into other industries. Those with access to sufficient capital may decide to start their own consulting firms.

Education and Training

A bachelor's degree in finance, accounting, economics, or business administration is the minimum academic preparation for financial managers. Many employers now seek graduates with a master's degree, preferably in business administration, economics, finance, or risk management. These academic programs develop analytical skills and teach the latest financial analysis methods and technology.

Financial officers often choose to broaden their skills by earning a professional certification. Although experience, ability, and leadership are emphasized for promotion, advancement may be accelerated by this type of special study.

Finance Directors can earn the Certified Public Accountant (CPA) from the American Institute of Certified Public Accountants (AICPA) or the Certified Management Accountant (CMA) designation. The CMA is offered by the Institute of Management Accountants to its members who have a four-year degree, have at least two years of work experience, and pass the institute's four-part examination. They must also fulfill continuing education requirements to maintain these credentials.

Experience, Skills, and Personality Traits

Beyond hands-on experience, financial managers need many different skills. Most employers look for candidates who have had some public accounting experience, preferably in real estate. Generally, three to five years' experience in real estate finance or underwriting—or a combination of academic training and experience—is what employers want to see.

Finance Directors have to be creative thinkers and problem solvers, applying their analytical skills to business. An ability to think conceptually and creatively is a valuable skill. Strong computer skills are essential tools on the job, especially an advanced knowledge of the Excel spreadsheet program. Also, a good knowledge of compliance procedures is essential because of the many recent regulatory changes in financial reporting. Financial managers should have excellent verbal and written communication skills to explain complex financial data.

Unions and Associations

Several real estate professional associations, including the CCIM Institute and CoreNet Global, have business networking and continuing education programs for real estate finance officers. Finance Directors with a CPA professional designation may also want to become members of the American Institute of Certified Public Accountants.

Tips for Entry

1. Attend real estate professional conferences sponsored by professional associations and local affiliates and get to know people who can help in your search.
2. College job fairs are another way to make useful contacts with potential employers.
3. Explore internship opportunities and interim assignments to gain valuable experience.

INVESTOR RELATIONS OFFICER

CAREER PROFILE

Duties: Distributes financial information to investors and the public; issues press releases about corporate events; organizes teleconferences and meetings with financial analysts

Alternate Title(s): Investor Relations Executive

Salary Range: $85,000 to $162,000

Employment Prospects: Good

Advancement Prospects: Fair

Prerequisites:

Education or Training—Four-year degree, with courses in finance, economics, and journalism

Experience—Two to five years' experience

Special Skills and Personality Traits—Excellent verbal and written communication skills; ability to explain business strategy to financial analysts and journalists; good organizational skills

Special Requirements—Chartered Financial Analyst (CFA) certification required for advancement

CAREER LADDER

Chief Investment Officer

Investor Relations Officer

Junior Investor Relations Officer

Position Description

Investor relations are the activities publicly traded companies undertake to give an accurate picture of business performance and prospects, while gaining market feedback useful in planning and strategy decisions. Earnings releases, earnings forecasts, annual and quarterly reports, quarterly teleconferences with securities analysts—all these activities are part of investor relations and the responsibility of the Investor Relations Officer. IR Officers also issue the financial reports required by federal or state regulatory agencies.

Investor Relations Officers are the information gatekeepers for timely release of any information affecting a company's stock price—a change from the practice years ago when the emphasis was on delivering only financial information. Credit this transition to the 24-hour news cycle and growing recognition that, in the information age, almost anything a company does will eventually have an impact on earnings and stock price.

Investor Relations Officers, or IROs, typically deal with several important audiences: insurance companies, pension funds and other big investors; sell-side analysts who work alongside brokers in the big Wall Street firms; buy-side analysts who advise the big investors on stocks to buy; financial media, the news channels that report on markets and events impacting stock prices; and to a lesser extent, private investors, or individual investors who own shares of a company's stock. Investor Relations Officers can expect to have contact with corporate finance advisors, IR consultants, financial printers, and public auditors who have a higher profile in the wake of several highly publicized accounting scandals.

Investor Relations Officers distribute information on financial events, such as corporate earnings and acquisitions, to the investing public and help develop corporate strategy. The IR professional today is one of the most influential individuals in the corporation.

The investor relations professional issues press releases to explain significant events and organize meetings or teleconferences with investors and financial analysts. Investor Relations Officers also are responsible for preparation of the company annual report, organizing the annual meeting with shareholders, and meetings with financial analysts who follow the company's performance. Investor Relations Officers have frequent contact with senior company executives.

The investor relations position may be a staff position or a function performed by a public relations firm specializing in financial public relations. Large corporations, or companies with sales above $500 million, usually have a designated Investor Relations Officer. The Investor Relations Officer's job is challenging.

Events of the last 10 years have redefined and broadened the job functions of the Investor Relations Officer. Besides communicating with investors and key constituencies (shareholders, financial analysts, strategic business partners, and even employees), IR professionals are assuming a leadership role in managing risk, shareholder activism issues, and the increased involvement of regulatory agencies such as the Securities and Exchange Commission in corporate governance.

Salaries

Earnings of Investor Relations Officers are competitive with annual compensation paid out to other senior finance officers. Larger public companies offer the most generous pay packages, compensating for the increased responsibilities of their IR professional.

Investor Relations Officers in public real estate companies can earn salaries ranging from $85,000 to $162,000, according to a salary survey by CEL & Associates, Inc., a benefits consulting firm. In addition to their base salary, IR Officers typically receive bonus compensation which is tied to financial performance of their company. Often there is a signing bonus.

Employment Prospects

There is strong demand for investor relations professionals. The stock market boom of the 1990s and the number of corporate initial public offerings have contributed to increased job demand for IR professionals. Investor Relations Officers come from varied backgrounds, including law, marketing, and communications.

Demand for investor relation specialists will be concentrated in the largest publicly owned development and property owning companies. Corporate mergers, acquisitions, and corporate downsizing—all of which are impossible to predict—are likely to have a strong influence on future employment growth.

Advancement Prospects

Investor relations professionals have several career advancement options. They can advance to a more senior position in the corporate finance department, such as chief investment officer, and assume responsibility for developing relationships with business partners and capital formation to finance new developments. IR professionals with the right credentials have the potential to move up into senior management, potentially to the chief financial officer (CFO). Another option is moving into an investor relations consulting firm specializing in financial public relations.

Education and Training

An undergraduate degree is required. Most investor relations professionals have college backgrounds in finance or economics, with courses in business, business law, or communication. A background in the liberal arts is helpful because IR managers deal with a wide variety of people in the course of their jobs. Some universities offer an investor relations certification program for indi-

viduals interested in moving into investor relations from another career, such as law, finance, or communications, or IR practitioners interested in improving their on-the-job skills. These certification programs are endorsed by the National Investor Relations Institute.

Experience, Skills, and Personality Traits

Investor Relations Officers entering the field generally have at least three to five years' experience in financial public relations or have previously worked in the corporate finance department. Key skills required for the position include strong verbal and written communication skills, strong analytical skills, and computer spreadsheet literacy. It is also helpful to have a knack for problem solving and to be able to present management with different scenarios for handling a particular situation.

Special Requirements

The investor relations position requires a broad view of corporate structure, a general understanding of financial markets, public relations, developed communication skills, and a comprehensive understanding of federal and state laws and regulations relating to securities. Also important are well-developed skills in strategic planning and operations management. The Chartered Financial Analyst (CFA) designation awarded by the CFA Institute is often a requirement for advancement to more senior positions in the largest public companies.

Unions and Associations

Investor relations managers can become members of the National Investor Relations Institute for networking opportunities and career advancement. NIRI has local chapters in most states. IR Officers who have the CFA professional designation—Chartered Financial Analyst—can become members of the CFA Institute, which has local chapters in major cities around the world.

Tips for Entry

1. Attend local or regional meetings of the National Investor Relations Institute to learn more about job opportunities.
2. Management recruiters are another source of job leads; recruiters can also help negotiate salary and benefits.
3. Build a file of key job skills on your home computer, such as negotiating or communicating, and chart your progress over time.
4. Periodically check the National Investor Relations Institute Web site (http://www.niri.org) for career management tips and publications available in the NIRI bookstore.

PENSION FUND PORTFOLIO MANAGER

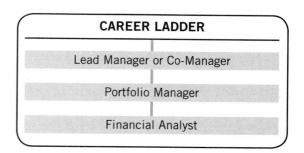
Position Description

Managing real estate investments for pension funds offers plenty of opportunities for people with the right skills. The commercial real estate market in the United States is valued at $4.8 trillion, only a small fraction of which is owned by public or private employee pension funds. For comparison, real estate investment trusts, another type of managed portfolio, have assets of $340 billion. Pension funds are seen likely to increase their investment allocations in real estate as more Baby Boomers reach retirement age, says Institutional Real Estate, Inc., a financial publisher.

Many fund managers view real estate as an income-producing asset with equity-like returns. Largely for this reason, pension funds can be expected to be more income-oriented in the years ahead, which tends to favor income-oriented investments like real estate. As an investment class, real estate has the benefits of a continuous stream of rental income and a low correlation with the overall stock market, which reduces volatility in the overall portfolio.

Pension funds are managed to guarantee payment of a certain dollar amount per month to retired workers, based on earnings and the number of years worked. The primary role of a fund manager is to help define portfolio objectives, and then to build and manage a portfolio so as to achieve those objectives while keeping the pension fully funded—or as close to being fully funded as possible, so the fund has sufficient assets to cover future obligations.

Financial portfolio management is different from asset management, another type of financial management in real estate. Portfolio managers operate at the strategic level, focusing on investment performance over a long time period, usually over the next five to 10 years. Asset managers, on the other hand, have a tactical focus, looking instead at the implementation of portfolio strategy. They spend their time managing collections of assets (as opposed to portfolios), often properties in a specific region of the country.

A pension fund's investment strategy may be expressed in terms of the following:

- scale of its desired investment in real estate. A typical range might be five to 12 percent of the portfolio.
- type of investments the fund will consider buying, such as REIT securities, securitized debt instruments, direct ownership, or investments via third party funds
- sector allocations (office, retail, multi-family, industrial, etc.)
- geographic allocation (by domestic region or international)

- requirements for current income versus future growth
- risk tolerance and return expectations as measured by quarterly investment performance reviews

Pension fund managers work for banks, insurance companies, and investment management companies that oversee the investments of client companies. Money managers get to face the challenges of investing. If you like the excitement of selecting investments and can deal with the uncertainty of waiting for the payoff, this field can be a rewarding career.

Salaries
Salaries vary by geographic region, experience, level of responsibility, type of investment portfolio managed, and employer. Fund managers with several years' experience are highly compensated. Salaries can range from the low $30,000 range for newly hired managers to $100,000 and up. Investment manager compensation may be pegged to portfolio performance, although incentive compensation is more common in the institutional fund management industry. The investment management field is highly competitive, and investment management firms place great importance on manager performance. Being in the top quartile of manager rankings can earn you a substantial annual bonus.

Employment Prospects
The money manager field can be difficult to break into, but there are good opportunities in regional investment advisory firms, hedge funds, bank trust departments, and government pension funds. Because real estate investing is a specialized field, pension funds typically outsource the actual money management to third-party firms specializing in real estate portfolios.

There are plenty of money managers who began their careers working in sales for investment banking firms. Another way to break in is to first get involved in marketing. Another entry path is through investment research. Many portfolio managers begin their careers as securities analysts who follow specific companies and report their investment research to a portfolio manager or portfolio management team.

Advancement Prospects
Hard work pays off in the money management industry. Managers whose investment picks perform well are rewarded with regular salary increases and annual performance bonuses. Investment professionals who make poor decisions for their investors or shareholders tend to have fairly short careers.

Managers who show an aptitude for stock selection are promoted to higher profile positions, and they take on the responsibility for managing larger portfolios, directing the activities of a group of investment managers. Fund managers also advance their careers by changing jobs and moving to another investment advisory firm, often with an increase in salary and responsibility.

Education and Training
A four-year undergraduate degree is required. Portfolio managers come to the field from a variety of academic backgrounds, but most have had courses in business management, economics, finance, and related fields. Managers specializing in a particular industry may have a post-graduate degree.

Special Requirements
An industry designation, Chartered Financial Analyst (CFA), awarded by the CFA Institute, may be a requirement for advancement to more senior positions.

Experience, Skills, and Personality Traits
Important skills for portfolio managers are good math and analytical skills. Individuals who can make good decisions under pressure, who can analyze large amounts of data and quickly reach two or three major conclusions, will do well in this industry. Some experience in real estate financial management is usually a requirement, anywhere from three to 10 years' experience, depending on the position.

Individuals entering this career should have strong quantitative and analytical skills and also a working knowledge of accounting, legal, and regulatory issues. Those who have a bias toward action and who are passionate about their careers will do well in this career path.

Unions and Associations
Portfolio managers can become members of professional associations such as the National Association of Real Estate Investment Managers or the Pension Real Estate Association for networking opportunities and career advancement.

Tips for Entry
1. Check out the National Association of Real Estate Managers job board (http://www.nareim.org) for a list of current job openings.
2. Working in financial marketing for an investment firm for a few years is one way to get your foot in the door.
3. Take courses in investment theory and portfolio management to get a head start on the CFA examination.

PROPERTY ACCOUNTANT

CAREER PROFILE

Duties: Prepares monthly reconciliation of accounts; calculates monthly expenses; reviews accounts payable

Alternate Title(s): Property Accounting Manager

Salary Range: $40,000 to $70,000

Employment Prospects: Good

Advancement Prospects: Good

Prerequisites:

    Education or Training—Four-year degree in accounting, finance, or related area

    Experience—Two to five years' accounting experience; two-plus years' experience in property accounting

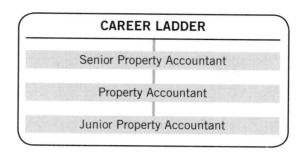

CAREER LADDER

Senior Property Accountant

Property Accountant

Junior Property Accountant

Special Skills and Personality Traits—Proficiency with spreadsheet accounting and accounting systems; strong organizational skills and time management skills; good written and verbal communication skills

Position Description

Property Accountants prepare accounting reports for management in a property management firm to ensure timely and accurate financial reports. They summarize activity reports on managed commercial properties and ensure compliance with applicable state or federal regulations. Property Accountants work collaboratively as members of a management team, which means they have an opportunity to apply their numbers-crunching skills while gaining real world experience.

Property Accountants prepare tenant account bank reconciliations, monitor all billing aspects of lease administration, manage cash balances in bank accounts, and disburse funds from bank accounts as needed for payment of invoices. Property Accountants calculate common area maintenance charges, or CAM charges, paid by tenants in multi-tenant commercial buildings. CAM charges cover such things as parking lot maintenance, snow removal, and common area utilities. Property Accountants prepare and distribute management reports and financial statements to property management departments and the property owner's financial group. They assist in annual operating expense audits and prepare updated cash flow forecasts throughout the year.

In larger organizations, Property Accountants may also assist in performing internal audits—a control function to make sure financial records are accurate. Internal audits cannot be done by accountants who regularly handle the information to be checked in an audit review. Many companies hire outside accounting firms to perform these audits.

Computers are changing the nature of the work performed by Property Accountants. With the aid of special software packages, accountants summarize transactions in standard formats used by financial records and organize data in special formats employed in financial analysis. These accounting packages greatly reduce the amount of tedious manual work associated with data management and record keeping. As a result, a growing number of accountants are specializing in correcting problems with software or in developing software to meet unique data management and analytical needs. Accountants also are beginning to perform more technical duties, such as implementing, controlling, and auditing systems and networks, developing technology plans, and analyzing and devising budgets.

In their regular duties, Property Accountants review monthly financial statements and reports the property management firm submits to business partners. They review tenant billing calculations to make sure the management company is charging the proper rents. They review cash balances and bank statements. They review auditing reports for compliance with the Sarbanes-Oxley Act, a federal law requiring public companies to ensure they have adequate record keeping and internal financial controls.

Property Accountants may also perform any of the following:

- reviewing general ledger reconciliations
- responding to auditor inquiries

- preparing billing statements
- preparing monthly, quarterly, and annual financial statements and reports
- reconciling accounts receivable and accounts payable

Property Accountants work in an office setting and typically work a 40-hour week. They work for real estate investment companies, property management companies, hotel management companies, and other companies involved in day-to-day management of commercial real estate.

Salaries

Earnings are based on experience, industry specialization, and specific position requirements. Property Accountants can earn salaries of $40,000 to $70,000 a year or more, depending on the employer. Property Accountants may also receive part of their compensation in the form of incentive bonuses if the firm or department meets certain performance goals. Non-salaried benefits typically include company-sponsored health insurance, a 401(k) employee savings plan, paid life insurance, and other fringe benefits.

Employment Prospects

Working for an accounting firm with real estate clients is good preparation for a career in real estate. Working as an accountant is an excellent way to learn the financial side of the business. Property management companies frequently have openings for entry-level accountants with good academic credentials but limited real estate experience. Part-time or interim assignments can lead to permanent hiring.

Advancement Prospects

This position reports to a senior Property Accountant, if there is one, or the firm's chief financial officer. The typical advancement path on the financial side of the business is to move into more senior positions with increasing responsibility. This often requires attaining a professional accounting designation such as Certified Public Accountant (CPA) credential given by the American Institute of Certified Public Accountants, or a post-graduate degree in finance. Experience in property accounting can also be a door-opener to careers outside finance. Accountants have first-hand knowledge of the operational side of real estate—how commercial leases are structured, for instance.

Education and Training

Education requirements to become an accountant vary according to specialization, but generally begin with earning a four-year degree. The basic academic foundation is a degree in accounting or finance. Accountants who want to advance their careers will often take college courses beyond the four-year degree requirements to earn a Certified Public Accountant (CPA) designation and become licensed accountants. The CPA designation requires 150 college education hours and a passing grade on the uniform CPA exam. After passing the exam, candidates can apply to their state licensing board and attain a state license. After licensing is granted, CPAs must take 40 hours of continuing education annually.

Experience, Skills, and Personality Traits

Employers generally look for individuals with at least two to five years' experience in accounting and two years' experience in real estate accounting or fixed-asset accounting. Many employers prefer candidates with some experience in property management. The position requires experience with budget reconciliations, accruals, balance sheet analysis, bank reconciliations, financial statement preparation, and property reclassifications. Property Accountants are expected to have excellent skills in spreadsheet accounting software and a working knowledge of real estate accounting software. Also important is an ability to interpret documents and to write reports and correspondence. Strong planning and time-organization skills and excellent verbal and written communication skills are essential.

Unions and Associations

Property Accountants can become members of professional associations such as the American Institute of Certified Public Accountants or real estate associations such as CoreNet Global or the National Association of Industrial and Office Property Managers.

Tips for Entry

1. Some accounting firms and property management firms have part-time work or internship programs for college students.
2. Check accounting job boards such as Tax Talent (www.taxtalent.com) for current openings.
3. Search out someone in your field who can offer helpful career advice. Entry-level accountants have to take it on themselves to find people willing to help them up the career ladder.
4. After landing that first job, seek out a more experienced professional who can serve as your mentor. Most firms don't automatically assign mentors to newly hired employees.

REAL ESTATE ACCOUNTANT

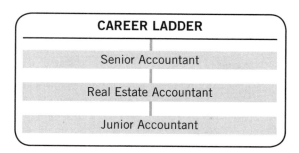
Position Description

Accountants help to ensure that businesses are run efficiently, records kept accurately, and taxes paid properly and on time. The Real Estate Accountant is a key player in a real estate management company. He or she has broad responsibility for managing accounting reports from property managers and preparing financial reports to senior management. Real Estate Accountants have frequent contact with investors, lenders, residential property managers, independent auditors, and various government agencies. They may also manage the accounts payable function and assist in managing relations with banking institutions. The accountant reviews rent collections, journal entries and reporting, quarterly reporting, annual budget preparation, annual report filings, and any other duties assigned.

Beyond carrying out the fundamental tasks of the occupation—preparing, analyzing, and verifying financial documents in order to provide information to clients—many accountants now are required to possess a wide range of knowledge and skills. Accountants are broadening the services they offer to include budget analysis, financial and investment planning, information technology consulting, and limited legal services.

In some organizations the Real Estate Accountant may be responsible for staffing in the accounting department, internal audit, quality control, employee training, and fixed-asset management. The Real Estate Accountant prepares monthly, quarterly and annual financial reports. The Real Estate Accountant may

also assist in preparation of annual audit and tax work reports and oversee special projects.

Essential duties of Real Estate Accountants typically include:

- preparing monthly consolidated financial statements
- checking monthly, general ledger, and other reports for accuracy
- performing monthly balance sheet and bank statement reconciliations
- providing reconciliations of inter-company accounts
- assisting in special projects as assigned
- participating in budgeting and forecasting analysis
- preparing monthly or bimonthly payroll journal entries
- supporting cash sweep investments and electronic banking (automated clearing house) payments

Most accountants work a standard 40-hour work-week, but many work longer hours, particularly if they are self-employed and have numerous clients. Real Estate Accountants in public companies often work long hours during the tax season or when quarterly financial reports are due.

Salaries

Salaries in many accounting and auditing professions have been rising in response to heightened demand for skilled professionals. Research shows that nationwide demand for accounting professionals is strongest in commercial real estate, as well as in financial services.

Real Estate Accountants can earn $45,000 to $52,000 annually, plus a bonus pegged to financial performance of the company.

According to a salary survey by the National Association of Colleges and Employers, bachelor's degree candidates in accounting received starting offers averaging $43,269 a year in 2005. Master's degree candidates in accounting were offered $46,251 initially.

Earning a professional certification, an advanced degree, or an M.B.A. can lead to a substantially higher salary. Accountants with at least one professional certification, whether it is a Certified Public Accountant (CPA) license or an M.B.A. degree, typically earn a much higher average salary—averaging 30 percent higher—than those without a CPA license.

Employment Prospects

Overall job opportunities should be favorable; jobseekers who obtain professional recognition through certification or licensure, a master's degree, proficiency in accounting and auditing computer software, or specialized expertise will have the best opportunities. The U.S. Bureau of Labor Statistics says certified public accountants are among the most sought-after professionals.

There is strong demand for accounting graduates about to enter the job market. Business expansion and ongoing compliance requirements have led to an increase in hiring in many positions. An increase in the number of businesses, changing financial laws and regulations, and greater scrutiny of company finances will drive faster-than-average growth of accountants and auditors.

Accountants with auditing or Sarbanes-Oxley reporting experience—two areas where demand is strongest—should have their pick of employment opportunities. In addition, some vacancies will occur from the need to replace accountants who retire or transfer to other occupations. Individuals starting their careers with limited real estate experience generally begin as entry level (or junior) accountants, advancing with experience to Real Estate Accountant.

Advancement Prospects

Experienced accountants have plenty of occupational mobility. As they rise in the organization, Real Estate Accountants can advance to senior accountant, the highest non-supervisory position. Those interested in management positions can move up to accounting manager, finance director, or a similar position. Some will eventually become controllers, treasurers, financial vice presidents, or chief financial officers. Academic credentials beyond college, such as a master's degree, can provide the additional credentials necessary to move into a senior management position or possibly a career as a financial consultant.

Education and Training

Most jobs require at least a four-year degree in accounting, finance, or a related field. If you're interested in pursuing a career in accounting, take math courses while in high school and economics or accounting electives. While in college you will have to take accounting courses. Earning the Certified Public Accountant (CPA) credential can improve your chances of promotion, so begin taking college courses qualifying for the CPA designation while in school. CPA candidates must pass the uniform CPA exam and apply to their state board of accountancy to get a CPA license. Further information on testing and licensing can be found at the National Association of State Boards of Accountancy (http://www.nasba.org) or the CPA exam Web site (http://www.cpa-exam.org).

Most states have raised their education requirements for CPA licensing. Starting in 2009, 47 states and the District of Columbia require CPA candidates to have completed 150 hours of college education—30 hours beyond the usual four-year degree. Many colleges and universities offer CPA candidates the opportunity to earn a master's degree while working toward the 150 hours in required college courses. Licensed CPAs must also take 40 hours of continuing education annually to maintain their state certification.

Experience, Skills, and Personality Traits

Some experience in real estate accounting, from one to five years, is recommended. Real Estate Accountants should have strong organizational skills, a commanding knowledge of spreadsheet accounting software, and a working knowledge of U.S. accounting principles (Generally Accepted Accounting Principles, or GAAP). Depending on the position, some experience in real-estate specific software programs, such as Argus or Yardi, may be recommended or required. Some prior experience in public accounting can be helpful background for those interested in working at a larger firm.

Unions and Associations

Many accountants join professional associations to keep up with developments in the field and take advantage of networking opportunities with like-minded professionals.

Real Estate Accountants can become members of professional accounting associations such as the International Management Accounting Association, the

American Institute of Certified Public Accountants, and top real estate industry associations for networking opportunities and career advancement through seminars, conferences, and continuing education courses.

Tips for Entry

1. Previous experience in accounting or auditing can be a real door opener to a career in accounting. Many colleges offer summer employment and part-time internships, which are useful in acquiring practical knowledge and industry contacts.
2. Take courses in computer science and communication to build up job-related skills that can help advance your career.
3. Temporary or interim assignments can often lead to longer-term employment.
4. State Certified Public Accountant societies often sponsor internships for accounting majors.

REAL ESTATE BOOKKEEPER

CAREER PROFILE

Duties: Records transactions in accounting journals; posts entries to ledger accounts

Alternate Title(s): Accounting Clerk

Salary Range: $35,000 to $45,000

Employment Prospects: Good

Advancement Prospects: Fair

Prerequisites:

    Education or Training—High school diploma; associate's degree or four-year degree optional

    Experience—Three or more years' accounting experience; real estate experience recommended

    Special Skills and Personality Traits—Computational skills; facility with accounting software and

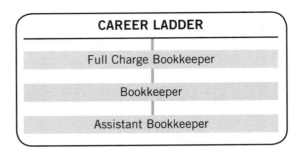

CAREER LADDER

Full Charge Bookkeeper

Bookkeeper

Assistant Bookkeeper

Microsoft Excel spreadsheet software; good verbal and written communication skills

Special Requirements—Insurance bonding normally required

Position Description

Bookkeepers and accounting clerks are financial record keepers. They work with a business to manage its financial ledgers, keep track of purchases, and process the company payroll. A bookkeeper is also responsible for submitting taxes and other deductions from payroll to the appropriate government agencies. Each company will have slightly different expectations for the bookkeeper, and these are typically established when the bookkeeper first begins working with business.

Actual day-to-day responsibilities of a bookkeeper will vary according to the office and the scope of business, but there are some general guidelines. Typically, the bookkeeper has overall responsibility for updating and maintaining daily accounting records, periodic accounts payable and receivable, and profit and loss statements. In a real estate brokerage office, bookkeepers and bookkeeping clerks produce financial statements and prepare reports for supervisors and managers. Bookkeepers also prepare bank deposits, verify and balance receipts, and send checks or other payments to banks and creditors. They may also handle payroll, make purchases, prepare invoices, and keep track of overdue accounts.

Bookkeepers are often designated by the range of duties performed on the job. Bookkeepers are responsible for recording transactions in accounting journals and subsidiary journals and posting entries to general ledger accounts. They may, or may not, do adjusting entries, file federal or state payroll tax returns, and

compute related deposits. Full-charge bookkeepers can maintain an entire company's books, including monthly bank reconciliations, current-period error corrections in the general ledger, and payroll accounting.

Typical duties performed by bookkeepers include the following:

- paying and recording all accounts and bills for both incoming and outgoing transactions
- issuing payroll at the required time schedule, including legally required deductions or withholdings for tax purposes or for other reasons
- verifying accuracy of work performed by others when updating ledgers and other financial statements
- correcting and reconciling any discrepancies in ledgers, accounts, or other financial statements
- maintaining general ledgers in accordance with accepted bookkeeping and accounting principles
- recording and summarizing financial data using journal books, ledgers, or computers
- calculating and issuing bills, invoices, and account statements
- compiling statistical, accounting, or auditing reports for cash receipts, accounts payable, accounts receivable, profit and loss
- accessing computerized records to answer general questions or questions relating to specific accounts
- reporting to government agencies as required
- meeting business owners to discuss ledgers and answer any questions

Bookkeeping and accounting clerks normally work a standard 40-hour workweek in an office setting. They may work longer hours during the tax filing season, when monthly or year-end accounting audits are performed, or at the end of the fiscal year. About 25 percent of bookkeepers work part time, according to the U.S. Bureau of Labor Statistics.

Salaries

Wage and salary earnings of bookkeepers and bookkeeping clerks ranged between $35,000 and $45,000 in 2006, according to the U.S. Bureau of Labor Statistics. The top 10 percent earned more than $46,000 annually. Non-salary benefits offered by employers vary according to company size and type of organization. Company-paid health insurance and vacations are common.

Employment Prospects

Employment opportunities for bookkeepers are favorable through 2016, according to the U.S. Bureau of Labor Statistics. Full-charge bookkeepers do many of the routine duties performed by accountants, increasing their value to employers. Higher corporate accountability standards, namely those outlined in the Sarbanes-Oxley Act of 2002, are expected to have a positive impact on demand for bookkeepers. More bookkeeping work will go to independent, or freelance, bookkeepers, as companies continue outsourcing accounting operations to reduce costs. Certified bookkeepers and those with several years of bookkeeping or accounting experience will have the best employment prospects.

Advancement Prospects

Bookkeeping and accounting clerks normally advance by taking on more duties for higher pay or by transferring to a related occupation. Most employers fill administrative and support positions by promoting individuals from within their organizations. Bookkeepers who acquire additional skills, experience, or training will improve their advancement opportunities. Bookkeepers who can carry out a wide range of bookkeeping or accounting activities, or who have demonstrated experience with real estate accounting software, will have more promotion opportunities. Earning an industry certification—certified bookkeeper—will also improve chances for promotion. According to the American Institute of Professional Bookkeepers, more than 40 percent of certified bookkeepers have been promoted or have found new jobs as a result of being certified. With additional training, some bookkeepers could become accountants or internal auditors.

Education and Training

A high school diploma is the minimum educational requirement. Increasingly, employers are looking for candidates who have earned at least an associate's degree or four-year college degree with a concentration in accounting courses. Some college-level courses in spreadsheet accounting software or database software would be helpful. Once hired, bookkeeping and accounting clerks normally receive on-the-job training, learning company procedures under the supervision of a more experienced employee. Some formal classroom training in computer software may also be necessary. A number of colleges offer preparatory courses for certification. Some community colleges and four-year colleges offer online business administration and accounting courses.

Bookkeepers who want to further their careers will find it beneficial to become certified bookkeepers. The Certified Bookkeeper designation, awarded by the American Institute of Professional Bookkeepers (AIPB), demonstrates that individuals have the competence to handle payroll and general ledger accounting according to accepted accounting practices. To become eligible for certification, bookkeepers must have at least two years' experience, pass a four-part exam, and adhere to a code of ethics.

Special Requirements

Since bookkeepers have direct access to accounts, they are typically required to maintain insurance bonding indemnifying the business against any loss arising from theft or misuse of company funds.

Experience, Skills, and Personality Traits

Bookkeeping and accounting clerks must be careful and detail-oriented in their work and have a strong aptitude for financial calculations. Some prior bookkeeping or accounting experience, three years or more in an office setting, is generally preferred. Extensive experience may not be necessary. Bookkeepers who start out as assistant bookkeepers can learn most of the job requirements under supervision by another, more experienced employee.

Good bookkeepers are problem solvers; a mathematical aptitude goes hand in hand with the ability to spot errors in calculations and correct errors as soon as discovered. They should have a working knowledge of common PC software, including the Microsoft Office suite, and have an intermediate knowledge of Excel spreadsheet software. Good communication skills—verbal and written—are also important as bookkeepers have to communicate the results of their work to supervisors. Bookkeepers working in a real estate office should have some knowledge of real estate accounting software such as Yardi. Bookkeepers should be discreet and trustworthy because they are entrusted with financial records and frequently come into contact with sensitive information.

Unions and Associations

The American Institute of Professional Bookkeepers (http://www.aipb.org) sponsors continuing education and training programs for bookkeeping professionals. Most are self-paced, home study courses. The association also has an online job bank listing current employment opportunities.

Tips for Entry

1. Take high school or college courses in accounting, mathematics, computer science, and related subjects to get a good background in the fundamentals of bookkeeping.
2. Some colleges offer courses qualifying toward certified bookkeeper designation.
3. Summer employment and part-time employment are opportunities to get valuable on-the-job experience.
4. Check the American Institute of Professional Bookkeepers job board lists for current job openings in your area.

REAL ESTATE ADVISORY ANALYST

CAREER PROFILE

Duties: Provides clients with research and valuation analysis; works with financial models; provides guidance on technical issues in asset management, development, and finance

Alternate Title(s): Real Estate Advisor, Real Estate Consultant

Salary Range: $60,000 to $90,000 and up

Employment Prospects: Good

Advancement Prospects: Good

Prerequisites:

Education or Training—Four-year degree in business, economics, finance, or real estate; master's degree preferred for some positions

Experience—Two to five years' experience in real estate financial analysis, asset management; expe-

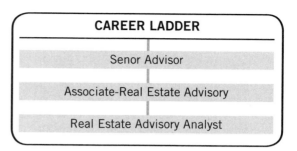

CAREER LADDER

Senor Advisor

Associate-Real Estate Advisory

Real Estate Advisory Analyst

rience calculating financial ratios and investment returns; strong communication skills; facility with spreadsheet accounting and database software

Special Skills and Personality Traits—Strong analytical skills, research skills; excellent presentation skills

Special Requirements—Real estate sales license may be required in some positions

Position Description

Real estate advisors and consultants give advice about property. They help investors evaluate and select a property by recommending geographic areas and property types that will likely experience price appreciation in the future. For example, institutional investors and pension funds require detailed studies to determine their real estate investment strategies. Advisors are a source of professional, independent advice, based on the advisor's professional experience and sound judgment. They help clients make decisions when purchasing, investing, or using property.

Real estate advisors are the experts others turn to when they want answers to a wide range of real estate questions. Counselors must know every phase of the real estate business because they use that knowledge in nearly every consultation. Often they will be asked about income opportunities and productive uses of different kinds of properties.

Advisors work for development firms, financial and business consulting firms, and real estate consulting firms. Services offered vary depending on consulting activities of individual firms. Some consultants are more involved in planning and property development; others are more active in quality control screening and pre-purchase or pre-sale due diligence assessments.

Real estate advisors work differently from real estate agents or brokers who hold themselves out to clients as

consultants. A real estate advisor does not represent the client as an agent, and has no financial interest in the sale or purchase of property. Real estate agents and brokers, notably those selling residential properties, often call themselves "consultants" to position themselves as more than sales agents.

Real Estate Advisory Analysts and advisory associates perform a variety of analytical services, including the following:

- property acquisitions and sales (dispositions)
- site analysis and inspections
- deal reviews
- 1031 tax-free property exchanges
- property appraisals
- asset management
- investor due diligence
- litigation support
- development assistance
- lease advisory services

Analysts research and resolve problems, and they provide guidance on technical topics.

On the brokerage side, analysts advise senior brokers and investment bankers in preparing a disposition analysis. They research and write investment offering memorandums and provide support for transaction closings.

Real Estate Advisory Analysts work in an office setting, usually a standard 40-hour workweek, but occasional travel is required to visit and inspect properties throughout North America.

Salaries

Annual earnings of Real Estate Advisory Analysts are competitive with other types of high-end consulting. The typical salary range is $60,000 to $90,000 a year in base salary with some type of incentive bonus (10 percent of base salary or more) that is tied to performance goals. Analysts may also receive an annual profit-sharing bonus. They may also receive non-salary benefits such as educational assistance, health insurance, flextime working schedules and paid vacations.

Employment Prospects

This is a growth field, with more opportunities for real estate advisors likely over the next eight to 10 years as investors become more comfortable with real estate as part of a diversified investment portfolio. There are relatively few brokers specializing in counseling, but the field will grow as investors and owners realize the value of expert advice in developing property and improving income. While accumulating experience in other real estate specialties, people planning to become real estate counselors also continue to study in continuing education programs in financial management.

Advancement Prospects

Advancement is often difficult, but those who are successful can have very successful careers. Real Estate Advisory Analysts can advance to management level positions, such as manager of strategic consulting or senior consultant, and deliver advice across a diverse range of assignments—residential, hotels, office, and recreational properties. Some consultants advance their careers by upgrading their academic qualifications, earning a master's degree in real estate, urban studies, or a related field of study.

Education and Training

Most positions require at least a four-year degree, although few require a specific major. Most candidates have a bachelor's degree in business, finance, accounting, or economics, although this is not necessarily a requirement. Many firms hire summer interns before their last year of college, and those who are most successful are offered full-time jobs after they graduate. An M.B.A., post-graduate degree in real estate or

finance, or professional certification can also be very helpful.

Many employers provide intensive on-the-job training, especially for newly hired employees. While college course work is helpful, most firms have a specialized business model which employees must learn. Trainees in large firms may receive classroom instruction in securities analysis, effective speaking, and the finer points of real estate analysis.

Professional credentials beyond a college degree are desirable, such as Member—Appraisal Institute (MAI), Member, CCIM Institute, or Counselor of Real Estate (CRE), conferred by the Counselors of Real Estate. Membership in the Counselors of Real Estate is by invitation only, and is awarded to real estate professionals with at least 10 years' experience in real estate counseling or consulting.

Experience, Skills, and Personality Traits

Employers usually look for analysts who have at least two to five years' experience in commercial real estate. Candidates with less experience may qualify if they have a high grade point average in relevant college courses.

Real Estate Advisory Analysts should have strong analytical and effective communication skills. Financial modeling skills are equally important, and analysts should have a proficiency in Microsoft's Excel spreadsheet software. Some experience with ARGUS software, useful in calculating real estate cash flows, is helpful.

Unions and Associations

Analysts can become members of several professional associations: the CCIM Institute (http://www.ccim.com), the Society of Industrial and Office Realtors (http://www.sior.org), or the Counselors of Real Estate (http://www.cre.org). These associations sponsor professional development seminars and conferences for continuing education in the field and maintaining professional credentials.

Tips for Entry

1. Contact real estate consulting or advisory firms to learn about specific opportunities in real estate consulting services.
2. Some companies offer paid internships for motivated undergraduates looking to explore careers in real estate consulting.
3. Many colleges and universities now offer their alumni free job search and career advice. Check your college alumni offices for details.

REAL ESTATE INVESTMENT ANALYST

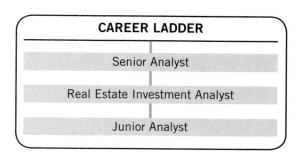

Position Description

Successful real estate development depends on solid numbers-crunching analysis of potential opportunities. Real Estate Investment Analysts, or project analysts, concern themselves with evaluating the feasibility of a particular development—whether it will pay for itself in a given number of years. Analysts collect and interpret large amounts of proprietary and public information, prepare reports, and work closely with real estate brokers, agents, development managers, and the sales staff. They are highly organized and detail-oriented in their work.

Real Estate Investment Analysts provide analytical support for property acquisitions. They evaluate the merits or risks of a particular investment, both long-term and short-term. They review and analyze real estate property operating statements. They prepare journal entries for operating activity and changes in valuation. They work closely with the asset management and acquisition team to identify properties suitable as additions to the real estate investment portfolio.

Real estate analysts do more than assemble data into a spreadsheet and submit reports. They ask some hard questions and stay with the process until answers have been secured and verified. By taking a broad approach to gathering data, they are able to develop possible trends for the investment opportunity, based on the indicators that make up the analysis.

Real Estate Investment Analysts also perform research on currently owned properties. They review the portfolio of owned properties to identify properties that are underperforming, and they assist the accounting staff in preparing data for quarterly reports to senior management. Real Estate Investment Analysts are sometimes involved in database management, trend analysis, and preparation of new business presentations to senior management, developers, or clients.

Real estate analysts focus their attention on preparing financial analysis, environmental assessments, and land-use issues. Their primary duties typically include the following:

- assisting in financial analysis of existing portfolio assets
- conducting pre-acquisition due diligence or market research of real estate development opportunities
- preparing financing packages for prospective lenders
- coordinating lender visits to development sites and investment presentations to lenders
- qualifying underwriting, financial modeling, scenario analysis, budgeting, forecasting and reporting on investments in office, hotel, retail, and residential properties

Real estate investment analysts typically work a 40-hour week in an office setting. They may work longer hours, including weekends, during peak production periods, for example when working on a project deadline.

Salaries

Salaries of Real Estate Investment Analysts usually range from $55,000 a year for individuals starting their career to $90,000 or more. Analysts employed in the larger banks, which typically approve the multimillion dollar loans to real estate developers, can earn upwards of $100,000 a year. They may also earn a performance bonus tied to the success of the department or the lender's overall return on assets in a particular year.

Employment Prospects

Qualified financial analysts are always in demand. Analysts who can grasp the differences between market sub-sectors (shopping centers or office markets, for example) are more important than ever in commercial real estate. Opportunities for real estate analysts with some experience analyzing real estate investment opportunities are expected to remain strong over the next five to 10 years.

Some job opportunities for entry-level staffing come about through staffing turnover. More applicants are interested in the development and leasing side of the business than in a supporting role as a back-office numbers cruncher. Brokerage teams need an experienced supporting team at the back office so they can go out and bring in new business.

Advancement Prospects

Real estate analysts can advance to positions of increasing responsibility, such as senior analyst or research director. Advancement may require upgrading job skills to stay current with industry trends and changes in regulation. An M.B.A. or master's degree may be required for advancement to management positions. Some of these positions may require a master's degree in real estate or a related field of study.

Education and Training

Most employers look for people with a four-year degree in accounting, business, or related academic courses and a proficiency in financial analysis. Candidates should be detail-oriented, with in-depth analytical aptitude, excellent written and verbal communication skills, and strong knowledge of Excel spreadsheet program and ARGUS real estate database software.

While technical skills are important to the job, there is more to the job than knowing how to read spreadsheets and interpret financial data. If you don't have any ARGUS training, you can pick up the basics by attending an ARGUS class or taking an online course.

The software is more user-friendly today, and courses are available from real estate schools. A general background in real estate fundamentals—how properties are valued and investment returns measured—can be a good place to start.

Experience, Skills, and Personality Traits

Some prior experience analyzing real estate investment reports is normally a requirement, usually one to three years. Analysts should have good analytical and communication skills and an ability to create accounting journal entries based on their analysis. Also important are good decision-making skills and problem-solving skills and a proficiency in working with spreadsheet accounting programs.

Strong communication skills and report writing are integral to the job. Investment analysts use real estate–specific analytical software such Skyline, Timberline, PROJECT, or ARGUS, and a working knowledge of these software programs would be very useful. Also important is having an ability to produce designs and graphs for presentation and some proficiency with Excel spreadsheet software.

Unions and Associations

The National Association of Industrial and Office Properties offers networking and career management opportunities for Real Estate Investment Analysts through schools, conferences, and industry specific seminars.

Tips for Entry

1. Real estate firms will sometimes hire college graduates with strong academic records and a desire to work in real estate. Check Web site job boards for entry-level financial analyst opportunities.
2. College courses in accounting, finance, and statistics are helpful, as are courses in ARGUS, a real estate financial management software. Take an ARGUS course to brush up on your ARGUS skills.
3. Attend trade association career events and networking events to make contacts with real estate investment firms in your area.
4. Check career tips on interviewing techniques and résumé writing on Specialty Consultants Web site (http://www.specon.com) and other real estate Web sites.
5. Internship opportunities, both paid and unpaid, are a great way to make connections with potential employers while still in school.

CHIEF INVESTMENT OFFICER

Duties: Senior officer responsible for acquisition of income-producing real estate, portfolios, or other investment opportunities; assists in securing equity investors or project financing

Alternate Title(s): None

Salary Range: $339,000 to $433,000

Employment Prospects: Good

Advancement Prospects: Fair

Prerequisites:

    Education or Training—Four-year degree in finance or real estate; advanced degree in real estate or M.B.A. preferred

    Experience—Three to five years' experience in investment real estate and real estate development; experience with real estate syndication

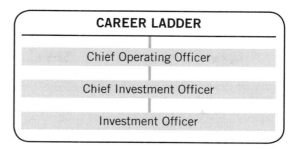

CAREER LADDER

Chief Operating Officer

Chief Investment Officer

Investment Officer

Special Skills and Personality Traits—Thorough understanding of real estate lending and finance; fluency in Excel spreadsheet accounting and financial analysis software; excellent communication skills

Position Description

The Chief Investment Officer (CIO) oversees development and execution of investment strategy for all classes of real estate investments. He or she is responsible for identifying, recommending, and negotiating the acquisition of income-producing properties, real estate portfolios, or other value-creating opportunities. In some companies the Chief Investment Officer also serves as the chief financial officer and has overall responsibility for all financial activities.

As senior investment officer, the CIO may be involved in raising equity capital from business partners or securing financing from commercial banks or other funding sources. The CIO also directs the due diligence process, or the careful examination of relevant financial records and reports, when considering an acquisition or a minority share investment in income property.

As senior investment officer, the CIO will search out potential business partners, including developers and construction firms, and identify potential investors. The Chief Investment Officer coordinates the risk management assessment of pending projects, reviewing projects for potential weaknesses and strengths. The Chief Investment Officer provides senior-level guidance on acquisition or disposition opportunities and maintains a network of real estate brokers and investors for portfolio properties. The CIO makes strategy

recommendations to the management committee and follows up on committee recommendations.

The Chief Investment Officer plays an integral role in securing capital for real estate acquisition from bank lenders, investment partners, or directly from investors. If the company is a real estate investment trust (REIT), financing can be secured through sales of investment shares directly to the public.

Typical responsibilities of a senior investment officer include the following:

- negotiating contracts, terms, and prices of properties marked for disposition and preparing letters of intent
- overseeing all financial reporting functions related to investments, including preparation of budget projections and tax compliance
- overseeing a staff of financial analysts and investment officers to ensure accurate financial modeling
- providing advice to in-house legal staff or external real estate attorneys regarding key elements of acquisitions, dispositions, due diligence, and negotiations
- writing property-by-property analysis using cash flow projections for all portfolio properties
- assisting senior officers in writing internal and external financial reports to investors, business partners, and government agencies

Investment officers typically work long hours, often 50 or 60 per week. They have frequent job-related travel, visiting business partners or associates, and may also attend meetings of financial and economic associations to give business presentations.

Salaries

Chief Investment Officers are well compensated for their efforts. CIOs receive a combination of salary and annual bonus tied to company performance. Compensation is influenced by a wide number of factors, such as company size, industry, geographic location, and professional experience. CEL & Associates, Inc., a compensation consulting firm, reports real estate companies paid out base salaries in 2006 ranging from $339,000 to $433,000. About 400 real estate companies participate annually in this survey. CIOs typically receive an annual performance bonus equal to 50 percent or more of their base salary.

Employment Prospects

There is nationwide competition for experienced real estate investment officers, although the number of openings available at any given time is likely to be small. There are several paths to becoming a CIO. Many candidates have previous experience as an investment officer or have worked in a similar position managing property acquisitions or dispositions. The typical entry level path is as a junior investment officer, or assistant investment officer. An assistant investment officer is responsible for a portfolio of investment partnerships and provides back-up administration support to the Chief Investment Officer.

The long-run prospects for financial managers of all types should be favorable, because more people will be needed to handle increasingly complex financial transactions and manage portfolio investments. Some companies hire financial managers on a temporary basis to see the organization through a short-term crisis or to make recommendations on ways to boost profits or reduce costs.

Advancement Prospects

As the top ranking investment officer, the CIO occupies a senior-level position. Further advancement is possible, but in practice is often difficult to achieve. A CIO can advance to chief operating officer, chief executive officer, or company president. Most CIOs advance their careers by starting their own real estate investment firms or real estate advisory firms.

Education and Training

Most employers look for candidates with a four-year degree in finance or real estate. A post-graduate degree such as a master's degree in real estate or an M.B.A. degree is a plus. Candidates with an M.A. or M.B.A. degree may receive preferential consideration. Experienced investment officers have a solid academic background in financial theories, principles, and concepts commonly used in real estate investments.

Continuing education is vital to financial managers, who must cope with changes in federal and state laws and regulations and the proliferation of new and complex financial instruments. Financial management associations sponsor numerous national and local training programs, often in cooperation with local colleges and universities. Many firms pay all or part of the costs for employees who successfully complete courses. Although experience, ability, and leadership are emphasized for promotion, advancement may be accelerated by special study.

Experience, Skills, and Personality Traits

Experience may be more important than education for real estate investment officers. Prior experience with income-producing real estate or real estate investments is a prerequisite. Typically, five to 10 years' experience in real estate investments and real estate syndications is preferred. A senior investment officer is expected to have a strong track record in real estate asset management, project management, and financial analysis. Some experience in real estate sales or marketing is also a very useful background. Investment officers spend a fair amount of their time giving presentations, so excellent communication skills, both verbal and written, are important on-the-job skills. A fluency in Microsoft Excel spreadsheet accounting software and financial analysis software is an essential skill.

Unions and Associations

As financial professionals, CIOs can become members of several professional associations. Among these are the Association for Financial Professionals, the CCIM Institute, or the Financial Executives Institute for professional networking and career advancement.

Tips for Entry

1. Personal contacts with friends or former business associates are always useful, particularly when approaching a company for the first time.
2. Contacts with executive search can pay off here. Aside from in-house promotions and personal

referrals, search firms are a top source of senior-level candidates when vacancies occur.

3. Temporary assignments can lead to a longer-term career at a new employer; recruiters are a good source of temporary or interim employment opportunities.

4. The Internet is an excellent source of information about positions at all levels. Use the Internet to do research on prospective employers and keep up with trends, especially if you are considering changing industries.

CHIEF FINANCIAL OFFICER

CAREER PROFILE

Duties: Directs accounting, finance, and treasury functions; prepares internal and external financial reports; communicates frequently with investors and capital partners

Alternate Title(s): None

Salary Range: $209,000 to $291,000

Employment Prospects: Good

Advancement Prospects: Fair

Prerequisites:

    Education or Training—Four-year degree with emphasis in accounting and finance; M.B.A. often preferred

    Experience—Four to 10 or more years' experience in corporate finance with increasing levels of responsibility

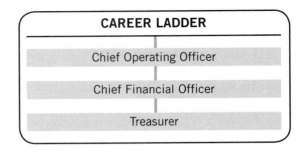

CAREER LADDER

Chief Operating Officer

Chief Financial Officer

Treasurer

Special Skills and Personality Traits—Visionary or strategic thinking; strong leadership skills and interpersonal skills; ability to delegate responsibility

Special Requirements—Professional certification such as Certified Public Accountant (CPA) designation

Position Description

The Chief Financial Officer (CFO) is the top financial officer of an organization, usually a public corporation. CFOs direct all accounting and financial functions, preparation of financial reports and fiscal reports, and investment activities. They formulate, through subordinate officers, finanacial plans and policies and relations with key outside organizations, including leading institutions, shareholders, and the financial community. The CFO is normally a senior officer, reporting directly to the president, chief operating officer, or chief executive officer.

In carrying out their duties, CFOs function principally as the financial architects of their organizations. He or she works closely with senior executives to provide financial support for the achievement of strategic goals. The CFO directs the financial activities of the accounting groups, ensuring the integrity of financial data, providing timely and accurate analysis and management reports, and ensuring adequate accounting controls.

As a high-level executive, the CFO must know how to delegate responsibility to subordinates, allowing trusted managers to take charge of various accounting, treasury reporting, and other functions. The CFO must be able to present budget and planning proposals to the chief executive officer (CEO), the highest corporate executive, or to the board of directors.

Strategic planning and visionary skills are becoming more important in what is becoming a global economy. Corporations are starting to run their business activities with an integrated or enterprise-wide approach to management, examining the cumulative impact of various business functions on corporate earnings, market share, and so on. Increasingly, it is the CFO's responsibility to bring together the corporate treasurer, controller, risk manager, and other senior officers to try to develop creative solutions to business problems.

In performing his or her duties, the Chief Financial Officer will:

- direct all accounting, treasury, and financial functions
- supervise payroll, tax accounting, and relationships with bank lenders
- monitor the company's cash position
- determine accounting and financial reporting policy
- direct the preparation of internal and external financial reports
- communicate frequently with investors and capital partners
- direct company financial reporting in quarterly conference calls with financial analysts

As a senior level executive, the Chief Financial Officer works long hours, often 50 or more hours a week.

Frequent travel is a part of the job, and the CFO is often on the road visiting affiliated companies, financial partners, or attending business conferences and trade shows.

Salaries

As high-profile officers, Chief Financial Officers are generously compensated for their efforts. Typically, CFOs receive a combination of salary, annual bonus tied to company performance, and stock options. Signing bonuses have become common, especially for experienced CFOs. A smaller number of companies offer retention bonuses to keep valued employees on staff.

Actual compensation earned by CFOs varies according to a wide number of factors, including company size, industry, geographic location, and professional experience. CFOs of real estate companies reporting their salary data to CEL & Associates, Inc., a compensation consulting firm, reported paying base salaries ranging from $209,000 to $291,000 in 2006. About 400 real estate companies participate annually in this survey. CFOs typically receive an annual performance bonus equal to 50 percent or more of their base salary.

Employment Prospects

There is nationwide competition for experienced CFOs, although the number of openings available at any given time is likely to be small. Competition for the choicest assignments, says a CFO for a Fortune 100 company, can be especially intense. Vacancies in top companies are often filled by executive search firms.

There are several paths to becoming a CFO. Many CFOs have previous experience as corporate treasurer, investment officer, or financial controller. Treasurers could move up to become CFOs, filling job vacancies, as long as they are well-rounded individuals experienced in computer systems and strategic planning in addition to corporate treasury functions. An individual who has created an impressive record as a manager may be in a position to move up to a CFO position being created for the first time, but there are no guarantees. Most CFO vacancies are filled from within the company, by personal referrals, or by executive search firms.

Advancement Prospects

As the top financial officer, the CFO already occupies a senior-level position. Further advancement to chief operating officer, chief executive officer, or company president is possible, but in practice difficult to achieve. Most CFOs advance their careers by leaving their companies to take similar positions at other firms or starting their own real estate investment firms or development firms.

Education and Training

The foundation for a Chief Financial Officer is a strong undergraduate and graduate background, usually with a high grade point average. A four-year degree with an emphasis in accounting and finance or related courses is the minimum academic criteria, and many employers look for candidates with an M.B.A. degree or a postgraduate degree in finance. Courses in information technology and database management are also helpful.

Special Requirements

Professional certification is generally a standard requirement. Most CFOs have achieved at least one certification, and often several, from recognized professional groups. Perhaps the most common is the Certified Public Accountant (CPA) designation.

Experience, Skills, and Personality Traits

Most employers want to interview individuals with a strong track record and four to 10 years' or more experience in a variety of corporate finance positions. Strong written and interpersonal communication skills are essential to the job; CFOs spend much of their time making presentations to senior executives, financial analysts, and the board of directors.

In recent years, the skill requirements of CFOs have tightened; employers want people who can help develop strategy and function as business partners to the CEO in addition to performing their financial duties. Strong communication and interpersonal skills are important for CFOs, but these are not the highest ranked skills, according to a survey of senior executives by *CFO Magazine*. This survey ranked communication skills third on the list, after financial expertise and a strong sense of personal integrity and professional ethics.

Unions and Associations

As financial professionals, CFOs can become members of several professional associations. Among these are the Association for Financial Professionals, the CCIM Institute, or the Financial Executives Institute for professional networking and career advancement.

Tips for Entry

1. As in other finance positions, contacts and connections are always useful, particularly when approaching a company for the first time. Executive recruiters can also help with initial contacts leading to an interview.

2. People who demonstrate entrepreneurial flair or who add value by getting projects done on schedule will always be in demand.

3. Contacts with executive search can pay off here. Aside from in-house promotions and personal referrals, search firms are a top source of CFO candidates when vacancies occur.

4. The Internet is an excellent source of information about positions at all levels. Use the Internet to do research on prospective employers and keep up with trends, especially if you are considering changing industries.

RISK MANAGER

CAREER PROFILE

Duties: Identifies risks and risk mitigating measures; prepares credit assessments and monitors performance; manages compliance with government regulations

Alternate Title(s): Risk Officer

Salary Range: $100,000 to $127,000

Employment Prospects: Good

Advancement Prospects: Good

Prerequisites:

Education or Training—Four-year degree in finance or a related field of study, master's degree or M.B.A. recommended

Experience—Five to 10 years' progressive experience in commercial or residential real estate

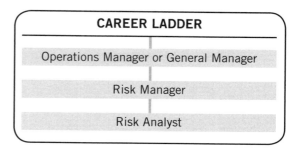

CAREER LADDER

Operations Manager or General Manager

Risk Manager

Risk Analyst

Special Skills and Personality Traits—Excellent communication and organizational skills; strong analytical and problem-solving skills; strong leadership skills

Position Description

In the world of commercial real estate, risk is anything that creates uncertainty about a property or portfolio. The Risk Manager is the senior executive responsible for financial management functions associated with insurance, safety, and disaster recovery. The Risk Manager also oversees emergency procedures and compliance with government regulations covering workplace safety. The manager may also be responsible for workplace safety issues in construction management, vendor relationships, and contracts with subcontractors or outside service firms.

Property Risk Managers develop policies across a broad spectrum of potential risks, including but not limited to fires, flooding, and other natural disasters, environmental risks from mold and hazardous materials, and terrorism risk. The Risk Manager develops, administers, and monitors a risk management program to assist in the prevention and reduction of claims, loss, and insurance litigation activity and maintains a library of risk management policies and procedures. The Risk Manager may appoint and manage independent insurance brokers to provide insurance marketplace access and risk management services.

An important part of risk management is computing the risk versus reward trade-off. Take for example a hot tub or swimming pool on the property. The property manager has to balance the value of the pool with the associated risks (accidental drowning being the worst

possible outcome). In this example there are three ways to deal with the swimming pool risk:

- avoidance: Remove the hot tub or pool if the additional expected income is not worth the cost of insurance.
- control: If the hot tub is retained, a coded lock or border fence might be installed to keep out younger children.
- risk transfer: Take out an insurance policy to transfer risk to the insurer—the most common way that property managers deal with identifiable risks.

Risk Managers are also important participants in managing the global risks affecting a business and devising strategies to manage these risks. A recent evolution in risk management is enterprise-wide risk management, in which the company takes a holistic view of all financial and non-financial risks to the business. Risk Managers spend much of their time in an office setting but are required to travel on a regular basis to production departments.

In performing their duties, Risk Managers are active in many different ways. Typical duties performed often include the following:

- participating in the management and coordination of insurance programs, either self-insured or commercially purchased insurance
- working with senior management to secure constant improvement in risk management procedures

- reviewing contracts and agreements with respect to insurance and indemnity language
- reviewing vendor, tenant, investor, and partner insurance requirements and ensuring compliance with these requirements
- developing and monitoring an emergency preparedness program at all facility locations
- coordinating the development of a business continuity plan
- developing an annual departmental budget and corporate insurance expense budget

Risk Managers work in an office setting and typically work a 40-hour workweek. As salaried employees, they may work longer hours during peak periods, for example during a project deadline. This is normally uncompensated overtime.

Salaries

Risk Managers' salaries vary by company size, level of responsibility, academic training, and level of experience in the industry. According to the U.S. Department of Labor, earnings for financial managers (including Risk Managers) varied from a low of $21,800 to $80,000 in 2006. Senior Risk Managers employed in real estate finance earned base salaries of $100,000 to $127,000 in 2006, according to CEL & Associates, Inc., a compensation consulting firm specializing in real estate. Risk Managers may also receive performance bonuses pegged to department or company performance over the prior year. They typically receive a standard benefits package, including health and life insurance, paid vacations, and other non-financial compensation.

Employment Prospects

There are excellent opportunities for risk analysts and Risk Managers over the next several years. Risk management is an accepted discipline in real estate finance, creating numerous employment opportunities for skilled practitioners. Salaried opportunities for Risk Managers are expected to grow faster than the overall economy through 2014. Organizations recognize risk management as an integral and effective tool in cost containment and business strategy. Risk Managers can enter the profession from careers in accounting, personnel, or insurance. The usual entry is from a risk analyst position or financial analyst position.

Advancement Prospects

Risk Managers can advance to positions of increased responsibility, ultimately advancing to the position of general manager or operations manager. Risk Managers can also work in related fields, such as human resources or employee benefits management. Some leave the corporate world to become risk management consultants for major accounting firms and management consulting firms.

Education and Training

Employers generally prefer college graduates with a bachelor's degree in real estate, finance, or accounting. If the position is highly specialized, employers often prefer to hire individuals with a post-graduate degree in finance or real estate or an M.B.A. degree. The risk management position requires a broad background in business management and finance. Some universities have academic programs in risk management and insurance. Courses in accounting, finance, business law, engineering, management, and political science are also helpful.

Earning an industry certification can bolster an individual's qualifications and prospects for advancement to more senior, and higher paying, positions. The Risk and Insurance Management Society, Inc. (RIMS) offers a Risk and Insurance Management certificate to individuals who have completed a college-level risk management course or have equivalent experience and attended a risk management workshop. The Global Risk Management Institute, Inc., confers the Risk Fellow designation to individuals who have attended an approved risk management educational program, attend a certain number of continuing education courses annually, and meet certain other requirements.

Experience, Skills, and Personality Traits

The position requires at least five years' experience in risk management, treasury, or insurance. Important job-related skills are excellent communication skills, good organizational skills, and negotiating skills. Risk Managers should have an ability to build consensus among departmental managers and corporate staff in devising solutions to specific situations. Mastery of spreadsheet accounting programs is also an essential part of the job.

Unions and Associations

Risk management professionals can join the Risk and Insurance Management Society, the Public Risk Management Association, and other organizations for networking and career advancement opportunities. They can also become members of professional real estate associations such as the CCIM Institute.

Tips for Entry

1. College placement officers can help arrange job interviews with prospective employers.
2. Attend industry meetings sponsored by the Risk Insurance Managers Society to learn about new developments in the field.
3. Get a broad academic background and learn how business works; managing risk is an integral part of the business world.
4. The Spencer Educational Foundation, affiliated with RIMS, offers academic scholarships to academically outstanding students pursuing careers in risk management and insurance.

RESEARCH DIRECTOR

CAREER PROFILE

Duties: Responsible for overall management of the research department; monitors economic, demographic, product, and competitor trends; may write market trend reports for marketing

Alternate Title(s): Manager of Research, Research Services Manager

Salary Range: $75,000 to $100,000

Employment Prospects: Good

Advancement Prospects: Fair

Prerequisites:

Education or Training—Four-year degree in business administration, economics, finance, real estate, or a related field of study

Experience—Three or more years' experience in real estate analysis and market research; excellent

CAREER LADDER

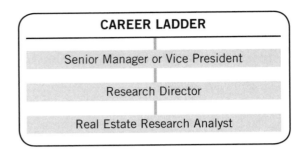

Senior Manager or Vice President

Research Director

Real Estate Research Analyst

database and systems management experience; advanced Excel spreadsheet experience

Special Skills and Personality Traits—Excellent analytical and decision-making skills; strong organizational skills and communication skills; proficiency in database and Web-based research

Position Description

The Research Director is responsible for day-to-day management of the real estate research department. Research Directors work closely with senior management and sales brokers to address their research needs and develop appropriate solutions. They are responsible for personnel management, database management, market analysis, forecasting, and producing market reports and overviews. They may assist in training of research staff and sales brokers.

Research Directors conduct analysis and market studies to provide information to make informed business decisions supporting new business opportunities. They serve as an information resource to professional staff and convey a broad understanding of market conditions and relative values of markets and property types. When working with an investment advisory firm or investment management firm, the Research Director is an active partner in developing and defining investment strategy.

The Research Director reviews published information on prevailing market conditions, attends seminars, and makes recommendations on specific markets and investment types. Research findings are summarized in reports and published articles for use internally or for distribution to clients.

The head of research follows economic and demographic trends and real estate market data to identify trends and make conclusions guiding investment strat-

egies and decisions. Research Directors review the market and macroeconomic variables to be used in testing the feasibility of investment opportunities. They make recommendations based on analysis on investment strategy, that is, whether to continue to hold or sell specific properties in the investment portfolio.

Research Directors provide market data and real estate analysis for front-line departments, including capital markets, tenant representation, appraisal, real estate brokerage, and others. They collaborate with the brokerage staff to generate reports on specific properties, markets, and market activities. They maintain proprietary internal databases on properties in specific, targeted market areas and update these records to ensure that reports are both timely and accurate.

Their day-to-day responsibilities typically include the following:

- gathering data on national or regional and local economic, demographic, and socio-economic trends and analyzing their impact on real estate markets
- producing quarterly market statistics for local and national markets
- researching commercial real estate markets, analyzing supply, demand, vacancy, and rent trends for various real estate products
- tracking market rental information, employment data and demographic data for specific markets

- preparing studies of the competitive environment for current and future portfolio property acquisition
- making recommendations on pricing, product mix, and investment strategy
- reviewing newspapers, journals, third-party market reports, and other sources of information
- compiling high-level summaries for the company's acquisition and investment management staff
- managing the purchase and use of purchased market research data and other sources of information
- mentoring and supervising junior analysts

Research Directors may also be involved in the selection of independent third-party research for use in decision making, assisting senior management in developing the company business plan, and assisting the management team in introducing non-U.S. investors to the U.S. real estate market. Research Directors work in an office setting, usually working a 40-hour workweek.

Salaries

Salaries vary with experience and position responsibilities. Real estate Research Directors with several years' experience can expect to earn base salaries of $75,000 to $100,000 and up. They may also receive annual performance bonuses equal to 10 percent or more of base salary, based on the success of the department or the lender's overall return on assets in a particular year. As salaried employees, Research Directors receive a standard benefits package, including paid health insurance, sick leave, vacations, and tuition reimbursement.

Employment Prospects

Employment opportunities for Research Directors are tied to the overall success of the real estate industry. Market demand is expected to remain strong as the industry becomes more research-focused in identifying and bringing to market new development opportunities. Real estate investment professionals who can meet the information needs of investors will always be in demand.

Financial analysts who understand the differences between market sub-sectors (shopping centers or office markets, for example) have become essential players in commercial real estate. In a highly competitive market, there is little margin for error as profit margins get squeezed tighter and capitalization rates (or cap rates, a measure of real estate return on investment) come under increasing pressure. Opportunities for real estate analysts with some experience analyzing real estate investment opportunities are expected to remain strong over the next five to 10 years.

Advancement Prospects

Advancement opportunities for Research Directors are more limited than for junior real estate analysts. A director of research who has strong supervisory skills can advance to become a managing partner or managing director in the firm. Advancement may require earning an M.B.A. degree, a master's degree in real estate, or an advanced certification in investment research such as Chartered Financial Analyst (CFA) designation conferred by the CFA Institute.

Education and Training

A four-year degree in economics, business administration, real estate, urban studies, or a related field of study is a minimum requirement. Financial analysts who move into this position are expected to have a solid foundation in the fundamentals of finance and investment theory and have a hands-on understanding of performance measurement and attribution analysis. A solid knowledge of real estate markets and commercial real estate fundamentals is normally a pre-requisite to a position in real estate market research.

Experience, Skills, and Personality Traits

Qualified candidates have a strong track record of providing insightful market analysis and making strategic investment recommendations. Most firms look for individuals who have at least three to five years' experience in real estate market research and real estate investment analysis. A director of research should have excellent analytical and decision-making skills; strong organizational skills and communication skills; proficiency in database and web-based research technology.

Research Directors have a high level of interaction with senior management. They should have excellent oral communication skills and ability to deliver clearly written summaries of research findings and recommendations. Proficient computer skills are an important skill, notably a facility with the Microsoft Office suite, and an ability to present statistical data in charts and graphs for client and senior management presentations.

Unions and Associations

Professional associations such as the CCIM Institute or CoreNet Global, among others, offer many opportunities for networking with other real estate professionals and staying up with developments in the field by attending association meetings and seminars. Much of this activity occurs within regional affiliates of national real estate organizations.

Tips for Entry

1. Get to know recruiting firms specializing in placement of real estate professionals.

2. Check industry job boards on association Web sites for leads on current employment opportunities.

3. Attend trade association career events and networking events to make contacts with real estate investment firms in your area.

TAX MANAGER

CAREER PROFILE

Duties: Prepares corporate, partnership and/or limited liability company tax returns; projects tax obligations; researches tax and compliance issues; oversees federal and state audits; may have supervisory responsibility

Alternate Title(s): Tax Accountant

Salary Range: $91,000 to $115,000

Employment Prospects: Good

Advancement Prospects: Fair

Prerequisites:

   Education or Training—Four-year degree in accounting, finance or taxation; master's degree optional

   Experience—Four or more years' experience in public accounting; real estate experience

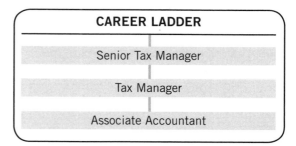

CAREER LADDER

Senior Tax Manager

Tax Manager

Associate Accountant

Special Skills and Personality Traits—Problem-solving skills; strong Microsoft Office skills; excellent Excel spreadsheet skills; strong verbal and written communication skills

Special Requirements—CPA license required for mangers filing Securities and Exchange Commission reports

Position Description

Real estate Tax Managers prepare corporate, partnership, and/or limited liability company tax returns. They are responsible for tax compliance for their clients and are frequently consulted on tax planning strategies. They review the tax-related issues in real estate acquisitions or property sales.

Tax Managers are typically involved in the life cycle of real estate ownership—from acquisition due diligence to disposition (property sales) and related federal or state tax compliance issues. They estimate future tax obligations, research tax and compliance issues, and oversee federal and state audits. They typically have supervisory responsibility and help train associate accountants assigned to work on tax-related issues.

Tax Managers assist in identifying new business opportunities and offer their advice on deal structuring, tax planning and compliance, and business advisory services. They take the lead in resolving complex tax issues.

Typical duties include, but are not limited to, the following:

- calculating quarterly projected taxable income
- preparing and filing business licenses, personal property tax returns, and annual reports
- evaluating and selecting alternative actions to mitigate the tax burden and cost of compliance

- recognizing and communicating potential risks
- identifying potential changes in tax policy
- developing new policies in tax compliance
- assisting in handling routine inquiries from federal or state regulators

Most accountants work in an office setting. They work a standard 40-hour workweek, but may work longer hours in the weeks or months proceeding tax filing deadlines or during periods of peak business activity.

Salaries

Salaries vary with experience, individual background, and industry specialty. Real estate Tax Managers earn annual compensation of $91,000 to $115,000 in base salary and are eligible for additional compensation through annual performance bonuses or participation in profit-sharing plans. They may also participate in employer-sponsored pension plans and get employer funded health insurance, vacation pay, and other fringe benefits.

Employment Prospects

Strong growth of accountants and auditor jobs over the 2006–16 decade is expected to result from stricter accounting and auditing regulations, along with an expanding economy. The best job prospects will be for accountants and auditors who have a college degree or any certification, but especially a Certified Public Accounting (CPA) designation.

In general, employment of accountants and auditors is expected to grow by 18 percent between 2006 and 2016, according to the U.S. Bureau of Labor Statistics, which is faster than the average for all occupations. This occupation will have a very large number of new jobs, almost 226,000 over the projection decade. An increase in the number of businesses, changing financial laws, corporate governance regulations, and increased accountability for protecting an organization's stakeholders will drive growth.

Overall, job opportunities for accountants and auditors should be very favorable. Those who earn a CPA should have excellent job prospects. After most states instituted the 150-hour rule for CPAs, enrollment in accounting programs declined. However, enrollment is again growing as more students have become attracted to the profession by the attention from the accounting scandals.

In the aftermath of the accounting scandals, professional certification is even more important to ensure that accountants' credentials and knowledge of ethics are sound. Regardless of specialty, accountants and auditors who have earned professional recognition through certification or licensure should have the best job prospects. Applicants with a master's degree in accounting or a master's degree in business administration with a concentration in accounting also will have an advantage.

Advancement Prospects

Tax Managers generally advance their careers by developing competency in a specialty area or by developing strong management skills. Accountants with public accounting experience usually have plenty of occupational mobility. As they rise through the organization, they may advance to accounting manager, budget director, controller, treasurer, or financial manager.

Education and Training

A four-year degree is generally a requirement with a concentration in accounting, finance, or taxation. A master's degree or course work toward a master's degree in finance may be a requirement in competitive positions. Real estate consulting firms and accounting firms that typically hire Tax Managers offer on-the-job training, mentoring, and career development coaching to help newly hired managers reach their potential and become more effective managers.

College graduates who are proficient in accounting and auditing computer software or have expertise in specialized areas—such as international business, specific industries, or current legislation—may have an advantage in getting some accounting and auditing jobs. In addition, employers increasingly seek applicants with strong interpersonal and communication skills. Many accountants work on teams with others who have different backgrounds, so they must be able to communicate accounting and financial information clearly and concisely. Regardless of qualifications, however, competition will remain keen for the most prestigious jobs in major accounting and business firms.

Special Requirements

Any accountant filing reports with the Securities and Exchange Commission is required by law to be a Certified Public Accountant (CPA). CPAs are licensed by their State Board of Accountancy. As of 2007, 42 states and the District of Columbia require CPA candidates to complete 150 hours of college course work—30 additional hours beyond the usual four-year bachelor's degree. Nearly all states require a certain number of hours of continuing education courses before CPA licenses can be renewed.

Experience, Skills, and Personality Traits

Previous experience in accounting or auditing can help applicants get a job. Most employers look for individuals with at least four years' experience in real estate auditing or accounting. Some previous experience in real estate partnerships or real estate tax management is recommended and may be a requirement with some employers. If the position requires supervising or training junior employees, some management experience, normally two years, is often a requirement.

Individuals should have strong problem-solving skills, a proficiency with the Microsoft Office software suite and excellent Excel spreadsheet skills. Strong verbal and written communication skills are also important. A strong work ethic and a desire to succeed are very helpful personality traits. Employers look for candidates with a desire to develop professional skills and leadership skills.

Unions and Associations

Many tax professionals choose to join an industry association to keep up with developments in the accounting field and to network with their peers at industry events. Real estate Tax Managers can become members of professional real estate associations such as the CCIM Institute or professional accounting associations such as the American Institute of Certified Public Accountants.

These associations sponsor frequent conferences, seminars, and other meetings to help accountants maintain their job skills and stay current with industry trends.

Tips for Entry

1. Many colleges offer students the opportunity to get experience through summer jobs or internships with public accounting firms or businesses.
2. Information on accredited accounting programs at colleges or universities can be found at the Association to Advance Collegiate Schools of Business Web site (http://www.aacsb.edu).
3. Get information on the Certified Public Accountant (CPA) licensing requirements from the National Association of State Boards of Accountancy (http://www.nasba.org).
4. The Institute of Management Accountants (http://www.imanet.org) has information on careers in management accounting.

ADMINISTRATION

BENEFITS ADMINISTRATOR

CAREER PROFILE

Duties: Assists in management of personnel-related policies and programs; administers corporate health, life, and disability insurance; negotiates contracts with service providers

Alternate Title(s): Benefits Manager, Benefits Supervisor

Salary Range: $49,970 to $89,340

Employment Prospects: Good

Advancement Prospects: Good

Prerequisites:

Education or Training—Four-year degree in business, insurance, accounting, or a related field

Experience—Several years' experience in claims analysis and management

Special Skills and Personality Traits—Excellent communication and interviewing skills; excellent organizational skills; knowledge of claims processing and filing; working knowledge of employee welfare and benefit programs, health insurance, workers' compensation, and legal issues

Special Requirements—Certification optional

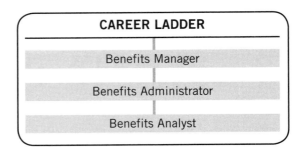

CAREER LADDER

Benefits Manager

Benefits Administrator

Benefits Analyst

Position Description

Employee Benefits Administrators and managers handle the company's employee benefits program—health insurance and pension programs. Expertise in this field continues to gain importance as employer-provided benefits account for a growing percentage of overall compensation costs, and also as benefit plans grow in size and complexity. Pension plan benefits typically include employee savings and thrift plans, profit sharing, and stock ownership plans.

Health benefits may include long-term catastrophic illness insurance, parental leave (paid or unpaid), dental insurance, and short-term disability benefits. Familiarity with health insurance has become a top priority, as health insurance costs have been increasing faster than consumer prices over the last decade, forcing companies to find new ways to provide affordable, yet comprehensive, employee health benefits.

In addition to health and pension programs, some firms offer life and accidental death and dismemberment insurance, child and elder care, long-term nursing home care insurance, employee assistance and wellness programs, and flexible benefit plans.

These professionals help design and implement employee health and life insurance programs for employers. They manage third-party insurance programs purchased from life insurance companies, health maintenance organizations (HMOs), and other healthcare providers. Benefits Administrators supervise the handling and submission of health insurance, workers' compensation, and general liability claims filed by employees. They also function as an intermediary, or liaison, between the employer, health insurers, and healthcare providers.

Administrators are involved in day-to-day management of insurance programs to ensure adequate coverage for employees. They negotiate policy renewals with HMOs and other health insurers. Benefits Administrators responsible for employee health benefits coordinate plan management with third-party administrators and insurance companies. They handle retiree billing and death benefits.

When acting as managers of company-sponsored 401(k) employee savings plans, Benefits Administrators notify employees of plan diversification options, process rollovers from other qualified retirement plans, and plan distributions to employees. They handle hardship withdrawals from a company-sponsored plan, 401(k) loans, and locate recipients of unclaimed benefits and dividend checks.

These administrators also perform retirement calculations, process inquiries from retirees about their benefits, and coordinate payment of retiree benefits. They also prepare quarterly statements and annual statements of account balances required by federal law.

Workplace safety, employee absenteeism, and health issues are handled by the human resources staff, including the Benefits Administrator. The manager may work directly with outside agencies to provide on-site counseling, as needed, or even specialized programs such as crisis intervention if these services are included in the benefits package. The benefits manager may act as bridge, or liaision, between management and workers in non-union companies.

Common workplace activities often include ensuring that all record keeping relating to workers' compensation, health and medical insurance, and other state or government regulations is completed as required and is up-to-date. The manager may also assist the human resources department and staff in handling all issues involving employee complaints regarding health or pension benefits that cannot be answered by other staffers.

Other duties performed may include the following:

- preparing benefits cost analyses of new employee benefits or additions to existing programs
- reporting changes in employee benefit plans to senior management
- notifying employees of benefit plan changes
- directing clerical support functions, such as updating records and processing insurance claims
- providing in-service training for new department employees and periodic training for all staff as required by changes to state or federal regulations
- assisting in hiring, supervising, and monitoring staff

Benefits administrators typically work a 40- to 50-hour workweek in an office setting. They may work longer hours during a benefit enrollment period. This position reports to the director of human resources.

Salaries
Annual salary rates for Benefits Administrators vary according to occupation, level of experience, training, location, size of the firm, and whether they are union members.

Benefits administrators earned salaries between $49,970 and $89,340 in 2007. The average compensation package in 2007, according to Abbot, Langer & Associates, Inc., was $57,682. This figure includes base salary, cash bonuses, and cash profit-sharing paid. Non-salary benefits in addition to salary usually include paid life and health insurance, paid vacations and sick leave, and participation in employer-sponsored retirement plans.

Employment Prospects
Employment opportunities should grow at a rate faster than overall job opportunities over the next several years. More employers are offering company-funded health and welfare programs to attract qualified employees. Also contributing to job growth is the widespread popularity of defined contribution pension plans such as 401(k) plans, which are funded through payroll deduction programs, usually with matching employer contributions up to a certain dollar amount of salary.

Advancement Prospects
With experience, Benefits Administrators can advance to more senior positions with increased management responsibility. They might advance to higher positions in human resources management, eventually becoming manager of human resources. Advancement to higher salaried positions is often linked to continuous improvement of job-related skills and industry certification. Earning a post-graduate degree in benefits administration increases the opportunities for promotion in most organizations.

Education and Training
A four-year college degree is recommended, with courses in accounting, communication, human resources management, business administration, or insurance. Courses in spreadsheet accounting, database management, and other popular computer programs are helpful. Employer-sponsored training is available from a number of sources, including the Institute for Insurance Education and Research, which sponsors training programs in benefits management, and the Society of Human Resources Management (SHRM). Four out of 10 human resources professionals say a college degree is essential to landing a position in benefits administration or human resources.

Special Requirements
Earning a professional certification is optional, though not required for entry. Certifications available to Benefits Administrators include the Certified Employee Benefits Specialist, which is co-sponsored by the International Foundation of Employee Benefit Plans and the Wharton School of the University of Pennsylvania.

Experience, Skills, and Personality Traits
Some prior experience in benefits or claims processing or claims administration is considered essential. Experience as a service provider with an insurance company is helpful. Benefits Administrators should have excellent communication skills and interviewing skills, good organizational skills, analytical skills, and interpersonal skills. Benefit managers must keep abreast of changing federal and state regulations and legislation that may affect employee benefits.

The position requires a working knowledge of corporate benefits and legal issues affecting corporate benefit programs. Administrators of employee pension plans and 401(k) employee savings plans should be familiar with federal or state regulations governing employer-sponsored employee savings plans.

Unions and Associations

Benefits Administrators can join several industry associations for networking and career advancement opportunities. Among these are the American Association of Professional Group Insurance Administrators, the Health Insurance Association of America, the American Payroll Association, and the 401k Association.

Tips for Entry

1. Take college-level courses in finance business management and law for a well-rounded academic background.
2. Internship programs provide opportunities to gain a practical understanding of industry practices and build contacts with potential employers.
3. Attend industry conferences, seminars, and job fairs and make personal contact with potential employers.

CONTROLLER

Duties: Prepares and maintains company records and issues financial reports; manages day-to-day budgeting and forecasting; coordinates auditing with internal and external auditors

Alternate Title(s): Financial Controller

Salary Range: $61,250 to $147,250

Employment Prospects: Good

Advancement Prospects: Good

Prerequisites:

Education or Training—Four-year degree in accounting, business, or finance. An M.B.A. degree is desirable.

Experience—Several years of increasing responsibility in budgeting, financial planning, and cost accounting; senior level positions require at least eight years' experience

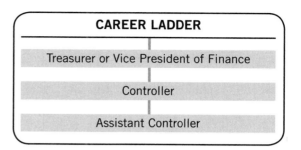

CAREER LADDER

Treasurer or Vice President of Finance

Controller

Assistant Controller

Special Skills and Personality Traits—Strong analytical, interpersonal, and organizational skills; ability to lead projects; excellent communication skills; detailed knowledge of manual and automated accounting systems; familiarity with real estate database systems

Special Requirements—Certified Public Accountant (CPA) certification often required in larger organizations

Position Description

As chief accountant, a financial Controller holds an important position in any business.

The Controller prepares short-term and long-term budgets and accounting reports for senior management and supervises audits and reports filed with government agencies. The Controller has responsibility for day-to-day funds disbursements, including the company's payroll, and coordinates activities of internal and external auditors.

Real estate companies perform audits for different reasons. Companies do audits to determine which businesses are performing well and which ones need attention, or why a certain business strategy worked well and others didn't work out. Some audits are required by government regulations. Controllers of public companies have to be familiar with the Sarbanes-Oxley Act, a federal law that requires that public companies attest that they have sufficient internal controls (as detailed in Sarbanes-Oxley Section 404) to prevent any financial misconduct that could be harmful to investors.

Controllers are the main budget planners in a company. They may function at the division or business-unit level or be responsible for overall budgeting and expense-related disbursements for an entire corporation. In large corporations, the Controller has a high-profile job, reporting directly to the chief financial officer and the corporate finance committee.

At the corporate level, the Controller's duties include:

- ensuring the timely and accurate processing of accounting and financial reports to management and audit staff
- managing all aspects of accounting, including accounts payable, accounts receivable, and general ledger
- ensuring timely monthly and year-end reporting and tax filings
- managing investor financial reporting, including return on investment and internal rate of return calculations
- formulating goals and objectives for financial and accounting activities
- maintaining internal accounting controls
- supervising the activities of business unit Controllers and corporate treasury
- developing annual operating budgets and monitoring the achievement of these plans
- coordinating the activities of outside auditors to ensure that each audit performed by the auditing firm is performed in a timely and cost-efficient manner

- contributing to senior management decision-making on special projects, acquisitions, reorganizations, and in long-range planning activities
- managing annual budget preparations and expense reconciliations

The Controller's job requires extensive accounting experience. Holders of the position often come from big accounting firms, or have previously been employed by accounting firms. In large organizations, the corporate Controller is responsible for day-to-day financial and accounting functions. In addition to coordinating financial reporting, the Controller is responsible for managing professional development of subordinate managers. In a small organization, the Controller may have responsibility for all financial and budgeting controls in the firm.

Salaries
Salaries tend to increase with size of the organization, years of experience, responsibilities, and geographic location. Salaries of corporate Controllers employed in real estate firms earned a median annual salary of $101,000 in 2006. Salaries of corporate Controllers varied from $61,250 to $147,250, according to search firm Robert Half International. Typically, corporate Controllers are compensated with a combination of salary and performance bonus plus stock options.

Employment Prospects
Opportunities are likely to grow through 2014 as the economy expands and increases the need for managers with expertise in auditing, budgeting, and financial management.

Businesses have an ongoing need to refresh their professional ranks with people who can handle increasingly complex financial transactions, and assess global risks as required by internal and external users of information. As in other managerial occupations, job seekers will face competition because the number of qualified applicants can exceed the number of available positions at any one time. Many businesses have raised compensation packages significantly to recruit the most qualified applicants.

Advancement Prospects
Real estate Controllers generally start out as division Controllers, where they handle financial reporting for a business unit and gain experience. The typical advancement path is from divisional Controller to corporate Controller, where they manage budgeting and accounting at the holding company level. Another advancement option is taking a similar position at another company, often with a hefty increase in salary and benefits. Controllers have excellent prospects for advancing to more senior positions, moving eventually to chief financial officer. Some Controllers change careers, becoming consultants with large accounting firms or setting up their own consulting firms.

Education and Training
A four-year degree in accounting, finance, or a related course of study is a minimum requirement for employment. However, many employers now seek graduates with a master's degree, preferably in business administration, economics, finance, or risk management. These academic programs develop analytical skills and teach the latest financial analysis methods and technology.

Continuing education is vital for financial managers, who must cope with the growing complexity of global trade, changes in federal and state laws and regulations, and the proliferation of new and complex financial instruments. Firms often provide opportunities for workers to broaden their knowledge and skills by encouraging employees to take graduate courses at colleges and universities or attend conferences related to their specialty. Many companies pay all or part of the costs for employees who successfully complete courses. Although experience, ability, and leadership are emphasized for promotion, advancement may be accelerated by this type of special study.

Special Requirements
Financial managers can broaden their skills and increase their marketability in a very competitive job market by earning a professional certification such as the Certified Public Accountant (CPA) designation from the American Institute of Certified Public Accountants.

Experience, Skills, and Personality Traits
Controllers usually have several years' experience performing complex tasks, such as leading cost management projects, and team leadership skills are preferred. Also important is an aptitude for abstract reasoning and excellent inter-personal skills and communication skills.

Well-developed financial analysis skills and managerial skills are also important. Advancing in the field usually requires a proven ability to recruit, train, and motivate employees to meet revenue and sales goals. Accounting systems in large organizations are highly automated operations. The Controller's position requires a working knowledge of both manual and automated accounting and financial controls systems and financial management software. A working knowledge of real estate database systems such as ARGUS or MRI is usually a requirement for this position.

These financial managers should be creative thinkers and problem solvers, applying their analytical skills to business. They must be comfortable with the latest computer technology. Financial managers must have knowledge of international finance because financial operations are increasingly being affected by the global economy. A working knowledge of auditing and compliance procedures is essential because of the many recent regulatory changes.

Unions and Associations

As professional employees, Controllers can belong to professional associations, including the Financial Executives Institute (FEI), and join special interest groups devoted to networking issues. Real estate Controllers can become members of any of several professional associations, such as the National Association of Industrial and Office Property Managers (NAIOP), a trade group for commercial property managers.

Tips for Entry

1. Join professional organizations for networking and career advancement opportunities.
2. Experience managing money for nonprofit or college organizations can provide useful experience.
3. Internships and summer employment arranged through a university can lead to job opportunities in finance or accounting.

PROJECT CONTROLLER

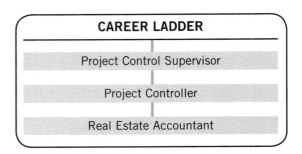

Special Skills and Personality Traits—Strong analytical, communication, and organizational skills; facility with Web-based management and accounting software

Position Description

Project Controllers direct financial reporting and analysis for designated real estate development projects. They participate in assigned accounting activities, audits, tax reports, cash management, and vendor payments. They prepare monthly, quarterly, and annual financial reports. They assist in the development of project financing studies, or feasibility studies. They produce financial presentations for delivery to the finance committee, board of directors, and investors. They participate in drafting of operating budgets.

These financial managers have duties very similar to those of senior-level corporate controllers, although their role is limited to managing a line of business or a designated project. They are responsible for managing the business unit's budget, accounts payable, and accounts receivable. They may also be responsible for the auditing function within that business unit. Project Controllers play an increasingly important role in managing companies with multi-state operating divisions or that have business operations outside the United States.

These areas require extensive, specialized knowledge on the part of the financial manager to reduce risks and maximize profit. The role of the financial manager, particularly in business, is changing in response to technological advances that have significantly reduced the amount of time it takes to produce financial reports. Project Controllers perform more complex data analysis and use it to offer senior managers ideas on how to maximize profits. They often work on teams, acting as business advisors to top management.

Typical duties of Project Controllers include the following:

- producing monthly, quarterly, and annual reports for investors and lenders
- managing accounts receivable and accounts payable
- reviewing contracts, accounts payable, and disbursements
- monitoring debt covenants and ensuring compliance with lending agreements
- performing financial modeling and analysis to support asset managers and the chief financial officer
- maintaining banking relationships with primary banks
- performing common area and maintenance (CAM) reconciliations on tenant properties
- investing excess corporate cash and managing treasury operations
- supervising and mentoring property accountants and accounting staff
- participating in drafting of internal accounting and auditing controls
- preparing documentation for internal and external auditors at year-end audit review
- participating in special projects as assigned

Project Controllers work in comfortable offices, often close to top managers and the departments that originate financial data these managers need. They usually work long hours, often up to 50 or 60 per week. They may travel occasionally to visit heads of operating divisions, subsidiary firms, vendors, or clients.

Salaries

Project Controllers can earn salaries of $50,000 to $85,000 a year and are eligible for incentive bonuses of 10 to 20 percent of their base salary. Experienced controllers may receive additional compensation in the form of signing bonuses. Non-cash compensation usually includes health insurance, company-sponsored 401(k) plan, and tuition reimbursement.

Employment Prospects

There is adequate demand for financial managers with real estate accounting experience. The U.S. Bureau of Labor Statistics expects hiring of financial controllers will grow at about the same pace as hiring in all occupations through 2014.

The long-run prospects for financial managers in that industry should be favorable. They are needed to handle increasingly complex financial transactions and manage a growing amount of investments. Some financial managers increasingly are hired on a temporary basis, or in interim contracts, to advise senior managers on these and other matters. Small firms routinely contract out all their accounting and financial functions to specialist accounting companies that provide such services. Computer technology has reduced the time and staff required to produce financial reports. Financial managers who are familiar with computer software that can assist them in this role will be needed.

Opportunities are best for candidates who have at least a four-year degree and have begin working toward a professional certification such as the Certified Public Accountant (CPA) designation from the American Institute of Certified Public Accountants.

Advancement Prospects

Well-trained, experienced Project Controllers who display a grasp of the operations of various business units are candidates for promotion to top management positions. Financial controllers advance their careers by moving into more senior management positions, such as controller. Some financial managers transfer to closely related positions in other industries. Those with extensive experience and sufficient capital may start their own consulting firms.

Education and Training

A four-year degree in accounting or finance is a basic requirement. Some companies prefer candidates who have a professional designation, such as Certified Public Accountant (CPA). Continuing education is vitally important to financial managers, who must cope with the growing complexity of global trade, changes in fed-eral and state laws and regulations, and the proliferation of new and complex financial instruments. Firms often provide opportunities for workers to broaden their knowledge and skills by encouraging them to take graduate courses at colleges and universities. Many pay all or part of the costs for employees who successfully complete courses.

Experience, Skills, and Personality Traits

Most employers look to hire candidates who have some experience with real estate accounting practices. Actual on-the-job experience, up to three to five years in the field, may be considered equally important to formal academic training, as these managers are familiar with the complexities of real estate accounting. Some employers want people who have prior team leader or management experience if the position involves supervising and mentoring junior staffers. Project Controllers should have strong analytical, communication, and organizational skills and some facility with Web-based management and accounting and database software specific to real estate.

Advances in computer technology in recent years have reduced the amount of time and the staff required to produce financial reports. Countering this trend, financial managers who are familiar with real estate–specific software will be needed to produce financial reports and provide accounting guidance for property owners and developers.

Candidates for financial management positions need a broad range of skills. Interpersonal skills are important because these jobs involve managing people and working as part of a team to solve problems. Financial managers must have excellent communication skills to explain complex financial data. Because financial managers work extensively with various departments in their firm, a broad overview of the business is essential.

Financial managers should be creative thinkers and problem solvers, applying their analytical skills to business. They must be comfortable with the latest computer technology. Financial operations are increasingly being affected by the global economy, so financial managers must have knowledge of international finance. Proficiency in a foreign language also may be useful in multinational companies.

Unions and Associations

Professional associations such as CoreNet Global, the Institute of Management Accounting, and others sponsor numerous trade shows and conferences and also have year-round education programs for improving skills and staying current in the field.

Tips for Entry

1. Professional organizations provide ample opportunities for networking and career advancement.
2. Temporary or interim employment can open the door to making contacts with hiring managers and a job offer a few years down the road.
3. Internships and summer employment arranged through a university can lead to job opportunities in finance or accounting.

CONSTRUCTION

CONSTRUCTION ESTIMATOR

Duties: Forecasting project costs; determines resources necessary for project completion

Alternate Title(s): Planner-Estimator, Cost Estimator

Salary Range: $33,872 to $48,929

Employment Prospects: Good

Advancement Prospects: Good

Prerequisites:

    Education or Training—Four-year degree

    Experience—Up to two years' experience in real estate development or construction

    Special Skills and Personality Traits—Computer literacy in Microsoft Word and Excel; problem-

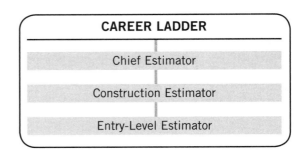

CAREER LADDER

Chief Estimator

Construction Estimator

Entry-Level Estimator

solving skills and project management skills; working knowledge of cost estimating software; ability to read and interpret construction drawings and blueprints

Position Description

Accurately forecasting the cost of future projects is vital to the survival of any business. Cost estimators develop the cost information that business owners or managers need to make a bid for a contract or to decide whether a proposed new product will be profitable. They also determine which endeavors are making a profit.

On a construction project, the estimating process begins with the decision to submit a bid. After reviewing various preliminary drawings and specifications, the estimator visits the site of the proposed project. The estimator gathers information on access to the site and the availability of electricity, water, and other services. The information developed during the site visit usually is recorded in a signed report that is included in the final project estimate.

After the site visit, the estimator determines the quantity of materials and labor the firm will need to furnish—a process known as the quantity survey or takeoff. A cost estimator working for a general contractor estimates the costs of all of the items that the contractor must provide. The general contractor's cost estimator often analyzes bids made by subcontractors as well. During the takeoff process, the estimator must make decisions concerning equipment needs, the sequence of operations, the size of the crew required, and physical constraints at the site. Also, any allowances for wasted materials, inclement weather, shipping delays, and other factors are included in the estimate.

After completion of the quantity surveys, the estimator prepares a cost summary for the entire project, including the costs of labor, equipment, materials, subcontracts, overhead, taxes, insurance, markup, and any other costs that may affect the project. The chief estimator then prepares the bid proposal for submission to the owner.

Construction Estimators spend most of their time in an office, but they must make visits to project worksites that can be dusty, dirty, and occasionally hazardous. Frequent travel between a firm's headquarters and its subsidiaries or subcontractors may be required.

Although estimators normally work a 40-hour week, overtime is common. Cost estimators often work under pressure and stress, especially when facing bid deadlines. Inaccurate estimating can cause a firm to lose a bid or to lose money on a job that was not accurately estimated.

Salaries

Salaries of cost estimators vary widely by experience, education, size of firm, and industry. Median annual earnings of cost estimators in May 2004 were $49,940. The middle 50 percent earned between $38,420 and $65,620, according to the U.S. Labor Department's Bureau of Labor Statistics. The lowest 10 percent earned less than $30,240, and the highest 10 percent earned more than $84,870. College graduates with degrees in fields that provide a strong background in cost estimating, such as engineering or construction management, can start their career in construction management at a higher salary.

Employment Prospects

Overall employment of cost estimators is expected to grow faster than average for all occupations through the year 2014. In addition to openings created by growth, some job openings will arise from the need to replace workers who transfer to other occupations or leave the labor force. In construction and manufacturing—the primary employers of cost estimators—job prospects should be best for those with industry work experience and a bachelor's degree in a related field.

Employers prefer individuals with a degree in building construction, construction management, construction science, engineering, or architecture. However, most Construction Estimators also have considerable construction experience, gained through work in the industry, internships, or cooperative education programs. Applicants with a thorough knowledge of construction materials, costs, and procedures in areas ranging from heavy construction to electrical work, plumbing systems, or masonry work have a competitive edge.

Advancement Prospects

For most estimators, advancement takes the form of higher pay and prestige. Some move into management positions, such as project manager for a construction firm or manager of the industrial engineering department for a manufacturer. Others may go into business for themselves as consultants, providing estimating services for a fee to government or to construction or manufacturing firms.

Education and Training

Regardless of their background, estimators receive much training on the job, because every company has its own way of handling estimates. Working with an experienced estimator, newcomers become familiar with each step in the process. Those with no experience reading construction specifications or blueprints first learn that aspect of the work. Then they may accompany an experienced estimator to the construction site or shop floor, where they observe the work being done, take measurements, or perform other routine tasks. As they become more knowledgeable, estimators learn how to tabulate quantities and dimensions from drawings and how to select the appropriate prices for materials.

Many colleges and universities include cost estimating as part of bachelor's and associate's degree curriculums in civil engineering, industrial engineering, and construction management or construction engineering technology. Organizations representing cost estimators, such as the Association for the Advance-

ment of Cost Engineering (AACE International) and the Society of Cost Estimating and Analysis (SCEA), also sponsor educational and professional development programs.

These programs help students, estimators-in-training, and experienced estimators stay abreast of changes affecting the profession. Specialized courses and programs in cost-estimating techniques and procedures also are offered by many technical schools, community colleges, and universities.

Experience, Skills, and Personality Traits

Cost estimators should have an aptitude for mathematics; be able to quickly analyze, compare, and interpret detailed but sometimes poorly defined information; and be able to make sound and accurate judgments based on this information. Assertiveness and self-confidence in presenting and supporting one's conclusions are important, as are strong communications and interpersonal skills, because estimators may work as part of a project team alongside managers, owners, engineers, and design professionals. Cost estimators also need knowledge of computers, including word-processing and spreadsheet packages. In some instances, familiarity with special estimation software or programming skills also may be required.

Unions and Associations

Voluntary certification can be valuable to cost estimators because it provides professional recognition of the estimator's competence and experience. In some instances, individual employers may even require professional certification for employment. Both the Association for the Advancement of Cost Engineering (AACE International) and the Society of Cost Estimating and Analysis (SCEA) sponsor certification programs. To become certified, estimators usually must have between two and eight years of estimating experience and must pass an examination. Certification requirements may also include publication of at least one article or technical paper in the field.

Tips for Entry

1. Read up on industry trends in construction industry periodicals such as *Construction News Daily*.
2. Check industry Web sites for job leads, job fairs in your area, and job search techniques.
3. College courses in construction management and engineering are recommended by career experts in this field.

CONSTRUCTION LENDER

Duties: Originates construction loans for commercial loan clients and prospects; provides construction lending expertise to other business units.

Alternate Title(s): Commercial Construction Lender

Salary Range: $45,500 to $75,000

Employment Prospects: Good

Advancement Prospects: Good

Prerequisites:

    Education or Training—Four-year degree in business or a related field of study

    Experience—Three or more years' experience in commercial lending or construction loan underwriting

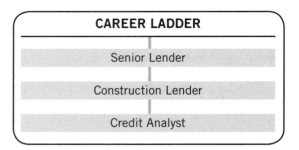

Special Skills and Personality Traits—Good analytical skills; good negotiating skills; facility with spreadsheet accounting software; working knowledge of commercial credit

Position Description

Construction lending is the most complicated part of real estate financing. By definition, construction lending involves a high degree of risk. The construction loan officer must take into consideration everything that could delay a project or put it at risk—construction delays, cost overruns, and so on. A Construction Lender needs to have a comprehensive knowledge of the construction and leasing process and a thorough understanding of the project being financed.

Construction Lenders make the decision whether or not to invest large amounts of capital in real estate projects. The builder prepares a request for funds, called a construction draw, to the lender to pay for work completed up to that date. The Construction Lender has to be skilled at managing the risks associated with development. An experienced Construction Lender knows full repayment is unlikely until the construction phase has been completed and the project realizes its expected value. If the project fails to produce the expected rental income, its value after completion will not provide a means of loan repayment. Very few lenders will approve a construction loan without being assured that a longer term or permanent mortgage loan will pay off the construction financing at project completion.

Loan officers frequently perform as salespeople. Construction loan officers contact firms to determine their needs for loans. If a firm is seeking new funds,

the loan officer will try to persuade the company to obtain the loan from his or her institution. Once the initial contact has been made, loan officers guide clients through the process of applying for a loan. The process begins with a formal meeting or telephone call with a prospective client, during which the loan officer obtains basic information about the purpose of the loan and explains the different types of loans and credit terms that are available to the applicant. Loan officers answer questions about the process and sometimes assist clients in filling out the application.

A recent trend in residential construction is a combination loan, called a "temp to perm loan," that wraps the construction loan and a longer-term loan in a single financing. The construction financing converts to a permanent, fully amortizing loan when construction is completed.

Typical duties of construction lenders include the following:

- recommending marketing and business development strategies for construction loan financing
- ensuring that construction loans meet the lender's loan guidelines and audit requirements
- communicating on a regular basis with credit administration, loan servicing, and senior management on loan activity
- assisting other business units in construction loan underwriting

A Construction Lender manages his or her loan portfolio and works with other bankers as part of a team. Construction Lenders work in an office setting, working a 40-hour week, and make regular inspection visits to construction sites. They typically spend 25 to 75 percent of their time on business development, or prospecting clients for new loans.

Salaries

Construction loan officers earn a base salary plus an incentive bonus or are paid entirely in commissions from loan production. Commercial loan officers with one to three years' experience earn between $45,500 and $70,000. Commercial loan officers with more than three years of experience can earn $61,750 to $100,000 annually. Earnings of loan officers with graduate degrees or professional certifications are higher. Loan officers who are paid on a commission basis usually earn more than those on salary only. Construction Lenders typically get a generous expense allowance, and proven lenders with an established track record may receive a signing bonus.

Employment Prospects

Job opportunities for construction lenders are influenced by the volume of loan applications, which is determined largely by interest rates and by the overall level of economic activity. Besides openings created by economic growth, some openings will result from the need to replace workers who retire or otherwise leave the occupation permanently.

College graduates and those with banking, lending, or sales experience should have the best job prospects. Employment growth stemming from economic expansion and population increases—factors that generate demand for loans—will be partially offset by increased automation that speeds lending processes and by the growing use of the Internet to apply for and obtain loans.

Most construction lenders start out as analysts or mortgage loan officers, where they learn real estate and finance fundamentals. Once they've mastered the fundamentals, the job path varies according to an individual's particular strengths and skills. Those who are more marketing-oriented become loan originators or loan officers.

Those who have a preference for analytics are more likely to become loan underwriters or credit officers who approve loans and assemble loan documentation for loans originated by someone else. Construction Lenders are often hired from the ranks of experienced mortgage lenders.

Advancement Prospects

Experienced loan officers can advance to managerial positions, supervising other loan officers and clerical staff. Loan officers with less work experience—or weak academic preparation—could find their advancement opportunities limited without obtaining training to upgrade their skills. Another option is working on larger, more complex projects as senior loan officers with a corresponding increase in compensation.

Education and Training

Most employers look for individuals with a four-year degree in business, finance, or an equivalent background. A graduate degree in finance or a professional certification can be very helpful for individuals looking to move into higher paying, more senior positions in commercial lending. Formal credit training at a banking school may be a requirement, depending on the position.

Professional associations and private schools offer continuing education courses and programs for experienced loan officers who want to keep their skills current. The Certified Mortgage Banker (CMB) designation from the Mortgage Bankers Association of America demonstrates the holder's superior knowledge, understanding, and competency in real estate finance. The Mortgage Bankers Association offers three CMB designations: residential, commercial, and master's. To obtain the CMB, candidates must have at least three years of experience, earn educational credits, and pass an exam. Completion of one of these programs enhances a Construction Lender's employment and advancement opportunities.

Experience, Skills, and Personality Traits

Construction Lenders should have broad knowledge of construction techniques and commercial lending to property developers. They should have excellent negotiating skills and marketing skills. There are a large number of lenders competing to make the same loans, so the most successful people in the business tend to be good marketers. Good lenders also have strong analytical skills and a facility with spreadsheet accounting software.

Unions and Associations

The Mortgage Bankers Association sponsors career training seminars for credit officers and loan officers through its Campus MBA program (http://www.campusmba.com). The American Bankers Association and the Risk Management Association also sponsor education programs and networking events for commercial loan officers.

Tips for Entry

1. Contact the Mortgage Bankers Association's Campus MBA program to learn about skills and information needed to begin a career in commercial real estate finance.

2. Get some on-the-job experience in a bank credit department and learn firsthand how real estate loans are made. College internship programs may also be available.

3. As in other financial careers, informal networking through college alumni associations and local business organizations can put you in contact with hiring managers.

4. Employment opportunities posted on Internet job boards can lead to job interviews for the right applicant. Check out American Bankers Association's career Web site (http://www.aba.careersite.com) or Select Leaders (http://www.selectleaders.com).

CONSTRUCTION PROJECT MANAGER

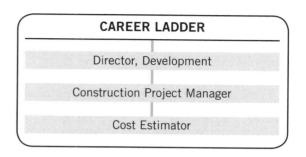

CAREER LADDER

Director, Development

Construction Project Manager

Cost Estimator

Position Description

Construction managers plan, direct, and coordinate a wide variety of construction projects, including the building of all types of residential, commercial, and industrial structures, schools, and hospitals. Construction managers may oversee an entire project or part of a project. While they usually play no direct role in the actual construction of a structure, they typically schedule and coordinate all design and construction processes, including the selection, hiring, and oversight of specialty trade contractors.

Construction managers are salaried or self-employed managers who oversee construction supervisors and workers. They often go by the job titles program manager, constructor, construction superintendent, project engineer, project manager, general contractor, or similar designations. Construction managers may be owners or salaried employees of a construction management or contracting firm. Some may work under contract or as salaried employees of the property owner, developer, or contracting firm overseeing the construction project.

Construction managers coordinate and supervise the construction process from the conceptual development stage through final construction, making sure that the project gets done on time and within budget.

They often work with owners, engineers, architects, and others who are involved in the construction process.

Large construction projects, such as an office building or industrial complex, are often too complicated for one person to manage. Therefore, these projects are divided into many segments: site preparation, including land clearing and earth moving; sewage systems; landscaping and road construction; building construction, including excavation and laying of foundations and erection of the structural framework, floors, walls, and roofs; and building systems, including fire-protection, electrical, plumbing, air-conditioning, and heating. Construction managers may be in charge of one or more of these activities.

Construction managers work out of a main office where the construction project is monitored or out of a field office at the construction site. They work long hours and are often on call 24 hours a day to deal with the effects of weather delays or emergencies at the job site.

Specific duties performed may include any of the following:

- coordinating and overseeing the design process
- negotiating contracts with subcontractors or vendors on projects

- scheduling subcontractor work schedules and construction scheduling milestones
- ensuring projects are built in compliance with plans, specifications, owner's requirements, and best construction practices
- ensuring compliance with various "Green Building" standards and initiatives
- ensuring compliance with federal or state accessibility standards
- approving and reconciling payments to subcontractors and vendors
- assisting in due diligence reviews for prospective new property acquisitions
- securing permits and approvals from federal, state, or local permitting authorities
- supervising site superintendents and laborers
- coordinating tenant relocation when necessary

Salaries

Earnings of salaried construction managers and self-employed independent contractors are influenced by the size and scope of projects managed, their geographic location, and the local economy. The median annual salary in 2007 was $82,648, according to an industry survey by Salary.com. The middle 50 percent had earnings between $68,743 and $100,301. Earnings are affected by such factors as employer size, industry, industry credentials, and years of experience. Many salaried construction managers also receive benefits such as performance bonuses, paid health insurance, company funded retirement plans, and use of a company car.

Employment Prospects

Excellent employment opportunities for construction managers are expected through 2014 because the number of job openings will exceed the number of qualified individuals seeking to enter the occupation. This situation is expected to continue even as college construction management programs expand to meet the current high demand for graduates. The construction industry often does not attract sufficient numbers of qualified job seekers because it is often seen as having poor working conditions.

The increasing complexity of construction projects is boosting the demand for management-level personnel within the construction industry. Laws setting standards for buildings and construction materials, worker safety, energy efficiency, and environmental protection have further complicated the construction process. Advances in building materials and construction methods and the growing number of multipurpose buildings and energy-efficient structures will increase the demand for more construction managers. More opportunities for construction managers also will result from the need for greater cost control and financial management of projects and to oversee the numerous subcontractors being employed.

Prospects for individuals seeking construction manager jobs in construction management, architectural and engineering services, and construction contracting firms should be best for persons who have a bachelor's or higher degree in construction science, construction management, or civil engineering—but also practical experience working in construction. Employers will increasingly prefer applicants with college degrees, previous construction work experience including internships, and a strong background in building technology.

College graduates entering the field are usually hired as assistants to project managers, field engineers, schedulers, or cost estimators.

Advancement Prospects

Construction Project Managers typically advance by moving into more senior positions where they become responsible for supervising a group of construction managers or a division within a company. Advancement opportunities for construction managers vary depending upon their performance and the size and type of company for which they work. Within large firms, managers may eventually become top-level managers or executives. Highly experienced individuals may become independent consultants; some serve as expert witnesses in court or as arbitrators in disputes. Those with the required capital may establish their own construction management services, specialty contracting, or general contracting firms.

Education and Training

Individuals interested in becoming construction managers should have a solid background in building science, business, and management. They need to understand contracts and be familiar with construction methods, materials, and regulations. Employers prefer hiring people who have a four-year degree in business, construction management, engineering, architecture, or a related field if study is typically required. Many colleges and universities, including two-year colleges, have degree programs in construction management. Several colleges also offer a master's degree program in construction science or construction management.

Experience, Skills, and Personality Traits

Employers generally prefer hiring managers who have had some previous experience in construction-related occupations. There is a growing movement toward certification of construction managers to ensure that construction managers have a working knowledge of industry practices and standards. Attaining certification provides evidence of competence and experience. Both the American Institute of Constructors (AIC) and the Construction Management Association of America (CMAA) have voluntary certification programs for construction managers. AIC awards the Associate Constructor (AC) and Certified Professional Constructor (CPC) credential to candidates who successfully meet its requirements and pass written exams. The CMAA awards the Certified Construction Manager (CCM) designation to those who meet work-experience requirements and pass a technical exam. A working knowledge of construction practices and a knowledge of spreadsheet and project management software is also recommended.

Unions and Associations

The American Institute of Constructors and the Construction Management Association of America have career advancement programs and offer continuing education programs for maintaining industry credentials. Annual or regional conferences provide opportunities for networking with other industry professionals.

Tips for Entry

1. Industry periodicals are an excellent source of information on current employment trends in the construction industry.
2. Check trade association Web sites for current openings in your area or in your specialty.
3. College job fairs are another opportunity to make connections with companies looking to hire college graduates.

DEVELOPMENT

ACQUISITION ANALYST

Duties: Identifies and analyzes real estate investment opportunities; reviews financing options; negotiates financing with lenders, real estate brokers, and others

Alternate Title(s): Acquisition Associate

Salary Range: $94,800 to $116,400

Employment Prospects: Good

Advancement Prospects: Good

Prerequisites:

　Education or Training—Four-year degree in accounting, finance, or real estate

　Experience—Two to three years' real estate and financial analysis experience

CAREER LADDER

Director—Acquisitions

Acquisition Analyst

Research Analyst

Special Skills and Personality Traits—Strong analytical and computer skills; strong organizational and communication skills; sound research skills related to identifying real estate trends

Position Description

Companies investing in real estate employ specialists to evaluate property acquisition recommendations. The process can vary, but it typically involves collecting, modeling, and analyzing a wide array of financial, market, and project specific information provided by the real estate property owner (the party interested in selling) or the property developer.

Real estate professionals know that upfront due diligence, a thorough review of an investment property under consideration, is an essential part of the acquisition process.

Acquisition Analysts support the investment decision-making activities of a real estate developer or real estate investment firm by conducting various financial analyses of real estate opportunities, such as purchase of existing office and industrial properties, redevelopment of existing sites, or ground-up development of acquired sites. These analysts are critical members of the due diligence team. They use sophisticated financial modeling software to summarize the financial effects of tenant turnover (renewals and replacements of tenants), operating costs, and capital improvement costs required to maximize the performance of a real estate asset. They perform market research—comparable "in-the-field" rental surveys—to determine rental rates, absorption rates (time needed to lease comparable space), capital costs associated with re-leasing, and other qualifying criteria.

In addition, they may help maintain the company's internal database of managed properties or properties under consideration for purchase, and they prepare investment offering memorandums. They are in frequent contact with key business partners and maintain relationships with office property owners, advisers, and bank lenders.

The Acquisition Analyst will underwrite commercial investment opportunities by collecting all the background information necessary to decide whether to acquire the property, review tenant credit reports, financial statements, property surveys, and title searches. The analyst may also visit the property location and perform an on-site inspection. This time-consuming process is intended to identify potential problems that may have to be dealt with before the purchase is finally approved. If the problems uncovered are serious enough, the acquisition will not be completed. The analyst performs a financial analysis to estimate future cash flows using discounted cash flow (DCF) and internal rate of return (IRR) analysis from rents and other sources, using financial spreadsheet software.

Acquisition Analysts may focus their attention on specific property types, such as office, industrial, retail, multifamily, or hotel properties. They may focus on key geographic markets. They develop contacts with real estate brokers, property owners and developers, real estate consultants, asset managers, and suppliers of market research data.

Typical responsibilities of Acquisition Analysts include the following:

- contacting commercial real estate brokers, landlords, and developers to acquire properties
- underwriting potential acquisitions
- assisting in preparation of documents to be presented to the investment committee
- completing rent surveys, reviewing financing options, and obtaining supporting documents
- coordinating due diligence reviews of properties under consideration with sellers, institutional partners, and other key players
- traveling to properties to complete property inspection
- submitting written findings and recommendations on prospective acquisitions
- writing letters of intent describing key business terms of a transaction

Acquisition Analysts work a 40- to 60-hour workweek in an office setting. Some light travel is required occasionally to conduct site visits and meet other members of the site acquisition team or development team.

Salaries

Acquisition Analysts earn salaries competitive with earnings of entry-level financial analysts. Compensation is typically salary with an incentive bonus tied to financial performance of the department or the company as a whole. Base salaries of office-industrial property analysts ranged from a low of about $94,800 to a high of $116,400, depending on experience and qualifications, according to a 2007 salary survey by CEL & Associates, Inc. The bonus paid out in early years may be subjective or could be determined based on the amount of capital invested during the prior year. More senior positions in property acquisition may be compensated based on the performance of the company or the assets acquired. Residential analysts earned between $83,700 and $100,600 in base salary (excluding annual bonuses) in 2007. Annual bonuses based on performance profitability can increase total compensation 30 percent or more.

Employment Prospects

There are several entry paths to this position. The typical entry path is starting as a research analyst, credit analyst, or asset manager. Employment opportunities for Acquisition Analysts should grow at about the same rate as employment opportunities in real estate development in general. Real estate development is sensitive to the cost of financing, supply and demand, and local economic conditions. There may be fewer opportunities available after a period of strong growth. Acquisition Analysts work for real public and private investment companies or independent consulting firms that provide third-party due diligence services.

Advancement Prospects

Advancement is generally through taking on projects of increasing complexity. Typically, these projects involve supervising other analysts or working as a team leader (project manager) on a development team. Analysts can move into related positions, such as disposition analyst, where they review underperforming properties that are candidates for sale. An Acquisition Analyst interested in a managerial position can advance to site selection manager and assume overall responsibility for property acquisitions. More senior positions are director of real estate and chief investment officer.

Education and Training

Most companies want to see candidates who have a four-year degree with a concentration in accounting, finance, or real estate. Some firms prefer hiring candidates with an advanced degree such as a master's degree in real estate or an M.B.A. degree. Entry-level analysts should have some experience working in an analytical role, including summer internships. College courses in property valuations or appraisals are recommended. Also helpful is some familiarity with real estate analytical programs, such as ARGUS, which is commonly used to evaluate potential acquisitions. Acquisition Analysts continue to refine their skills by attending industry seminars or taking continuing education courses sponsored by an industry trade association.

Experience, Skills, and Personality Traits

Most companies look for candidates who have had at least two years' experience analyzing financial statements and leases and preparing financial models. Some employers want people who have had some development experience. Acquisition Analysts should have exceptional analytical, written, and interpersonal skills and have a proficiency in Microsoft Office suite with a strong emphasis in Excel spreadsheet software. They need to be adept at handling multiple assignments in a fast-paced working environment and have a strong problem-solving aptitude. Individuals should have the ability to work cohesively in a team environment as well as independently.

Acquisition Analysts need to have an understanding of the equity and debt capital markets, an ability and desire to negotiate transactions, and an ability to make and support investment recommendations to constituents who ultimately approve or disapprove of the recommendations. Analysts should have at least two to three years' experience in real estate or real estate accounting. Experience in real estate modeling software, such as ARGUS, which estimates future cash flows from a real estate development, may be a requirement in some companies.

Unions and Associations

Several professional associations, including the CCIM Institute (http://www.ccim.com) and the National Association of Industrial and Office Property Managers (http://www.naiop.org), are available to property acquisition managers for networking opportunities and career advancement. CCIM Institute's CCIM credential (Certified Commercial Investment Member) is a widely recognized standard for professionalism and competence in managing commercial real estate.

Tips for Entry

1. Take college courses in property appraisal, finance, economics, and related fields of study.
2. College and industry job fairs are another opportunity to meet industry recruiters.
3. Check out internship programs at real estate development or property management firms.
4. Career Web sites such as Select Leaders (http://www.selectleaders.com) list many currently open positions.

DEVELOPMENT ANALYST

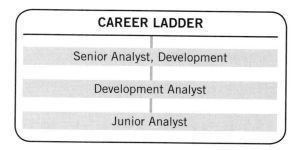
Position Description

The Development Analyst plays a key role in real estate project management and new business development. The Development Analyst is responsible for assisting development acquisitions managers and project managers by doing various types of financial analysis and market research to determine the economic feasibility and return on investment of development projects. The developer is the person or company responsible for taking a project from initial concept to reality.

Development Analysts assist the development team by figuring out the key variables affecting the project's return on investment (ROI) and understanding how they affect the economics of a project. A good part of the work is spreadsheet analysis to keep track of debt and interest payments and investment returns to the investors. Whenever there is a change in the design plans or construction schedule, which can happen frequently in a real estate project, the Development Analyst will have to rework the numbers and come up with a new set of financial calculations. Analysts conduct various financial analysis calculations, including sensitivity analysis and investor projections for projects in the pre-development phase and also projects currently in operation.

In their duties, Development Analysts maintain accurate development start, schedule, progress, change order, and completion reports on each development project in Europe and Asia through a development tracker system. They work closely with development teams in each office to maintain accurate records of

to-date project costs and final budgets. They track individual and cumulative land carry costs, absorption schedules, and projected land-banking requirements relative to specific plans.

Development Analysts also perform financial analysis of land acquisitions and vertical development using an established development model, ARGUS, and an in-house discounted cash flow model. They conduct financial analysis of projected value upon completion, estimated gain on sale/contribution, and sensitivity analysis of change in timing, scope, cost, and leasing assumptions.

Typical day-to-day responsibilities of Development Analysts include:

- working with financial spreadsheet models to examine return on investment (ROI) for the developer
- assisting in reviewing development underwriting assumptions and related investment committee presentations for development deals, cross-referencing cost and schedule information with prior completed deals and active projects to ensure market-based costs are accurate
- working closely with development financial managers to ensure that the quarter-end reporting process is accurate and reflects current and projected conditions for each development project
- assisting with site selection research and analysis
- conducting development scenario analysis related to new acquisitions

- working with the finance group to prepare information project packages for the purpose of obtaining debt and equity financing
- constructing various "what-if" scenarios to determine the impact of any changes in financing or construction scheduling to the developer and equity partners
- conducting market research and comparable project analysis

Development Analysts work in an office setting, normally working a 40- to 50-hour workweek with occasional travel to visit construction sites and meet other members of the project development team.

Salaries

Development Analysts can earn salaries of $40,000 to $50,000 or more a year. There is potential for an annual performance bonus, although bonuses depend on the firm's financial performance in any given year and may not amount to much. Development firms usually offer generous fringe benefits covering health insurance, 401(k) savings plans, and other company-funded perks. Salaries increase significantly as analysts gain experience and move up to more senior positions. Salaries increase with an advanced degree. Development associates with an M.B.A. or a master's degree in real estate can earn $80,000 to $90,000 a year at large development firms. Associates are typically rewarded with larger annual bonuses, as much as 10 to 20 percent of their base salary.

Employment Prospects

This is an entry-level position in real estate development. Entry level hires typically start their careers as analysts. Market demand for Development Analysts should grow in step with the economy through 2014. Real estate development is a cyclical business and some segments, notably residential development, are very sensitive to trends in the larger economy. An over-supply of newly constructed housing can lead to a pullback in new housing construction, dampening the job prospects for new Development Analysts.

Advancement Prospects

With experience, Development Analysts can move into more senior positions offering increased compensation and more responsibilities. Associates are assigned to a specific project and typically only that project. Associates also have responsibility for financial analysts and Development Analysts on their team but also have regular contact with investors, attorneys, or the development firm's design team. The next level up is vice president. A vice president is involved in all aspects of a project, including leasing and potential sale of the property. Vice presidents are ultimately responsible for a project's success or failure. Above the vice president level are the principals in a development firm. Principals typically contribute their own funds to a project or solicit seed money funding from outside investors. They may also provide development concepts on future projects.

Education and Training

A solid academic foundation in business or construction practices is a good starting point for a Development Analyst. Development firms want to hire individuals who have a four-year degree in business, construction management, engineering, or project management. An advanced degree may be very helpful if you are trying to get into a top development firm. Most firms provide on-the-job training in their methods and practices, but they expect Development Analysts to have core skills essential to performing their jobs. For example, Development Analysts should be familiar with general financial analysis concepts, including discounted cash flow analysis.

Experience, Skills, and Personality Traits

Some experience in construction management, cost estimating, and project scheduling are considered essential to the job.

Development firms expect their analysts to have a working knowledge of real estate finance, strong analytical skills, an attention to detail, and an ability to see the big picture. They should also have a facility with financial spreadsheet programs such as Microsoft Excel. Analysts should have the capacity to learn pro forma and profitability analysis, which are commonly used in the real estate industry. Some familiarity with project management software is also important.

Previous experience in real estate is also important. Development firms look for new employees who have at least two to three years' experience in real estate development, including project management and financial analysis. Most real estate people agree that development is the riskiest, but also the most rewarding, part of the industry. Successful developers are people with outgoing personalities who like working hard and enjoy getting involved in all aspects of their work.

Unions and Associations

Several real estate associations offer opportunities for networking with peers and maintaining job skills through continuing education courses and seminars.

Development Analysts can become members of various real estate trade associations, such as the CCIM Institute. Some may also become members of the Urban Land Institute to develop contacts with other people in their field.

Tips for Entry

1. Getting hired by a development firm can be challenging. While still in college be ready to do an independent job search, because most placement offices don't bring a lot of real estate firms on campus.

2. Read up on development trends by reading publications like *Urban Land* (Urban Land Institute), *Realtor* (National Association of Realtors), *Journal of Real Estate Portfolio Management*, or *National Real Estate Investor.*

3. When in an interview, be prepared to answer questions on the specifics of local real estate markets or how to value a particular property.

DEVELOPMENT MANAGER

Position Description

Real estate developers work in one of the most challenging areas in real estate—land development. Developers buy land or buildings at the lowest possible price and try to add as much value as they can before selling a property. Sometimes they buy neglected buildings and develop them for new uses (adaptive re-use).

As an example, they may acquire an old factory building and redevelop the property into a modern apartment complex or office complex.

Developers are first and foremost visionaries. They have a creative mindset—an ability to see the future of a designated property and bring that vision to life. The process begins with careful site selection. Once the site is acquired, the development process begins with conceptual project planning and filing for regulatory approvals. Ideally, the site is secured with limited funds, known as taking an option or placing a deposit on the site, subject to securing the appropriate use approvals from local governments.

After securing approvals and commitments of prime tenants, the developer's team must then secure financing to complete the project. Developers may rely on their own capital or secure "risk capital" from partners to initiate the development process. This start-up phase is typically the riskiest phase, as all funds invested in the project are at total risk of loss until the appropriate approvals are secured.

Developers begin the planning process working extensively with architects and site engineers to gain the necessary approvals for groundwater management, traffic control, and other key approval issues. Concurrently, the leasing team begins work to secure prime tenants. The naming of a significant tenant may be key to getting the project approved and is typically a prerequisite for financing. Once these hurdles are satisfied, detailed engineering studies are commissioned and a contractor is selected. When construction begins, the developer manages the project construction by hiring a general contractor or a construction management firm. Projects built for eventual sale are often developed as "built to suit" projects, meaning the building was constructed for a designated tenant and designed according to the tenant's specifications.

In their work, developers wear many hats. They are both creative in their vision and analytical in that they "know the numbers," meaning they understand the many phases of the construction process and can make quick decisions as needed. They are very detail oriented, being careful to see that the smallest details are not overlooked, potentially resulting in costly construction delays or occupancy delays—all of which can damage the viability of the project, not to mention the developer's longer-term reputation.

Typically, developers specialize in certain types of real estate, such as commercial or residential construction, retail shopping mall, or office complex, and within these broad groups they tend to specialize by geographic region (such as Northeast versus Sunbelt), population center (suburban versus urban), or some other industry grouping.

In their work, developers wear many hats. They oversee the construction process, manage subcontractors, and negotiate any building and construction permits required before construction can begin. They have to pay attention to the smallest details, for example, obtaining the necessary environmental permits.

A Development Manager may be assigned overall responsibility for an entire project, or be given a small portion of the project to manage.

Specific duties on the job may include any of the following:

- assessing potential development sites in their geographic area
- presenting development proposals to a management committee for approval
- securing all required state or federal approvals and permits
- overseeing internal and external consultants
- working with real estate brokers, legal counsel, title companies, city planners, and others
- reviewing construction pricing and contracts to ensure delivery on time and within pre-set budget estimates
- monitoring and managing the construction process
- reporting on project status to clients, business partners, and senior management

Real estate developers have no calendar or watch. Because time erodes the value of a project, extraordinary efforts are at times required to gain approvals from government agencies, make presentations during evening public hearings, or redraft development plans based on the input from community groups or public agencies. The result can frequently be a working schedule going well beyond the typical 40-hour workweek, extending the work day into evenings and weekends to meet important project deadlines and milestones. This is one of the most challenging fields in the real estate industry.

Salaries

Earnings of real estate developers are influenced by many factors, including geographic location, the size and success of projects, and the condition of the economy. Some experienced real estate developers who own their own firms earn more than $1 million a year. On the other hand, developers who invest their money in an unsuccessful project may lose their entire investment. Development Managers starting out as project managers can expect to earn $40,000 to $50,000 initially and from $60,000 to $80,000, plus any incentive compensation or performance bonus, after five years' job experience. Some development executives can earn $187,000 to $240,000 in base salary and performance bonuses of 50 percent or more, depending on property type, company size, and even market conditions.

Employment Prospects

There is no standard entry path to a career as a developer. Many started their careers in a related profession, including architecture, construction management, engineering, or planning. Some got involved in development as property investors. Still others learned from the ground up, working in the building trades and gaining enough experience to set up their own businesses.

The very large property development firms usually prefer hiring college graduates who have had some post-graduate experience in property management, engineering, law or real estate asset management. Recent graduates are typically hired as project managers, assigned to manage a small piece of a large development project, such as an office building or shopping mall.

That said, property development is a cyclical business, and hiring patterns tend to move in lockstep with the economy as a whole. The real estate industry is greatly affected by economic trends. Employment prospects for the industry as a whole are expected to be good through 2014. Opportunities for prospective developers will vary in different areas around the country, depending on a region's specific needs and economic health.

Aside from the big name development firms that grab most of the news headlines, the development industry is dominated by small names. The majority of development firms are small independent businesses, and a sizable number are run by self-employed developers who make their money one project at a time. Small independent businesses, medium-sized commercial developers, and engineering firms are the best target companies to approach if you are looking to break into the field.

Advancement Prospects

Real estate developers who stay in the field advance by taking on increasingly larger and more complex projects. Some will move into management positions or become equity owners, or partners, in their firms. A surprising percentage—about 20 percent—will leave within five years, according to industry data, to pursue careers in other aspects of the real estate industry or go into occupations offering more predictable incomes and less job stress.

Education and Training

Real estate developers must have broad knowledge of the various aspects of real estate and strong skills in financial management. To obtain this knowledge, most prospective developers pursue a four-year college degree. Development firms prefer hiring candidates with degrees in architecture, engineering, real estate, or a related field of study. College courses in accounting, construction technology, business law, and property investments also can be very helpful. As the industry has become more specialized, academic requirements have changed, notably those for higher-paying, advanced positions. Many developers return to school after a few years to earn an advanced degree or an M.B.A. Earning an advanced degree can net a substantial boost in salary, while also increasing the number of job offers.

Experience, Skills, and Personality Traits

Property developers are risk takers. To succeed in this business, you have to be enterprising and be willing to take risks. Property development involves speculating with money and putting in large amounts of work before a project pays off. Many people interested in becoming developers start off as contractors, salespeople, leasing agents, or brokers. Real estate developers need to have strong entrepreneurial instincts and communication skills, because they need to sell their ideas to succeed.

Developers have one overriding personality trait: confidence in the success of their endeavor.

Unions and Associations

The National Association of Industrial and Office Properties, the International Council of Shopping Centers, and the Corporate Real Estate Network offer opportunities for career development and networking through conferences, educational programs, and job search tips available on their Web sites.

Tips for Entry

1. This is a good career choice if you want a hands-on job, like dealing with people, and enjoy the challenges in juggling a variety of tasks.
2. Regional development firms are a good place to start your career and gain some experience in a variety of assignments.
3. Developers are always looking for people with some hands-on experience in construction or construction planning.
4. Financial skills can pay big dividends if you can apply what you've learned in college accounting or business management courses.

DISPOSITION ANALYST

CAREER PROFILE

Duties: Identifies and analyzes property disposition (asset sale) opportunities; negotiates sale transactions for clients, the company, or a business unit

Alternate Title(s): Property Disposition Analyst, Real Estate Owned (REO) Disposition Analyst

Salary Range: $61,000 to $90,000

Employment Prospects: Good

Advancement Prospects: Good

Prerequisites:

Education or Training—Four-year degree in accounting, business administration, finance, or a related field of study

Experience—One to three years' experience in investment analysis or loan servicing

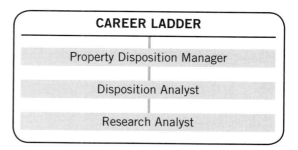

CAREER LADDER

Property Disposition Manager

Disposition Analyst

Research Analyst

Special Skills and Personality Traits—Proficiency in real estate investment analysis; working knowledge of mortgage loan servicing; strong organizational, communication, and computer skills

Position Description

When organizations grow through mergers, expansions, and changing strategic objectives, they often have to deal with closing facilities they no longer need. Sometimes a company will sell off unused properties or reduce its leased space to improve its cash flow and secure a funding source that might be used for other purposes.

Depending on prevailing market conditions, there are different strategies for disposing of vacated or closed facilities to realize the highest possible value from a property sale or sublease while at the same time minimizing costs and tax liabilities. When properties are identified as candidates for a possible sale, the property Disposition Analyst calculates the property owner's adjusted cost basis, deductible losses, and net capital gains from sale of the property.

The Disposition Analyst is responsible for identifying and analyzing disposition opportunities—real estate properties eligible for sale—and then negotiating sale of the designated properties. Disposition Analysts screen properties held in portfolio and develop disposition strategies for non-qualifying properties. If employed by a bank or mortgage company, the Disposition Analyst attempts to manage credit losses through effective disposition of properties acquired through foreclosure proceedings. Disposition Analysts employed in a financial institution may also determine the appropriate loan loss reserves during various stages of default.

In performing their duties, Disposition Analysts review income and expense projections on portfolio properties to identify ones that can be sold. They check these holdings against similar properties to determine offering and selling prices. They determine the fair market value of identified properties by analyzing appraisals and broker price opinions. They may assist in marketing properties marked for sale and negotiate contracts.

Disposition Analysts research portfolio properties to determine rents, vacancy, and competitive advantages or disadvantages of selling identified properties. They approve pending leases as they relate to disposition properties; they conduct market research to verify assumptions of financial models. The Disposition Analyst may also be a member of the loss mitigation team in reviewing alternatives to foreclosure with an emphasis on reviewing market values.

Typical job duties may include the following:

- reporting to the disposition executive committee on a regular basis, weekly
- overseeing the creating of all written disposition-related investor communications
- developing sales and marketing strategies
- conducting and leading conference calls with investors and investor representatives
- negotiating sales contracts and broker commission agreements

- overseeing the process of identifying potential dispositions
- identifying properties available for disposition using internal rate of return (IRR) and discounted cash flow (DCF) analysis
- coordinating the placement of liability and hazard insurance and settlement of mortgage insurance claims
- ensuring compliance with departmental and corporate policies
- compiling and maintaining departmental records

Disposition Analysts typically work in an office setting, working a standard 40-hour workweek, with occasional travel to inspect bank-owned or investor-owned properties identified as properties eligible for disposal.

Salaries

Earnings vary according to experience and position requirements. Compensation is typically a base salary plus an annual incentive bonus tied to department performance or performance by the property management company. Base salaries can range from $61,000 to about $90,000 for experienced property Disposition Analysts. Analysts may also receive an incentive bonus of 10 to 15 percent of base salary. Incentive bonuses in the early years of employment are typically based on the amount of invested capital in a property management firm. Disposition Analysts typically receive non-salary benefits, including paid vacations and holidays and company-funded health insurance.

Employment Prospects

This is an entry-level position for recent college graduates. There is continuing market demand for experienced real estate analysts with some experience in property management and financial analysis. The typical entry path is starting as a research analyst, credit analyst, or asset manager. Employment opportunities for Disposition Analysts should grow at about the same rate as employment opportunities in all financial occupations. Real estate development is sensitive to the cost of financing, supply and demand, and local economic conditions, which means that employment opportunities will vary from one region to another.

The services performed by Disposition Analysts are often provided by real estate advisory firms or accounting firms—companies that typically have a need to periodically replenish their analyst pool as Disposition Analysts move into higher ranking positions or leave the company.

Advancement Prospects

There are numerous advancement opportunities in a property management company.

Disposition Analysts can advance to more senior positions in the department, such as property disposition manager. Another option is through taking on projects of increasing complexity and projects that require supervising other analysts. More senior positions in the field are director of real estate or chief investment officer.

Education and Training

Most employers want to hire candidates with a four-year degree with a concentration in accounting, business, finance, or a related field of study. Courses in real estate fundamentals and property management are also very helpful. Some employers will hire individuals who do not have a four-year degree but have equivalent work experience in loan servicing or loss mitigation. Entry-level analysts should have some experience working in an analytical capacity, including summer employment or internships (paid or unpaid). Most real estate companies have continuing education programs to help their new employees learn important job skills, or they assign new employees to work as junior members of a property management team.

Experience, Skills, and Personality Traits

Candidates need to be well versed in the fundamentals of real estate financial analysis and mortgage loan servicing. Most employers look for people who have had some understanding of the property acquisition disposition process. Some experience in default management is helpful.

As in other financial analyst positions, disposition associates should have exceptional analytical, written, and interpersonal skills, a strong problem-solving ability, a proficiency in the Microsoft Office suite, and some working knowledge of real estate specific software. Public speaking skills are a plus. Proficiency in ARGUS software, a software program that estimates future cash flows from a real estate development, may be a requirement in some companies.

Unions and Associations

The CCIM Institute and CoreNet Global sponsor educational and networking programs throughout, which are available to property analysts. CCIM Institute's CCIM credential (Certified Commercial Investment Member) is a widely recognized standard for professionalism and competence in managing commercial real estate.

Tips for Entry

1. Take college courses in finance, economics, real estate, and related fields of study, and check into internship programs with real estate management companies.
2. College and industry job fairs are an excellent opportunity to meet industry recruiters.
3. Check out internship programs at real estate development or property management firms.
4. Career Web sites such as Select Leaders (http://www.selectleaders.com) list many currently open positions.

REAL ESTATE ENTREPRENEUR

CAREER PROFILE

Duties: Buys and rehabilitates apartment buildings and houses; may rent properties or resell to other owners or investors

Alternate Title(s): Real Estate Investor

Salary Range: $20,000 to $100,000 and up

Employment Prospects: Good

Advancement Prospects: Fair

Prerequisites:

    Education or Training—High school diploma; some college courses helpful

    Experience—Up to three years' experience in real estate

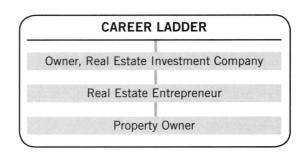

Special Skills and Personality Traits—Strong analytical skills and negotiating skills; good written and verbal communication skills; good self-discipline

Position Description

You've probably seen the late night television programs touting "no money down" strategies and similar ways to invest in real estate. The opportunities are real even if the successful stories seen on television are anything but typical results. Many people dabble in real estate, but few hit it big like Donald Trump. Superstars in real estate are the exception. For most people, real estate investing is a side business or maybe a second career.

Some Real Estate Entrepreneurs are people looking for the quick sale. These are people doing what is called wholesaling. They take title to the property and try to sell for a few dollars more—the classic "property flipper." Others take the longer view, buying an apartment building, for instance, and renting the units until they are ready to sell.

There are many ways to make money in real estate. The typical approach is buying properties at a discount to their market value, expecting to sell at a higher price at some future date. Some investors buy houses from people in financial trouble, people who, for one reason or another, have taken on more debt than they can handle. They cannot make their mortgage payments or need to raise cash quickly. They're willing to negotiate on pricing and closing dates. They're looking for a quick solution to a financial problem. Buying properties in foreclosure is another way to buy houses at less than market price, but it's a hard market to compete in. Non-professional investors who don't have a network of real estate agents and attorneys to feed them information about upcoming sales will often find the better deals are snapped up by competitors.

Another approach to the market is buying houses in distressed condition, properties that have market values below comparable houses in their neighborhood. Buying a "fixer-upper" house needing rehabilitation carries some risk to the investor—the biggest risk being overbidding on a property needing extensive renovation to bring it into salable condition. Building code violations can drain precious cash reserves, adding weeks if not months of costly repairs before the property can be listed for sale.

Successful real estate investors know how to size up a property offered for sale. They look for properties they can rehabilitate and quickly bring to marketable condition. They're constantly talking to developers, real estate agents, property owners, and others who follow the real estate market closely. Being a real estate investor is a lot like being a salesman: the investor has to get to know the people who have properties they want to sell—or may need to sell.

Much of the work isn't very glamorous. Real Estate Entrepreneurs spend a lot of time on the phone taking phone calls from real estate agents and others offering properties for sale. If they own rental properties, they collect rent from tenants or look for new tenants when a tenant moves out. They also attend property auctions and regular meetings of real estate investor groups to maintain their network of contacts. Real Estate Entrepreneurs who make it a full-time occupation can work a 40-hour week , or they can work much longer hours—

including evenings and weekends—when they are busy working on their properties.

Salaries

A six-figure income is possible although many Real Estate Entrepreneurs earn far less than that amount. Even successful entrepreneurs don't expect to make much during the first several years in business. Consequently, incomes can vary from $20,000 or less to more than $100,000 for someone in the business more than 10 years. Incomes can rise or fall with the cyclical nature of the real estate market and local market conditions. One real estate deal that goes sour at the wrong time can wipe out a good part of one year's income.

Employment Prospects

The majority of Real Estate Entrepreneurs are self-employed business owners. Anyone can own real estate and anyone who has sufficient cash on hand can become a real estate investor. While there is no direct career path for Real Estate Entrepreneurs, many who do become investors have had some prior experience in the market. Some started out as bank lenders, learning the financial side of the business. Many real estate agents have a side business in real estate investing or have moved from selling properties to investing in them. Still others come from backgrounds outside real estate.

Population trends over the next 20 years are expected to create many investment opportunities for entrepreneurs to find their niche in the real estate market with the growing market for second homes and vacation homes and the increase in the number of people in the rental housing market. Demographers expect the U.S. population will increase by at least 30 million over the next 20 years, creating many opportunities for investors owning small apartment buildings.

Advancement Prospects

Real Estate Entrepreneurs usually advance their businesses by owning more properties and building a portfolio of properties. They may hire on-site property managers, carpenters, and others to handle repairs and renovations. Some investors will set up their own full-service property investment company, offering a full range of investor services—everything from investor training to private money lending and property management for other property owners.

Education and Training

A four-year college degree is a useful background, although not essential. What is important is having a solid foundation in real estate economics. College courses in accounting, business, and economics are a good starting point. Working for a few years in mortgage lending or mortgage underwriting is valuable experience, because you will learn first-hand how deals get financed and also what happens when loans go bad. Some familiarity with legal contracts and loan documents is important because sellers want to believe they are dealing with people who know what they are talking about. Real estate investor associations are an excellent source of information and can be very helpful to investors getting into the business.

Experience, Skills, and Personality Traits

Real Estate Entrepreneurs have to be quick thinkers, able to size up a deal and perform calculations mentally. They meet a lot of people all the time so they have to enjoy socializing and getting to know people. Successful investors have a natural curiosity and are always asking questions about how a particular deal was structured and what new properties may be coming on the market. Owning a rental property can be a hands on experience; owner-investors have to know how to do small repairs or have a network of contractors on call to make any necessary repairs.

Unions and Associations

Real estate investor associations provide a wealth of information to entrepreneurs entering this field. The National Real Estate Investors Association (http://www.nationalreia.com) has chapters in all 50 states. The association also sponsors real estate training classes for new members.

Tips for Entry

1. Attend local or state chapter meetings of the National Real Estate Investors Association to learn about activities and opportunities in your area.
2. You've got to have a clear vision and a certain amount of self-discipline. Mistakes can be very costly.
3. Read U.S. census data reports for updates on local housing market conditions and projections over the next five to 10 years.
4. Have sufficient cash on hand to finance your business for at least six months to a year. You don't want to have to wait 30 to 60 days to get bank financing when an attractive deal comes along.

LAND DEVELOPMENT PROJECT MANAGER

CAREER PROFILE

Duties: Responsible for overseeing development projects from the design phase through construction and project completion; manages relations with engineers, architectural consultants, and other professionals

Alternate Title(s): Land development project engineer

Salary Range: $65,000 to $100,000

Employment Prospects: Good

Advancement Prospects: Fair

Prerequisites:

Education or Training—Four-year degree in engineering or real estate

Experience—Three to five years' experience in construction project management, site selection, or development

CAREER LADDER

Senior Project Manager

Land Development Project Manager

Project Manager

Special Skills and Personality Traits—Up-to-date knowledge of local building codes and regulations; ability to read construction drawings and legal documents; good verbal and written communication skills

Position Description

Land development is the process of acquiring undeveloped land (raw land) and obtaining entitlements—the right to build on it. The strategy can offer high returns on investment, especially when the developer has a good track record. The term *land developer* has many different meanings—as many as the various forms of land development: single-family, multifamily, commercial retail, commercial office, or mixed-use industrial.

Land development refers to altering the landscape in any number of ways, such as subdividing real estate into lots, typically for the purpose of building homes, or changing undeveloped landforms to construct commercial, industrial, or residential buildings. Land developers are the risk takers in real estate, much like the wildcatters in the oil industry put their capital at risk—sometimes their entire fortunes—in the hopes of developing a new oil field and the chance for a big payoff.

After rights to the property are acquired, the Land Development Project Manager guides the project through the planning and construction phase to project completion. Much of the work is done before ground is actually broken. These professionals investigate, calculate, and analyze the proposed project. They are respon-

sible, either directly or indirectly, for the key decisions made in almost any land development project.

For single-family residential development, a land developer manages the transformation of undeveloped raw land into lots for home construction. Behind every major land developer is a project manager whose skills and experience can determine the success for the entire team. Project managers stay current with ever-changing city, town, or county regulations on land development. The project manager works with city and county planning departments (for zoning, subdivision platting, street layouts, and other urban planning items), state environmental protection agencies, public works departments (for water, sanitary sewer, storm sewer, and flood control issues), and often directly with electric, gas, and water utility companies.

Environmental issues must be handled or negotiated before project lenders will commit to financing. Nearly every project begins with an environmental report or assessment of the project's impact on wetlands and flood-prone areas. Effective land planning is critical to the success of a development project. A project manager must be well versed in various land planning strategies, incorporating landscape improvements and flood abatements to improve the project's appeal and its overall marketability. One of the first tasks of the project manager is directing a market analysis, which helps determine the market demand, absorption rate (sale or lease potential), and project pricing.

Typical duties performed include the following:

- providing a cost analysis for each phase of a development project
- negotiating contracts with consultants and subcontractors
- filing the necessary building or construction permit applications
- selecting the project's civil engineer or design engineer, who is responsible for the design and operation of all utility and infrastructure aspects of the project
- working with the project engineer to coordinate bidding for infrastructure construction
- supervising the creation and initial operation of the homeowner's association
- coordinating the design and construction of project amenities, including landscaping, open space, golf courses, and other recreational features
- managing the design and construction activities throughout the development process to keep the project on schedule and on budget
- managing design consultants
- managing contractors, governmental agencies, utility providers, and others to deliver projects on time
- issuing contracts to subcontractors
- managing cost controls to keep the project within budget
- working with leasing and the tenant coordinator to develop budgets and deliver leased spaces on time and to the requirements of tenants

Project managers work independently or as members of a development team. They are often politically active, working to retain or improve property rights regulations in communities where they are active.

Development project managers typically work a 40- to 50-hour workweek and have frequent local travel to visit construction sites and meet with architects, other professionals, and other members of the development team.

Salaries

Earnings of land developers are influenced by many factors, including geographic location and the size and success of projects. Managers starting out as project managers can expect to earn $40,000 to $50,000 initially and from $60,000 to $80,000, plus any incentive compensation or performance bonus, after five years' job experience.

Employment Prospects

Employment prospects are expected to be good through 2014. Opportunities for prospective developers will vary in different areas around the country, depending on a region's specific needs and economic health. Major development firms prefer college graduates who have had some post-graduate experience in property management, marketing, or sales. Recent graduates are typically hired as project managers, assigned to manage a small piece of a large development project, such as an office building or shopping mall. Medium-sized commercial developers and engineering firms are the best target companies to approach.

Advancement Prospects

Real estate developers increase their status and earnings potential by taking on larger and more complex projects. Some will move into management positions or become equity owners, or partners, in their firm. About 20 percent will leave within five years, according to industry data, to pursue careers in other occupations offering more predictable incomes. Developers who switch careers often move into banking, investment banking, construction financing, and real estate sales.

Education and Training

Development firms prefer hiring candidates with degrees in construction or building sciences or civil engineering. College courses in accounting, architecture, business law, and property management can be very helpful. As the industry has become more specialized, academic requirements have changed, notably those for higher-paying, advanced positions.

Experience, Skills, and Personality Traits

Development project managers typically have prior experience as an owner's representative or have worked for a general contractor for at least three to five years. Real estate developers need to have strong entrepreneurial instincts and communication skills, because they need to sell their ideas to succeed. Development project managers need to have an ability to read and comprehend complex construction drawings and legal documents and a working knowledge of Microsoft Office software, scheduling, and project management software.

Also important are strong written and verbal communication skills and an ability to communicate effectively with employees, consultants, contractors, tenant representatives, and governmental agencies. Quantitative problem-solving skills to resolve project issues and a positive, team-oriented attitude are good personality traits.

Unions and Associations

The National Association of Industrial and Office Properties, the International Council of Shopping Centers, and the Corporate Real Estate Network offer opportunities for career development and networking through conferences, educational programs, and job search tips available on their Web sites.

Tips for Entry

1. Regional development firms are a good place to start your career and gain some experience in a variety of assignments.
2. Developers are always looking for people with some hands-on experience in construction or construction planning.
3. Financial skills are in demand if you can apply what you've learned in college accounting or business management courses.

LAND PLANNER

CAREER PROFILE

Duties: Develops comprehensive growth plans for urban and suburban communities; works closely with developers, government agencies, and others

Alternate Title(s): Regional Planner, Urban Planner

Salary Range: $51,000 to $86,000

Employment Prospects: Good

Advancement Prospects: Good

Prerequisites:

    Education or Training—Four-year degree, master's degree preferred

    Experience—One to three years' experience in community or urban development

    Special Skills and Personality Traits—Professional written and verbal skills; ability to work indepen-

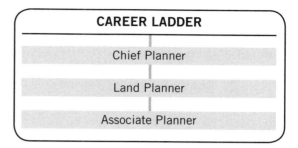

CAREER LADDER

Chief Planner

Land Planner

Associate Planner

dently; detail-oriented; proficiency with Microsoft Office suite.

    Special Requirements—Licensing required in some states

Position Description

Professional Land Planners create a broad vision—the big picture—for the community.

Almost all planners have an area of specialization, the most common being community development or redevelopment and land-use or code-use enforcement, according to the American Planning Association. Other specializations include transportation planning, environmental and natural resources planning, urban design, and economic planning. About two-thirds work in public agencies, and another 25 percent find employment in private consulting firms.

The planning process starts with writing a plan. Planners develop a plan by analyzing mounds of data and identifying goals for the community or project. When working with a property developer, planners often come up with several alternative plans, drawing from the developer's initial concepts. Land Planners come up with plans for the location, orientation, and design of buildings, open space, traffic, and other considerations. Planning is a team effort. Planners spend much of their day meeting with engineers, architects, health professionals, landscape architects, and others to review the specifics of a proposed plan. Planners also do presentations. Senior planners function as team leaders and have more direct contact with public officials and heads of local planning organizations. Planners frequently make presentations to business groups, city councils, and neighborhood groups.

Planners are responsible for knowing federal and state legislation and court rulings that could have some impact on their project. Planners also do research on their own, gathering data from a variety of sources, including economic development or market research studies, census reports, or environmental studies. Planning is done with the aid of various tools such as computer-aided visualization, Geographic Information Systems (GIS), financial analysis spreadsheets, and demographic databases.

Other duties of Land Planners typically include the following:

- managing work of consultants, civil engineers, and technical support
- negotiating and managing consultant contracts
- assisting in preparation of cost estimates
- coordinating public comments, including local neighborhood organizations
- managing approval process with government agencies
- making presentations before community groups
- acting as liaison with third-party suppliers and consultants
- assisting with maintaining master project schedule
- maintaining a database of project land uses

Local governments employ seven out of 10 urban and regional Land Planners. Planners in private industry work with utility companies, law firms, real estate developers, and planning consultants. Planners also work with nonprofit agencies such as the United Way, community development organizations, or advocacy groups for the elderly.

Although most planners have a scheduled 40-hour workweek, they frequently attend evening or weekend meetings or public hearings with citizens' groups. Planners may experience the pressure of deadlines and tight work schedules, as well as political pressure generated by interest groups affected by proposals related to urban development and land use.

Salaries

Median total compensation was $65,000 in 2006, according to the American Planning Association. The middle 50 percent earned between $51,000 (the 25th percentile) and $86,100, according to the American Planning Association. As in other professions, actual earnings are influenced by an individual's experience, responsibility, and employer. Earning a professional certification is an important step toward higher salaries as well as career advancement.

Land Planners who have earned a professional designation from the American Institute of Certified Planners earn, on average, $17,000 more than planners lacking certification. Another key variable is the place of employment; planners employed by federal agencies, private consulting firms, law firms, and development firms have potential for annual earnings significantly above the median earnings.

Employment Prospects

Most entry-level jobs require a master's degree. Graduates from accredited bachelor's degree programs qualify for some entry-level positions, but their advancement opportunities often are limited, unless they acquire an advanced degree.

Looking out over the next decade, planners are in high demand throughout North America, according to the American Planning Association. There are promising careers in nearly every planning specialization, although some specialties are more in demand than others. Most new jobs will be in affluent, rapidly growing urban and suburban communities.

Advancement Prospects

The typical advancement path is to more senior positions, often designed on job boards as Planner II or Planner III. After a few years of experience, planners can advance to assignments requiring a high degree of independent judgment, such as designing the physical layout of a large development or recommending policy and budget options. Some public-sector planners are promoted to community planning director and spend a great deal of time meeting with officials, speaking to civic groups, and supervising a staff.

Further advancement occurs through a transfer to a larger jurisdiction with more complex problems and greater responsibilities or into related occupations, such as director of community or economic development. Planners also may advance their careers by moving back and forth between public and private employers.

Education and Training

People enter this occupation from a variety of academic backgrounds. A four-year degree from an accredited planning program, coupled with a master's degree in architecture, landscape architecture, or civil engineering, is good preparation for many entry-level planning jobs. (A list of accredited colleges and universities can be found in Appendix I.) A master's degree from an accredited planning program provides the best training for a wide range of planning fields.

Some planners have four-year degrees in the social sciences, such as public administration, sociology, economics, or government. Others have more formal backgrounds in architecture, urban design, or landscape architecture. Many planners have graduate degrees from colleges or universities accredited by the Association of Collegiate Schools of Planning or the Association of Canadian University Planning Programs.

Special Requirements

Licensing may be required in some states, so check with your college's career planning department or state board of licensing for more information on specific requirements. A passing grade on a civil service exam is normally required for government jobs. Land planners hired by public agencies must also pass a background check.

Experience, Skills, and Personality Traits

Land planning is a high-profile occupation. Attending public meetings and making public presentations before boards or community groups is part of the job. Planners need to have highly professional written and verbal communication skills to be proficient at making group presentations. An outgoing professional demeanor and ability to build and maintain effective working relationships are important personality traits. Planners also need to be proficient in computer skills and have a working knowledge of the Microsoft Office suite of computer programs.

Unions and Associations

There are several professional associations, including the American Planning Association and the Urban Land Institute, both of which offer continuing professional development.

The American Institute of Certified Planners, a professional institute within the American Planning Association, grants certification to individuals who have the appropriate combination of education and professional experience and who pass an examination. Earning a certification in planning may be helpful for promotion.

Tips for Entry

1. Lay the groundwork for a career in planning before graduating from college. It's a great idea to join the American Planning Association or the Canadian Institute of Planners, because you get all the benefits of membership at a low entry fee.
2. Check for colleges that offer internship programs and learn about a career in planning before graduating.
3. Check for job listings in American Planning Association's JobMart, which lists current openings in the United States and Canada.

RIGHT-OF-WAY AGENT

CAREER LADDER

Chief Right-of-Way Agent

Senior Right-of-Way Agent

Right-of-Way Agent

ten reports, make verbal presentations of findings or recommendations
    Special Requirements—Working knowledge of property appraisal methods, contract negotiating

Position Description

Right-of-way Agents negotiate with property owners to secure the purchase or lease of land and right-of-way for utility lines, pipelines, and other construction projects. They negotiate with landholders for access routes and determine roads, bridges, and utility systems to be maintained during construction. They may examine public records to determine ownership and property rights. To obtain this right-of-way, a Right-of-way Agent works out the legal details with property owners who have legal title to the property. Right-of-way Agents will:

- search public records for the title and owner to determine the legal condition of the property
- prepare and issue policies regarding title and right-of-way
- negotiate contract details with property owners
- meet with the public and business owners to discuss right-of-way issues

They often investigate the routes or sites needed by their employers, usually with the help of engineers. One of their primary duties is accurately investigating the value of private property and negotiating a purchase price. The U.S. Constitution requires that owners be paid a reasonable sum of money. It is important in these negotiations for the property owners to be offered fair market value for their land. Right-of-way Agents prepare estimates of property value and evaluate third-party appraisals. Through this process, their

goal is to arrive at a price that represents the fair market value.

Agents sometimes examine public records to determine who owns or has a legal interest in the land. Agents then open negotiations with these parties, striving for an end result of buying or using the land. When they reach an agreement with the owner, they prepare escrow instructions and secure signatures. If the agent cannot reach a settlement with the landowner, the government or company may take the case to court in order to obtain the property. This is usually a tactic of last resort because of the negative publicity and costs involved. Some Right-of-way Agents negotiate with all levels of government and private companies. Sometimes they manage properties that have been acquired but are not needed immediately.

The agent will perform research on existing and proposed easements, permits, deeds, and other entitlements relating to land title matters. The agent will produce a variety of comprehensive reports involving provisions, restrictions, and other terms relating to the land rights of the company.

Salaries

Government Right-of-way Agents usually earn between $30,000 and $42,000 a year. Agents with a few years' experience can earn between $42,000 and $51,600 a year. Agents whose jobs entail administrative duties may earn between $62,400 and $74,400 annually. Agents normally work a typical 40-hour workweek but may be required to put in overtime hours. Most employees receive benefit packages that include paid vacations, sick leave, holidays, retirement, and health insurance.

Employment Prospects

Between 2002 and 2012, employment of Right-of-way Agents is expected to increase faster than the average. Because most agents work in government, employment is dependent on construction budgets. The overall economy is expected to grow at a healthy rate, creating more construction projects and thus more demand for Right-of-way Agents. Employment in the private sector will increase more slowly than for government jobs. Opportunities will be best for those who have experience in real estate or acquisitions. Government agencies, utilities, pipelines, and companies with active land management programs are the most active recruiters of Right-of-way Agents.

Advancement Prospects

With experience, a Right-of-way Agent can advance to a more senior position with higher earnings and more responsibility. Promotion in private companies depends largely on the initiative of the individual Right-of-way Agent in obtaining advanced training, industry certification, and on-the-job experience. Company size also influences promotional opportunities; there may be relatively few levels of responsibility in small companies. Promotions in government agencies usually are determined by competitive examination or a merit system. Advancement may be to senior right-of-way agent, supervising agent (chief right-of-way agent), or Right-of-way Agent handling more difficult assignments.

Education and Training

For government Right-of-way Agent positions, applicants must have at least a four-year degree, pass a civil service examination, and possess at least two years of experience in appraisal work. Those who have taken courses in such topics as law, economics, real estate management, or engineering usually receive preference in the hiring process. Positions at private companies require college degrees, and most jobs are filled by applicants who have work experience in related fields.

Private companies usually prefer applicants with a college degree or who have demonstrated skills in a related area of work or who have taken real estate–related courses. Large employers will have training courses for employees who have been assigned as Right-of-way Agents. Both government and private industry employers prefer applicants who have knowledge of federal and state acquisition regulations and a working knowledge of appraisal and negotiation procedures.

Special Requirements

Right-of-way Agents need to have knowledge of the methods and techniques used in property appraising, acquisition, and management. They must be familiar with legal instruments used for executing the transfer, sale, or lease of property.

Experience, Skills, and Personality Traits

Right-of-way Agents need to have a number of personal qualities to succeed in this occupation. They must have excellent communication skills, particularly verbal skills. They need to be motivated. They should be tactful when dealing with landowners. They also need to be able to make sound business decisions.

Right-of-way Agents spend much of their time analyzing survey maps and public land records; an ability to read and interpret maps and property descriptions is an essential skill.

Unions and Associations

The International Right of Way Association sponsors an annual conference and educational courses for career advancement. The association's Right of Way certification is a professional designation given to members who have achieved professional status through experience, education, and a written examination. Certification is available in five disciplines: appraisal, property management, environmental, negotiation and property acquisition, and relocation assistance. Additional career-related resources are available from the American Society of Appraisers and the Appraisal Institute.

Tips for Entry

1. Contact utility, railroad, and oil companies directly for possible openings.
2. Applicants should check government agency announcements for openings and exam dates.
3. Local chapters of professional associations and state employment agencies are additional sources of job leads.
4. Check career centers on industry Web sites for current job openings. The International Right of Way Association (http://www.irwaonline.org) is free to non-members but site registration is required.

SITE SELECTION MANAGER

Position Description

Site Selection Managers handle a number of duties associated with the acquisition of land or other resources. These professionals are responsible for all the processes involved in the purchase of undeveloped land. They locate and negotiate sites for purchase or lease and supervise the leasing of owned properties. They supervise the administrative management of leased or owned properties.

Site acquisition managers are responsible for all the duties relating to purchase of land for real estate development. These professionals are responsible for all the processes involved. They undertake surveys and property inspections or contract with other professionals to perform these inspections. They work closely with outside vendors, engineering and construction staffs, and other professionals to obtain zoning permit approvals. They review local zoning ordinances, determine the requirements to obtain a zoning permit, and prepare and file zoning applications. They represent the company or their client at any public hearings on the zoning request. They order property surveys or inspections and make sure that all required legal documents are prepared.

Acquisition managers work independently to negotiate land acquisitions. They perform detailed land use analysis and financial analysis, execute purchase agreements, and oversee due diligence reviews required

before purchase. These reviews typically include concept land planning, environmental reviews, utility system review, and title analysis. These managers work for shopping center managers, industrial developers, telecommunication companies, residential home builders, and other real estate development companies. Site Selection Managers, usually specialize by type of development, such as single-family residential, office, industrial, or other commercial development.

Typical day-to-day duties of site acquisition managers include the following:

• setting rental rates or leasing policies
• providing adequate documentation of lease or purchase transactions
• conducting demographic analysis to anticipate demographic trends
• developing an extensive network of property owners, developers, economic development officials, and other industry professionals
• performing a zoning analysis to identify permitted use areas
• preparing a specific analysis of the zoning requirements for each proposed site
• preparing the zoning application and related zoning application exhibits
• traveling to target markets to inspect property sites and gather information on prospective acquisitions

- assisting in structuring transactions, negotiating pricing, and drafting letters of intent
- making presentations to commissions and boards
- obtaining permits by researching requirements, and completing zoning and land use applications
- studying existing and pending legislation and advising management on needed actions

Site Selection Managers may work independently or as part of a team. They normally work a 40- to 50-hour workweek in an office setting. Overnight travel to inspect properties under review is often required as part of the Site Selection Manager's job, up to 50 percent of a selection manager's working time.

Salaries
Compensation varies according to qualifications and experience. Site Selection Managers can earn salaries ranging from $45,000 to $80,000 annually. A manager's base salary may be supplemented by an annual performance bonus equal to 10 percent or more of base salary for achieving departmental or company goals. More experienced Site Selection Managers can earn salaries above $100,000 annually. Managers typically receive a standard benefits package, including paid vacations, sick leave, and health insurance.

Employment Prospects
Employment prospects for site selection specialists who have the experience and contacts to secure property sites are likely to remain strong through 2014. There is strong demand for real estate professionals who are skilled at locating, securing, and gathering approvals for hard-to-develop sites in the build-to-suit market, meaning properties that are developed according to a tenant's specifications. There is very good demand for site selection specialists who can bring in tenants with investment-grade credit ratings.

Most development firms prefer college graduates who have a strong academic background coupled with some post-graduate experience in property management, site development, or sales. Recent graduates are typically hired as project managers, assigned to manage a small piece of a large development project such as an office building or shopping mall. Medium-sized commercial developers or regional developers are the best prospects for new graduates to approach.

Advancement Prospects
Site Selection Managers report to the director of real estate. Site Selection Managers advance their careers and their earnings potential by taking on larger and more complex projects. A Site Selection Manager might advance to senior project manager and head up a site selection team or become a land development manager and take on responsibility for a project after the development site has been acquired. Some will leave the real estate field after five years to pursue careers in other occupations offering more predictable incomes. Developers who switch careers often move into banking, investment banking, construction financing, and real estate sales.

Education and Training
The recommended academic background is a four-year degree in civil engineering, land planning, or a related field. Some employers look to hire candidates who have a law degree in addition to a bachelor's degree. College courses in accounting, construction technology, business law, and property investments can be helpful. A master's degree is preferred in some more specialized situations.

As the industry has become more specialized, academic requirements have changed, notably those for higher-paying, advanced positions. Extensive knowledge of land surveying, property inspections, and real estate legal contracts, whether acquired in college or post-graduate on-the-job experience, is normally a requirement.

Special Requirements
A real estate sales license may be required if the Site Selection Manager has a role in the actual purchase of undeveloped land.

Experience, Skills, and Personality Traits
Employers look for people who have some prior experience in real estate development or land planning. Site Selection Managers have to be fast thinkers, be able to make quick decisions, and have strong negotiating skills. They should have a working knowledge of land planning, zoning, real estate development, and contract law. Good computer skills and a working knowledge of the Microsoft Office suite also are important job skills. Strong communication skills and presentation skills are very important, as site selection specialists have to be comfortable making group presentations.

Unions and Associations
Real estate associations such as the National Association of Industrial and Office Properties, the International Council of Shopping Centers, and the Corporate Real Estate Network offer career development and

networking opportunities through conferences. Most have job search tips on their Web sites.

Tips for Entry

1. Take college courses in land planning or real estate development to learn the fundamentals of the development process.

2. Some companies offer internships (paid or unpaid) to qualified applicants.

3. Join a Toastmaster club in your area to beef up presentation skills. Find a club nearby on the Toastmasters International Web site (http://www.toastmasters.org).

LENDING AND UNDERWRITING

COMMERCIAL MORTGAGE-BACKED SECURITIES UNDERWRITER

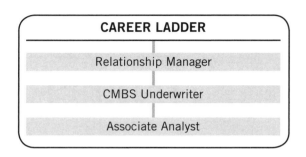

CAREER LADDER

Relationship Manager

CMBS Underwriter

Associate Analyst

Position Description

Commercial Mortgage-backed Securities (CMBS) Underwriters are bonds backed by commercial mortgages rather than residential real estate. This pooling of commercial mortgage loans financing shopping centers, hotels, and industrial properties into securities is a process known as securitization. The CMBS Underwriter gathers up sufficient information about the property (or properties) to enable the bond-issuing bank (the underwriting firm) to be able to sell the bond offering to investors. This examination covers anything related to the performance of the underlying properties, including rental income from tenants, occupancy rates, and ability to make debt-service payments.

Commercial real estate debt is generally divided into two distinct categories: loans to be securitized as commercial mortgage-backed securities, and portfolio loans (also known as "whole loans") that are originated by a lender and remain on its balance sheet through maturity. The loan is reported as an earning asset by the lender.

The typical structure of a CMBS transaction is the following: many single mortgages of varying size, property type, and location are pooled together and transferred to a trust. The trust then issues a series of bonds of varying maturity, payment priority, and credit quality. Nationally recognized credit rating agencies such as Standard & Poor's or Moody's Investors Service assign credit ratings ranging from

investment grade (AAA/Aaa through BBB/Baa3) to below investment grade (BB+ through B-B3). Finally, there is an unrated class which is subordinate to the lowest rated bond class. Interest received from the pooled loans is paid out to investors, starting with those investors holding the highest rated bonds, until all the accrued interest on these bonds has been paid. Interest is then paid to the holders of the next highest rated bonds.

In their duties, CMBS Underwriters perform financial analysis, review analytical models to see how the loan would perform under various changes in market interest rates, and have other related functions. The CMBS Underwriter is responsible for underwriting commercial mortgage loans from the application stage through loan closing and securitization. This process is also known as due diligence, a careful review of the qualifying criteria to determine whether the loans being considered for securitization actually meet the issuing bank's requirements, as well as regulatory agency requirements, for a new offering of mortgage-backed securities.

An important difference between underwriting a loan for a CMBS mortgage pool and underwriting one to be held in the lender's own portfolio is that CMBS underwriting puts more emphasis on cashflow—primarily the income stream from rental payments. By contrast, traditional lenders rely on their initial underwriting at the time a loan is originated to assure the loan will be repaid, either by the borrower or through foreclosure.

The capital markets require, above anything else, certainty about knowing whether the mortgaged property can generate enough rental income to make the debt service payments on the mortgaged property. The goal of the underwriting process is to come up with a net cash flow figure that will be sustained throughout the term of the loan. The CMBS Underwriter does this by examining four basic components: cash flows, property appraisals, engineering reports, and borrower credit reports. They look closely at a borrower's financial strength in terms of net worth, liquidity, credit history, and other publicly available or proprietary information.

CMBS Underwriters work closely with originators, bank representatives, borrowers, and brokers and maintain close contacts with outside legal counsel in negotiation of loan documents. They prepare and present the loan package to the credit committee, or loan committee, for approval. They prepare investor files for submission to credit-rating agencies and investors. They work on a daily basis with other professionals involved in loan securitization and with external investors. CMBS Underwriters work for real estate investment trusts, real estate investment management firms, life insurance companies, and other investment groups.

Mortgage securities underwriters work in an office setting and typically put in long hours, 50 to 60 hours a week or more. The working conditions are very similar to those in other investment banking jobs, which means the hours are long, and bankers are under constant stress to get their deals done.

Salaries

CMBS Underwriters earn competitive salaries. Entry-level base salaries generally range from $50,000 to $75,000 and up. Combined annual compensation, including annual incentive bonuses and signing bonus, if any, can be well in excess of $100,000 annually. Annual compensation usually includes bonus or incentive compensation for reaching performance goals, a generous employee benefit package, and paid vacations.

Employment Prospects

This is a growing field, though one that requires highly specialized skills. Career opportunities should exceed those for all occupations in general through 2014. Employment opportunities are driven in part by the trend toward carving up commercial loans into pieces that can be sold to various classes of investors, depending on the investor's funding requirements and willingness to commit their client's assets to commercial real estate investments.

Advancement Prospects

The typical advancement path is to a more senior position, such as senior underwriter or lead underwriter (often called a relationship manager). That individual is responsible for putting a deal together and negotiating with clients, using the information gathered from junior underwriters. The eventual career path would lead to a position as head of department or a position on the trading desk where mortgage securities are bought and sold to other investors.

Education and Training

A four-year degree with emphasis in accounting, finance, economics, real estate, or a related field of study is a basic requirement. Many firms prefer candidates with a master's degree in real estate or accounting. People entering this field should have a solid academic foundation in financial analysis and have an ability to create spreadsheets for construction, interest, and other development costs, along with future income and operating expenses.

Experience, Skills, and Personality Traits

The CMBS Underwriter needs to have a firm understanding of the fundamentals of real estate and be able to apply these to pending transactions. Applicants should have at least three to five years' experience handling commercial mortgage loans destined for securitization as CMBS securities. Also important is having some understanding of the secondary mortgage market for commercial mortgage loans. This is a fast-paced business environment, and underwriters have to be proactive in coming up with solutions that mitigate risks and potential for losses and keep deals moving forward.

Specific job-related skills are a thorough understanding of financial modeling, including calculation of cash flow models, cash-on-cash yield, internal rate of return, and discounted cash flow analysis. Fluency in Microsoft Office suite programs is important as is a working understanding of ARGUS real estate modeling software.

Unions and Associations

CMBS Underwriters can become members of the Commercial Mortgage Securities Association or the American Securitization Forum for networking opportunities and educational programs designed to keep members informed about current industry or regulatory issues in the industry.

Tips for Entry

1. Internship programs and summer employment can be door openers. Securities firms like to hire people with some prior experience in the firm.
2. Check industry job boards such as the Commercial Mortgage Securities Association's Web site (http://www.cmbs.com).
3. If you're good with numbers and like the challenge of taking risks for big rewards, this may be a good career choice.
4. Events such as job fairs and college campus recruiting events are opportunities to meet recruiters from investment banks and learn more about a career in mortgage securities.

COMMERCIAL LOAN UNDERWRITER

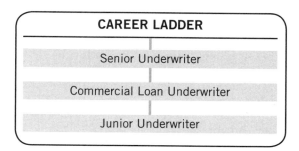

Position Description

Commercial Loan Underwriters are the fact-checkers and gatekeepers in commercial real estate. Once a business's financial records have been collected by the loan officer and a loan application completed, the information is sent to an underwriter. The underwriter decides whether to approve the loan, get more information from the borrower, or deny the loan application.

Underwriters use information provided by the loan officers in the application to determine whether a client's financial status fulfills a lender's pre-established credit conditions. Underwriters then decide with their supervisors whether a loan will be approved. If the application is accepted, the details for repayment are laid out with the customer. In commercial lending the client typically pledges property as collateral for repayment of the loan.

Loan underwriters or officers gather information about clients and businesses to ensure that an informed decision is made regarding the type of loan and the probability of repayment. They analyze the borrower's creditworthiness by asking the right questions to determine if it is a "do-able" deal.

For example, if the loan is a construction loan, the underwriter will evaluate the adequacy of funding and the project's capacity to achieve permanent financing. This review is known in the industry as a due diligence review. The underwriter prepares the credit approval

package for review and approval. The underwriter may work directly with the client and play an active role in building the client relationship. Documentation requirements vary, depending on property type and if the property is considered an investment property or an owner-occupied business. A personal guarantor may be required regardless of the property type.

Unlike residential loans, commercial loan underwriting can greatly differ case by case. There are, however, certain basic ratios with every commercial loan: the debt-service coverage ratio (DSCR), which measures whether the business can make mortgage payments and meet other obligations; the loan-to-value ratio (LTV), which determines the percentage of the property being financed; and net operating income (NOI), which measures the profitability of a property after expenses are paid.

A Commercial Loan Underwriter usually approves loans originated by mortgage banking firms (wholesalers) that have a business relationship (known in the mortgage industry as correspondent firms) and sell their loan production to consolidators who package loans with similar characteristics into investment pools for sale to secondary market investors. Loans over a certain dollar amount are typically reviewed and approved by a loan committee consisting of senior loan officers. The underwriter may package loans with similar characteristics, such as comparable rate and terms, for sale to investors. Many commercial loans are packaged as investment securities (commercial mortgage-backed securities) for sale to institutional investors, including real estate investment trusts, mutual funds, and hedge funds.

Typical duties of Commercial Loan Underwriters often include the following:

- soliciting, negotiating, and committing commercial mortgage loans consistent with investment guidelines
- maintaining relationships with mortgage banking officers (lenders)
- ensuring that mortgage bankers originate and close a consistent flow of quality business
- reviewing property appraisals, lease agreements, and other documents to determine whether a property will generate sufficient cash flow to repay any bank loans
- communicating department policies ad mortgage loan investment guidelines to investment sources
- providing appraisal, analytical, and technical support to the investment division
- providing market research information regarding trends in supply and demand, construction costs, rental rates, land values, and competitor lending policies
- maintaining a working knowledge of applicable lending laws of each assigned state in their market territory

Many Commercial Loan Underwriters have a home office and are often on the road, visiting clients. Many rely on laptop computers, cellular phones, and pagers to keep in contact with their offices and clients. They sometimes travel to other cities to prepare complex loan agreements. Commercial real estate underwriters typically work a 40-hour workweek in an office setting, corresponding with clients by telephone, fax, or e-mail.

Salaries
Commercial mortgage loan underwriters typically earn salaries of $45,000 to $60,000 or more, depending on their responsibilities. Annual compensation may also include an incentive bonus tied to financial performance of the department, business unit, or the entire company. Non-salaried benefits usually include a company-sponsored retirement plan, paid vacations, and health and life insurance.

Some loan underwriters are employed on an hourly basis. Hourly underwriting typically involves working on temporary assignments for two to four months, depending on business volume, and relocating periodically.

Employment Prospects
With qualified loan underwriting training, candidates can become salaried employees of a bank or mortgage company. Employment opportunities for Commercial Loan Underwriters should grow about as fast as demand for all occupations through 2014. While mortgage lending and underwriting is a cyclical business, the commercial side of the business is more diversified than residential lending and less sensitive to market cycles. Loan originators have a continuing need for people who have the analytical skills to evaluate complex loan applications and make judgments about a borrower's ability to repay a loan.

Advancement Prospects
Most loan underwriters begin as junior loan underwriters, working closely with the senior loan underwriter until they are familiar with the proper procedures. Career advancement includes moving into the position of senior loan underwriter or underwriting manager. Some loan underwriters become trainers and train the staff in conventional and government underwriting guidelines. Some will advance their careers by moving into related careers with real estate development firms.

Education and Training
A four-year degree in business, finance, or a related field is a minimum requirement. An advanced degree such as a master's degree in finance is often useful for advancing to higher paying positions with more responsibility. Partly due to the competition for positions at top employers, some post-graduate education is seen as the entry-level educational background in this field. Loan underwriters typically go through a period of on-the-job training after being hired to become familiar with the bank or mortgage company's loan policies and procedures.

Experience, Skills, and Personality Traits
Loan underwriters usually have some prior experience, generally three years or more, as loan processors or a combination of education and qualifying experience. Strong analytical skills, including a working knowledge of commercial real estate valuation techniques and commercial real estate loan analysis, are essential skills. Mortgage loan underwriters must have good communication and negotiation skills; they should be able to express their ideas and opinions clearly in both written and oral communication. Also important is an ability to analyze and apply technical procedures to each loan investment through a review of appraisals, leases, and financial information.

Good common sense, coupled with a complete knowledge of underwriting guidelines, is required in order to be able to make a fair decision on whether to accept or decline a loan application. Guidelines are only guidelines, not rules. Being too lenient could lead to foreclosures; being too strict could result in unfair denial of loans.

Unions and Associations

Commercial Loan Underwriters can become members of the Mortgage Bankers Association of America or the Commercial Mortgage Securities Association for networking and career advancement opportunities.

Tips for Entry

1. If you're good with numbers, and like the challenge of working on multiple projects, this can be a good career choice.
2. Get more information from trade associations with career Web sites: Mortgage Bankers Association or the Commercial Mortgage Securities Association.
3. Get a good background in math, economics, and related courses. An advanced degree or M.B.A. is helpful to those who want to advance their career in this field.

COMMERCIAL REAL ESTATE LOAN OFFICER

Duties: Structures mortgage loans for commercial properties; solicits new business; acts as financial adviser to commercial clients

Alternate Title(s): Commercial Real Estate Lender

Salary Range: $40,000 to $65,000 and up

Employment Prospects: Good

Advancement Prospects: Fair

Prerequisites:

Education or Training—Four-year degree in accounting, finance, or a related field

Experience—Three to five years' credit analysis or commercial lending experience

CAREER LADDER

Senior Lender

Team Leader, Commercial Mortgage Lending

Commercial Real Estate Loan Officer

Special Skills and Personality Traits—Working knowledge of commercial lending; strong PC skills and strong negotiation skills

Position Description

Commercial Real Estate Loan Officers develop and structure mortgage loans for office buildings, shopping centers, hotels, and other commercial properties. They manage loan transactions from origination through credit analysis, loan documentation, loan committee review, and follow-up loan monitoring after the loan closing. They oversee and provide guidance for the bank's credit analysis staff and documentation assistants. They also act as financial advisors for commercial loan clients; commercial loan borrowers view their bankers as a source of information or advice on deal structuring in addition to the mortgage financing. Commercial mortgage officers are sometimes known as "investment bankers" in the world of commercial banking because they originate loans on properties that are held for investment purposes by real estate developers or investor groups.

The job description of commercial bank loan officers has broadened in the last five years, partly the result of intensified competition for bank deposits and other customer relationships. Commercial mortgage lenders wear multiple hats; they have responsibility for cross-selling other bank products such as deposit accounts and generating other business relationships with their loan customers. The loan officer has responsibility for individual loan production, loan quality, loan profitability, and compliance with loan terms as stated in the loan documentation and compliance with banking laws and regulations.

Origination of commercial mortgages is broken down by loan size: once the loan application is received, smaller loans are reviewed by a credit analyst, who prepares an analysis and review of financial statements; larger loans—usually loans over $1 million in size—are referred to the bank's loan committee for final approval.

Some travel is required to visit clients though most travel is regional.

Among their various duties, commercial loan officers perform the following tasks:

- analyze and prepare commercial loan and commercial real estate transactions
- prepare formal loan analysis presentations for approval
- assemble loan documents such as appraisals, financial statements, or borrower tax returns prior to loan closing
- oversee first-level administration of all loan accounts in their portfolio
- manage the borrower's relationship with the bank, analyzing client needs for other banking products
- conduct continuous reviews of the borrower's compliance with loan terms and covenants
- direct activities supporting the company's image in areas of responsibility
- comply with state or federal lending laws and internal policies and procedures

Commercial lenders entering the business can spend the first five years of their careers building relationships with prospective borrowers.

Salaries

Salaries vary according to experience and qualifications when hired. Commercial Real Estate Loan Officers with at least five years' experience earn an average $54,000 a year according to a salary survey by Payscale.com. Salaries range from a low of $40,000 to a high of $65,000 and up. Salary is usually a combination of base salary plus commissions and incentive bonus for reaching performance goals.

Employment Prospects

Commercial real estate lending has its ups and downs. Lenders are most in demand when the real estate market is booming and loan interest rates are low, as happened in the 2001–05 real estate bull market. When the real estate market bottomed in the early 1990s after several years of speculative development, many lenders pulled back from the market, reduced staffs, and cut back their loan portfolios.

While most financial institutions want experienced lenders, there are ways to break into the business by working in a related area and gaining experience. One way to break in is working for a few years in loan workout, where you are given a basket of problem loans or delinquent loans. That's a good way to learn from the ground up, by learning from what can go wrong with a loan. By learning at the back end of the loan cycle how to research the fundamental weaknesses in a loan that goes bad and how to fix those problems, you can learn how to originate loans that perform as expected and that stay as high quality loans.

Advancement Prospects

Advancement is a function of time and experience gained on the job. The more a lender learns, the faster he or she can grow into more senior positions with more responsibility. Learn how to do the more complex types of loans and advise less experienced lenders. An experienced lender can become a team leader. A team leader may oversee a team of three to five lenders and have loan approval authority in concert with the loan officers. Other advancement possibilities are to more senior positions in the bank such as senior lender or department head. Experienced lenders can move laterally into careers in commercial lending at life insurance companies or commercial finance companies that make commercial property loans.

Education and Training

A four-year degree in finance, accounting, or economics with a concentration in finance is generally a minimum requirement. Many financial institutions prefer hiring lenders with a Master's of Business Administration. Financial recruiters seem to prefer people who have the M.B.A. degree.

Experience, Skills, and Personality Traits

Commercial loan officers should have some experience in commercial credit analysis in a bank credit department or in commercial lending, usually three to five years' experience.

Problem-solving and organizational skills are considered paramount, along with leadership, initiative, and ability to forge professional relationships with real estate professionals and others. As with other banking positions where interaction with peer-level professionals and clients is important to success, individuals must have strong written and verbal communication skills.

Some knowledge of the commercial loan business and deal structuring is important, but most employers are looking for individuals who have some experience in financial sales, people who can manage the bank's entire relationship with its customers. Also important is a working knowledge of commercial loan underwriting and some familiarity with Microsoft Office suite (Word, PowerPoint, and Access) of common PC programs.

Unions and Associations

There are no unions or association requirements for commercial loan officers. Loan officers can become members of associations such as the Mortgage Bankers Association of America for professional development, and also for networking opportunities.

Tips for Entry

1. Look into internship positions as a way to get your foot in the door. Most banks will review internships on a case by case basis. They like the free labor, and it's a valuable way to learn the business first hand and make contacts with potential employers.
2. Networking through business networking associations or nonprofit organizations helps build visibility.
3. Contact recruiters. Many positions in high growth fields such as mortgage lending are getting filled through recruiters and search firms.
4. It's all about sales; banks today are more comfortable hiring people who have a sales orientation.

ESCROW OFFICER

Duties: Prepares real estate settlement (closing) documents; reviews property records; issues escrow instructions

Alternate Title(s): Escrow Agent

Salary Range: $30,000 to $75,000

Employment Prospects: Good

Advancement Prospects: Good

Prerequisites:

    Education or Training—Four-year degree or associate's degree plus equivalent work experience

    Experience—Two to four years' escrow or related real estate experience

    Special Skills and Personality Traits—Ability to follow detailed instructions and real estate clos-

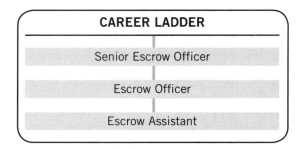

CAREER LADDER

Senior Escrow Officer

Escrow Officer

Escrow Assistant

ing procedures; good organizational skills; background in accounting, real estate law, and escrow procedures

    Special Requirements—Licensing required in some states

Position Description

In a property sale, the transfer of ownership and legal title is commonly known as the property settlement, or closing. On the East Coast, settlements typically involve a meeting of the parties around a table, typically in a real estate lawyer's office. The Escrow Officer position is unique to California and several other states, mostly in the western United States. In most other states real estate attorneys do the work performed by Escrow Officers. Escrow Officers are usually licensed to do business on any property within their respective states.

An Escrow Officer is an independent agent for buyer and seller at settlement time. The Escrow Officer carries out instructions of both parties and facilitates the transaction by receiving, holding, and transferring funds, deeds, and other legal papers. The agent collects all the funds necessary to close the transaction and disburse funds from the closing to the appropriate parties. The agent will contact mortgage lenders and other lien holders to obtain loan payoff information—the amount needed to fully pay off the debt.

The transfer of property is completed upon fulfillment of certain conditions specified in the sales agreement, at which time the necessary deeds and other instruments of ownership are recorded in public land records.

As a neutral third party, the Escrow Officer reviews the title search and pest inspection reports, insurance policies, and loan applications. He or she checks for liens, unpaid taxes and other encumbrances. Escrow Officers maintain a running tally of expenses (and credits) in property sale and calculate the amount payable to either buyer or seller.

The duties of a settlement agent can extend to examining land titles for accuracy, pro-rating property fees for the current year of the transaction, and interacting with local and state agencies to notify them about the transfer of ownership.

Typical job responsibilities of escrow agents can include the following:

- interviewing customers placing property in escrow and gathering pertinent information to complete the transaction
- holding deeds from sellers and funds from buyers and transfering these to appropriate parties when contract terms are met
- opening title reports and preparing escrow instructions
- obtaining loan payoff information from mortgage lenders
- reviewing title searches for unpaid liens, insurance coverage, and other questionable reports
- providing buyers and sellers with reports of all charges and claims left unsettled, and making payments as required
- reviewing all necessary escrow documents for completeness and accuracy

- ensuring that all escrow documents are completed, signed, and delivered
- working with legal staff to ensure that all escrow work is correct

Some Escrow Officers handle the transaction details for more complex commercial property sales, involving multiple parties. Some transactions may involve disbursement of funds from a construction loan. Escrow Officers may also handle 1031 property exchanges, named for a section of the U.S. tax code that allows investors to defer capital gains taxes when selling one property and buying another, comparable property. Escrow Officers work for title insurance companies, financial institutions, and real estate brokerage companies.

Escrow agents work a 40-hour workweek in an office setting. Some travel within the agent's jurisdiction to meet clients and handle real estate closings is normally required as part of the job. Agents may receive compensation for travel mileage, overtime pay, or compensatory time off for any hours worked beyond the standard 40-hour week.

Salaries
The salary range for Escrow Officers is from $30,000 a year to about $75,000, not including commissions. If a commission is paid, the Escrow Officer typically receives a commission based on the sale price of the property, paid out as a draw against future commissions. Earnings are determined in part by the complexity of a transaction and whether the Escrow Officer is performing a residential or a commercial escrow, and also whether capital gains from the sale are taxable or tax-deferred. Escrow Officers can earn higher commissions on more complicated commercial property sales.

Employment Prospects
Employment opportunities for Escrow Officers are tied to the fortunes of the real estate market. Opportunities in California and other fast-growing western states such as Arizona should be above average through 2014, due to continued growth in real estate sales and a strong residential market.

Most Escrow Officers begin their careers by first working as escrow assistants. Escrow assistants help process all the paperwork associated with escrow closings, real estate contracts, deeds, titles, and closing statements. Escrow assistants also help audit closed files.

Advancement Prospects
Escrow Officers can advance into higher paying, more responsible positions in their careers by taking on more administrative responsibility as senior escrow officers

who manage a team of Escrow Officers. Escrow Officers with experience handling the more complex commercial property sales and who have an established book of business with local clients can move into higher paying positions with national title insurance companies offering escrow services for their clients.

Education and Training
There are no formal training requirements for becoming an Escrow Officer. Taking courses in escrow practices and real estate at a local community college or four-year college is one way to learn the business. Numerous colleges offer courses in escrow principles, real estate economics, and real estate practices. Many employers look for individuals with at least a high school diploma who have taken courses in bookkeeping and mathematics. Some familiarity with industry-specific escrow accounting software is helpful, although employers often provide this training on the job. Some training in accounting or real estate law may also be helpful.

Special Requirements
State licensing is required in some states, such as Utah. Escrow Officers in California may also be required to maintain a notary public license and take state-approved courses and a written exam every four years. Check with your state's real estate licensing board or escrow association for further information in continuing education and licensing requirements.

Experience, Skills, and Personality Traits
Real estate transactions are complex. Some experience handling real estate closings is typically required, typically two years or more, or a combination of college degree and experience.

The settlement process can vary from one state to another and even from one county to another in the same state. Escrow Officers need to be familiar with the settlement and title (or deed) recording requirements in the jurisdiction where they are doing business. They have to be able to follow detailed instructions and maintain contact with all the parties involved in a real estate closing.

Strong organizational skills and written communication skills are important for escrow officers. Working in a real estate office, assisting in property closings, can provide some practical, hands-on experience leading to a career as an Escrow Officer.

Unions and Associations
Escrow Officers in California and several other western states can join the California Escrow Association or

the American Escrow Association for career advancement and networking opportunities. Both associations promote industry-best practices and sponsor member educational programs at annual conferences.

Tips for Entry

1. Check the California Escrow Association's Internet job board (http://www.ceaescrow.org) for current job openings.
2. Get experience in a real estate office handling property sales and loan closings.
3. If you are well organized, detail-oriented and good with numbers, this can be a good career choice for you.
4. Attend industry events such as American Escrow Association's National Networking Symposium, an annual event.

MORTGAGE-BACKED SECURITIES ANALYST

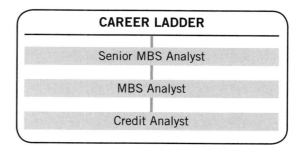

Position Description

Mortgage-backed Securities Analysts are the numbers crunchers in the world of real estate finance. Analysts have become important players in the field known as structured finance, or the business of packaging mortgage loans into investment pools and selling these pools to third-party investors. In the United States today more than half of all residential mortgage loans and about 25 percent of commercial mortgages are routinely bundled into securitized products and sold to secondary market investors. The proceeds from a sale of securities are channeled back to the loan originator and used to finance new loans. The securities created in this process have various names, depending on how the deals are structured. Residential mortgage-backed securities (RMBS), commercial mortgage-backed securities (CMBS), asset-backed securities (ABS), and collateralized debt obligations (CDOs) are some of the more common varieties.

A Mortgage-backed Securities Analyst works with sophisticated financial analysis models to analyze a portfolio of securities and identify the ones offering the best investment value. The methodology is similar to the financial modeling used in analyzing bond portfolios, except that mortgage-backed securities have some additional quirks. Mortgage-backed securities are very interest-rate sensitive. When homeowners refinance their mortgages or pay off the loans before

the maturity date, portfolio values can fluctuate wildly, adding another degree of uncertainty which has to be accounted for by an MBS Analyst.

Mortgage-backed Securities Analysts do a lot of data entry to create financial models that attempt to estimate future security values under various interest rate scenarios. They must be comfortable working with Excel spreadsheet software. They work within teams of associates to prepare reports detailing their findings. The reports are presented to upper-level management.

Specific responsibilities may include the following:

- analyzing investment opportunities in mortgage securities and preparing investment recommendations
- monitoring portfolio holding for changes in value of the underlying securities
- meeting regularly with other team members to exchange ideas and insights into market trends
- analyzing subsectors of the mortgage market to determine fundamental economic value and relative value versus other securities with similar characteristics
- assigning debt ratings to a pool of mortgage-backed securities

Mortgage-backed Securities Analysts work for debt rating agencies such as Fitch Ratings, Moody's or Standard & Poor's, asset management firms, mutual funds, hedge funds, and life insurance companies. Mortgage-backed Securities Analysts typically work a 50-hour week but can work longer hours during peak periods when dealer pipelines are loaded up with new offerings of securities.

Salaries

Entry-level Mortgage-backed Securities Analysts earn starting salaries of $40,000 to $45,000 plus an incentive bonus that is tied to profitability of the firm. Salaries increase with promotion to more senior positions, such as senior analyst or team leader. Analysts performing quantitative modeling, which involves plenty of numbers crunching and theoretical mathematics, can earn salaries of $100,000 or more.

Employment Prospects

This field is a growth opportunity in real estate finance. Demand for qualified mortgage analysts is expected to grow in step with financial innovation, which should stimulate employment growth through 2014. Analysts with quantitative modeling skills or who have experience in high-growth market sectors will have their choice of employment opportunities.

Advancement Prospects

Mortgage-backed Securities Analysts have several advancement options. With experience, they can move up to more senior positions and additional responsibilities. The typical advancement path is promotion to senior analyst and eventually to department head—the most senior position in the MBS research department. The department head is usually a managing director. MBS Analysts employed at a credit rating agency can advance their careers by moving to an investment management firm, mutual fund company, or hedge fund, usually with a sizable increase in annual compensation.

Education and Training

A four-year degree is a standard requirement for this position. Most candidates have a degree in econometrics, mathematical finance, statistics, or a related field of study. Senior-level positions often require an advanced degree, an M.B.A., or a CFA (Chartered Financial Analyst) professional designation. Many employers look for individuals who have a high grade point average, 3.2 or better.

Experience, Skills, and Personality Traits

Individuals should have at least one to two years' experience in credit research with an investment banking firm, credit rating agency, government-sponsored enterprise (Fannie Mae or Freddie Mac), or equivalent work experience. Another entry path is working for a few years in mortgage loan servicing or loan due diligence at a commercial bank or investment bank.

Because they spend much of their day crunching numbers, a working knowledge of Excel spreadsheets is an essential job-related skill. A strong intellectual curiosity and an interest in research are good personality traits. Earning an advanced degree or a CFA designation from the CFA Institute (http://www.cfainstitute.org) can open the door to more advanced positions.

Unions and Associations

MBS Analysts can become members, through their sponsoring firm, of the Securities Industry and Financial Markets Association (http://www.sifma.org), created in 2005 when the Bond Market Association merged with the Securities Industry Association. Another option is the American Securitization Forum, a professional forum specializing in market regulation issues.

Tips for Entry

1. Check current job postings on American Securitization Forum's Web site (http://www.american-securitization.com).
2. This is a fast-changing industry. Read industry publications to learn more about what's happening in structured finance.
3. Check newspaper or online classified ads and apply directly to the firm.
4. Internships and summer employment opportunities are a great way to gain practical experience.

REAL ESTATE CLOSING MANAGER

CAREER PROFILE

Duties: Prepares, assembles, and coordinates documents relating to commercial real estate property sales, known as closing transactions

Alternate Title(s): Closing Coordinator, Closing Specialist

Salary Range: $64,000 to $84,000

Employment Prospects: Good

Advancement Prospects: Good

Prerequisites:

Education or Training—Four-year degree in business administration, finance, or a related area preferred

Experience—Three to five years' experience with commercial real estate firm, mortgage lender, law firm, or escrow firm

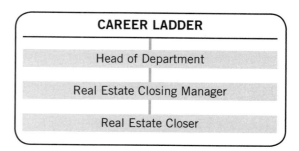

Special Skills and Personality Traits—Strong organizational, written and verbal communication skills; good negotiating skills; working knowledge of commercial real estate; excellent computer skills

Special Requirements—Paralegal certification may be required

Position Description

The Real Estate Closing Manager is responsible for preparing, assembling, and coordinating all the appropriate documents with the various parties involved in a property sale, including lenders, buyers, sellers, developers, attorneys, investors, escrow and title agents, and notary public. Closing is the consummation of a property transaction. The closing process involves delivery of a deed, signing of the mortgage note (if the transaction is financed via a mortgage), and disbursement of funds.

The closing manager collects all the information required to make the transaction a reality and effect transfer of title from seller to buyer or a change of terms in an existing transaction. Real estate transactions can include any of the following: property acquisitions, dispositions and exchanges, real estate debt and equity financings, refinancings, and loan draw-downs.

The closing manager provides advice and counsel in structuring real estate transactions. The manager also is responsible for maintaining all relevant documents relating to property, development project, and partnership, in both hard copy and digital image (soft copy) format. The manager prepares loan documentation with instructions from management or obtains a

review of draft documentation from legal counsel to ensure accurate representation of business terms and compliance with credit quality standards.

The closing manager identifies items and conditions to be satisfied as well as the party responsible for meeting these requirements. The manager obtains or provides a due diligence review of the transaction documents to ensure that the documentation is complete and there no errors or omissions. At closing, the closing manager coordinates the transfer of any loans to the administrator servicing the loan.

Other key job functions include the following:

- maintaining checklists for all development activity in process
- monitoring the status of active development projects, properties for sale, and escrow closings
- updating standard legal documents such as partnership agreements and limited liability company operating agreements for approval by outside counsel
- reviewing with management any proposed documentation changes
- preparing closing instructions for legal counsel or title company
- setting up ticklers (reminders to check) for financial information relating to loan covenants, project cov-

enants, and any outstanding items and following up to make sure these issues are dealt with

- authorizing closing funding and initial funding
- identifying and assisting in resolving issues affecting client service or the real estate management company's risk management procedures

Real Estate Closing Managers work in an office setting and typically work a 40-hour workweek with some limited overtime required during peak financing periods. Overtime work may, or may not, be compensated employment.

Salaries

Earnings of Real Estate Closing Managers vary according to experience and qualifications. Closing managers earned base salaries of $64,000 to $84,000 in 2006, according to a national salary survey by Salary.com. Closing managers may also qualify for an annual bonus program based on accomplishment of specific goals. Besides salary, managers typically receive a standard benefit package, including health and life insurance, paid vacations, flexible spending account, and company-sponsored 401(k) savings or retirement plans.

Employment Prospects

There is ample demand for experienced loan officers and loan closers. Employment of loan officers is projected to increase 11 percent between 2006 and 2016, comparable to the average for all occupations, according to the U.S. Bureau of Labor Statistics. Employment growth stemming from economic expansion and population increases—factors that generate demand for loans—will be partially offset by increased automation that speeds the lending process. Some job openings will result from the need to replace workers who retire or otherwise leave the occupation permanently. College graduates and those with banking, lending, or sales experience should have the best job prospects.

Advancement Prospects

There are several advancement options. Experienced closing managers who have demonstrated supervisory expertise can advance into management positions, taking over responsibility for the entire back-office department responsible for transaction closings. Some may advance their careers by changing jobs and taking similar positions, at a higher annual compensation, with other real estate management firms. Others will opt for similar positions at commercial banks that are active in commercial real estate finance.

Education and Training

Most employers prefer candidates who have earned a four-year degree in business administration, finance, or a related field of study. Beyond having a bachelor's degree from an accredited college or university, candidates can enhance their qualifications with paralegal training from an approved program of study or earning a paralegal certificate from an approved program.

Earning a professional certification can improve opportunities for advancement for closing officers. The Mortgage Bankers Association of America offers a Certified Mortgage Banker (CMB) designation to loan officers in real estate finance. The association has three CMB designations: residential, commerce, and masters to candidates who have at least three years of experience, earn educational credits, and pass an exam.

Special Requirements

A paralegal certification is optional and may be required in some positions.

Experience, Skills, and Personality Traits

Mastering the complexities of commercial real estate transactions takes years of experience. Most employers want to see candidates who have had several years of experience handling closing transactions. Prior experience working for a real estate property management company, mortgage lender or mortgage banking firm, law firm, or escrow firm—usually three to five years—counts as qualifying experience. A broad knowledge of commercial real estate practices and procedures, including real estate law, title insurance, and escrow procedures, can be very useful in this position.

Advanced computer skills in the Microsoft Office suite (Word, Excel, Outlook, and PowerPoint) are essential on-the-job skills. Problem-solving skills are also very important, as loan closers often work under extremely tight deadlines. Closing managers should have the investigative skills to research and resolve complex issues that often come up during a real estate deal.

Excellent communication skills are strongly recommended. Closing managers should have strong verbal and written communication skills, good decision-making skills, negotiating skills, and an ability to perform their duties under deadline pressure. Because they deal constantly with confidential information, an ability to maintain confidentiality and a good sense of tact in dealing with business associates and clients are important personality traits.

Unions and Associations

Professional associations such as the CCIM Institute and the Mortgage Bankers Association of America offer numerous opportunities for improving job skills through continuing education programs and professional certification. Association-sponsored conferences are excellent networking events to build or maintain a personal contact file.

Tips for Entry

1. College courses in math, finance, and economics can provide insights into the fundamentals of credit.

2. Prior experience in a commercial bank, law firm, or escrow firm can build valuable on-the-job experience.

3. As with other positions involving lending, experience gained through summer jobs or interim employment can be a source of useful contacts while job hunting.

REAL ESTATE OWNED MANAGER

Duties: Prepares marketing plan for properties acquired through foreclosure; attempts to sell owned at highest price possible; may negotiate rental, lease, or sale agreements

Alternate Title(s): Manager, REO; REO Asset Manager, REO Property Manager

Salary Range: $45,000 to $50,000 plus incentive bonus

Employment Prospects: Good

Advancement Prospects: Good

Prerequisites:

Education or Training—Four-year degree in business, finance, real estate, or equivalent

Experience—Five to seven years' experience in real estate dispositions or related experience

CAREER LADDER

Manager, Servicing Department

Real Estate Owned Manager

Assistant REO Manager

Special Skills and Personality Traits—In-depth knowledge of real estate finance, accounting, and law; excellent communication, project management, and negotiating skills

Position Description

A real estate owned (REO) property is a property that goes back to the bank lender or mortgage company after an unsuccessful foreclosure auction. The unpaid loan balance—what the mortgage lender is owed—may be more than what the property is worth. When this happens, the property reverts to the lender and the mortgage loan no longer exists. Since the property isn't earning any income, the mortgage company wants to find a buyer as quickly as possible. The Real Estate Owned Manager has overall responsibility for selling, or disposing, any properties acquired this way.

After an unsuccessful auction, the mortgage lender will remove some of the liens on the property and try to resell it to the public, either through future auctions or direct marketing through a realtor. Generally speaking, bank REO properties are in poor shape in terms of repairs and maintenance; however, real estate investors will often go after these properties as banks are not in the business of owning homes and so, in some cases, the low price can more than compensate for the condition of the property.

Each bank or lender works a little bit differently, but they all have similar goals. They want to get the best price possible and have no interest in "dumping" real estate cheaply. Most mortgage companies or banks have an entire department set up to manage their REO inventory.

Typically, the mortgage company wants to sell the property in "as is" condition. When a willing buyer is found, the lender will allow a property inspection at the buyer's expense but may not agree to do any repairs. Sometimes the lender will re-negotiate to save the transaction instead of putting the property back on the market.

REO Managers obtain property valuations and reports, including broker price opinions, property appraisals, and repair bids and write marketing plans for sale of foreclosed properties. They communicate frequently with real estate agents, contractors, closing attorneys, and escrow and title agencies. They are responsible for loss prevention and loss mitigation on defaulted loans, including contracting for preventive maintenance and repairs.

In performing their duties, Real Estate Owned Managers are responsible for the following:

- developing real estate marketing strategies, management plans, and budgets for owned real estate
- recommending criteria and performance goals for property disposition and effectively communicating such information to internal management throughout the ownership cycle
- hiring, coordinating, and managing brokers and on-sight property managers
- working closely with asset managers prior to foreclosures to coordinate a smooth transition

- working with brokers and counsel to assemble diligence packets, negotiate sales offers, and coordinate closings
- tracking income and expenses for owned real estate
- negotiating lease agreements for commercial tenants in inventoried properties

Real Estate Owned Managers work in commercial banks, savings associations, mortgage companies, and real estate management firms specializing in disposal of properties acquired through foreclosure. They work in an office setting, usually working a 40-hour workweek. Some travel to inspect properties in foreclosure is normally required—as much as two to three days a week.

Salaries

Salaries of Real Estate Owned Managers are in the $45,000 to $50,000 range. REO Managers may also receive an incentive bonus determined by individual performance or performance of the department for meeting goals in disposal of troubled real estate. As in other financial manager positions, compensation is based on skills and experience and will vary according to local market conditions and cost of living expenses.

Employment Prospects

Real Estate Owned Managers are in demand when times are bad, which can happen when borrowers have trouble meeting their loan payments, and loan delinquencies and property foreclosures are rising. This can happen after a period of rapid expansion in mortgage lending, when lenders made it harder for borrowers to refinance low-interest loans.

During the subprime mortgage meltdown of 2007–08 borrowers who took out variable-rate home loans with very low down payments were unable to refinance their loans. Foreclosed commercial properties often have unique characteristics, requiring specialized skills and custom-tailored solutions before they can be successfully sold off.

In such a market, job opportunities for loan specialists skilled in marketing distressed properties will exceed those in other occupations, at least until the inventory of properties acquired through foreclosure has been worked down.

Advancement Prospects

Real Estate Owned Managers generally advance to positions of increasing responsibility in the mortgage loan department. Those with strong leadership skills can move into a management slot, eventually moving into senior level management. Another option might be moving into a similar position in a real estate investment firm, such as dispositions manager—the manager in charge of selling properties that, for one reason or another, no longer fit the portfolio requirements of the property investor or owner.

Education and Training

Most employers prefer candidates with a four-year degree in accounting, finance, real estate, or a related field. Some employers will hire high school graduates with several years' experience in real estate property management, bank lending, or loan servicing. Some knowledge of the residential real estate market and loan servicing is very helpful. Banking schools offer classroom courses and correspondence courses in both areas. REO Managers need to maintain their technical skills and knowledge of industry practices, which can be done by taking continuing education courses sponsored by a professional trade association.

Experience, Skills, and Personality Traits

Two to three years' experience in real estate asset management, foreclosure management, or loan servicing is recommended. REO Managers should have strong qualitative and quantitative analytical skills, be computer literate, and have a working knowledge of spreadsheet accounting software. They should have a hands-on working knowledge of real estate contracts and some experience writing real estate contracts and be able to work under deadline pressure.

Good verbal and written communication skills, project management, and problem-solving skills are essential job skills. A working knowledge of Microsoft Excel spreadsheet software is also very useful. Real Estate Owned Managers often work independently, so they should have good time-management skills.

Unions and Associations

The American Bankers Association (http://www.aba.com) and the Institute of Real Estate Management (http://www.irem.org) are useful trade associations for real estate asset and REO Managers. Both associations have continuing education programs to upgrade job skills and maintain contacts with other industry professionals.

Tips for Entry

1. Networking at local bank associations or property management associations can lead to job tips.

2. Some of the best opportunities can be found on industry job banks such as the ones found on the Institute of Real Estate Management or Select Leaders (http://www.selectleaders.com).
3. Take college courses in finance or accounting to get a good foundation in credit management.

4. Prior experience in real estate sales or working for a bank lender or a property management firm can be very helpful; you'll learn firsthand how lenders and investors manage problem loans.

RESIDENTIAL MORTGAGE BROKER

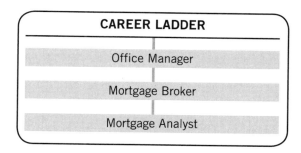

Position Description

Mortgage brokers are the middlemen in the mortgage lending industry. They contact borrowers seeking mortgage financing and negotiate loans with mortgage lenders. Mortgage brokers use their network of contacts with mortgage lenders to negotiate financing at the best interest rate and terms.

Brokers work on a commission basis only; effectively they are an unpaid sales force for mortgage lenders—until they bring in a customer. A mortgage broker hired by a lender is paid at the time of loan closing, when mortgage contracts are finalized and money passes from the buyer of the mortgaged property to the seller. Brokers save money for their clients by arranging financing at a lower cost than would be possible if the loan were made directly by the mortgage lender without using an intermediary to broker the loan.

By providing borrowers with financing at wholesale prices, mortgage brokers are able to save their clients money. Brokers maintain contacts with a large number of lenders, so they can shop around for the best rate and mortgage terms. Brokers work to understand the borrower's financial situation and personal goals. Every mortgage borrower is different, so there is not one loan package that's right for everyone. Many home mortgage borrowers have special needs, such as a desire to buy a home with little or no money down. Others may have less than perfect credit, which makes them a high-risk borrower from the typical lender's perspective. Even if the borrower's loan application is turned down, the mortgage broker will continue to work on the borrower's behalf.

In residential mortgage lending, the mortgage broker performs a number of services that normally would be done by the lender. Among these are the following:

- obtaining credit reports
- providing a good faith estimate of the loan and appraisal costs
- arranging for other work, such as property inspections and appraisals

Brokers are paid for their work by collecting a loan origination fee, or broker's commission, at loan closing time. Mortgage brokers are no longer the lender of last resort in the complex, and constantly changing, world of mortgage finance. Financial services companies, including commercial banks and thrift institutions, employ mortgage brokers to locate qualified borrowers, and reduce their loan origination costs. Brokers bring to the table an in-depth knowledge of the many different types of mortgages rarely found at the local bank.

There is a great deal of specialization in the mortgage brokerage field. Many brokers specialize in commercial or industrial property and multi-family residential property. Some commercial brokers specialize their work according to transaction size or the number of lenders they work with.

Developing and maintaining relationships with mortgage lenders is an important aspect of a mortgage broker's job. Mortgage brokers starting their careers spend much of their time building a contact file of mortgage lenders and prospective clients. Brokers can work 40- to 50-hour weeks, or longer, in the first few years of starting a career.

This is a good career choice if you are sales-oriented, have good math ability, and enjoy helping people meet their financial goals.

Salaries

Mortgage brokers are normally paid commissions rather than salary. Typically, this commission is in the form of a draw or advance against anticipated future commission earnings. Some brokers may receive a base salary plus commission. However, the trend in the industry over the last several years has been toward performance-based broker compensation and a gradual reduction in base salaries. Experience and geographic location, among other factors, determine salaries. Brokers working in the northeastern United States or in metropolitan areas have higher earnings than brokers in non-metropolitan areas.

Mortgage brokers entering the field directly from college can earn salaries of $60,000 to $80,000, plus an annual performance bonus of 10–15 percent. There may also be a signing bonus paid at the time of hiring. Experienced commercial mortgage brokers can earn up to $300,000 a year in total compensation.

Employment Prospects

Employment opportunities for mortgage brokers are relatively good over the next several years. Mortgage brokers have become a significant channel of prime business origination for most financial institutions. Opportunities should continue to look good as long as the financial services industry continues to employ independent wholesalers to locate mortgage-qualified borrowers.

On the other hand, employment in this field is closely tied to overall growth in the economy. A sharp reduction in loan originations, which might occur in a recession or an economic slowdown, could severely limit employment opportunities, as well as starting salaries of newly hired mortgage brokers.

Advancement Prospects

Mortgage brokers usually advance their careers, and compensation, by taking on more complex projects, usually commercial projects, requiring more job-related experience. Residential Mortgage Brokers with leadership skills might advance into management positions, such as office manager. Mortgage brokers seeking career stability might move into mortgage banking, which has an additional source of income—the servicing fees mortgage bankers collect for processing mortgage payments from borrowers.

Education and Training

Mortgage brokers come from varied academic backgrounds. A four-year college degree with courses in business, finance, or related courses, is generally the minimum education requirement. Continuing education beyond college is required to maintain professional competency in the field and is also a prerequisite in some states to the brokerage licensing exam.

The National Association of Mortgage Brokers Educational Foundation and the Institute for Financial Education, now part of Bank Administration Institute, both offer continuing education and correspondence courses to mortgage brokers.

Special Requirements

Mortgage brokers must pass a written exam and obtain a state license, usually from the state banking department or chief regulator of financial institutions. Mortgage broker regulations vary widely from state to state. Some states issue licenses to individual brokers while others license brokerage offices. A number of states have stringent educational requirements, requiring brokers to attend professional training courses, while some require that brokers maintain a surety bond or pass a background investigation.

Experience, Skills, and Personality Traits

Two to five years' experience in financial services marketing is a general requirement for the position. Mortgage brokers should have strong written communication and interpersonal skills and negotiating skills. Some knowledge of computers and personal computer programs used in business, such as word processing and financial spreadsheet programs, is also useful. Mortgage brokers should be entrepreneurial in personality, goal-oriented and willing to work long hours.

Unions and Associations

Mortgage brokers can become members of the National Association of Mortgage Brokers for career development and professional networking through state chapters of the association. The mortgage brokers association offers two certification programs, the Certified Residential Mortgage Specialist and the Certified Mortgage Consultant.

Tips for Entry

1. Take college-level courses in economics, finance, and related areas to get a good academic background in business and finance.

2. Licensing requirements for mortgage brokers can vary widely. It's a good idea to check into the education requirements of the state where you plan to work and take college courses in those subjects.

3. Contact industry associations such as the National Association of Mortgage Brokers (http://www.namb.org) for possible job leads.

RESIDENTIAL MORTGAGE ORIGINATOR

CAREER PROFILE

Duties: Markets residential mortgage loans and related mortgage loans to financial institution customers; responsible for loan closing and preparation of loan documents; contacts appraisers, real estate brokers, and others for new business leads

Alternate Title(s): Home Mortgage Consultant, Residential Mortgage Specialist

Salary Range: $20,400 to $92,571

Employment Prospects: Good

Advancement Prospects: Fair

Prerequisites:

    Education or Training—Four-year degree with courses in business management, finance, or related courses

    Experience—Two years in mortgage or consumer lending, or equivalent experience in related areas

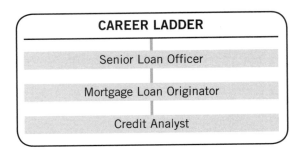

CAREER LADDER

Senior Loan Officer

Mortgage Loan Originator

Credit Analyst

Special Skills and Personality Traits—Excellent communication, organizational, and marketing skills; ability to work independently with minimal supervision; good computer skills; knowledge of state and federal laws relating to real estate closings.

Position Description

Mortgage loan originators work for commercial banks, credit unions, savings institutions, and mortgage companies. They work with realtors, property appraisers, attorneys, and bank business development officers to develop new business opportunities. Loan originators interview mortgage applicants and monitor progress of loans from the loan application to loan closing. They work closely with the bank's loan processors to make certain that new loans are compliant with the bank's underwriting guidelines. The mortgage originator interviews customers applying for loans, analyzes and screens preliminary loan requests, and packages loans for review by senior loan officers or a loan committee.

Mortgage originators solicit new loans from prospective borrowers, gather background financial information, help the borrower fill out mortgage loan applications, and submit loan applications for processing. They determine whether loan applicants meet the lender's credit criteria or loan standards. The loan originator may call the applicant to resolve discrepancies in the credit application, such as a credit report showing late payments.

Residential Mortgage Originators spend much of their time out of their office, working with laptop computers, cellular phones, and pagers to stay in contact with their offices and clients. Mortgage loan officers may work from their homes, and usually are assigned a geographic territory to work. They work closely with branch office managers and will frequently call on potential customers referred by a branch office in their region. Mortgage loan officers may work a 40-hour week, but may work evenings and weekends, especially when there is a heavy volume of mortgage originations and loan refinancings.

Specific job functions may include the following:

- interviewing loan applicants and explaining loan terms and conditions
- analyzing the applicant's financial status, credit history, and property to determine the feasibility of granting a loan
- ordering appraisals, credit reports, and reference checks
- verifying borrower's salary or requesting copies of tax returns if self-employed
- preparing loan documentation in accordance with financial institution standards
- screening loan requests according to financial institution policies and types of loans offered

- providing status reports to bank management on residential loan production
- coordinating loan closings with buyers, sellers, real estate agents
- counseling delinquent borrowers or referring delinquencies to loan collection department
- resolving customer complaints

The residential mortgage field has numerous specialty positions that service market subsegments. Subprime mortgage originators process loan applications of applicants who have had past credit problems or limited borrowing experience. (Subprime mortgage lending accounted for one out of every five mortgage loans originated in 2005.) Home renovation specialists process loan applications for home renovation financings; in a renovation loan the lender advances funds to renovate a property along with the funds necessary to purchase the mortgaged property. Funds are advanced based on the expected appraised value of the property after completion of the renovations.

Renovation loans can be any of several types; some lenders offer a construction-to-permanent-loan—a single loan covering renovation construction and home purchase. The Federal Housing Administration's 203(k) loan program, which offers low-downpayment mortgage financing on owner-occupied homes, is another popular option. Reverse mortgage specialists originate loans to senior citizens in which the lender advances funds to the borrower, providing income after retirement, in exchange for a lien on the borrower's property.

Salaries
Residential mortgage lenders earn much of their income from sales commissions. There are a number of possible salary arrangements, such as a base salary plus commissions based on loan production volume. Newly hired loan officers receive a base salary plus a drawdown against future commissions. The base salary is gradually reduced as lenders become more experienced and their loan production increases. Salaried mortgage loan officers earned 2006 salaries (excluding commissions) ranging from a low of $20,400 to $88,572.

Employment Prospects
Residential Mortgage Originators usually start out as credit analysts or mortgage loan underwriters, where they learn how to read financial statements and gather all the information needed to approve a loan application. Employment opportunities for commissioned mortgage lenders will grow about as fast as employment opportunities in general, according to the U.S.

Department of Labor's Bureau of Labor Statistics. The mortgage market is very interest rate sensitive, which means job opportunities may shrink during periods when mortgage lending is declining. Regions where home values have appreciated but home buyers and homeowners need financing to upgrade their homes may have greater demand for renovation loans—and home renovation lenders.

Advancement Prospects
Advancement opportunities for residential mortgage lenders are dependent on experience, as with other fields in bank lending. Mortgage lenders with successful track records—those who have met or exceeded production goals with average or lower-than-average loan losses—may advance to handle more complicated loan financings such as construction loans or commercial mortgages. They can advance to become team leaders, overseeing a group of lenders plus supporting loan processors and clerical staff. Some opportunities will come about through turnover when other lenders move to positions with another financial institution or reach retirement age.

Education and Training
Most financial institutions want to see candidates with at least a four-year college degree with courses in business, finance, and marketing. Also helpful are courses in the social sciences and the liberal arts. Financial institutions normally provide extensive on-the-job training to starting mortgage originators, supplemented with periodic seminars as new types of mortgage financing are introduced. The training requirements vary by financial institution and by the specific requirements of the position.

Experience, Skills, and Personality Traits
Mortgage lenders should have at least two years' experience, preferably in consumer lending or mortgages. Prior experience in mortgage lending or commission-paid financial sales is helpful, though not a requirement. As there is a high degree of customer contact, excellent communication skills, organizational skills, and marketing skills are important. Productive mortgage lenders have excellent people skills when interviewing prospective loan customers and have excellent organizational and marketing skills. Getting a mortgage approved has many separate steps, so attention to detail is important. Also important is an ability to work closely with builders, appraisers, and other professionals.

The mortgage lending position requires a general understanding of the various types of mortgage instruments and financial institution policies and procedures, plus federal and state regulations concerning residential mortgages. Industry certification is optional, and is generally not a requirement to enter the field.

Newly hired lenders go through a short training program in which they become familiar with mortgage underwriting guidelines of federal agencies, such Fannie Mae and Freddie Mac, that purchase loans from mortgage originators in the secondary mortgage market, or the Federal Housing Authority, an agency within the Department of Housing and Urban Development that insures mortgage loans. Most lenders have loan origination guidelines that match or exceed the federal agency guidelines.

Unions and Associations

Mortgage lenders can become members of the Mortgage Bankers Association through their employer for networking opportunities and skills improvement. The Mortgage Bankers Association sponsors seminars and distance learning courses for individuals involved in real estate lending. Industry certification is available through sponsoring trade associations. Among these are the Accredited Residential Underwriter and Certified Mortgage Banker designations awarded by the Mortgage Bankers Association of America.

Tips for Entry

1. Attending job fairs sponsored by state mortgage bankers associations is an effective way to get to know potential employers.
2. Check job opportunities at one of the many banking industry Web sites for available positions in your area.
3. While one to two years' experience is usually a requirement, lenders will sometimes hire individuals with no previous banking experience. Contact employers in your area directly or ask for referrals from friends or associates.

PROPERTY MANAGEMENT

ASSET MANAGER

Duties: Reports to property owners on building occupancy, lease expirations, and other issues; prepares financial statements on owned properties

Alternate Title(s): Asset Property Manager, Owner's Representative, Real Estate Asset Manager

Salary Range: $74,300 to $114,700

Employment Prospects: Good

Advancement Prospects: Good

Prerequisites:

Education or Training—Four-year degree in accounting, business administration, finance, or a related field of study

Experience—At least three to five years' experience in commercial real estate

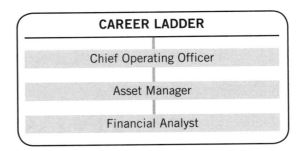

CAREER LADDER

Chief Operating Officer

Asset Manager

Financial Analyst

Special Skills and Personality Traits—Good written communication skills, organizational skills, and negotiating skills; proficiency in Microsoft Excel and ARGUS, a real estate analytical software

Position Description

Some real estate managers act as advisers to the property owners or investors. They plan and direct the purchase, development, and disposition of real estate on behalf of the business and investors. These specialists, known as Asset Managers, are responsible for one or more portfolios of real estate. These managers focus on long-term strategic financial planning, rather than day-to-day operations. They oversee the on-site property managers and determine the best time to sell or refinance the properties. They evaluate portfolio performance, advise owners on acquisition and disposition strategies, and identify opportunities for future real estate investments.

Asset Managers evaluate the financial terms and other critical factors associated with a particular lease or contract. They report to the property owners on building occupancy, lease expirations, lease market conditions, property marketing plans, future capital improvements, and redevelopment opportunities.

The Asset Manager functions as the primary manager of a property's profit and loss (P&L) statement, reporting directly to the property owner or a portfolio manager responsible for a group of properties. The Asset Manager rarely negotiates deals, but works closely with the leasing and property managers to monitor achievement of operating goals and profitability goals. The Asset Manager is more of a reviewer than a negotiator. The manager keeps tabs on the performance of

designated properties to make sure the properties are meeting the property owner's operating goals (occupancy, tenant mix, etc.) and profitability targets. In some organizations, the Asset Manager has authority to approve decisions about property management and leasing activities related to the assigned properties.

When evaluating potential acquisitions, real estate asset managers examine property values, taxes, zoning, population growth, transportation, and local traffic volume to determine how well they might fit in the overall portfolio. After a site has been selected, they often participate in contract negotiations for purchase or lease, securing use of the site on the most beneficial terms. Real estate asset managers review their company's real estate holdings periodically and identify properties that are no longer financially profitable or contributing to the property mix desired by the owner. They may recommend sale, or disposition, of chronically unprofitable properties.

Some employment opportunities are with relocation firms. These companies have specialized departments or wholly owned subs to advise sellers about property values and marketability. Some work directly with lenders that have large real estate owned (REO) inventories. Most work is done in an office setting, although some travel is required occasionally for on-site inspections of managed properties.

Specific duties of real estate asset managers typically include the following:

- overseeing performance of a regional portfolio of properties
- recruiting the property management team members
- reviewing and approving service agreements and contracts
- responding to requests for information from investors and capital clients
- preparing an annual operating plan, which includes lease objectives for each property, operating and capital budgets
- assisting property managers in evaluating and resolving operational issues
- completing quarterly valuations and reports for portfolio properties
- representing the owner before government agencies
- analyzing tax assessments
- reviewing rental collections and revised financial terms for delinquent tenants

Salaries

Earnings of Asset Managers are comparable to property manager compensation. Annual earnings are determined in part by the type of property under management, years of experience, industry credentials, and academic background. An Asset Manager who oversees industrial or office properties can earn anywhere from $74,300 to $114,000, according to CEL & Associates, Inc., a Los Angeles real estate consulting firm. Asset Managers of retail properties, including shopping malls, can earn salaries of $87,000 to $130,000. Most property management companies also have bonus and extensive fringe benefits plans including dental care, health insurance, and 401(k) employer match plans. Bonus payouts are tied to property performance.

Employment Prospects

There is growing demand for experienced real estate Asset Managers. Employment opportunities for Asset Managers are projected to grow about as fast as employment growth in all occupations through 2014, according to the U.S. Department of Labor's Bureau of Labor Statistics. Some Asset Managers gain experience working as property managers; some start out as financial analysts and learn how to spread financial statements and prepare financial reports for management and investors. Demand for Asset Managers is being driven in part by the institutionalization of real estate as an investment category. Growth in the number of managed properties owned by pension funds, real estate investment trusts, and other types of investors will create new employment opportunities for Asset Managers.

Advancement Prospects

Asset Managers typically advance their careers by moving up in the organization, taking more senior positions. Experienced managers can move into higher paying positions managing multiple properties or larger properties. Further opportunities can be found in the upper management levels of property management firms. As their careers advance, Asset Managers are given larger, more complex properties, to manage. They may specialize in the management of one type of property, such as apartments, office buildings, or industrial properties. This role is an excellent mid-level position, with potential to move into an acquisition role and eventually into a senior management position.

Education and Training

Most employers prefer to hire college graduates with a degree in business administration, finance, real estate, or public administration. Larger property management firms provide some on-the-job training by pairing newly hired managers with more experienced property managers. Many Asset Managers earn a professional certification, such as the CCIM, Certified Commercial Investment Member, awarded by the CCIM Institute to individuals who have sufficient work experience, complete a specified number of courses, and pass a competitive exam. A professional designation can effectively increase their advancement opportunities and positively impact their annual compensation. Some employers prefer managers who have earned a master's degree in real estate or finance.

Experience, Skills, and Personality Traits

Real estate Asset Mangers should be good negotiators and skilled in handling or analyzing data in order to assess the fair market value of property or its development potential. Resourcefulness and creativity in arranging financing are essential skills for managers who are active in land development. They need to have an ability to handle multiple tasks without losing focus on the details. They should also have detailed knowledge of commercial real estate practices and legal documents commonly used in real estate transactions. Proficiency in Microsoft Excel and ARGUS, real estate database software, is highly recommended.

Unions and Associations

There are several professional associations for Asset Managers: the Building Owners and Managers Institute (http://www.BOMI-edu.org), the Institute of Real Estate Management (http://www.irem.org), the CCIM Institute, and the Community Association Institute. Several associations have professional certification or designation programs for professional advancement. More information on these can be found in Appendix III.

Tips for Entry

1. College students can look at Institute of Real Estate Management's free booklet, Careers in Real Estate Management, for more information on careers in real estate management.

2. Learn on the job through industry-supported internship programs such as the one sponsored by the Institute of Real Estate Management.

3. Take courses toward the CCIM designation at colleges or universities participating in the CCIM academic program.

4. Look for employment opportunities listed on Select Leaders (http://www.selectleaders.com) and other industry sponsored Web sites.

ASSISTANT PROPERTY MANAGER

Duties: Supports the property manager in day-to-day operation of an apartment complex, office building, or other real estate facility; assists in financial records maintenance

Alternate Title(s): Property Manager Assistant

Salary Range: $48,000 to $54,600

Employment Prospects: Good

Advancement Prospects: Good

Prerequisites:

  Education or Training—Four-year degree in business administration, finance, or real estate

  Experience—One to three years' experience

  Special Skills and Personality Traits—Good communication skills and financial skills; good organizational skills

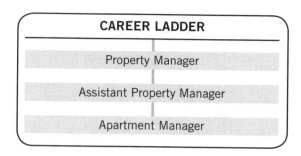

CAREER LADDER

Property Manager

Assistant Property Manager

Apartment Manager

Special Requirements—Industry certification usually required for managers of federally assisted housing developments

Position Description

Assistant Property Managers provide operational support to property managers in day-to-day implementation of policies and procedures, assuring that facilities are well managed. The Assistant Property Manager has an important role in vendor relations and tenant relations, and also in capital improvement project planning.

Assistants work closely with a property manager and learn how to prepare budgets, analyze insurance coverage, market property to prospective tenants, collect overdue rent payments, and negotiate contracts with suppliers and vendors. Under general supervision, Assistant Property Managers perform a wide variety of routine and more complex office, administrative, and support tasks. They serve as liaisons with tenants, assist in overseeing facility projects, and perform other related duties.

Assistant managers help local property managers in all activities associated with a property or a group of properties. These activities may include invoice processing, researching discrepancies in invoices, securing tenant and vendor certificates of insurance, tenant and vendor correspondence, assisting the property managers with property inspections, securing bids from vendors, and preparing vendor contracts.

Typical duties performed may include the following:

- writing contracts with service partners
- maintaining up-to-date records of vendor contracts
- inspecting work performed by service partners and vendors
- conducting building site inspections
- assisting the accounting department with accounts payable and tenant accounts receivable
- conducting needs analysis for project improvements, issues, requests for proposals (RFPs), and selecting vendors
- assisting in preparation of monthly management reports, budgets, and forecasts

Salaries

Earnings of Assistant Property Managers are determined by the type of property under management and, if it is a commercial property, the size of the property in square feet. Assistant managers of commercial or industrial properties earned base salaries ranging from $48,000 to $54,600 in 2007, according to CEL & Associates, Inc., a Los Angeles real estate consulting firm. Assistant managers of residential facilities earned slightly lower base salaries, from $31,300 to $37,700 annually. Assistant Property Managers may also receive an annual bonus averaging about 10 to 12 percent of base salary. In addition to salary, most employers also have a standard benefits package, including paid vacations, company-funded health insurance, and a 401(k) employee savings plan.

Employment Prospects

Large apartment developers and property owners are a primary source of employment. Job growth in property management will rise with construction of new apartment complexes, offices, and other rental properties.

While employers say they prefer to hire property managers with some real estate experience, labor market conditions often dictate otherwise. Employers are increasingly hiring inexperienced college graduates with a bachelor's degree or master's degree to fill position vacancies and placing them under the supervision of a property manager for a period of several months to a year or more. Someone starting directly from college may work for a few years as on-site manager of a single apartment building, gaining experience on the job while attending seminars to learn about property management.

The graying of America, as seen in the burgeoning over-65 age group, is increasing demand for suitable housing, assisted living facilities, and retirement communities. Employment opportunities for property managers will be due to growth in commercial real estate and planned residential communities. As planned communities become more prevalent across the country, property management firms will increase their hiring of on-site administrators to take on the on-site management duties in these facilities. Opportunities are likely to be brightest in states experiencing population growth compared to the rest of the country. Overall, employment of property managers is expected to grow about as fast as employment growth in all occupations through 2014, according to the U.S. Department of Labor's Bureau of Labor Statistics.

Advancement Prospects

People who prove their worth as apartment managers can advance to positions with greater authority, working as assistants to property managers. Working under the supervision of a property manager, Assistant Property Managers with little or no previous experience can advance to on-site manager within two or three years after hiring. More experienced managers can advance to positions with more responsibility and more pay while managing larger properties. Additional opportunities can be found in higher level positions in property management firms, such as regional manager. For example, a regional manager has responsibility for a number of managed properties in a designated geographic region.

Education and Training

Most employers prefer to hire college graduates with a bachelor's degree. A four-year degree in business, finance, accounting, real estate, or a related field of study is a basic requirement. Many employers encourage their new employees to attend short-term formal training programs given by professional trade associations. Employers send managers-in-training to these programs to improve their management skills and expand their knowledge of industry specific subjects, such as building maintenance, insurance, risk management, and real estate law.

Special Requirements

There are no special requirements for most Assistant Property Managers. Property managers of public housing facilities financed with federal assistance may be required to have an industry certification.

Earning a professional certification at association-sponsored seminars is optional, but getting a recognized credential helps new employees upgrade their business skills and is useful for career advancement. The Certified Property Manager (CPM) credential conferred by the Institute of Real Estate Management is designed for property and asset managers working with large portfolios of all property types. The CPM designation is regarded as the property management industry's premier real estate credential. The Real Property Administrator (RPA) designation or the Facilities Management Administrator (FMA) program available from the Building Owners and Managers Institute serve the educational needs of third-party property managers and corporate property managers. College courses in real estate may qualify for credit toward a Certified Property Manager designation and an undergraduate degree.

Experience, Skills, and Personality Traits

Individuals entering this field should have some property management experience, anywhere from three months to four years, depending on the position. Employers look for individuals who can work independently, read and follow instructions, and maintain financial records.

Good communication and public contact skills also are important, as are an ability to manage subordinates, including maintenance and clerical staff. Some experience in real estate sales may become handy because the negotiating skills learned in selling properties can be used in dealing with vendors and tenants.

Assistant Property Managers should have a general understanding of accounting and finance, budgeting, business planning, contract administration, and tenant relations. The major property management companies have on-the-job training programs to supplement college courses with real world training in important job-related management skills.

Unions and Associations

Assistant Property Managers can join several professional associations for career management and networking opportunities. Among these are the Building Owners and Managers Institute (http://www.BOMI-edu.org), the Institute of Real Estate Management (http://www.irem.org), the CCIM Institute, and the Community Association Institute. Several of these have professional certification or designation programs for professional advancement. See Appendix III for more information on certification programs.

Tips for Entry

1. Check newspaper classified ads or apply directly to property management firms listed in the telephone directory under "Real Estate Management."
2. Don't have experience? Consider part-time or summer jobs or internships to develop valuable contacts that will be useful in your job search.
3. Internet resources such as the Institute of Real Estate Management's Web site for college students (http://www.GetRealGetReady.org) have career tips for those interested in a career in property management.
4. Negotiating skills learned from real estate sales can be applied to a career in property management.

APARTMENT MANAGER

CAREER PROFILE

Duties: Oversees day-to-day operations of apartment complexes; handles lease negotiations and renewals; oversees building maintenance

Alternate Title(s): Community Manager, Resident Manager

Salary Range: $46,400 to $64,800

Employment Prospects: Good

Advancement Prospects: Good

Prerequisites:

    Education or Training—High school diploma or equivalent

    Experience—Three months' to four years' experience in real estate management or customer service

CAREER LADDER

Business Manager

Apartment Manager

Lease Consultant

Special Skills and Personality Traits—Strong managerial, interpersonal and computer skills; knowledge of building maintenance; ability to work independently

Position Description

Apartment Managers are the primary link between the property owner and tenants who rent apartments in a residential community. They oversee the day-to-day management and supervise maintenance workers and other on-site employees. They negotiate contracts for construction, maintenance, security, garbage removal, and groundskeeping services. They periodically report the status of the property to the property owner.

Many Apartment Managers are on-site managers. They show units to prospective tenants and review rental applications. They check an applicant's credit history and verify employment or other sources of income. Most managers are also responsible for completing and signing the rental agreement. When screening applicants for subsidized housing, managers must determine and certify each applicant's eligibility according to government standards.

In larger apartment complexes, the Apartment Manager may train leasing consultants, the sales people who negotiate leases and handle marketing to new tenants. The Apartment Manager may recruit and train the building staff. The staff will vary according to community size, but generally consists of an Apartment Manager, assistant manager, leasing consultants, and the maintenance workers.

On-site Apartment Managers handle the financial operations of the apartment building or assist the management company's business manager in

collecting rents, security deposits, insurance, and maintenance. On-site managers routinely inspect the property to see if any repairs are needed and make arrangements to fix the problem. Each month they collect rents, keep a record of all transactions, and submit reports to building owners showing income, expenses, and vacancies. Some Apartment Managers' duties may include cleaning hallways and other common areas, changing light bulbs, and making minor repairs to the property. Managers are expected to enforce building rules and regulations and also to investigate residents' complaints. When necessary they serve eviction notices.

Typical duties of an on-site Apartment Manager include the following:

- touring apartments with prospective tenants
- completing lease and lease renewal paperwork
- explaining lease information to tenants
- assisting in resolution of tenant and employee issues
- supervising rent collections and tenant evictions
- coordinating work with contractors
- assisting the business manager in inspecting vacancies

Resident Apartment Managers generally work a 40-hour week. Part-time managers work between 10 and 30 hours a week.

Apartment Managers usually don't have a separate business office and are often required to live in the apartment complex where they work, so they are available to handle any emergencies that may occur on weekends or at other times when they are off-duty. They work flexible hours as needed and are usually on call evenings and weekends to deal with tenant problems or emergencies.

Salaries

Apartment Managers can earn salaries of $46,400 to $64,800 annually, according to the National Apartment Association. Earnings will vary according to the number of units in the apartment complex. In addition to salary, on-site Apartment Managers typically get the use of a rent-free apartment in the building complex. They may be entitled to compensatory time off for night and weekend work or overtime pay for hours worked beyond a 40-hour workweek.

Apartment Managers working for large multi-apartment owner-operators may also have generous fringe benefits, including company-paid health and life insurance and a company-sponsored retirement plan.

Employment Prospects

Job opportunities for Apartment Managers are expected to grow about as fast as opportunities in all occupations through 2014, according to the U.S. Bureau of Labor Statistics. The real estate industry is growing in response to a growing—and aging—U.S. population, and building more rental housing to meet that market demand. About one-third (30.5 percent) of U.S. households lived in rental apartment units in 2006, according to the National Multi-Housing Council.

Demand for rental housing comes from several sources: people who lack the income to become homeowners or who choose to rent rather than own a home and older Americans who move into retirement communities with on-site property management. Most employment opportunities will be found in major metropolitan areas, which typically have the highest concentrations of rental housing. This expected growth in multi-family housing units of all types will increase job opportunities for Apartment Managers.

Advancement Prospects

After some on-the-job experience, an Apartment Manager can grow in the business to pursue other managerial and supervisory opportunities. Earning an industry certification in property management from any of the professional real estate associations can open the door and provide additional qualifications for promotion to senior positions, such as business manager, with increased responsibility and higher annual income. Further advancement to higher levels is possible for

managers employed by a property management company that owns and operates residential facilities in several states.

Education and Training

While a high-school diploma is the minimum academic requirement, many employers prefer hiring college graduates. A four-year degree in business administration, real estate, or public administration would be a solid academic foundation. Employers typically provide some on-the-job training to orient new employees. In some metropolitan areas, industry associations offer basic and advanced courses in apartment management. The Institute of Real Estate Management (http://www.irem.org) and the National Apartment Association (http://www.naahq.org) offer apartment management courses. Employers often encourage employees to take these introductory courses and may pay tuition and other costs.

Experience, Skills, and Personality Traits

Apartment Managers have to be comfortable dealing with all types of people. Managers have to be effective communicators with good interpersonal skills and public contact skills. Some experience is helpful, from three months' to four years' experience in real estate property management. Employers look for people who can work independently, read and follow instructions, and maintain financial records. Legible and effective handwriting, a working knowledge of business math, and the ability to plan and organize the work of others are job skills highly ranked by employers. Other useful skills are a working knowledge of word processing, e-mail, spreadsheet, and other generic computer software.

Apartment Managers should have some knowledge of state or federal regulations covering rental housing and have some familiarity with building maintenance. Managers can often work long hours, so physical conditioning and a dedication to getting the job done are important. The work can be physically and emotionally demanding, with very little uninterrupted free time.

Unions and Associations

Apartment Managers can become members of the National Apartment Association for career advancement and networking opportunities. The NAA sponsors the Registered in Apartment Management (RAM) professional designation and Certified Apartment Manager (CAM). Another designation option is the Accredited Resident Manager (ARM) awarded by the Institute of Real Estate Management

Tips for Entry

1. If you're interested in general business management, administration, and real estate, this may be the career for you.
2. Apply directly to major owner-operators of rental apartment units, such as American Investment Management Company of Denver, which manages apartment units across the country.
3. Courses in property management, available from community colleges, four-year colleges, or real estate training schools, can provide the background for a successful career in real estate management.

COMMUNITY ASSOCIATION MANAGER

Position Description

Community Association Managers manage the common property and services of condominiums, cooperatives, and planned communities through their homeowners or community associations. Their responsibilities are limited to managing residential communities. Some association-managed communities encompass thousands of individual homes and are large enough to employ their own on-site staff and managers.

In many ways, the work of Community Association Managers parallels that of property managers. Community Association Managers collect monthly assessments, prepare financial statements and budgets, negotiate with contractors, and resolve homeowner complaints. There are some important differences. Community Association Managers work with homeowners and other residents every day. They are hired by a volunteer board of directors and oversee the management of property and facilities the homeowners own and use jointly through the association. They also assist the board and owners in complying with association bylaws and government regulations.

These managers are responsible for the financial administration and daily supervision of properties they manage. They oversee everything from the marketing of vacant space, negotiation of leases, collection of rental fees, maintenance, and other essential services. They often negotiate contracts for on-site maintenance workers such as janitors and groundskeepers and monitor their performance. They also handle the bookkeeping duties, including payment of taxes, mortgages, and insurance.

Apartment complexes and other large properties have a full-time, on-site manager who reports to the property manager or owner. On-site managers train, supervise, and assign duties to the maintenance staff, handle daily service and repair problems, and keep records of operating expenses. They must understand and comply with city, state, and federal legislation pertaining to local building codes, fair housing laws, and accessibility requirements of the Americans with Disabilities Act. Condominium managers or homeowner association managers may have additional responsibilities for maintaining streets, parking areas, and grounds and operating swimming pools, golf courses, and community centers.

Community Association Managers work in offices, but they spend much of their time at the properties they manage. On-site managers must check regularly on building maintenance. Evening or weekend meetings are often held with property owners or association members to discuss legal issues that may affect the owners and also to review any proposed changes or improvements by homeowners to their properties.

Community Association Managers typically work a 40- to 50-hour workweek, including some evenings and weekends. They often must attend evening meetings with residents, property owners, association boards of directors, or civic groups. Many put in long hours in preparation of quarterly reports and community board annual meetings.

Salaries

Earnings of real estate association managers vary according to their level of responsibility, years of experience, and community size. Annual earnings are often linked to the number of units in a condominium or apartment development. On-site managers of housing complexes with less than 300 units typically earn $43,800 to $52,300 a year in base salary, according to CEL & Associates, Inc. Association managers of developments with more than 300 units can earn $56,700 to $63,600 a year. Property and association managers receive other benefits, such as paid vacations and health insurance, and may also have the use of a company car or a rent-free apartment. Performance bonuses add another 12 to 15 percent to annual compensation.

Community managers in California and the South (excluding Florida) earn higher salaries than their counterparts in Florida, the Northeast, the Midwest, and West, according to the Community Associations Institute. Community managers who hold a professional designation (such as Professional Community Association Manager) have significantly higher earnings potential than managers who do not hold a professional designation.

Employment Prospects

Most employers prefer to hire college graduates with some real estate management experience and a business background. Newly hired managers usually start out in entry-level positions as assistants to on-site apartment managers or Community Association Managers. Some openings will come about from vacancies created when more senior managers approach retirement age.

Also stimulating hiring demand for Community Association Managers is continued growth in retirement communities, limited-access gated communities, and other planned unit developments with on-site property managers and association managers.

Advancement Prospects

After a few years of on-the-job experience, assistant managers can advance to community association or property management positions. On-site managers can move from managing small apartment buildings or community associations to handling more complex management duties at larger properties. Another option is advancing to a more senior position in a property management firm that has a management contract to provide services for multiple residential communities. Another option for managers who want to go out on their own is opening their own association management firm or consulting firm. Earning a competency-based professional certification can be helpful for those interested in advancing to higher paying mid-level and senior management positions.

Education and Training

A four-year degree in business administration, public administration, finance, real estate, or a related field is the preferred academic background. Individuals with a liberal arts background who have taken additional courses on business or finance may also qualify if they have some relevant work experience.

Some on-the-job training is typically provided for new employees, usually by pairing newly hired managers with more experienced property managers. Association managers can increase their advancement opportunities by earning a certification from a professional association, because an industry designation means formal recognition of their achievements and it often leads to an increase in salary.

Special Requirements

Managers of government-subsidized public housing must be certified. Various professional and trade organizations offer accredited continuing education programs for managers to improve their skills and learn about more specialized subjects such as business law. Completion of one of these programs, along with job experience and passing a written exam, can lead to certification or a professional designation such as Professional Community Association Manager, awarded by the Community Associations Institute. More information on available designations can be found in Appendix III.

Experience, Skills, and Personality Traits

Community Association Managers spend much of their day dealing with property owners or tenants and community association boards. Strong speaking, writing, and interpersonal skills are an essential part of the job. Community managers have a high level of personal contact with tenants, maintenance workers, and others. Problem-solving skills and negotiating skills are important job-related skills.

Unions and Associations

Community Association Managers can become members of the Community Associations Institute or the National Association of Residential Property Managers. Both have extensive continuing education and career advancement programs.

Tips for Entry

1. Get more information on a career in property management from organizations such as the Community Associations Institute (www.caionline.org) or the National Association of Residential Property Managers (www.narpm.org).

2. You may also want to apply directly to community associations or property management firms.

3. Check association Web sites for job search tips and activities by local or regional chapters in your area.

FACILITY MANAGER

Duties: Manages day-to-day operations of specific properties; supervises maintenance workers, groundskeepers, and others; maintains contact with tenants

Alternate Title(s): Administrative Services Manager, Corporate Facility Manager, Facilities Services Supervisor

Salary Range: $83,900 to $109,800

Employment Prospects: Good

Advancement Prospects: Good

Prerequisites:

    Education or Training—Four-year degree in business, finance, real estate, or a related field

    Experience—Three to five years' property management experience

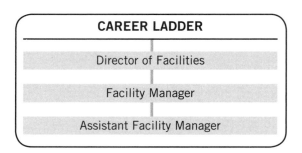

Special Skills and Personality Traits—Proficiency in accounting and financial analysis; working knowledge of project management activities; good computer skills

Special Requirements—Professional designation preferred

Position Description

Facility Managers plan, direct, or coordinate the day-to-day facility operations of companies, colleges, and nonprofit organizations. They manage buildings and grounds in addition to people. Their duties include formulating policies, managing daily operations, and planning the use of materials and human resources. Actual duties usually vary by degree of responsibility and authority.

First-line Facility Managers directly supervise a staff that performs various support services. In a small organization, a single manager may oversee all support services. Larger organizations, on the other hand, have first-line managers reporting to mid-level managers, who in turn report to owners or top-level managers. In larger organizations, manager duties are often broken out by specific activity or job function.

Often, Facility Managers negotiate contracts for janitorial, security, groundskeeping, trash removal, and other services. When contracts are awarded competitively, managers solicit bids from several contractors and advise the owners on which bid to accept. They monitor the performance of contractors and investigate and resolve complaints from residents and tenants when services are not properly provided. Facility Managers also purchase supplies and equipment for the property and make arrangements with specialists for repairs that cannot be handled by regular property maintenance staff.

The Facility Manager's job requires integrating business management and other disciplines. Specific tasks can vary substantially depending on the organization, but their duties fall into several broad categories: operations and maintenance, real estate management, project planning and maintenance, finance, quality assessment, technology integration, and management of human and environmental factors. Specific tasks can include architectural planning and design, budgeting, workplace planning, purchase and sale of real estate, lease management, and renovations. Facility Managers may oversee renovation projects to ensure the facilities meet government regulations and environmental, health, and security standards. Facility Managers also monitor the facility to ensure that it remains safe, secure, and well-maintained.

Typical day-to-day responsibilities of Facility Managers include the following:

- managing real estate and buildings to maximize use of the facilities
- managing in-house maintenance and engineering staff and coordinating work assignments
- overseeing the scheduling, maintenance, and monitoring of heating, ventilating and utility systems to ensure efficient operation
- supervising equipment repairs and maintenance by on-site staff

- performing or contracting for emergency repairs
- inspecting facilities (or supervising inspections) and generating reports
- negotiating and administering service contracts
- training and developing staff; maintaining active certification program where applicable
- managing space planning and facilities acquisition services
- negotiating leases and handling tenant communications
- preparing capital budgets and operating budget reports
- acting as security officer in the absence of the security manager

Most Facility Managers work a standard 40-hour week. Facility Managers are often on call to address a variety of problems that can occur during non-working hours, which is normally treated as non-compensated overtime.

Salaries

Salaries of full-time Facility Managers have trended upward over the last several years as companies have begun hiring more college-educated managers. Facility Manager salaries in 2007 varied from $83,900 to $109,800, according to CEL & Associates, Inc. Performance bonuses add another 16–19 percent to total compensation. Facility Managers who have earned an industry certification generally earn higher salaries. Those who have earned International Facility Management Association's (IFMA) Certified Facility Manager (CRM) credential have salaries 13 percent higher than those who have not attained it, the association says.

Employment Prospects

The U.S. Department of Labor says employment of Facility Managers should grow about as fast as employment growth for all occupations through 2014. However, demand for experienced Facility Managers should be strong because businesses are realizing the importance of maintaining, securing, and efficiently operating their facilities. Some openings are expected to occur as managers transfer to other occupations or leave the labor force. Opportunities should be best for those with a college degree in business administration, real estate, or a related field and for those who attain a professional designation.

Administrative managers in management consulting or management services should also be in demand as both public and corporate organizations contract out their facilities management to third-party facilities management firms. Demand for professional managers is expected to remain strong with non-real estate corporations that own large numbers of properties. Large real estate owners and developers also employ facility management firms.

Advancement Prospects

Advancement is usually determined by the practices and size of individual companies. Some Facility Managers advance their careers by moving into positions offering additional responsibilities. Some work their way up from technical positions into positions offering managerial responsibility.

Attaining competency-based professional certification can be helpful for those interested in advancing to higher paying mid-level and senior management positions. An experienced Facility Manager can advance to a mid-level position, such as director of administrative services, and eventually to a senior management position, such as executive vice president for administrative services. Those with enough money and experience could also set up their own management consulting firms.

Education and Training

Most employers look for individuals who have a four-year college degree majoring in business, finance, real estate, or a related field of study. Regardless of college major, the curriculum should include courses in office technology, accounting, business mathematics, computer applications, human resources, and business law. Many Facility Managers have some background in real estate and have worked in a real estate management company before being hired as Facility Managers.

Special Requirements

Certification, while not a requirement for entry-level managers, is recommended for Facility Managers who want to make a career in facility management. Candidates for the IFMA's Certified Facility Manager designation must meet certain educational and experience requirements. Individuals who are starting their careers can earn the Facility Management Professional (FMP) credential, a springboard for eventually attaining the CFM certification.

Experience, Skills, and Personality Traits

Individuals interested in becoming Facility Managers should have good communication skills and an ability to establish effective working relationships with people with varying skills and competencies. They should be analytical, detail-oriented, and decision-makers. They must be able to coordinate several different tasks at the same time, quickly analyze and resolve specific problems, and cope with deadlines. Some proficiency in accounting and financial analysis is important, as is having a working knowledge of project management activities and good computer skills.

Unions and Associations

Facility Managers can become members of the International Facility Management Association or Building Owners & Managers Institute International (BOMI International) for networking and career management opportunities. Those in higher education can join the Association for Higher Education Facilities Officer.

Attaining an industry-approved certification or designation demonstrates a commitment to staying involved in the industry. Examples include the International Facility Management Association's Certified Facility Manager (CFM) designation or the Building Owners and Managers Institute's Facility Management Administrator (FMA) designation. Earning a certification or designation can also help earn a pay raise. Facility Managers with a certification earn on average 24 percent higher than those without it, according to industry salary surveys.

Tips for Entry

1. Read industry publications like *Today's Facility Manager* (http://www.todaysfacilitymanager.com) for the latest trends in employment and hiring.
2. Attend college- or trade association–sponsored job fairs.
3. Do a Web search and contact third-party facility management or property management companies in your area.

LEASING CONSULTANT— MULTIFAMILY

CAREER PROFILE

Duties: Locates and qualifies residential housing tenants; handles lease renewals and rent collections

Alternate Title(s): Leasing Agent, Leasing Representative

Salary Range: $26,800 to $33,800

Employment Prospects: Good

Advancement Prospects: Fair

Prerequisites:

    Education or Training—High school diploma or equivalent

    Experience—One to three years' customer service or sales experience

    Special Skills and Personality Traits—Ability to work effectively in a sales environment; good customer service skills; good verbal and written communication skills

    Special Requirements—Pre-employment background check, drug and alcohol screening may be required

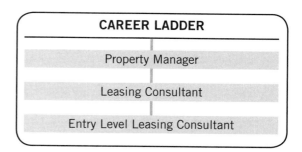

CAREER LADDER

Property Manager

Leasing Consultant

Entry Level Leasing Consultant

Position Description

Leasing Consultants coordinate all phases of apartment leasing. The consultant's primary responsibility is leasing apartments available for rent, collecting rents, and keeping apartments close to fully occupied. A Leasing Consultant is the first line of contact for prospective apartment tenants, vendors, and the public. They coordinate move-ins and move-outs, lease negotiations and renewals, and apartment showings. They attempt to maximize occupancy rates by pre-selling available apartments, contacting interested prospects by telephone soliciting or other means. They ensure that lease paperwork of current and prospective tenants is completed accurately and is well maintained. They work under the general supervision of an on-site property manager or supervisor.

Leasing Consultants may work for a government-assisted affordable housing development. Housing costs in low-to-moderate income affordable housing are capped at 30 percent of gross monthly income. The federal government determines the fair market rent for the apartments and pays the difference between what the tenants pay and prevailing fair market rents in that community. The federal program is commonly referred to as Section 8 housing, named after the legislation that first authorized government-assisted housing: the U.S. Housing Act of 1937.

Tenants participating in an affordable housing program need to meet certain guidelines, typically called obligations, to become eligible for the program. Their income must be verified, and they have to report any changes in income or dependents. There are no time limits to participation in an affordable housing program as long as tenants continue to meet the qualifying guidelines.

Leasing Consultants have various administrative and front-line support duties. They handle inquiries from prospective tenants and maintain records of the inquiries. They conduct apartment and general facility tours, greet future residents, and take rental applications. They check the accuracy of the applicant's personal data, verifying income with employers or other sources. They process the applicant's security deposit against property damages and deposit these funds into an escrow account. They provide written information or brochures to interested tenants. They notify prospects whose applications were turned down in accordance with company procedures, federal Equal Housing Opportunity (EHO) requirements, and any other applicable state or federal regulations.

In performing their duties, Leasing Consultants may do any of the following:

- answer telephone calls, Internet inquiries, or in-person requests for information from prospective tenants

- schedule sales appointments with prospects
- make group presentations on available model apartment units to prospects, tenants, and other employees
- enter applicant information into a central database
- tour model apartments or market units daily, confirming readiness for presentation to prospective tenants
- maintain a record of apartment showings and follow-up contacts with prospects
- notify prospective tenants of application acceptance or rejection
- receive and record resident service requests and post completed service requests
- conduct tenant surveys and make recommendations for residential improvements based on an analysis of the information collected
- promote residency to prospective tenants by composing newspaper advertisements and ads for placement on Internet Web sites or in other media
- accept checks, money orders, and certified checks for daily deposit
- report any property loss or damages to the property owner's insurance company
- assist in reporting any claims for workers' compensation for on-the-job injuries

Apartment Leasing Consultants work in an office setting and usually work a 40-hour workweek. They may be assigned to work more than a 40-hour week or work weekends or evenings periodically to fill on-site staffing needs.

Salaries

Leasing Consultants can earn base (excluding bonuses) salaries of $26,800 to $33,800. In addition to salary, leasing agents may earn overtime pay for any hours worked past the standard 40-hour week. They usually receive generous fringe benefits such as paid vacations and sick leave, health and life insurance, and employer-sponsored 401(k) savings plans, and performance bonuses of 10–15 percent of base salary.

Employment Prospects

Market demand for affordable housing will drive employment growth in rental housing for the foreseeable future. Nearly one-third of the U.S. population—31.5 percent of all households in 2006—lives in apartment units of all types, according to the National Multi-Housing Council. There are fairly good employment opportunities for apartment leasing consultants at both public housing agencies and privately owned and managed apartment complexes. Some opportunities

will come about when individuals holding these positions move into other occupations or reach retirement age. Apartment management companies may also have part-time positions available.

Advancement Prospects

This position reports to an on-site or off-site property manager. Experienced Leasing Consultants can advance to more senior positions, such as assistant manager, community relations manager, or property manager. The best opportunities for advancement are in the large apartment management companies that own and operate apartment buildings across the United States. Denver-based Apartment Investment and Management Company, the largest U.S. apartment management company, owns and operates more than one million apartments and has plenty of employment opportunities for those interested in a career in residential property management.

Education and Training

The minimum education requirement is a high school diploma or GED equivalent diploma. Some employers prefer candidates who have taken some college courses or have a four-year degree in business or a similar field of study.

This is a trainable position, so most employers have some kind of on-the-job training or orientation for new employees. Newly hired Leasing Consultants usually receive an unspecified number of hours of training, as directed by the property manager.

Individuals who want to advance their careers to higher paying positions will want to have taken some college courses. Four U.S. colleges currently have degree programs in residential property management. See Appendix I for more details on available programs.

Special Requirements

Because this position has a high degree of contact with the public, a pre-employment background check and drug and alcohol screening may be required.

Experience, Skills, and Personality Traits

Some prior experience, usually one to three years' experience, in real estate sales or customer service is desirable. Leasing Consultants should be familiar with standard lease terms, concepts, and practices and federal fair housing laws. Working as a Leasing Consultant means working in sales, which means good interpersonal skills and strong verbal and written communication skills are essential job skills. Also important are sound math skills—being able to easily compute rates, discounts, interest, and commissions.

Leasing Consultants should have some working knowledge of office equipment and basic computer programs such as word processing and e-mail applications.

Unions and Associations

The National Apartment Association (http://www.naahq.org) is the primary trade association for apartment leasing consultants. The association offers a professional designation for Leasing Consultants, available to individuals who have at least six years' experience, complete a specified number of courses in apartment management, and get a passing grade on a written exam.

Tips for Entry

1. Check the National Apartment Association's Education Institute to learn more about careers in apartment management.
2. Industry Web sites such as Apartment Careers (http://www.apartmentcareers.com) and the National Apartment Association list currently open positions across the country.
3. Major employers, including Apartment Investment and Management Company, have numerous openings listed on their Web sites.

MAINTENANCE SUPERVISOR

CAREER PROFILE

Duties: Responsible for all physical operations of an apartment complex, condominium association; supervises maintenance staff and groundskeepers

Alternate Title(s): Building Operator

Salary Range: $62,600 to $77,600

Employment Prospects: Good

Advancement Prospects: Fair

Prerequisites:

Education or Training—High school diploma or GED equivalent

Experience—Three to five years' experience in skilled or semi-skilled property maintenance

Special Skills and Personality Traits—Good communication skills; good leadership skills; working

CAREER LADDER

Assistant to Property Manager

Maintenance Supervisor

Maintenance Coordinator

knowledge of building maintenance practices and procedures

Special Requirements—Professional certification optional

Position Description

Maintenance Supervisors coordinate and manage the work of employees who repair and maintain buildings and facilities. They prepare work schedules, assign work, and inspect work performed by the maintenance staff. They provide training, scheduling, and job performance evaluations for maintenance, groundskeeping, and housekeeping workers. They provide technical knowledge and skills for maintenance projects and assist when needed. They serve as first-line of communication contact for off-hour emergencies and may be part of a 24-hour pager rotation in the event of a staffing shortage.

In supervising subordinates, the Maintenance Supervisor performs periodic evaluations of subordinates and recommends promotions or disciplinary action as required by department regulations. The manager is also responsible for ensuring that safety training is provided to staff and that proper safety practices have been followed. The manager makes sure that groundskeepers and other staff are trained in maintenance activities and are following recommended operating procedures. They also answer questions and provide information related to projects, including resolving complaints and approving expenditures.

Typical day-to-day duties of Maintenance Supervisors include the following:

- supervising the maintenance staff by determining workloads and schedules

- developing and implementing policies and procedures
- evaluating staff and making hiring or termination recommendations
- negotiating contracts and inspecting a contractor's work to ensure that safe work practices and operating procedures have been followed
- providing recommendations in development of a maintenance operating budget
- ordering materials and supplies
- performing a variety of field maintenance tasks, depending on experience and level of certification

In a residential apartment community, the Maintenance Supervisor typically reports to a manager, the property manager or assistant property manager. Maintenance Supervisors normally work a 40-hour week but may be required to work emergency overtime to supervise unscheduled maintenance or repairs.

Salaries

Earnings will vary according to qualifications, background and employment location.

Maintenance Supervisors can earn base salaries from $62,800 to $77,600 annually, according to CEL & Associates Inc. Supervisors working in urban areas or those employed by any of the major apartment management companies typically have earnings at the higher end of the scale. Most employers also have excellent fringe-benefit packages which include health, life, and disability insurance coverage, paid vacations, sick leave, and employer-sponsored savings and retirement plans. Annual performance bonuses increase base compensation 8–10 percent.

Employment Prospects

Strong employment growth is expected over the next several years, aided by development and construction of new and replacement office buildings, hospitals, hotels, motels, schools, and manufacturing facilities. Job entry is normally from the maintenance coordinator position, who performs similar duties but has limited supervisory experience.

Employment is related to the number of buildings—for example, office and apartment buildings, stores, schools, hospitals, hotels, and factories—and the amount of equipment needing maintenance and repair. One factor limiting job growth is that computers allow buildings to be monitored more efficiently, partially reducing the need for workers.

Job opportunities should be excellent, especially for those with experience in maintenance or related fields. The building maintenance field is a large occupation, generating many job openings due to growth and the need to replace those who leave the occupation. Replacement jobs should also be plentiful due to the normal occupational turnover. Many job openings are expected to result from the retirement of experienced maintenance workers over the next decade.

Advancement Prospects

Highly qualified Maintenance Supervisors with proven management abilities can advance their careers and their income potential by taking more senior management positions in a property management company. Some will advance by taking jobs with larger property owners, which typically employ more building maintenance workers and have need for more supervisory employees.

Maintenance Supervisors can increase their advancement opportunities by earning one or more industry certifications, qualifying them for more job responsibilities and an increase in compensation. Available certifications from the National Apartment Association (http://www.naahq.org) include the Certified Apartment Property Supervisor (CAPS).

Education and Training

Employers generally look for individuals who have at least a high school diploma or a general equivalency diploma (GED) or a combination of education and experience sufficient to successfully perform the duties required. College-level course work at a community college or technical college to obtain job-related licenses or certificates can provide additional qualifications.

Further educational opportunities are available through formal classroom or self-paced instruction leading to a professional certification or through on-the-job training by an on-site property manager or assistant property manager.

Special Requirements

A valid driver's license and a clean driving record are often required. Some Maintenance Supervisors may be required to pass certification tests demonstrating competency in the field. Check with the National Apartment Association's education department or state licensing board for further information on these requirements.

In 1990, the International Maintenance Institute (IMI) developed its first Maintenance Certification Program for General Industry. It offers three levels of certification for the skilled trades or technicians and two levels for maintenance management. The National Apartment Association offers a certification program, the Certified Apartment Property Supervisor (CAPS), for individuals who successfully pass a two-part exam. Courses in National Apartment Association–approved certification programs are scheduled by local and state NAA affiliates.

Experience, Skills, and Personality Traits

Broadly speaking, three to five years' experience in skilled or semi-skilled maintenance, including one year as a lead maintenance technician, is sufficient to adequately perform the on-the-job duties of a Maintenance Supervisor. Because they often have to perform heavy physical work outdoors in all weather conditions, Maintenance Supervisors must possess strength, stamina, and mobility. They may also need to have the skills to operate various hand tools and power tools, drive heavy construction equipment, and lift or move materials and equipment.

Maintenance Supervisors should have a working knowledge of building repair practices and procedures, be familiar with use of construction equipment, and have a basic knowledge of equipment and infrastructure, such as street lights and underground lines, commonly used in municipal areas. Good communication skills, leadership skills, a sense of tact, and sound judgment while working with subordinates are useful personality traits.

Unions and Associations

Maintenance Supervisors can become members of professional associations such as the National Apartment Association and NAA's affiliated state chapters. These associations, such as the National Apartment Association and the International Maintenance Institute (http://www.imionline.org), have education and certification programs for maintenance supervisors. Association-sponsored trade shows, continuing education programs, and conferences are opportunities to learn more about building maintenance as a career opportunity.

Tips for Entry

1. Take high school or vocational school courses in mechanical drawing, shop, math, science, and related subjects to get a solid background in maintenance and repair.
2. Check current job listings online at the National Apartment Association's Web site or the International Maintenance Institute's online job board. The IMI Web site also allows résumé posting.
3. Other sources of information are newspaper classified ads and job service offices of state labor departments.

PORTFOLIO MANAGER

Duties: Intermediary between real estate owner and on-site property managers and asset managers; represents the owner's interest to achieve the best use, property operation, and investment return

Alternate Title(s): Owner's Representative, Regional Director

Salary Range: $108,000 to $134,000

Employment Prospects: Good

Advancement Prospects: Good

Prerequisites:

Education or Training—Four-year degree in business management, finance, or real estate

Experience—Two to three years' commercial real estate management and property development experience

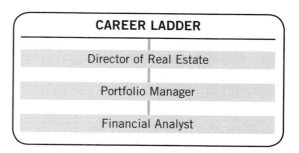

Special Skills and Personality Traits—Working knowledge of real estate asset management, portfolio valuation, and cash flow analysis; fluency in Excel spreadsheet software

Special Requirements—Real estate sales license may be required in some states

Position Description

The Portfolio Manager is the property owner's on-site "eyes and ears" in the day-to-day management of a development project. Portfolio Managers are typically selected by the client to represent their interests. Their responsibility is to create property-level strategies to meet the owner's objectives, with an emphasis on maximizing the property's income, cash flow, and long-term value.

To put that strategic plan into action, the Portfolio Manager develops and implements operating, financial, and capital budgets for the project, approves property marketing plans, and oversees lease negotiations with prospective tenants. The Portfolio Manager works closely with on-site professionals, including architects, engineers, and construction managers to resolve property issues and monitor compliance with partnership agreements among the property owners and loan agreements negotiated with bank lenders.

Portfolio Managers may not be involved in day-to-day activities, although they should be aware of any problem, so that they can take prompt corrective action. They can serve as an owner's representative when third-party property managers are employed to service a multi-property portfolio over a large geographic region. Alternatively, the Portfolio Manager may oversee a pool of assets managed by one or more asset managers. In this latter role, they take a broader perspective to ensure that the clients' overall goals and objectives are met and the properties are producing the highest possible investment return. They focus their attention on significant opportunities to add value to client investments.

Portfolio Managers evaluate the strengths and weaknesses of each property, taking into consideration such things as property type, geographic location, occupancy, income from leases and ownership structure. The Portfolio Manager is responsible for reviewing the operating and capital plans presented by third-party service companies or asset managers. They review financial projections and operating budgets to ensure that properties in the portfolio are meeting the owner's objectives. They approve property marketing plans and tenant leases, supported by recommendations of the asset manager and their knowledge of the regional economic climate. Portfolio Managers may work directly with on-site property managers to resolve property management issues or indirectly through an asset manager assigned to the properties.

The Portfolio Manager anticipates market changes to identify potential acquisition or disposition opportunities. The manager may also represent the owners during the project construction or redevelopment phase. When properties are no longer meeting the investment criteria of the owner, or when the owner decides to harvest a property's accumulated economic value, the properties are usually sold to other owners. During the sale process, the Portfolio Manager may be involved in approving the marketing strategy and presenting the disposition recommendation to the investment committee or owner. Other responsibilities often include preparing client reports and presentations and developing investment presentations.

Portfolio Managers work for real estate management companies that own real estate assets, real estate management service companies, pension and private equity funds, and consulting firms specializing in commercial property management. There are a number of real estate management firms offering portfolio management or owner representation services for commercial real estate investors. In larger organizations the Portfolio Manager may also be called a Territory Director or Regional Director.

Salaries

Portfolio Managers are well compensated for their work. Earnings are determined from experience, qualifications, and the requirements of the position. Typically, compensation is a combination of base salary and annual bonus, plus participation in a company-funded profit sharing plan. Starting salaries are comparable to those earned by financial industry investment professionals and can range anywhere from $108,000 to $134,000, according to CEL & Associates Inc. Portfolio Managers may also receive other non-salary benefits such as paid life and health insurance, vacation pay, and sick leave. Annual performance bonuses are determined by the firm's profitability and can be 30–50 percent of base salary.

Employment Prospects

The typical career path is starting out as a research analyst and moving into portfolio management after a few years on the job. Growth in employment opportunities will be influenced by such factors as pension funds and other managed funds increasing their ownership of income-producing real estate and non-U.S. investors buying properties in the United States to diversify their investment holdings. Employment of Portfolio Managers is expected to grow at a rate comparable to employment growth across all occupations through 2014, according to the U.S. Department of Labor.

Advancement Prospects

The Portfolio Manager typically reports to the director of real estate. College-educated or experienced Portfolio Managers can advance into more senior positions in a property management firm, such as director of real estate. Managers who have an advanced degree in real estate or an M.B.A. degree can move into higher paying positions managing multiple Portfolio Managers or large client relationships or working for a larger property management firm. Attaining an industry-recognized certification can be a door-opener to a more senior position.

Education and Training

Most employers want to hire individuals who have a four-year degree with a college major in business management, finance, or real estate. A master's degree in real estate or an M.B.A. degree may be required for more specialized positions.

Portfolio Managers are constantly learning on the job and adding to the knowledge gained while attending college. A thorough knowledge of construction techniques, procedures, plans, and specifications supplements what they learned in college and enables the manager to identify trouble spots and recommend solutions.

Special Requirements

A real estate sales license may be required in some states, though not in most regions if the Portfolio Manager is not directly involved in purchase or sale of real estate. State licensing requirements can vary so check with your state's real estate licensing board. A list of state licensing boards can be found in Appendix VI.

Experience, Skills, and Personality Traits

Prior experience in real estate development is the best qualifier. Most employers want to see some prior experience as a real estate investment analyst, generally two to three years. Some additional on-the-job experience may be required in more specialized positions. Individuals should have a track record analyzing, underwriting, and closing real estate transactions across a range of property types. Essential job-related skills are superior analytical and quantitative skills and a passion for accuracy in figures. Work is often done under deadline, so Portfolio Managers have to be able to work under pressure in a team environment. Some experience with discounted cash flow (DCF) analysis and real estate specific software, such as ARGUS, the standard tool for cash flow projections in commercial real estate, is a plus.

Portfolio Managers have to be effective communicators who can work effectively with professional staff and clients. Strong verbal and written communication skills are essential. The Portfolio Manager maintains frequent communication with the property owners and other professionals on the job site. The manager must be able to communicate effectively with all members of the development team and give periodic status reports to the property owner.

Globalization is also having an impact on this position. U.S.-based real estate investment funds and management companies are much more active internationally today compared to only a few years ago. A working knowledge of foreign markets and knowledge of a foreign language could be real pluses long term.

Unions and Associations

There are several professional associations: the Building Owners and Managers Institute (http://www.BOMI-edu.org), the Institute of Real Estate Management (http://www.irem.org), the CCIM Institute, and CoreNet Global. All have professional certification or designation programs for professional advancement. See Appendix III for additional information on certification programs for Portfolio Managers.

Tips for Entry

1. People who are good at financial analysis do very well in this field.
2. If you're ambitious, take an ARGUS course at a participating college (go to http://www.realm.com; the Web site lists schools offering ARGUS courses).
3. Contact firms specializing in owner representation services for real estate clients.

PROPERTY MANAGER

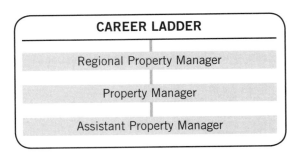

Position Description

For businesses and investors, managed property is a source of income and profits. Property Managers oversee the performance of income-producing properties and ensure that real estate investments achieve their expected revenues. When the owners of office buildings or retail and industrial properties lack the expertise for effective day-to-day management of their investments, they hire a Property Manager or real estate manager. People who buy second homes as investment properties typically hire a property management company to act as their local agent for rentals and property maintenance.

Generally, Property Managers handle the financial operations of the property, ensuring that rent is collected and mortgages, taxes, insurance premiums, payroll, and maintenance bills are paid on time. Property Managers typically negotiate contracts for janitorial, security, groundskeeping, trash removal, and other services. When contracts are awarded competitively, managers solicit bids from several contractors and advise the owners on which bid to accept. They monitor the performance of contractors and investigate and resolve tenant complaints when services are not properly provided. Managers also purchase supplies and equipment and make arrangements with specialists when repairs cannot be handled by the maintenance staff. Managers report periodically to the property owners on the condition of their properties.

On-site Property Managers are responsible for the daily operations of just one piece of property. The property may be an apartment complex, office building, or a shopping center. On-site managers routinely visit their properties to see if any repairs are needed and make arrangements for the necessary repairs. Property Managers employed by condominium or homeowner associations are known as condominium managers or community association managers. These managers have daily interaction with homeowners. They oversee the maintenance of the property and facilities that homeowners use, including golf courses, swimming pools, and tennis courts. Community association managers attend condominium association board meetings to handle legal and environmental issues and to resolve disputes between neighbors.

Property Managers who do not work on-site act as a liaison between the on-site manager and the property owner. They also market vacant space to prospective tenants through the use of a leasing agent by advertising or by other means. They set rental rates in accordance with prevailing economic conditions and market demand.

Full-time Property Managers work a 40- to 50-hour workweek, which typically includes some evenings and weekends. Property Managers often must attend evening meetings with residents, property owners, community association boards of directors, or civic groups. Many put in long workweeks, especially before financial and tax reports are due and before board and annual meetings.

Salaries

Salaries of Property Managers are determined by the type of property under management and, if it is a commercial property, the size of the property in square feet. Other factors are the type of job responsibilities and professional experience. Earning an industry certification demonstrating professional competence can result in a higher salary or an increase in total compensation.

A property manager of a 300,000-square-foot retail strip mall could earn base salaries anywhere from $68,200 to $83,400 annually, in 2007, according to CEL & Associates, Inc, a Los Angeles real estate consulting firm specializing in salary and compensation trends. A shopping mall manager in charge of a mall with 750,000 to 1 million square feet can expect to earn $78,400 to $102,300 a year, according to CEL & Associates, Inc. Annual performance, however, can increase compensation an additional 12–15 percent. Standard non-salary benefits include paid vacations and sick leave, health and life insurance, and employer-sponsored retirement plans.

Employment Prospects

Employment of Property Managers is expected to grow about as fast as employment growth in all occupations through 2014, according to the U.S. Department of Labor. Increased demand for Property Managers will be due to growth in commercial real estate and planned residential communities. Most employment opportunities will be found in urban areas. Another factor driving employment growth is changing demographics: an aging U.S. population will translate into growth in assisted living and retirement communities and more jobs for Property Managers.

Candidates with little or no property management experience can learn on the job under the supervision of an experienced Property Manager. To help properties become more profitable or to enhance the resale values of homes, commercial and residential property owners will place their investments in the hands of professional managers.

Some job openings will occur when managers transfer to other occupations or leave the labor force. Opportunities should be best for those with a college degree in business administration, real estate, or a related field and for those who attain a professional designation. More than one-third of Property Managers employed in the United States work for real estate agents and brokers, lessors of real estate, or property management firms. Others are employed by real estate development companies, government agencies, and corporations with extensive commercial properties holdings.

Advancement Prospects

College-educated or experienced Property Managers can advance into more senior positions in a property management firm. Experienced managers typically move into positions with more responsibility and more pay while managing larger properties. Further opportunities can be found in the upper management levels of property management firms.

Education and Training

Academic requirements for Property Managers are quite broad. Most employers prefer to hire college graduates with a degree in business administration, finance, real estate, or public administration. For most individuals entering the field, this is a trainable job. Larger property management firms provide some on-the-job training by pairing newly hired managers with more experienced Property Managers. Many Property Managers of privately owned properties voluntarily earn a certification from a professional association, because an industry designation means formal recognition of their achievements, and it often leads to an increase in salary.

Special Requirements

There are no licensing or other special requirements for most Property Managers. Property Managers of public housing subsidized by the federal government must be certified. Some states require licensing for community association managers.

Experience, Skills, and Personality Traits

Individuals entering this field should have some property management experience, anywhere from three months to four years, depending on the position. Employers look for individuals who can work independently, read and follow instructions, and maintain financial records. Good communication and public contact skills also are important, as are an ability to plan and organize the work of others.

Being in compliance with state or federal regulations is an important part of the job. Property Managers must have a working knowledge of federal, state, and local regulations covering rented or leased property and the Americans with Disabilities Act to ensure nondiscriminatory practices.

Unions and Associations

There are several professional associations for Property Managers: the Building Owners and Managers Institute (http://www.BOMI-edu.org), the Institute of Real Estate Management (http://www.irem.org), the CCIM Institute, and the Community Association Institute. Several associations have professional certification or designation programs for professional advancement.

Available programs include the following: the Certified Commercial Investment Member (CCIM), through the CCIM Institute; Certified Shopping Center Manager (CSM), through the International Council of Shopping Centers; Real Property Administrator (RPA), through Building Owners and Managers Institute. More information on these can be found in Appendix III.

Tips for Entry

1. Helpful high-school and college courses include courses in English, math, business management, and computer science.
2. Web sites to look for jobs: allpropertymanagement.com; CAIonline.org (Community Associations Institute) has resources for managing community associations, condo associations, and cooperatives. Job openings also listed.
3. Check out IREM Web site for college students considering careers in real estate management (GetRealGetReady.org).
4. College courses in real estate management can qualify for credits toward your CPM (Certified Property Manager) designation and your undergraduate degree.

PUBLIC HOUSING MANAGER

CAREER PROFILE

Duties: Responsible for the review of applications for admission to subsidized or rent-assisted public housing units and annual examinations for continued eligibility; supervises building maintenance and maintenance staff

Alternate Title(s): Fair Housing Manager, Housing Manager

Salary Range: $40,000 to $60,000

Employment Prospects: Good

Advancement Prospects: Good

Prerequisites:

    Education or Training—Four-year degree in business, public administration, or a related field of study

    Experience—Three or more years' experience in public housing or social services

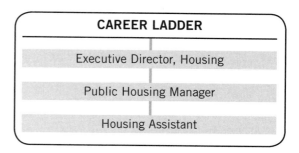

CAREER LADDER

Executive Director, Housing

Public Housing Manager

Housing Assistant

Special Skills and Personality Traits—Good communication skills and interviewing skills; working knowledge of public housing eligibility; computer proficiency

Special Requirements—Demonstrated competency (industry certification) normally a requirement upon hiring or within one year of hiring.

Position Description

Public Housing Managers oversee the management of federally subsidized (or state-supported) affordable housing developed for low-to-moderate income families. The manager coordinates all occupancy matters, including interviewing applicants and collection of rents. The manager is responsible for the review and clarification of applications for admission to public housing units and annual examinations for continued eligibility.

The manager oversees the planning and delivery of maintenance services, supervises the maintenance manager and maintenance staff, and monitors routine maintenance or project repairs. The manager also performs a variety of services designed to foster or improve relations between tenants and the public housing authority. The housing manager gathers information relating to eligibility through personal interviews and telephone interviews.

Typical duties performed include the following:

- supervising the work of subordinate staff
- determining apartment rents in accordance with federal housing guidelines
- preparing leases and executing lease agreements with prospective tenants
- preparing and maintaining reports and records

- advising and counseling tenants with respect to housing-related issues
- investigating tenant complaints and developing solutions
- maintaining a waiting list of eligible applicants for subsidized housing
- preparing monthly statistical reports for review by the executive director and the public housing board of commissioners

The Public Housing Manager reports to the executive director of public housing or director of property management. Public Housing Managers work a 40-hour workweek in an office setting, but may work longer hours to attend evening meetings of tenant association groups. On-site managers spend much of their time on tenant management issues, checking on building maintenance, and meeting with contractors or vendors. Some weekend work is often required to resolve maintenance problems or supervise project improvements.

Public Housing Managers usually don't have a separate business office and are often required to live in the apartment complex where they work, so they are available to handle any tenant problems or emergencies that may occur on weekends or at other times when they are off-duty. They may be compensated for any hours beyond the 40-hour workweek with overtime pay.

Salaries

Salaries vary according to experience, qualifications, and other factors, such as the number of rental units managed. Salaries can range from $40,000 to $60,000 a year, depending on location and size of the housing development. Manager working in urban areas can expect to earn higher salaries. Housing authority executive directors generally earn much higher salaries, averaging $60,000 to $80,000 a year or more. Public Housing Managers receive non-salary benefits, including health insurance, paid vacations, and paid personal days.

Employment Prospects

There is steady demand for housing management staff among local public housing authorities and housing associations. Demand is highest in metropolitan or urban areas where the concentration of public housing units is highest. Some position vacancies will come about through staff turnover when housing managers take positions in the private sector or change jobs within the public housing field. The initial entry is often to a housing support officer, customer service, or housing administration position. Advancement to a housing manager position, with line management for a team of housing officers, comes with experience and on-the-job training.

Most employment opportunities will be found in major metropolitan areas, which typically have the highest concentrations of rental housing and low-to-moderate income families.

Advancement Prospects

Public Housing Managers generally advance by moving up the management structure to more senior positions with a corresponding increase in salary. Above the Public Housing Manager, more senior positions are likely to focus on traditional management functions such as finance, strategy, research and development, and policy making. Earning an industry certification in property management from any of the professional real estate associations can open the door and provide additional qualifications for promotion to senior positions. After five to 10 years of management experience, promotion to housing authority executive director, regional manager, or chief executive is possible.

Education and Training

A career in public housing management is open to graduates from almost any discipline. However, a four-year degree in business management, public administration, or a related field of study is particularly relevant. College-level courses in facilities management, property management, urban studies, sociology, and property law are helpful. Candidates who have completed less than four years of college education may qualify for a career in housing management if they have five or more years of professional experience. College courses in finance or accounting are very important for candidates who intend to make a career in housing management, as it increases their advancement opportunities.

Special Requirements

Public Housing Managers maintain their job skills by earning a professional certification and taking continuing education courses to maintain their credentials. The National Center for Housing Management has several certification programs, including the Certified Occupancy Specialist, Certified Manager of Housing, and Registered Housing Manager. The National Affordable Housing Management Association has the following certifications: National Affordable Housing Professional, Certified Professional of Occupancy, and Specialist in Housing Credit Management. The National Association of Housing and Redevelopment Officials has two professional certifications: Professional Housing Manager and Senior Professional Housing Manager. The National Apartment Association offers a Specialist in Housing Credit Management certification for managers of properties operated under the federal Low-Income Housing Tax Credit (LIHTC) program.

Earning a Public Housing Manager certification from a nationally recognized certification authority or professional association is normally required at hiring or within one year of the hiring date.

Experience, Skills, and Personality Traits

In addition to a college degree, Public Housing Managers should have at least three years' or more experience with increasing levels of responsibility in housing administration, personnel evaluation and supervision, budgeting, manpower scheduling, and program analysis. Some prior experience in community relations, maintenance supervision, and redevelopment is very helpful.

Housing managers should have good interviewing skills, strong verbal and written communications skills, a working knowledge of public housing regulations and the low-income housing tax credit (LIHTC) program, and some proficiency in standard word processing, e-mail, and PC computer applications.

Unions and Associations

Public Housing Managers can become members of several professional associations: Public Housing Authority Directors Association (http://www.phada.org), National Association of Housing and Redevelopment Officials (http://www.nahro.org), the National Affordable Housing Management Association (http://www.nahma.org), or the National Apartment Association (http://www.nhahq.org.). All sponsor conferences and continuing education seminars to help managers maintain their professional certifications.

Tips for Entry

1. Learn more about the field of public housing by reading publications such as *Affordable Housing Finance*.
2. Attend meetings of local or regional chapters of professional associations to learn more about opportunities in your area.
3. Professional association Web sites often have job banks listing currently available career opportunities in public housing management.

TENANT COORDINATOR

CAREER PROFILE

Duties: Acts as liaison between landlord or property owner and commercial tenants

Alternate Title(s): Tenant Relations Coordinator, Tenant Services Coordinator

Salary Range: $27,000 to $59,400

Employment Prospects: Good

Advancement Prospects: Good

Prerequisites:

Education or Training—Four-year degree in business administration or marketing

Experience—Two to five years' accounting, bookkeeping, or real estate experience

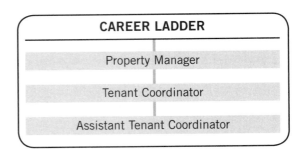

CAREER LADDER

Property Manager

Tenant Coordinator

Assistant Tenant Coordinator

Special Skills and Personality Traits—Excellent customer service skills and communication skills; strong computer skills

Position Description

In commercial real estate, the Tenant Coordinator is the middleman between building tenants and the building owner, or landlord. The Tenant Coordinator, also called the tenant services coordinator or the tenant relations coordinator, is a conduit between the tenants and the building's development, leasing, and property management teams. The Tenant Coordinator acts as a liaison to the tenants regarding any construction work in progress prior to occupancy.

The Tenant Coordinator handles all building improvements paid for by the landlord (or the tenant) as required in a lease agreement. In some real estate management companies the Tenant Coordinator will handle tenant relations for all the tenants located in a single property; in others, the Tenant Coordinator will handle negotiations with tenants in several properties with a shared administrative assistant for support. The Tenant Coordinator provides tenants with base building drawings and design specifications and keeps property managers informed about building improvements requested by the tenant.

The Tenant Coordinator performs all construction management duties for completion of on-premises work, such as contracting with architects and engineers, soliciting and analyzing construction bids, negotiating and awarding contracts, and administering contracts with construction firms and subcontractors. He or she maintains a construction management handbook and check-in procedures for building contractors entering the building during the construction or renovation phase. The tenant liaison also conducts a preconstruction meeting with the tenant's general contractor to collect all necessary documents, deposits, and payments owed the landlord as specified by construction documents.

When renovations are required as specified in a lease agreement, the Tenant Coordinator will furnish construction cost estimates for work paid for by the landlord or property owner and determine the work to be paid for or performed by the landlord or tenant.

When renovation or remodeling work is performed by a tenant, the Tenant Coordinator reviews all drawings submitted by tenants, compares them to the property owner's requirements to insure their compliance, and monitors their completion. The Tenant Coordinator manages the final punch list, or to-do list, immediately prior to project completion.

The Tenant Coordinator resolves tenant and landlord construction conflicts to ensure that the tenants open for business as quickly as possible. The coordinator also works with local government authorities to obtain the necessary permits, on-site building code inspections, and certificates of occupancy issued by local permit-issuing authorities.

Typical duties of Tenant Coordinators include the following:

- scheduling regular tenant meetings
- attending new tenant meetings
- participating in prospective tenant tours
- attending space planning, construction, and team meetings

- providing quick responses to tenant inquiries
- conducting daily property inspections
- planning and managing regional marketing events
- confirming compliance with approved tenant improvement plans
- assisting tenant contractors in meeting agreed-upon construction schedules
- updating tenant improvement records daily, weekly, or as needed

After tenants have moved in and opened for business, the Tenant Coordinator maintains close contact with tenants and maintenance crews to perform site maintenance as required. The Tenant Coordinator maintains regular communication with property management teams to report emergencies requiring immediate attention or any tenant requests for property improvements.

Tenant Coordinators normally work a 40-hour workweek, but may work longer when required. They may work from on-site offices or from a property management office. Some travel to managed properties is a normal requirement for off-site Tenant Coordinators.

Salaries

Salaries vary according to experience, qualifications, and the job market in a given region or locality. Annual 2006 earnings of most Tenant Coordinators (the middle 50 percent) range between $27,000 and $59,400 a year, according to the U.S. Labor Department's Bureau of Labor Statistics. The lowest 10 percent earned less than $18,510, and the highest 10 percent earned more than $89,840 a year.

Tenant Coordinators may receive an annual performance bonus, tuition reimbursement for attending courses at local colleges or universities, and a standard benefits package that includes paid health insurance, vacations, paid sick leave, and a company-sponsored 401(k) savings plan.

Employment Prospects

There are plenty of opportunities for Tenant Coordinators with good client management skills. General employment opportunities for Tenant Coordinators should increase at about the same pace as other opportunities in all occupations through 2014, according to Bureau of Labor Statistics employment forecasts. Some openings will come about when managers transfer to other occupations or reach retirement age. Opportunities should be best for those with a college degree in business administration, real estate, or a related field and for those who attain a professional designation

in property management or begin working toward a professional certification. The Institute of Real Estate Management's Certified Property Manager (CPM) designation is given to professionals who are up to date on the latest trends in commercial property development.

In markets where there is a shortage of experienced Tenant Coordinators, employers increasingly are hiring inexperienced college graduates with bachelor's or master's degrees in business administration, accounting, finance, or real estate for many of these positions. Tenant Coordinators with limited on-the-job experience typically start out as assistant tenant coordinators. They work closely with a more experienced manager or property manager and learn how to market properties to prospective tenants, work with development teams, and perform other duties. Many of these opportunities are in retail shopping mall and strip mall projects, where investors and property owners put an emphasis on bringing projects to completion as quickly as possible.

Advancement Prospects

With experience, Tenant Coordinators can advance to more senior positions, such as on-site property manager, or in a larger firm, to regional manager supervising a group of Tenant Coordinators, each assigned a specific property to manage. The typical advancement path is from assistant tenant coordinator for an office building to on-site coordinator.

Education and Training

Most employers prefer to hire college graduates for property management positions. Entrants with degrees in business administration, accounting, finance, real estate, public administration, or related fields are preferred, but those with degrees in the liberal arts also may qualify.

Experience, Skills, and Personality Traits

Strong customer service skills, communication skills, ability to manage multiple priorities, and ability to learn database management software are needed. Some prior experience in tenant servicing or customer service is normally expected for new college graduates.

Most employers expect Tenant Coordinators to have some proficiency with standard PC software such as word processing, spreadsheets and e-mail programs.

A working knowledge of engineering systems, such as electrical, heating and ventilating, plumbing, and sprinkler systems, is helpful. Some knowledge of architectural software or drafting programs is helpful though not necessary. Good speaking and writing skills, as well as developing an ability to deal tactfully with people, are important job skills.

Unions and Associations

Tenant Coordinators can become members of real estate professionals associations such as the Institute of Real Estate Management (http://www.irem.org) or the Building Owners and Managers Institute (http://www.bomi.org) for career advancement and professional networking with their peers. Both associations sponsor annual conferences and frequent educational events for their members.

Tips for Entry

1. Take college courses in marketing and business management to get a solid academic background in property management.
2. Check building management Web sites and industry billboards for job leads in your area and apply directly to the firm.
3. Some prior experience in customer service or real estate sales may be very helpful in a position with a lot of public contact.

TENANT REPRESENTATIVE

CAREER PROFILE

Duties: Negotiates leases for commercial real estate clients; performs related lease administration services

Alternate Title(s): Office Leasing Broker, Tenant Representative Broker

Salary Range: $70,000 to $100,000 and up

Employment Prospects: Good

Advancement Prospects: Good

Prerequisites:

Education or Training—Four-year degree in business or real estate

Experience—Two to five years' experience in commercial real estate

Special Skills and Personality Traits—Strong negotiating and closing skills, well-developed oral and written communication skills

Special Requirements—Real estate license required in most states and the District of Columbia

CAREER LADDER

Director of Leasing

Tenant Representative

Junior Real Estate Broker

Position Description

In commercial real estate there are two types of sales brokers: the sales leasing associates who represent landlords or property owners and those who represent tenants. A Tenant Representative works for companies and other corporate clients who want to buy or lease space for their business. Business development is a big part of the job. Tenant Representatives spend a fair amount of their time prospecting—cold-calling—potential clients. Tenant Representatives are responsible for building their own book of business. They may get direction and supervision from senior brokers and tenant reps in their office, but they still have to make the phone calls and build their own leads to bring in new clients.

Tenant Representatives usually work in teams to spread the workload around. A typical arrangement is pairing a junior broker (or several junior brokers) with a more experienced senior broker who acts as a team leader. The junior broker makes the phone calls, sets up client meetings, and arranges site visits to prospective rental or build-to-suit sites. The senior broker handles lease negotiations and tries to win the client's business. A list of all the possible market alternatives meeting the client's needs is presented to the client for approval. This pairing of junior and senior brokers has its benefits: the senior broker gets an assistant who does all the up-front client prospecting and market research; the junior broker learns the commercial real estate business firsthand by working alongside a more

experienced professional. Working hours can be long. Junior brokers can expect to work 50 to 60 hours a week while learning the business.

Tenant Representatives perform a range of client services: occupancy analysis, market research, lease negotiation, facility measurement, space planning, company relocations, expense audits, lease administration, and property disposition. They also check lease terms and conditions typical for the market and type of real estate.

Specific duties performed on the job may include the following:

- identifying desirable prospective clients and selling them on the benefits of working with their brokerage firm to lease office space
- qualifying potential tenants by reviewing their financial statements and checking references
- communicating with the legal department to have documents prepared incorporating the lease terms agreed upon
- visiting existing properties to determine suitability and arranging site visits for prospective clients
- reviewing industry publications to identify potential national and regional tenants and maintain an awareness of industry trends
- communicating with partners, lenders, and other parties and filing reports on the status of leasing activity as needed

The business can be very competitive. This can be a good career choice if you are a risk taker, someone who is willing to work hard for the big payoff when you bring in a major client.

Salaries

A Tenant Representative earns commissions on the property under lease, much like any other commercial real estate broker, or $70,000 to $100,000 and up after the first year. Top producers can expect to earn in excess of $200,000 annually. The commission is most often calculated as a percentage of the lease value, and is determined by the local market. Commissions are generally in the 4–6 percent range. Commissions are calculated from the total square footage of leased space and are divided among the team members.

Commissions depend on the deal size, market location, and lease term. Commissions are highest in the top markets: New York, Chicago, and Los Angeles. Top-producing brokers who switch to a new firm may also get a sizable signing bonus.

Employment Prospects

This is a competitive market. Tenant Representatives who have a solid Rolodex full of top clients and prospective clients will always be in demand. Junior brokers who put in the long hours required to learn the business can establish themselves as players in the market after a year or two working with a senior broker. Commercial real estate brokerage is going through a consolidation phase, giving a competitive edge to the biggest real estate brokers, the ones that have the clout to offer their corporate clients a full menu of consulting services. These mega-brokerages are also writing non-compete clauses into employment agreements, which forbid brokers from taking clients who were added while they were at the firm when they leave. The industry still revolves around one thing: brokers who hit the pavement and come back with the leases.

Advancement Prospects

With some on-the-job experience and after reaching certain earnings goals, junior tenant representatives are promoted to senior brokers. They will still make prospecting cold calls to generate leads, though not as much as junior brokers starting out. Brokerage firms rely on senior brokers for their contacts and industry experience. Senior brokers have the know-how to bring in the important clients and win their business. Senior brokers may also become members of the brokerage firm's policy committee or have an equity stake in the company. Entrepreneurial brokers who want to build a consulting practice will strike out on their own and start their own tenant representation firms.

Education and Training

Tenant Representatives should have a solid academic footing in real estate fundamentals. A four-year degree with concentration in real estate, business, or a related course of study is recommended for anyone entering the industry. Most commercial brokerage firms have an in-house training program where starting brokers are exposed to all facets of the business in their first year on the job.

Special Requirements

As with other specialties in commercial real estate, a real estate sales license is required in most states.

Experience, Skills, and Personality Traits

Two to four years' leasing or selling experience and a working knowledge of deal structures and leasing terminology are required. The biggest challenge in this business is acting in the best interests of the client while generating income for the firm, so the pressure to get deals done can be intense at times. Strong negotiating skills and closing skills are essential on-the-job skills in this position. Well-developed oral and written communication skills are also important.

Unions and Associations

Tenant Representatives can become members of the Alliance of Tenant Representatives, a national trade group. There are regional associations in some markets, for instance, Houston, Texas. Several associations have education programs, career networking, and other membership benefits for commercial real estate brokers. Commercial brokers can become members of AIR Commercial Real Estate Association, the CCIM Institute, the Society of Industrial and Office Realtors, or Hotel Brokers International, an association of hotel brokers and consulting specialists.

Tips for Entry

1. Find commercial brokerage firms in your area by doing a Web search for "office lease broker."
2. A sales background is helpful if you are changing careers.
3. Contact local or national associations to learn about networking meetings and attend meetings in your area.

SALES AND MARKETING

ADMINISTRATIVE ASSISTANT

Duties: Types contracts and legal forms used in property sales; performs routine clerical and administrative duties in support of real estate sales staff

Alternate Title(s): Administrative Coordinator, Administrative Associate, Personal Assistant

Salary Range: $26,250 to $34,000

Employment Prospects: Excellent

Advancement Prospects: Good

Prerequisites:

    Education or Training—High school diploma, some college helpful

    Experience—One to two years' administrative experience

Special Skills and Personality Traits—Competency with word processing, e-mail and other office computer programs; strong organizational and communication skills

Position Description

Administrative Assistants are the front line in the real estate brokerage office, performing many tasks once reserved for managerial and professional staff. Core functions performed by administrative staffers have remained much the same, despite their increased responsibilities: performing and coordinating an office's administrative activities; preparing documents related to a property sale; processing, storing, and retrieving information for clients and staff.

Administrative Assistants have broad responsibility for a variety of administrative and clerical tasks necessary to run a real estate office efficiently. They serve as information and communication managers for their office. They plan and schedule meetings and appointments, maintain paper and electronic files, conduct research on the Internet, disseminate information via e-mail, fax, telephone, and mail services. They may take part in new employee orientation and training.

Today's Administrative Assistants are more computer literate than their predecessors, thanks to the recent advances in personal computer technology. They create spreadsheets, manage databases, and create sales presentations for sales staff and clients. They may also negotiate vendor contracts, maintain equipment leases, purchase supplies, and retrieve information from various industry databases. Because they spend less time on routine tasks such as answering phones and typing correspondence—managers often type their own e-mails and answer their own telephone calls—Administrative

Assistants can function in a supporting role for office managers, sales agents, and brokers.

Specific job responsibilities will vary according to the type of real estate office but typically include the following:

- meeting and greeting clients; interacting with clients and staff daily, handling routine queries
- operating personal computer to access e-mails, electronic calendar, and other basic office support software
- coordinating meetings and travel arrangements
- compiling and organizing reports, managing projects and schedules
- responding to or initiating phone calls to clients to determine need for assistance or referring clients to the appropriate area for assistance
- preparing or composing correspondence
- preparing background or collateral materials for conferences, appointments, meetings, and conference calls
- monitoring and distributing correspondence and incoming mail
- maintaining a filing system and ordering office supplies as needed
- preparing minutes for departmental meetings
- serving as a back-up for sales support staff

Real estate Administrative Assistants work in an office environment and normally work a regular 40-hour week. Their schedule may include working evenings and weekends as needed to support the office sales staff, as may occur during peak periods in the residential property market.

Salaries

Administrative Assistants can earn anywhere from $26,250 to $34,000, according to a 2006 salary survey by International Association of Administrative Professionals. Base salary may be supplemented by incentive bonuses for reaching sales goals. Many factors influence salary, including seniority, work ethic, performance, and training. Another influencing factor is office size and the amount of business produced annually.

Forty-five percent of Administrative Assistants surveyed by IAAP said they earned more than $40,000 annually in total compensation. Assistants to top-producing real estate agents or brokers can routinely earn more than $40,000 a year.

Employment Prospects

Employers report strong demand for Administrative Assistants with proficiency in personal computer applications, such as word processing, contact management and e-mail. About 20 percent of real estate brokerage offices have Administrative Assistants on staff, according to the National Association of Realtors. While employment opportunities in real estate offices are tied to fortunes of the broader housing market and the economy as a whole, productive real estate agencies will always have a need for assistants to handle routine office chores, freeing agents to spend their productive time prospecting for new clients and handling real estate sales.

In the broader economy, job opportunities for Administrative Assistants are expected to grow more slowly than opportunities for all occupations through 2014, the U.S. Bureau of Labor Statistics reports. Continuing growth in office productivity, allowing workers to perform more tasks, is a contributing factor. Some opportunities will come about as older workers reach retirement age or change jobs. Opportunities should be best for those with extensive knowledge of software applications, including online research, spreadsheets, databases, and desktop publishing programs.

Advancement Prospects

As they learn more about the real estate business, Administrative Assistants can move into more senior positions in the office. Qualified Administrative Assistants who broaden their knowledge, and who also have a desire to advance into more challenging positions,

can become senior administrative assistants, executive assistants, or office managers.

Another option is becoming a real estate agent by studying for the state real estate licensing exam. State licensing laws prohibit assistants from taking listings or performing other real estate activities; however, they can learn a great deal about the field by working in a real estate office. This background knowledge about real estate sales can pave the way to a career selling real estate, starting with a passing grade on the real estate sales licensing exam.

Education and Training

Education requirements vary for Administrative Assistants in real estate. The minimum requirement in a residential brokerage office is a high school diploma or an equivalent GED diploma. A commercial real estate office may require assistants to have taken some college courses, including some computer courses or business courses. Business schools, vocational-technical schools, and community colleges also provide training in office systems and computers.

Informal training after job placement is very common, often supplementing formal educational programs. Office skills and computer skills are often acquired through on-the-job mentoring or personal instruction by more experienced employees. Temporary placement agencies may also provide instruction in computer systems and software as part of their service to employers.

On-the-job training can also help Administrative Assistants learn which tasks in a real estate office can be performed only by a licensed agent or broker, such as taking a new property listing from a client.

Experience, Skills, and Personality Traits

Administrative Assistants should have at least one to two years' experience in an office setting, have strong computer skills in the Microsoft Office suite (word processing, e-mail, Excel spreadsheet), have some proficiency with document preparation software, and have excellent verbal and written communication skills. Surveys by the International Association of Administrative Professionals (IAAP) rank computer proficiency as the number one skill requirement for administrative office workers. A changing workplace is pushing Administrative Assistants to brush up their computer skills on a regular basis. Administrative Assistants say that keeping up with changing office technology is one of their biggest challenges, according to an IAAP survey. Administrative Assistants handle many different tasks throughout the day, which means an ability to prioritize assignments and an attention to detail are key job skills.

Several professional organizations offer testing and certification for entry-level proficiency, including the International Association of Administrative Professionals (IAAP) and the National Association of Legal Secretaries. The IAAP offers two professional designations, the Certified Professional Secretary (CPS) and the Certified Administrative Professional (CAP). Both can be earned by meeting certain experience or educational requirements and passing an examination.

Unions and Associations

The International Association of Administrative Professionals sponsors an annual professional education conference, office trade show, and education related meetings for professional advancement and network opportunities. The IAAP has local affiliate chapters in most U.S. states and Canadian provinces.

Tips for Entry

1. Check the Real Estate Assistants Job Forum (www.indeed.com) Web site for latest tips.
2. Attend meetings of local chapters of the International Association of Administrative Professionals to learn about opportunities in your area.
3. Vocational school or trade school computer courses can help you brush up on essential job skills.

LEASING AGENT—COMMERCIAL REAL ESTATE

CAREER PROFILE

Duties: Leases commercial space for a property management company or real estate investment trust; negotiates lease renewals

Alternate Title(s): Commercial Leasing Agent, Leasing Representative, Space Sales Representative

Salary Range: $61,900 to $97,100

Employment Prospects: Good

Advancement Prospects: Good

Prerequisites:

Education or Training—Four-year degree in business administration or related field of study

Experience—Two to five years' experience in real estate or sales

Special Skills and Personality Traits—Effective written and verbal communication skills; profes-

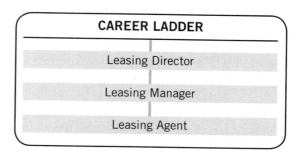

sional demeanor; familiarity with basic finance principles; good computer skills

Special Requirements—State licensing may be required if leasing agent handles real estate sales

Position Description

A Leasing Agent works for the landlords of shopping centers or office buildings to find tenants. Some work for a third-party owner such as a real estate investment trust (REIT). They locate tenants for vacant commercial space and negotiate leases for tenants waiting to renew their leases. Landlords expect the Leasing Agent to rent their properties to responsible commercial tenants for a fair price. Landlords expect to earn a fair return on investment (ROI) on their properties, while tenants want a fair rent and the right location for their business. A Leasing Agent earns a commission for finding tenants and usually handles all aspects of leases.

The Leasing Agent is hired to serve the property owner, which means the building tenants are responsible for ensuring the location and lease terms meet their requirements. Commercial tenants often hire a tenant representative, a leasing professional who acts in their interest and negotiates the best terms for the leased space.

In performing their duties, Leasing Agents attempt to collect as much information from prospective tenants as possible to ensure the lease is a good fit for both tenant and property owner. Topics for discussion typically include total lease cost, taxes and utilities, site improvements requested by the tenant, air condition-

ing, zoning regulations, access to on-site parking, and availability of additional space at lease renewal.

After gathering information from a prospective tenant, the Leasing Agent arranges a meeting with the prospect to review terms of the property lease. When an agreement is reached, the Leasing Agent sends a copy of the lease to the prospective tenants requesting a signature so that the landlord can then sign the lease agreement. The lease is not legally binding unless it is signed by both the tenant and the landlord.

Leasing commercial property requires an understanding of leasing practices, local economic trends, labor market conditions, business trends, and property location. Agents who lease industrial property need to know about the region's transportation, utilities, and labor supply. Agents who lease retail shopping mall space are in frequent contact with regional and national retail merchants regarding their space requirements. Whatever the type of property, the agent must know how to meet the client's unique requirements.

Leasing Agents make outbound cold calls or telephone calls to prospective tenants. They keep local and national prospects up to date on properties currently available for lease and projects currently in development.

Typical day-to-day duties of Leasing Agents include the following:

- collecting data on the local market and presenting their findings to the property owner or REIT
- preparing monthly status reports on all tenants and vacant space available for rent
- maintaining regular contact with tenants and carefully monitoring lease expirations
- maintaining a network of contacts with leasing market representatives in the local market
- preparing and generating all leases
- reviewing and signing leases with clients
- collecting lease deposit balances
- providing administrative support including preparation of letters and memos
- answering or directing client inquiries
- maintaining a visitor and client log
- preparing weekly rental reports, move-in inspections, and lease renewals
- marketing the building or available space at special events, such as golf outings, breakfast meetings, or business seminars

Leasing Agents also conduct research on market rents and absorption rates—the annualized occupancy rate in a building. They maintain databases on the market information collected. If tenants require additional square footage, the Leasing Agent will try to locate temporary space as needed. Leasing Agents typically work a 40-hour week including weekends. They may work longer hours as required during marketing or promotional events.

Salaries

Leasing Agents typically earn a salary plus commission, but this may depend on whether the position is temporary, part-time, casual, or whether the position is a contract, work-for-hire position as opposed to full-time employment. The commission earned by a Leasing Agent is usually based on a percentage of the monthly rent the new tenant will pay. Starting salaries of Leasing Agents begin at $25,000 but can be much higher, depending on experience and industry specialty. Base compensation, including commissions, ranged from $61,900 to $97,100 in 2007, according to CEL & Associates, a real estate consulting firm. Office and industrial positions usually pay the highest salaries. Annual performance bonuses can increase base salary by 40–50 percent, depending on property type and local market conditions.

Employment Prospects

Employment opportunities for Leasing Agents should grow at least as fast as opportunities in all occupations.

There is above average demand for agents with specialty industry knowledge, such as industrial sites or office parks in fast growing areas of the country. Demand is strong for agents with a successful track record of filling vacant commercial space.

Advancement Prospects

The typical advancement path is to a more senior position with additional responsibility in a property management company, such as leasing manager or leasing director. Some Leasing Agents will advance their careers by becoming leasing consultants employed by accounting firms or real estate consulting firms.

Education and Training

Some post-secondary education is preferred. Employers generally look for individuals with a four-year degree with a background in business administration or marketing. Courses in accounting, finance, or real estate are very helpful, as are courses in computer science and database management. A working knowledge of financial spreadsheet software is an important background.

Special Requirements

A real estate sales license may be required, depending on state regulations. Some states require a real estate license if the agent is engaged in property rentals, but not if the agent handles property leases exclusively. Check with your state's licensing board to learn about licensing requirements in your state.

Experience, Skills, and Personality Traits

Real estate experience is helpful in becoming a Leasing Agent, but knowledge of each particular property up for lease is essential. Leasing Agents should have some experience in real estate or sales through prior employment or college internship. More on-the-job experience is required in specialized industries, such as industrial property. Leasing Agents should have effective written and verbal communication skills, professional demeanor in working with clients, and some working knowledge of finance.

Excellent negotiating skills and the ability to recognize a qualified tenant are crucial characteristics of a good Leasing Agent.

Unions and Associations

Leasing Agents can become members of professional property management associations such as the National Association of Industrial and Office Properties or the Building Owners and Managers Institute for networking and career advancement opportunities.

Tips for Entry

1. Business courses such as marketing or accounting are as important as courses in real estate or finance.
2. Talk to friends with real estate experience or contact college alumni associations for career events in your area.
3. Read as much as you can about the real estate industry in business periodicals such as *Crain's*, *Commercial Property News*, or *National Real Estate Investor*.

COMMERCIAL REAL ESTATE BROKER

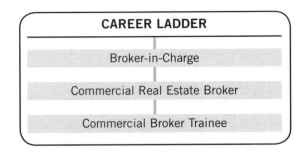

CAREER LADDER

Broker-in-Charge

Commercial Real Estate Broker

Commercial Broker Trainee

Position Description

Commercial Real Estate Brokers negotiate leases and sales for retail, high-tech industrial, and other industries that need office or industrial space. They can represent both landlords seeking to market office or industrial space and commercial tenants looking to relocate or expand. They also work with investors interested in buying properties for investment purposes. Commercial agents analyze property values, future income potential, and other market conditions to structure acceptable lease or purchase terms. Commercial Real Estate Brokers may specialize in a specific property type, such as office buildings, industrial properties, shopping malls, storage facilities, and warehouses.

By presenting an accurate picture of a property's potential value, commercial brokers are able to create a competitive market and extract the highest offers from prospective purchasers. This process requires extensive market research and sophisticated financial modeling, which enable the broker to put together a credible offering memorandum. The most successful brokers have deep relationships with senior level investors in the institutional and entrepreneurial real estate community. These relationships are developed through marketing success and a strong track record of previous sales.

Commercial brokers may also arrange financing, working with a network of banks and other sources of funding. They maintain a close watch over the markets to anticipate economic trends affecting the real estate industry. Many specialize in a particular property type because the commercial side of the real estate brokerage business is highly segmented around property type. Agents who sell industrial properties are knowledgeable about transportation costs, utility rates, labor supply, and other issues in their sales region.

Measured by the number of active brokers, Commercial Real Estate Brokers are a distinct minority in the real estate brokerage community. About 6 percent of licensed brokers were actively employed as commercial brokers in 2006, according to the National Association of Realtors.

Commercial brokers often work more than a standard 40 hours, may work evenings or weekends, and can work long and irregular hours—up to 60 hours a week, but each day is different and commercial brokers are out there meeting new people every day. They are always on call to service client needs.

Salaries

Commercial Real Estate Brokers earn a straight commission on deals actually closed, which makes commercial real estate a risky business for people just starting out. Brokers in their first year rely on their draw, or money paid in advance of future commissions. Most brokerage houses split the commissions 50/50 with the selling broker up to the first $350,000 in commissions. (Commercial brokerage commissions can vary from 2 percent of the listed price up to 10 percent, depending on the property type.) The broker's share of earned commissions typically increases in small increments as the broker writes more business throughout the calendar year. At the beginning of each year the commission split is readjusted back to a 50/50 split. Brokers need to have a lot of deals going at any one time because it normally takes four or five months to close a deal.

Commercial Real Estate Brokers shouldn't expect to earn too much in the first few years in business, but after four or five years' they can expect earnings of $70,000 to $100,000 or more. Successful brokers with five years' experience can expect to earn executive-level compensation of $200,000 or more in commissions and annual performance bonuses.

Employment Prospects

Commercial Real Estate Brokers generally start out as an underwriting or due diligence analyst, marketing associate, or research analyst. There is above average demand for Commercial Real Estate Brokers, which means the number of vacancies will grow faster than the average for all jobs through 2014. Because many areas of the country have a surplus of office space, demand is strong for successful marketing agents with a track record of filling vacant space. The demand for commercial agents is expected to increase in economically developing regions of the country.

Entry-level positions are typically due diligence and underwriting analyst, where future brokers learn how to evaluate prospective deals and build their personal network with successful brokers.

Advancement Prospects

Commercial Real Estate Brokers usually advance their careers by moving into more senior positions offering more responsibility and higher compensation. The typical advancement path is to senior manager or group leader. More senior positions are vice president, senior director or managing director.

Education and Training

A four-year degree with courses in economics, finance, accounting, or real estate is recommended for a solid foundation in real estate academic principles. Nearly half of commercial real estate firms operating in the United States have some form of on-the-job training for the staff and sales agents, the National Association of Realtors says. Training activities are slanted toward newly hired agents. One-third of all real estate firms require newly hired agents to complete 30 or more hours of training per year. Training activities can include scheduled training classes, informal training by a more senior employee, or training sessions scheduled in conjunction with other meetings. Continuing education to improve or upgrade job skills is available through various trade associations, including the associations listed below.

Special Requirements

State licensing is required, as in residential real estate brokerage. Check your state's real estate licensing board for details on licensing requirements in your state. A complete list of state licensing boards can be found in Appendix VI.

A professional certification helps commercial brokers maintain their job skills and improve their marketability as sales professionals. The Certified Commercial Investment Manager is awarded by the CCIM Institute for recognized experts in commercial and investment real estate. According to the CCIM Institute, only about 6 percent of the 125,000 Commercial Real Estate Brokers nationwide hold the CCIM designation. Candidates for the CCIM designation successfully complete 200 hours of classroom courses in financial analysis, market analysis, decision analysis and investment analysis, meet certain work experience requirements and pass a written exam. Courses leading to the CCIM designation are offered throughout the world.

Experience, Skills, and Personality Traits

Commercial Real Estate Brokers need to have good analytical skills and be aware of the economic growth possibilities in the region where a property is located, current state or federal income tax regulations, and financing/purchasing options that may give the buyer a greater return on investment. Also important are excellent people skills and some technical knowledge of the real estate markets, such as prevailing economic conditions in a local market area.

Unions and Associations

Several associations have education programs, career networking, and other membership benefits for Commercial Real Estate Brokers. Commercial brokers can become members of AIR Commercial Real Estate Association, the CCIM Institute, the Society of Industrial and Office Realtors, or Hotel Brokers International, an association of hotel brokers and consulting specialists. AIR Commercial Real Estate Association sets rules of professional conduct for commercial brokers engaged in sale or leasing of industrial and commercial properties. The CCIM Institute specializes in commercial and investment real estate. The Society of Industrial and Office Realtors is an affiliate of the National Association of Realtors.

Tips for Entry

1. Attend regional networking events of trade associations like AIREA, a California association of commercial agents.
2. Working toward an industry designation is helpful and can place you in contact with potential employers.
3. Industry Web sites such as Select Leaders (http://www.selectleaders.com) have the most current job openings for real estate professionals.

INVESTMENT SALES BROKER

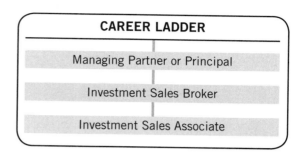

Position Description

Investment Sales Brokers represent property owners in the acquisition or sale of commercial properties. Their work covers the entire spectrum of commercial real estate: apartment buildings, shopping centers, office buildings, industrial properties, manufactured housing communities, hospitals, self-storage facilities, undeveloped land, and senior housing. Investment brokers provide their clients with strategic advice and market knowledge on specific markets and property types.

Brokers starting their careers spend much of their time cold-calling prospects and building a database of customers and potential customers and writing marketing materials. These materials include in-depth financial analyses, information about the local market and detailed property information. Investment Sales Brokers work in teams of associates to analyze data and prepare sales proposals and presentations.

Typical on-the-job duties include the following:

- pitching presentations to clients and prospective clients
- crunching numbers and performing financial analysis
- developing marketing materials to help facilitate property sales

Investment Sales Brokers normally have a long workweek, typically 50 to 60 hours, often working late nights and weekends when structuring a deal.

Salaries

Investment Sales Brokers earn very attractive salaries, compensating for long hours of hard work. Some earn a salary, but more commonly their earnings are 100 percent commissions. Investment Sales Brokers in most firms are independent contractors who receive no base salary and may not receive company-paid fringe benefits. Successful brokers can earn $60,000 to $90,000 in their first year of employment and a six-figure income by their second year. Top-performing brokers historically have annual incomes in the high six-figure to low seven-figure range.

Brokers collect a portion of the commissions earned from a property sale. Commissions are typically set at 2 percent of the total sale price, which means a $100 million sale yields a gross commission of $2 million. By industry practice, commissions are split equally between the property seller and buyer; in this example, the seller and buyer each pay their broker 1 percent. Broker commissions are then split among the team members and the company.

Employment Prospects

Getting in isn't easy. This field is challenging and hard to break into for individuals with limited experience. Entry-level associate broker positions can be the most difficult to obtain for recently graduated college students. Those entering the field from college start out as associates, working as junior members of a brokerage team. As members of teams, brokers are expected to be quick on their feet and juggle a lot of responsibilities.

Broker teams are small, making it harder for someone to break in right after graduating college. However, some brokerage firms do advertise entry-level positions for individuals who are working toward their undergraduate degree or are recent graduates. Their work would include assisting in research, preparing marketing packages, taking property photographs, and assisting in general day-to-day operations. No prior experience is required—only a desire to work in commercial real estate.

Commercial real estate brokers who have successful sales records may be able to make the career switch into investment brokerage. Another option is working for a while as a sales assistant to a broker. Some investment brokers have successfully started their careers after working for year or two as a sales assistant to an experienced broker and learning the business from the ground up.

Advancement Prospects

Individuals entering the business start out as sales associates, working as junior members of a team. Advancement is generally to vice president, a team leader position. Vice presidents are expected to bring in new business, manage transactions, and supervise a group of investment brokers. Above the vice president is managing director or managing partner, who is in charge of the brokerage office. Nationally ranked investment brokerage firms offer numerous career opportunities beyond working in a local office.

Education and Training

A four-year college degree in accounting, finance, real estate, or related studies is the basic academic background for a career in commercial real estate sales. Brokerage firms offer continuous on-the-job training and job coaching for individuals they hire out of college. The most successful brokers are also leaders in their field, and have earned an industry certification from one or more professional associations.

New brokers take part in an extensive training and development program designed to polish skills and prepare them to build their business in brokering investment real estate. Non-competing managers coach and develop new brokers one-on-one, in weekly sales meetings, and in workshops. Professional associations sponsor continuing education courses and seminars to help sales brokers stay up with developments in the field and maintain their job skills.

Special Requirements

A real estate sales license is generally required, though may not be a pre-requisite to get a job interview. Check with your state's real estate licensing board or a professional association to learn more about specific licensing requirements in your region.

Experience, Skills, and Personality Traits

Prior sales experience is helpful though not a requirement. Investment Sales Brokers must be dedicated, energetic, and willing to work long hours. They need to have an ability to develop sophisticated financial and asset valuation models using discounted cash flow (DCF), net present value (NPV), and other standard valuation techniques. This business is extremely competitive. To be successful, individuals starting out must be self-motivated and tenacious and have strong interpersonal and communication skills. Successful brokers have a balance of strong interpersonal and quantitative analysis skills. The top achievers are accomplishment-driven, consistently setting and achieving high goals.

Investment brokers should have strong computer skills, including a working knowledge of the Microsoft Office suite, and have a facility with Web-based research. Public speaking skills are important, as brokers spend much of their time making presentations to prospective clients.

Unions and Associations

Successful Investment Sales Brokers are active in professional associations such as the Urban Land Institute, CCIM Institute, or the International Council of Shopping Centers. These associations and others sponsor regularly scheduled conferences and educational seminars, providing opportunities for networking and improving job skills. Top performers also are active in their communities, serving on committees and planning boards of community organizations and charities.

Tips for Entry

1. Look for internship opportunities while still in college and get firsthand knowledge about the commercial brokerage business. Some internships with top firms are paid internships.
2. Get experience in real estate sales working as a sales assistant or real estate sales agent.
3. Be prepared to have answers to questions about how your talents would be a valuable addition to a brokerage team.
4. Bolster your speaking skills by joining a Toastmasters Club in your area. Find a club by visiting the Toastmasters International Web site (http://www.toastmasters.org).

LEASE ADMINISTRATOR

Duties: Provides financial analysis for property management and lease administration; collects data on property values and rental rates

Alternate Title(s): Commercial Lease Administrator

Salary Range: $50,000 to $70,000

Employment Prospects: Excellent

Advancement Prospects: Good

Prerequisites:

Education or Training—Four-year degree in accounting or finance

Experience—Three to five years' experience in commercial real estate or operational expense auditing

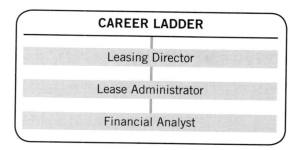

CAREER LADDER

Leasing Director

Lease Administrator

Financial Analyst

Special Skills and Personality Traits—Excellent computational skills and analytical skills; strong verbal and written communication skills; proficiency with Microsoft Office suite

Position Description

Staying on top of lease-related expenses is an important activity for both property owners and tenants, and for a very good reason. Lease expenses are one of the top five business expenses in most organizations that lease commercial or office space—accounting for as much as 15 percent of annual operating budgets. Errors in lease accounting can add up to millions of dollars a year in lease overpayments or missed revenue opportunities for property owners.

Lease administration is today viewed as a critically important function in controlling operating expenses. If the information in a Lease Administrator's records is inaccurate or incomplete, the risks can be substantial.

These business risks can include any or all of the following:

- unintended lease renewals. Missed notification dates can result in unintended lease renewals, sometimes adding up to millions of dollars in additional lease obligations.
- payment delays. Inaccurate payments can trigger penalties and incremental premiums charged to the tenant.
- compliance challenges. Inaccurate reporting could trigger penalties under Section 404 of the Sarbanes-Oxley Act, which requires public companies to have internal controls in place to ensure that financial reports are accurate.

Some of these business risks can be mitigated with technology applications that make the administrator's job easier to manage. Software systems can be programmed with automatic triggers that notify Lease Administrators of key dates, such as lease renewal dates, when some action is required.

The Lease Administrator is the person responsible for managing occupancy charges and keeping lease expenses (or revenues) within targeted ranges. A landlord or property owner who overlooks a simple rent bump, or rent increase, could be losing thousands or even millions of dollars in rental income, depending on the size of the tenant.

By keeping accurate and up-to-date records, Lease Administrators help ensure that all lease-related transactions—property rent, real estate taxes, property insurance, common area charges, tenant improvements and sublease payments—are properly recorded. They participate in lease negotiations. They do financial reviews on leased and owned properties. They maintain records on current leases, property values, capital expenses, and rental rates. They provide financial analysis for property management, facility planning, and financial reporting to senior management and investors.

Abstracting leases is an important part of the job. An abstraction of a commercial lease is just a summary of the main terms of the lease, taking all the important information (such as the amount of square feet leased, the base rent, and a list of documents modifying the terms of the lease) and condensing that information into a readable report. If the lease is for office space, for instance, the abstract might describe lease terms relating to lessee improvements.

Other job functions performed may include:

- maintaining records of rent schedules, including common area charges, taxes and insurance
- reconciling monthly payments and expenses
- processing utility charges and other monthly billings
- processing security deposits or amounts due at lease termination
- reviewing and processing invoices
- preparing correspondence with property managers, attorneys, and outside servicers
- coordinating insurance administration

Lease Administrators work in an office setting and generally work a standard 40-hour workweek. Uncompensated overtime may be required to resolve problems, meet deadlines, or manage excessive workloads during busy seasons. Lease Administrators employed by corporate tenants usually report to the corporate real estate department. Among property owners, they report to either corporate real estate or accounting departments.

Salaries

Salaries of Lease Administrators are competitive. Experienced Lease Administrators can earn from $50,000 to $70,000 in base salaries annually, according to a 2007 benchmarking survey by Deloitte FAS, a consulting firm. Individuals with less than three years' experience earn less than $50,000 annually, typically in the $30,000 to $45,000 range. Earnings can also vary according to industry segment and job requirements. Lease Administrators in office and industrial property management typically earn more than their counterparts in other industry segments, due largely to the fact they are expected to be more technically proficient and have more diverse experience.

Employment Prospects

Lease Administrators are finding their talents are in demand. Both property owners and tenants are reporting that recruiting talented Lease Administrators has become more challenging and that labor market conditions have tightened in the last several years. Recent college graduates may find their best employment opportunities are with corporate tenants. These companies often require no previous on-the-job experience.

Working for an independent servicing firm is an option for those with accounting or auditing experience. Much of the numbers-crunching, labor-intensive,

work such as lease abstraction or lease audits—two activities where demand has been greatest—is done by service firms working under outsourcing contracts with building owners or tenants.

Advancement Prospects

With experience, a Lease Administrator could advance to senior lease administrator, manage relationships with internal and external servicers, and act as a consultant to vice president of real estate or director of leasing for all Lease Administration issues. They may also get involved in mentoring junior lease administrators.

Education and Training

Most large employers look for college graduates with B.A. or B.S. degrees in accounting or finance. Some employers require only an associate's degree. Education requirements vary according to industry segment, but most employers expect their new hires to have some facility with numbers, accounting statements, and accounting spreadsheets and have some familiarity with accounting and auditing principles.

Experience, Skills, and Personality Traits

There are many opportunities for recent college graduates with the right academic background but limited real estate experience. Most employers look for individuals with up to three years' experience in the field who have some experience in operating expense audits. Individuals should have excellent oral and written communication skills, excellent computational skills, and strong computer skills.

Unions and Associations

Associations such as CoreNet Global and the CCIM Institute sponsor continuing education programs and industry conferences for networking and career advancement opportunities.

Tips for Entry

1. Contact third-party lease administration agencies or lease abstracting agencies in your area.
2. Get some experience in lease management software or maybe take a course in real state accounting software.
3. Attend regional meetings of CoreNet Global and other industry associations to learn about job opportunities and industry hiring trends.
4. Temporary or interim employment can lead to longer term opportunities.

MARKETING PROPOSAL COORDINATOR

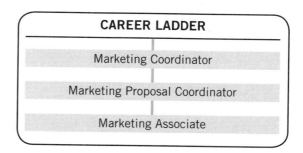

Position Description

Organizations seeking to hire vendors or suppliers often begin the selection process by requesting written business proposals from qualified vendors. By reviewing proposals from competing vendors, a company can select the vendor whose product line, servicing, and pricing best meets its current needs. The selection process often begins with the issuance of a Request for Information (RFI) or a Request for Quotations (RFQ) to a large number of vendors. After the initial responses are reviewed, a more detailed Request for Proposals (RFP) is usually issued to a smaller group of vendors, requesting answers to a more detailed questionnaire about their capabilities, staffing, and other qualifying criteria. The response for proposals writer produces marketing proposals in response to these formal solicitations for business.

Selecting vendors through a Requests for Proposals is very common in financial services. Some companies use RFP projects as a means to control their bank service costs. Others issue an RFP when they want to add services unavailable from their current vendor, are considering a technology upgrade, or are dissatisfied with their current vendor. Some organizations routinely rebid their vendor services every three to five years. This is more common in the public sector, where it may be required by statute.

RFP writers are skilled communicators with detailed knowledge of their company's objectives, practices, and position in their industry. As a member of their company's marketing team, the RFP writer works closely with the appropriate department managers to produce clearly written and concise responses to requests for proposals. The RFP writer edits written answers to an RFP for clarity and content, working to ensure the response document has sufficient quantitative information, such as tables or graphs, and that all questions have been answered. This role requires maintaining frequent contact with both the product development teams and sales managers in order to stay up to date on the company's product offerings and sales efforts. Because the turnaround time for gathering information and delivery of a completed RFP may be quite limited, RFP writers work under very tight production deadlines.

Full-time RFP writers wear many hats. An RFP writer's skills can easily translate into other tasks, such as technical writing or in-house communications. Some RFP writers have extensive backgrounds in marketing or corporate communications, which can come in handy when creating new advertising or marketing materials or when asked to assist in creating new sales or marketing initiatives.

Other duties of Marketing Proposal Coordinators typically include the following:

- responding to ad hoc information requests from client service or marketing

- analyzing RFP requirements to write, organize, and edit proposal content
- maintaining a database of common RFP questions and answers
- researching product information to update RFP responses

Long hours, including evenings and weekends, are common. About two-thirds of advertising, marketing, and public relations managers work more than 40 hours a week. Working under pressure is unavoidable when schedules change and problems arise, but deadlines and project goals must still be met.

Salaries

Starting salaries of $60,000 to $75,000 are fairly common, with higher salaries paid to more experienced Marketing Proposal Coordinators. Employers in the financial services field often require some previous experience producing marketing materials for an investment management firm, hedge fund, investment bank, or other financial company. Compensation packages often include annual incentive or performance bonuses for attaining department or company goals.

According to a National Association of Colleges and Employers survey, starting salaries for marketing majors graduating in 2005 averaged $33,873. Salary levels can vary substantially, depending upon the level of managerial responsibility, length of service, education, size of firm, and location. Many managers earn bonuses equal to 10 percent or more of their base salaries.

Employment Prospects

There is good demand for RFP writers, especially in the mutual fund and investment management industry. Individuals with some experience writing financial reports for investment firms or a strong background in financial journalism will find ample opportunities as RFP writers. More senior positions usually require some previous experience writing RFP documents. As RFP-format requests for bids are widely used in financial services, RFP writers with solid experience can find opportunities working at commercial banks, real estate development firms, real estate investment trusts, local development agencies, and other firms. Specific opportunities and job requirements will vary by industry.

Advancement Prospects

The Marketing Proposal Coordinator usually reports to the vice president of business development. Advance-ment is usually moving to more senior positions, such as team leader. The lead RFP manager is responsible for a team of marketing writers. Individuals with a post-graduate degree, such as an M.B.A. degree, which is not usually a requirement for entry, can move into a management level position as director of marketing. Some individuals can move laterally into related fields such as client servicing and client support.

Education and Training

A wide range of educational backgrounds is suitable for a career in marketing. A four-year college degree with concentration in sociology, psychology, literature, journalism, or philosophy, among other subjects, is acceptable. Candidates should also take some business and economics courses. A degree in journalism with a minor in finance would be a good academic background. RFP writers have to know their markets and have an ability to explain often complex topics in concise, readable copy. Most of this industry knowledge is gained through actual on-the-job experience after graduation from college.

For marketing, sales, and promotions management positions, some employers prefer a bachelor's or master's degree in business administration with an emphasis on marketing. Courses in business law, economics, accounting, finance, mathematics, and statistics are advantageous. In highly technical industries, such as computer and electronics manufacturing, a bachelor's degree in engineering or science, combined with a master's degree in business administration, is preferred.

Experience, Skills, and Personality Traits

RFP writers have to be adept at absorbing a large amount of information very quickly and preparing concisely written responses to detailed questions. Excellent verbal and written communication skills, plus an interest in writing about technically challenging subjects are important skills. RFP writers need to be assertive in obtaining required information from department managers, often working under very tight production deadlines. An ability to make decisions quickly and work as part of a marketing team is a very useful job-related skill. A working knowledge of standard PC software—the Microsoft Office suite—and some familiarity with database software is very useful in this position.

Unions and Associations

RFP writers can become members of professional associations such as the Financial Communications Society or any of the top real estate trade associations for career advancement and networking opportunities.

Tips for Entry

1. Executive search firms specializing in marketing communications are a good source of job leads.
2. Check online job boards such as the Select Leaders Web site (http://www.selectleaders.com) sponsored by leading real estate trade associations for current openings.
3. Marketing experience gained through internships or paid employment can be very useful background in this field.
4. Some background in finance or an in-depth familiarity with financial terms and deal structures is highly useful for anyone pursuing a career in this field.

MARKETING MANAGER

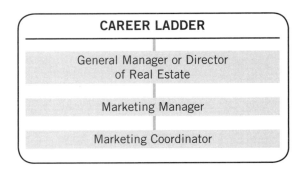

CAREER LADDER

General Manager or Director of Real Estate

Marketing Manager

Marketing Coordinator

Position Description

The Marketing Manager is responsible for implementing and executing the marketing, communications, and public relations strategy of a real estate development firm, real estate investment trust, or real estate management company. The Marketing Manager plays a key role in promoting the company's brand relationship with customers, retaining and expanding the client base through marketing activities. Marketing programs may include any of the following: direct mail, print, radio, television and Internet advertising; brochures and other collateral materials; graphic design and creative services; Web site management; market analysis and research; and product branding. In sum, the marketing director determines how to allocate the company's marketing resources to support its business strategy.

Marketing professionals stay abreast of changes in the marketing environment to best serve the objectives of the organization and adjust their plans accordingly. They research and develop pricing policies and recommend appropriate sales channels. In most real estate organizations they manage a group of marketing professionals. Marketing Managers typically report to a senior executive, such as the general manager, finance director, or director of operations.

Duties of the real estate Marketing Manager will vary according to business type. The Marketing Manager in a property management firm is responsible for prospecting new tenants, directing lease negotiations, coordinating the construction or renovation of tenant occupied space, and carrying out advertising or promotional campaigns to generate sufficient public exposure for managed properties.

The marketing director usually reports to a general manager, the director of property management, or a senior director of marketing, depending on the size of the firm. The marketing director of a real estate investment trust may report to the head of investor relations.

Duties of Marketing Managers typically include the following:

- managing a team of marketing and communications professionals
- coordinating with the business development team to plan business meetings, proposals, and client presentations
- identifying and evaluating conferences, events, and speaking engagements for professional staff
- conducting strategy and business development meetings with project and business development staff
- conducting research on specific strategies and planning, including competitive analysis, and client segmentation
- preparing marketing documents including Requests for Proposal (RFP) responses and presentations
- writing RFP proposal documents or assigned sections of proposal documents
- assisting in staff training on the proposal development process
- executing special projects as required

Marketing Managers work in an office setting, normally working a 40- to 50-hour workweek. They may work longer hours during peak periods and have occasional travel assignments to visit clients and business partners or to attend professional conferences and seminars.

Salaries

Earnings of real estate Marketing Managers are competitive with salaries of marketing professionals in other industries. Salaries can vary according to managerial responsibility, experience, educational background, and size of firm. Real estate Marketing Managers can earn salaries of $66,000 to $92,000 annually, plus an annual performance bonus. Many managers earn annual performance bonuses equal to 10 percent or more of their base salary. Earning an advanced degree or an M.B.A. can lead to higher starting salary.

Employment Prospects

There are excellent opportunities for Marketing Managers. Employment opportunities for marketing and public relations managers are expected to grow at a faster rate than opportunities for all occupations through 2014, according to the U.S. Bureau of Labor Statistics. College graduates who have some related experience in the industry, a high level of creativity, and strong communication skills will have the best opportunities. Completing an internship while still in school is highly recommended for the opportunity to make personal contacts with potential hiring managers. There are many highly qualified professionals in marketing and competition for choice assignments can be very strong. Many marketing positions will become available as marketing executives reach retirement age, resign, or move into other positions. Some will take senior management positions in their firm.

Advancement Prospects

Advancement opportunities are closely tied to the type of real estate firm. Many companies offer their employees continuing education opportunities, either in-house or at local colleges or universities, which can bolster their chances of getting promoted to positions with increased responsibility. Advancement is usually to a more senior position with operational responsibility. Some will advance their careers by going independent and setting up their own marketing consulting and advisory firms.

Education and Training

A four-year degree in business administration, marketing, or public relations is preferred. Academic background is an important qualifier; individuals who have more academic credentials or who have taken continuing education courses should find it easier to break into real estate marketing in a top firm than if they had not every opportunity to maintain or upgrade their job skills.

Marketing Managers who want to broaden their real estate management skills can earn a professional certification such as the Certified Property Manager (CPM) awarded by the Institute of Real Estate Management to individuals who have an undergraduate degree in real estate or property management from an accredited college or university and pass a qualifying examination.

Experience, Skills, and Personality Traits

Marketing Managers rely on experience and judgment to plan and accomplish goals.

Real estate marketers should be well versed in all the various marketing strategies commonly employed in real estate and should have a portfolio to demonstrate that experience. Real estate Marketing Managers should have at least three to five years' experience in sales and marketing and some exposure to working with construction development.

Unions and Associations

Marketing Managers can become members of any of several professional associations for continuing education and networking opportunities, including the following: the CCIM Institute, Building Owners and Managers Institute, the Community Associations Institute, or the International Council of Shopping Centers.

Tips for Entry

1. Take college courses in real estate or property management, marketing and related subject areas.
2. Establishing and maintaining a relationship with a recruiter can open doors to an interview.
3. Remember that real estate is a relationship-driven business, so contacting people in companies where you may want to work can pay off better than posting your résumé on Internet job boards.

NEW HOME SALES REPRESENTATIVE

CAREER PROFILE

Duties: Prospects qualified home buyers; sells homes in new communities; assists home buyers to real estate closing

Alternate Title(s): Community Sales Associate, New Home Sales Associate

Salary Range: $30,000 to $75,000 and up

Employment Prospects: Good

Advancement Prospects: Fair

Prerequisites:

Education or Training—High school diploma or equivalent; some college preferred

Experience—One to three years' sales experience

Special Skills and Personality Traits—Excellent prospecting skills; good problem-solving and communication skills; good computer skills

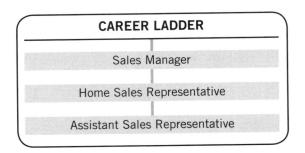

CAREER LADDER

Sales Manager

Home Sales Representative

Assistant Sales Representative

Special Requirements—Real estate sales license and valid driver's license required in most states

Position Description

New Home Sales Representatives, or sales agents, work with new home buyers in planned communities or new housing developments. They also assist buyers through the home closing process. They spend much of their time prospecting new home buyers and helping interested buyers qualify for a home mortgage. They maintain a detailed knowledge of local market competition, real estate laws and regulations relating to home sales, and local or national trends in regulations applicable to the home-buying industry.

Obtaining new accounts is an important part of the job for New Home Sales Representatives. Sales representatives follow leads from other clients, track advertisements in trade journals, participate in trade shows and conferences, and may visit potential clients unannounced. Compiling a list of potential home buyers, generally referred to as sales leads, is the first step in the sales process.

Developing a list of sales leads is generally done systematically. Sales leads are acquired from advertising inquiries, trade shows, direct mail marketing, Internet Web sites and other sources. Sales leads are also acquired through word-of-mouth referrals from sales managers or other sales representatives, real estate agents and brokers, real estate attorneys, and others. Typically, the sales leads are gathered together in a database and sorted by name, location, phone number, e-mail address, and any other relevant information.

Home sales representatives make outbound calls to potential and existing customers by telephone or e-mail to qualify leads and invite prospective home buyers to attend model home open houses and other marketing events. They emphasize salable features of homes offered for sale, quote prices and credit terms, and help buyers obtain mortgage financing on a new home.

Home sales representatives have several duties beyond selling housing to home buyers. After the initial contact has been made, home sales representatives prepare reports of business transactions and enter new customer data into the home seller's computer database. They analyze sales statistics, prepare reports, and handle administrative duties, such as filing expense accounts, scheduling appointments, and making travel plans. They also read about new and existing products and monitor the sales, prices, and products of their competitors.

Typical job responsibilities of a home sales representative include the following:

- planning an effective personal sales presentation and executing that plan
- attaining established sales goals
- conducting interviews with prospective home buyers for current and future home sales
- demonstrating model homes
- explaining mortgage payment terms, taxes, insurance, applicable deed restrictions, homeowner associations, and country club or golf club memberships
- preparing required paperwork for each home sale
- assisting in setting up home buyer appointments for design center, mortgage finance, home inspection, and settlement/ closing
- keeping buyers up to date and informed as to construction start and completion dates
- staying in contact with home buyers through loan closing

New Home Sales Representatives work in an office setting, often on weekends, and may work longer than a standard 40-hour week. They may spend time meeting with and entertaining prospective clients during evenings and weekends.

Salaries

Home sales representatives typically earn a base salary plus sales commissions. Base starting salaries vary according to experience and range from $30,000 to $75,000 annually. The sales rep may also be eligible for incentive rewards and annual bonuses for meeting personal or business office sales goals. Other forms of compensation are straight commission, in which no base salary is paid out, or a draw against commission. Working on a commission-only compensation can be a risky proposition in a slowing market, when the inventory of unsold homes exceeds market demand. You may go months without getting paid or have months in which you make a good percentage of the year's income.

Most home builders offer a generous benefits package, including employee discounts on mortgages, an employee stock purchase plan, employer-paid health insurance, and career training to maintain job skills. Top producers can expect to earn more than $100,000 a year, regardless of the compensation structure, including bonuses and other incentive payments.

Employment Prospects

Employment opportunities for home sales agents rise and fall with the fortunes of the home building industry. When new home sales are slowing, home builders cut back on production and hiring sales representatives, as occurred in the 2007–08 time period, when new home sales declined sharply after several years of record-setting growth. Employment opportunities are best in niche markets, such as planned communities, age-restricted communities, or retirement communities. Home builders usually look for experienced sales reps to fill these marketing positions.

Advancement Prospects

With two to three years' experience, home sales representatives can move up to more demanding positions with an increase in salary. They can advance their careers by taking more senior positions or management positions, such as directing a sales office. Another option is regional sales manager. Experienced home sales representatives can also work as account managers for companies marketing single-family housing to corporate clients.

Education and Training

A high school diploma or the equivalent is the minimum education requirement for entry. Most employers prefer hiring people who have a college degree or have completed some college courses in business, marketing, or related areas. New hires can expect to get an intensive training in a home builder's sales techniques during the first year of employment. Most home builders hiring sales agents provide on-the-job training for their new agents. They provide training in the way their products are sold and may also offer training in specific sales tactics.

Special Requirements

Home sales associates should have a real estate sales license in the state where they plan to be doing business, or be close to completing their training and qualifying for a real estate license. A valid driver's license is also required.

Experience, Skills, and Personality Traits

Home sellers have to be at ease cold-calling and working with people. They spend much of their day prospecting for new clients, which means strong interpersonal skills and negotiating skills are a must. Some prior experience in commission-paid sales, preferably real estate, is a very helpful background. Sales associates log their sales leads on computer, so good computer skills in word processing and spreadsheets are important job skills. Employers look for people who have some experience in real estate sales or new home sales, usually one to three years. Sales agents should have also have a general knowledge of residential real estate construction and the sales closing process.

Unions and Associations

The National Association of Home Builders offers career training opportunities for people who work in home sales The association has several professional designations for individuals involved in home sales, including Certified New Home Marketing Professional and Certified New Home Sales Professional. The association's MIRM designation (Member, Institute of Residential Marketing) is the top-level achievement for professionals in new home marketing.

Tips for Entry

1. Contact home builders directly for sales opportunities in your area.
2. Previous sales experience in a real estate office can pay dividends for anyone interested in a career with a home builder.
3. Take courses toward a real estate license if licensing is required in your state.

REAL ESTATE BUYER'S AGENT

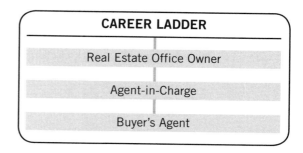

Position Description

Real estate brokers are licensed professionals who function as an intermediary between buyers and sellers of real estate. In the typical sales arrangement, the broker or agent tries to identify buyers who are looking for the type of property the seller is offering to sell. A Buyer's Agent is a real estate sales professional who, by agreement, seeks to represent the buyer in a real estate transaction rather than the seller.

The Buyer's Agent has a duty to locate the right home for the buyer, negotiate on the buyer's behalf for the best price and terms, maintain the buyer's confidentiality, and disclose all information known about the seller and the property. An exclusive buyer agent works for a real estate sales office that does not take property listings of any kind and represents only the buyers.

Buyer brokerage came about in the last 10 to 15 years as real estate agents in some states began to look around for ways to stand out from the competition and offer services catering exclusively to property buyers. Under prevailing laws in most states, real estate agents and brokers represented only sellers. About 15 states have since passed laws allowing buyer brokerage. The Buyer's Agent acts as a fiduciary for the buyer.

The practice of buyer representation differs from the practice in most states in which real estate agents (or brokers) have a dual agent role, representing both buyers and sellers. The seller's agent, also known as the listing agent, is legally obligated to represent the property seller. (The listing agent's name is the one displayed on the real estate sign.) Some states permit dual agency representation, which means the agent may represent either buyer or seller.

A buyer agency agreement means that the agent will do the following for the property buyer:

- find property meeting the buyer's needs, specifications and affordability
- take buyers to properties listed as available for sale
- prescreen buyers to ensure they are financially qualified
- negotiate price and terms, acting on the buyer's behalf
- prepare a standard real estate purchase contract

As in a listing agreement with sellers, a buyer's agreement must have a starting and ending date and specify how the buyer's broker is to be paid (by either seller or buyer). The agreement also spells out the duties and obligations of all parties involved in a real estate sale.

Salaries

Buyer's Agents and brokers are typically compensated 100 percent through commissions. The potential for higher annual earnings rises with experience. Nationally, real estate agents and brokers earned between $23,500 and $58,110 a year. Real estate sales agents earned a median $38,300 in 2005, meaning that 50 percent received earnings above this amount and half earned less, according to the National Association of Realtor's

2005 Member Profile. The NAR report does not break out annual incomes by type of real estate agent, which means these figures are average figures across the industry.

Sales associates with between six and 10 years experience earned a median $57,000, and those in business more than 26 years had earnings of $83,400, the NAR *Member Profile* reports. Many real estate agents earn substantially more and top producers can earn over $1 million a year. Buyer's brokers, because they represent the buyer, may earn less in commissioned income than agents or brokers representing the seller, because commissions are paid by the seller. Having a professional designation from a recognized trade association can also boost earnings.

Employment Prospects
Most real estate agents start off as sales trainees. Others begin as office assistants, rental agents, or assistants in a large real estate organization or the mortgage division of a commercial bank or savings and loan association. According to the National Association of Realtors, nearly 70 percent of sales agents come from non-real estate–related fields such as teaching, government, retail, and the armed forces. Only 25 percent have management or sales experience.

Advancement Prospects
Buyer's brokers advance their careers much like other real estate agents—by getting more clients and selling more properties. Agents in a large firm can become office managers or agents in charge. Agents who earn their state broker's license may decide to open their own offices. Agents who enjoy dealing with finances may become loan agents and help buyers get mortgage financing. Some agents may become property managers and help people find properties to rent. Successful agents may make real estate their full-time occupation.

Education and Training
A college degree is not required, although many real estate brokers and sales agents have some college. Most states require only a high school diploma or equivalency certificate. College level courses in business or communication will contribute to success as a real estate agent but are not essential. Some formal on-the-job or classroom training is necessary to become a real estate agent. Upon satisfactory completion of the training program, candidates can apply to their state's licensing board for a sales license.

Over three-quarters of residential real estate firms provide some type of on-the-job training and education for their sales agents and staff, according to the National Association of Realtors. Training helps both staff and licensed agents develop the skills necessary to grow their businesses and service clients. Nearly all large brokerage firms offer some form of training, whether formal scheduled training or training sessions combined with other meetings. The typical real estate firm schedules about 20 hours of training annually.

Special Requirements
State licensing is required in all states and the District of Columbia. Check with your state's real estate licensing board for more information on requirements in your area. The requirements for real estate agents are different from those for real estate brokers and are generally less stringent. A complete list of state real estate licensing boards and their contact information can be found in Appendix VI.

Experience, Skills, and Personality Traits
Buyer's Agents need to have strong interpersonal skills and have an interest in helping others meet their personal and financial goals. Also important is some technical expertise, because so much of what goes on in a real estate transaction—from finding a home to qualifying for a loan—is done over the Internet. Some experience with Internet browsers, word processing, and basic computer applications will be very useful.

Unions and Associations
Buyer's brokers can become members of the Real Estate Buyer's Agent Council (an affiliate of the National Association of Realtors) or the National Association of Exclusive Buyer Agents for career advancement and networking opportunities.

Tips for Entry
1. Look for internship opportunities to break into real estate sales. Some real estate brokers will pay real estate school tuition in exchange for an unpaid internship.
2. Do an Internet search under the term "buyer's broker" to find buyer broker agencies in your area of the country.
3. Real estate agencies that have the most for sale signs in your area are a good place to start your career search.

RESIDENTAL REAL ESTATE BROKER

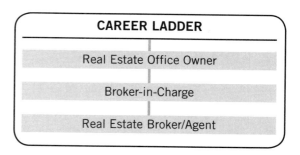

CAREER LADDER

Real Estate Office Owner

Broker-in-Charge

Real Estate Broker/Agent

Position Description

Real Estate Brokers assist property owners in selling their property at the highest price and the best possible terms. When acting as buyer's agents, they help buyers find property at the lowest price and best terms as outlined in a signed agreement. In most states, a real estate agent can represent either buyer or seller, acting in a dual agency capacity. The terms *broker* and *agent* are often used interchangeably, although agents are typically sales people employed by licensed Real Estate Brokers. Most states still use the term *salesperson* to describe a real estate agent.

Most real estate agents work as commission-paid independent contractors who set their own hours. A drawback is they are responsible for their own business expenses, which are paid from real estate commissions. Besides office expenses and selling costs, expenses can include phone calls, postage, advertising, increased insurance to cover liability for business passengers, and errors and omissions insurance coverage.

A recent trend is working in teams. Real estate agents share office workers and Web masters and pool resources to share the workload. Successful teams are actively courted by the big national agencies, which benefit from having agents with a local, personalized approach. One advantage is being able to offer personalized service even when busy elsewhere or doing something else.

Real Estate Brokers and agents do more than sell properties for clients. Most real estate firms also offer real estate–related services, either in-house or by contracting with third-party firms, such as relocation services, mortgage lending, title or escrow services, and home improvement. Many offer their clients a full menu of services, including consultation services, help with real estate closings, and assisting buyers in finding home improvement contractors. Some examples of services offered by real estate brokers and agents are the following:

- comparable market analysis
- marketing real property to prospective buyers
- guiding a buyer through the home buying process
- guiding a seller through the home selling process
- preparing the necessary paperwork for "Sale by Owner" Sellers
- full residential appraisal if the broker/agent is licensed as an appraiser
- home selling kits, or guides on marketing and selling a property
- hourly consulting for a fee
- leasing for a fee percentage of the gross lease value
- property management
- exchanging property in a tax-advantaged transaction
- auctioning property
- preparing contracts and leases where permitted by state law or regulations

Some real estate brokerages charge their salespersons a monthly fee for brokerage services and use of office space. The rent-your-space option generally works best for agents with an established clientele and regular closings, because fixed monthly fees can take a bite out of earnings, and each agent is responsible for every expense associated with doing business.

Salaries

Commissions are the main source of broker and agent earnings. The commission rate is determined by the value of the property sold and type of real estate agency handling the sale. Full commission brokers generally charge commissions up to the maximum permitted in their locality (split equally between the selling broker and the buying broker). Real estate brokerage commissions are normally divided between the listing office and the selling office. Each then pays its agent a percentage of the total received. If the office is part of a franchise system such as Century 21® or Coldwell Banker®, the commission paid to agents within that office is decreased by whatever amount the franchising company charges. Some agents are not commission-paid independent contractors and are compensated by salary, a share of brokerage firm profits, or a combination of salary and profits.

The potential for higher annual earnings rises with experience. Real estate sales agents earned a median $38,300 in 2005, meaning that 50 percent received earnings above this amount and half earned less, according to the NAR's *2005 Member Profile*. Sales associates with between six and 10 years' experience earned a median $57,000, and those in business more than 26 years had earnings of $83,400. Many real estate agents earn substantially more and top producers can earn over $1 million a year.

Employment Prospects

There are lots of openings in real estate sales but plenty of competition. This is a relatively easy field to start out in, but it can be a difficult way to make a living because there are so many agents and brokers competing for clients. Most real estate salespersons start off as sales trainees in a real estate brokerage office. Others begin as office assistants, rental agents, or assistants in a department of a large real estate organization or the mortgage division of a commercial bank or savings and loan association. According to the National Association of Realtors, nearly 70 percent of sales agents come from non-real estate–related fields such as teaching, government, retail and the armed forces. Only 25 percent have management or sales experience.

Advancement Prospects

Residential real estate agents advance by getting more clients and selling more properties. They can also advance their careers by selling more expensive properties and collecting bigger commissions on these sales. Agents who work at large firms may become office managers or agents in charge. Agents who earn their state broker's license may decide to open their own offices. Agents who enjoy dealing with finances may become loan agents and help buyers get mortgage financing. Some agents may become property managers and help people find properties to rent.

Education and Training

A college degree is not required, although many Real Estate Brokers and sales agents have some college. Most states require only a high school diploma or equivalency certificate. College level courses in business or communication will contribute to success as a real estate agent but are not essential.

Over three-quarters of residential real estate firms provide on-the-job training and education for their sales agents and staff, according to the National Association of Realtors. Training helps both staff and licensed agents develop the skills necessary to grow their businesses and service clients. Nearly all large brokerage firms offer some form of training, whether formal scheduled training or training sessions combined with other meetings. The typical real estate firm schedules about 20 hours of training annually.

Special Requirements

State licensing is required in all states and the District of Columbia. Before getting involved, Real Estate Brokers and agents need a real estate license. All future agents must first pass the real estate license exam in their states. State regulators in each state (the Department of Real Estate, Licensing, or Real Estate Commission) requires a specific numbers of hours in real estate principles before a new agent can take the state license exam.

Licensing requirements vary from state to state, but all states require prospective real estate sale agents and brokers to pass a written exam. Some states allow prospective agents to take pre-licensing educational courses at schools accredited by the state licensing agency before they qualify to sit for the exam. Other states allow taking these courses within a specified time after being licensed. More information on licensing and other requirements is available from the Association of Real Estate License Law Officials on their Web site (http://www.arello.org), from local real estate boards, or from real estate licensing commissions in the states where you would practice real estate sales. Most states require agents and brokers to take continuing education courses, usually 10 to 20 hours annually or biannually, to renew their sales licenses.

Experience, Skills, and Personality Traits

People who have found success in real estate have the same skills and personality traits as people who have met with success in any sales career. They have an almost intuitive understanding of what buyers and sellers want and are sensitive to their needs. Good communication skills really come into play in this job. Second, they are good at juggling all the parts of a real estate sale, including phone calls to attorneys, appraisers, property inspectors, and others, without getting overwhelmed by all the small details. Every real estate transaction has numerous legal contracts, and they all have to be filled out correctly. The third quality is a strong drive to succeed. Real estate agents have to maintain their enthusiasm in the face of long working hours and sales that fall through at the last minute. This is a typical sales job, and it is important to remain positive and full of enthusiasm.

Unions and Associations

Real estate agents and brokers can become members of several associations for career advancement and networking opportunities. The most common is the National Association of Realtors. Others include the Real Estate Buyer's Agent Council (an NAR affiliate) and the National Association of Exclusive Buyer Agents.

Professional designations awarded by industry associations are very popular among residential real estate agents. Agents holding one or more professional designations handle more real estate sales and benefit from substantially higher earnings. A listing of professional certifications and designations can be found in Appendix III.

Tips for Entry

1. Have extra cash on hand or savings to cover living expenses for the first several months while learning the job.
2. Because licensing requirements vary by state, it might be a good idea to visit or contact your state's real estate licensing commission to learn more about licensing requirements and regulations covering agents in your area before starting out.
3. Do you know any local agents? Ask them which agencies they recommend.
4. Visit your area Chamber of Commerce or visitor's center. Look for agencies that have handouts for potential residents. Are they promoting their services for the agency in general or just for the agents whose names appear on the flier?
5. Pick up a copy of your local real estate publication, the free magazine handed out in supermarkets and other businesses. Look for ads that pop out.
6. Real estate agencies that have the most for sale signs in your area are a good place to start your search.
7. Test your real estate aptitude by going online and taking an online self-test real estate simulator, and see if you have what it takes to be successful. Century 21 is an example.

SALES ASSISTANT

CAREER PROFILE

Duties: Assists in selling, leasing, and marketing of real estate properties; provides transactional support for real estate agents and brokers

Alternate Title(s): Marketing Assistant

Salary Range: $18,000 to $50,000

Employment Prospects: Good

Advancement Prospects: Good

Prerequisites:

Education or Training—High school diploma or equivalent

Experience—Up to two years' sales experience

Special Skills and Personality Traits—Facility with Microsoft Outlook e-mail software; good Internet research skills

CAREER LADDER

Real Estate Agent/Broker

Sales Assistant

Sales Trainee

Special Requirements—Real estate sales agent license or courses toward state licensing; valid driver's license

Position Description

Real estate Sales Assistants help with routine tasks in a real estate brokerage office or sale office. They answer phones, schedule appointments, sit in at open houses, and perform general administrative duties. They provide sales and transactional support for agents and brokers. They assist brokers in all aspects of client servicing and sales. They coordinate schedules for prospective buyers. They assist with open house sales, respond to client service requests, and deliver documents to attorneys, clients, and others involved in a real estate transaction.

Real estate sales offices often employ clerical employees, both licensed and non-licensed, to assist with administrative or management functions. The typical real estate office has one staff employee, according to the National Association of Realtors' 2006 *Industry Profile of Real Estate Firms*. The staff size, not surprisingly, tends to increase with business volume and the number of licensed real estate agents. At the opposite end of the scale, smaller real estate offices do not have Sales Assistants or clerical staff. Over one-third of the smaller offices (those with five or fewer licensed agents) do not have any administrative staff.

Sales Assistants plan and implement direct marketing and sales campaigns. They assist in pre-sale property preparation by getting keys made, closing packages, and contacting property inspectors and contractors. They answer client questions about properties offered for sale or a pending sale. They may also help with office accounting, do word processing or data entry, answer phones and respond to client e-mails.

Typical duties of Sales Assistants may include the following:

- meeting with clients and accompanying brokers and clients to property sites
- assisting in property showings and open house events
- collecting materials necessary for transactions, including listing and commission agreements, leases, and sales agreements
- preparing tenant surveys, summary or update reports, presentations for listing or for tenant representatives
- compiling property data for clients, with data tailored to client needs
- assisting sales agents with trouble-shooting or solving routine office problems
- coordinating marketing activities with sales staff—real estate agents, clients, and others and gathering necessary market data
- distributing sales brochures and other marketing materials

Real estate Sales Assistants typically work in an office setting, normally working a 40-hour workweek. They may work longer hours, including weekends, as needed during peak production periods. The spring and summer months are the busiest time periods in residential real estate.

Salaries

Salaries are determined by education level, prior real estate experience, and the requirements of the job. The typical salary range is $18,000 to $30,000 in residential real estate and $30,000 to $50,000 in commercial real estate. Earnings can be commission-based or computed at an hourly rate. If earnings are primarily from sales commissions, they are usually determined from sales activity and are treated as a draw against future commissions.

Sales Assistants receiving a combination of salary and commission generally get a low base pay plus a sales commission of 1 percent to 5 percent. The base salary is gradually reduced over a period of time until the earnings are 100 percent commission-based. Commercial real estate Sales Assistants generally earn higher salaries than residential assistants.

In addition to salary or commissions, real estate Sales Assistants typically receive non-salary benefits, such as paid health insurance, dental and vision care, paid vacations, and sick days, and may participate in employer-sponsored 401(k) savings plans or other types of retirement plans. More than 90 percent of large real estate offices or those with 51 or more licensed sales agents offer vacation and sick time benefits, the NAR say. Seventy-eight percent of these firms provide health insurance benefits for administrative staff.

Employment Prospects

There is adequate demand for real estate Sales Assistants. Some opportunities will come about as new Sales Assistants replace those who move up into full-time agent positions. Overall opportunities are determined by growth in the economy and local market conditions. Real estate brokerages need Sales Assistants to perform routine tasks, so there are plenty of ground floor opportunities. Starting as a Sales Assistant is a good way to take responsibility for tasks already performed while learning more about real estate sales.

Advancement Prospects

Advancement is normally done by obtaining a real estate sales license and becoming a full-time real estate agent. Sales Assistants are expected to seek a sales career as a licensed real estate agent within a certain period of time after being hired. Normally, they are not expected to remain in this position for more than a 12-month period. A Sales Assistant who decides not to pursue a career in sales can become an office manager, supervising other administrative employees in a real estate sales office.

Education and Training

A high school diploma is the minimum requirement in a retail sales agent position. More formal training about real estate marketing, lender financing, and client service is provided on the job after being hired. Sales Assistants work under the direct supervision of an experienced broker or team of sales professionals for several months, while learning all aspects of the real estate brokerage business.

Special Requirements

Sales Assistants need to have a valid real estate license in the state where business is conducted or have taken courses toward a state license. Licensing may not be required in some situations, if working part-time for instance, but is usually a requirement if working in an active sales office or working in commercial real estate sales. Check with your state's real estate licensing board for information on requirements in your state.

Experience, Skills, and Personality Traits

Some sales experience, up to two years, is helpful. Sales Assistants are expected to work independently and be able to assist sales agents in solving problems. They should have good communication skills, good Internet search skills, and a working knowledge of e-mail software programs. Also important is an ability to read and interpret instructions and meet production deadlines both independently and as part of a team. This is a good fit for candidates who have excellent people skills and like working with clients.

Unions and Associations

Sales Assistants can become members of the National Association of Realtors or one of its affiliates for networking and career management opportunities. Licensed sales agents must take a certain number of continuing education courses to maintain their licenses.

Tips for Entry

1. Test your real estate aptitude by going online and taking an online self-test real estate simulator, and see if you have what it takes to be successful.
2. Visit your area Chamber of Commerce or visitor's center. Look for agencies that have handouts for potential residents. Are they promoting their services for the agency in general or just for the agents whose names appear on the flier?
3. Licensing requirements vary by state. Contact your state's real estate licensing commission to learn more about licensing requirements and regulations covering real estate agents in your area.

TRANSACTION MANAGER

CAREER PROFILE

Duties: Coordinates and manages commercial real estate transactions; oversees property acquisitions or sales from due diligence review to escrow and closing

Alternate Title(s): Commercial Real Estate Transaction Manager, Office Administrator

Salary Range: $55,000 to $80,000 and up

Employment Prospects: Good

Advancement Prospects: Good

Prerequisites:

Education or Training—Four-year degree in business administration, real estate, or a related field of study

Experience—Three to five years' experience in commercial real estate

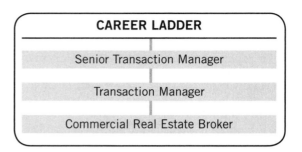

CAREER LADDER

Senior Transaction Manager

Transaction Manager

Commercial Real Estate Broker

Special Skills and Personality Traits—Report writing, presentations, intermediate Microsoft Office skills; working knowledge of property escrow and title process; good problem-solving skills

Special Requirements—Real estate sales license recommended or required in some states

Position Description

The Transaction Manager coordinates and manages commercial real estate transactions. He or she is responsible for the execution of all tasks related to the transactions of each project, through documentation, due diligence review, closing documents, and any post-closing obligations. The Transaction Manager acts as a liaison between the buyer and the seller to coordinate the processes necessary.

The manager prepares information for property listings through coordinating the final closing of a sale. The transaction manager coordinates the buyer's due diligence and closing processing, assembles the due diligence documents from the seller, and distributes this information to the buyer.

He or she coordinates transaction tasks related to real estate acquisitions and dispositions from letter of intent and purchase drafting agreement, title review, and escrow coordination, through to transaction closing. The manager oversees the due diligence review process to identify all issues that relate to underwriting standards, identifies potential problems, and communicates these issues to others on the management team.

The Transaction Manager reviews and negotiates changes to various documents, which may include confidentiality agreements, easements, etc., to minimize risk exposure.

The manager also prepares agendas, notices, and meeting minutes for distribution to executive boards, advisory boards, and investors. He or she prepares, recommends, and implements a transaction strategy for acquiring or disposing of property and monitors the portfolio for lease expirations.

This position coordinates with marketing and production staff for real estate offerings, marketing materials and proposals, and brochures. The manager also supervises the financial analyst staff, calculates sales value and listing value recommendations, conducts on-site inspection of each listing, abstracts loan documents and other legal documents, participates in marketing presentations to clients and to the public, etc. Typical duties performed may include the following:

- conducting weekly meetings to focus brokers on active listings, proposals, and leads
- assisting in developing and creating opportunities to achieve sales goals
- reading and analyzing business journals and government regulatory bulletins

The Transaction Manager works in an office setting, normally working a 40-hour workweek. However, the position requires occasional extended hours beyond the usual workweek during peak production periods.

Some travel to client sites and managed properties is required as a part of the job.

Salaries

There is a wide range of compensation, depending on how the Transaction Manager is compensated. This position can be either a salaried position or a commission-based position. If a salaried position, the Transaction Manager earns a base salary plus a percentage of commissions on deals closed. If the manager is paid entirely through sales commissions, he or she is usually treated as an independent contractor and receives no base salary or company-paid benefits. Annual earnings can range from $55,000 to $80,000 and up. Top performers can earn in excess of $100,000 annually.

Transaction Managers who receive a base salary plus commissions may also be entitled to a standard employee benefits package, including medical, dental, vision, life and short-term/long-term disability insurance, a flexible spending account, and 401(k) employee savings plan. Income usually increases as a Transaction Manager gains experience, but individual motivation, economic conditions, and the type and location of the property can also affect earnings.

Employment Prospects

Employment opportunities for commercial real estate Transaction Managers are generally very good because people with transaction skills are an essential part of the real estate management process. In addition to job growth, a large number of job openings will arise from the need to replace workers who transfer to other occupations or leave the labor force. Well-trained, ambitious people who enjoy selling—particularly those with extensive social and business connections in their communities—should have the best chance for success.

Advancement Prospects

As Transaction Managers gain knowledge and experience, they become more efficient in closing a greater number of transactions and can increase their earnings. In many large firms, an experienced manager can advance to become a full-fledged commercial real estate broker, sales manager, or general manager. Experienced managers with a thorough knowledge of business conditions and property values in their localities may enter mortgage financing or real estate investment counseling.

Education and Training

A strong financial background is normally a requirement. Most people entering this position have a four-year degree from a college or university with an accredited program in finance, real estate, business management, or a related field of study. College courses in real estate, finance, business administration, statistics, economics, law, and English are helpful. Advanced courses in mortgage financing, property development and management, and other subjects also are available. Many firms offer formal training programs for entry-level brokers and Transaction Managers. Larger firms usually offer more extensive in-house training programs.

Special Requirements

Some real estate firms want their Transaction Managers to have a state real estate sales license or have the capacity to get their license within a one- to two-year period after being hired. Most states require candidates for the general sales license to complete between 30 and 90 hours of classroom instruction. To get a broker's license, an individual needs between 60 and 90 hours of formal training and a specific amount of experience selling real estate, usually one to three years. Some states waive the experience requirements for the broker's license for applicants who have a bachelor's degree in real estate.

Experience, Skills, and Personality Traits

Prior experience in commercial real estate transactions is essential. Most employers want to see candidates with at least five years' experience in financial analysis and an extensive knowledge of the real estate due diligence process—the up-front fact checking that precedes a real estate acquisition or sale. Candidates who have a fluent knowledge of finance, real estate documents, market practices, and a working knowledge of commercial real estate dynamics are preferred.

Transaction Managers should have exceptionally strong interpersonal skills, both verbal and written communication skills, and strong presentation skills and be fluent in Microsoft Word, Excel, and PowerPoint software. They should be conceptual thinkers with good analytical and problem-solving skills. Knowledge of specific market segments, such as multifamily, office, hotel, would be helpful if applying to a market-specific real estate management company.

Unions and Associations

The CCIM Institute and CoreNet Global, among other professional associations, offer many opportunities for Transaction Managers to maintain or upgrade their on-the-job skills. Continuing education courses are available through online courses or are offered at association-sponsored seminars.

Tips for Entry

1. Attend meetings of professional associations to meet industry professionals and learn about current opportunities. CoreNet Global's New York City chapter, for instance, has mentoring meetings for young professionals.

2. Check job boards on industry association Web sites for the latest opportunities in your area.

3. College alumni offices can be another source of job leads. Many offer free career counseling and job search assistance.

OTHER CAREERS RELATED TO REAL ESTATE

APPRAISER—RESIDENTIAL REAL ESTATE

Duties: Conducts on-site inspections of residential properties to estimate current market value; summarizes findings in a written appraisal report

Alternative Title: Staff Appraiser

Salary Range: $30,820 to $60,110

Employment Prospects: Excellent

Advancement Prospects: Good

Prerequisites:

Education or Training—Two-year or four-year degree required for state licensing after 2008

Experience—Six months to one year of experience assessing real estate

Special Skills and Personality Traits—Excellent analytical and computer skills; ability to gather and

CAREER LADDER

Residential Appraisal Coordinator

Residential Real Estate Appraiser

Appraiser Trainee

analyze facts and make valuation judgments based on past experience

Special Requirements—State licensing and continuing education required for certified appraisers and licensed appraisers

Position Description

Residential Real Estate Appraisers conduct on-site inspections of residential properties to determine their estimated market value, usually in connection with a mortgage loan application. Appraisals are also performed when an estimate of value is required for tax or insurance purposes, when a piece of property is offered for sale, or for other reasons. Appraisers usually conduct their on-site inspections alone and are expected to provide their own car.

Appraisers work for commercial banks, thrift institutions, insurance companies, and independent appraisal firms. Staff appraisers work for commercial banks, savings associations, and other financial institutions. About four out of ten appraisers work as self-employed independent contractors, collecting a portion of the appraisal fee for their work. Independent contractor appraisers often work more than a standard 40-hour workweek and may work evenings or weekends writing reports. On-site visits usually take place during the daytime hours and are arranged according to the client's schedule.

Residential property appraisers gather and analyze data on sales of comparable properties, legal descriptions, and land values to determine a fair market appraisal value. They may inspect properties under construction, inspect properties for casualty losses, and

inspect properties before and after a foreclosure action. They may recommend repair and rehabilitation work if necessary to bring mortgaged properties into conformance with local building codes.

Appraisers prepare reports based on their findings for use by lenders, investment officers, and others. Commercial bank appraisers submit their written reports to the bank's loan committee, which approves or declines commercial mortgage applications.

Duties typically performed include the following:

- performing on-site property inspections
- checking local real estate listings for reports of recent comparable property sales
- submitting reports on the physical condition of properties
- making recommendations for repairs or replacement of mechanical systems such as heating, plumbing, and air conditioning in commercial buildings.
- maintaining a basic knowledge of local real estate market conditions, construction expenses, and property improvement expenses
- reporting results of appraisal inspections to supervisors
- testifying in court as to the value of a piece of property

- researching public records of sales, leases, outstanding liens, and property tax assessments relating to an individual property
- supervising clerical staff

Appraisers spend much of their time out of the office visiting and inspecting properties. This is a good career path if you are attentive to details and like the challenge of handling multiple projects at the same time.

Salaries

Earnings of Residential Real Estate Appraisers vary according to experience, qualifications, and compensation plan. Staff appraisers employed by financial institutions are paid an annual salary, plus employer-paid vacation, health, and pension benefits. The median annual earnings for all appraisers was $43,390 in 2004, according to the Bureau of Labor Statistics. The middle 50 percent earned between $30,820 and $60,110.

Earnings of independent appraisers, who are paid commissions but don't collect a salary, are determined by their ability to produce reports on a production schedule. The more reports they write, the higher their potential annual income. Experienced independent fee appraisers typically perform two to three appraisals a day, and they can have annual earnings in the six-figure range. Independent appraisers (sometimes called fee-split appraisers) receive a portion of the appraisal fee that varies from 30 percent to 50 percent of the gross billings charged to clients. The split is determined by an appraiser's prior experience and their compensation plan. Employer-paid benefits such as paid vacation or health insurance reduce the independent appraiser's share of fee income from appraisal work.

Employment Prospects

There is growing demand for residential property appraisers. Opportunities in this field are expected to grow faster than for most occupations through 2014, according to the Bureau of Labor Statistics. Appraisal firms will often hire trainees with no prior experience when they cannot find experienced appraisers. Trainee appraisers go through a training period of six months to a year, taking courses toward their appraisal licenses during this period. After successful completion of their exams, trainees begin working as unsupervised appraisers.

Individuals entering the field may find employment opportunities somewhat better working as independent fee appraisers because commercial banks, insurance companies, and other financial institutions have been contracting out their appraisal work,

assigning appraisals on a case-by-case basis to reduce staffing needs.

The cyclical nature of the real estate market has a strong influence on demand for residential appraisers. Demand tends to increase during periods of peak loan origination, as in the 2003–05 period when low interest rates pushed mortgage originations to new heights, and falls off when new loan activity is weak.

Advancement Prospects

Advancement is usually to a management position. An experienced residential appraiser can advance to a supervisory position, examining the work of fee-paid appraisers as a review appraiser. Review appraisers also coordinate the work flow for a financial institution, if appraisal work is done in-house, or an appraisal agency. With additional experience, an appraiser could become chief appraiser, becoming responsible for directing appraisal policy and managing the appraisal staff. Appraisers who earn the industry's top certification, the Member—Appraisal Institute designation from the Appraisal Institute, often leave an appraisal agency and set up their own independent appraisal agencies.

Education and Training

A two-year degree or four-year college degree with courses in business, finance, or a related field is recommended. While there is no required academic background, college-level courses in finance, accounting, and related fields are said to be very useful. Individuals entering this position must successfully complete a series of qualifying state licensing exams. Starting in 2008, appraisers taking their state licensing exams are expected to have completed a certain number of core college-level courses in finance, economics, or related studies before taking their state licensing exams. They must also complete 16 hours of continuing education courses annually to maintain their licenses.

Special Requirements

State licensing is a requirement in most states for both licensed residential property appraisers and certified residential real property appraisers. Certification is issued after the individual completes a series of qualifying exams.

Experience, Skills, and Personality Traits

This position requires the ability to gather and analyze factual information, read blueprints and architectural drawings, and perform mathematical calculations. Appraisers need strong quantitative measurement skills, analytical skills, and computer skills. They need to make valuation estimates and judgments based on previous real estate experience and become familiar with the Uniform Standards of Professional Appraisal Practice, or USPAP, a set of guidelines set by the Appraisal Standards Board. Appraisers must also be alert to minor details such as unusual activity or deterioration in maintenance that could adversely affect the resale value of property pledged as loan collateral. As they spend much of their day working directly with clients, appraisers also need be able to work independently with minimal supervision.

Unions and Associations

Real estate appraisers often join professional associations to maintain their license or certification through association-sponsored continuing education courses. Associations also provide ample networking opportunities. Appraisers can become members of the American Institute of Real Estate Appraisers (the Appraisal Institute), the Society of Real Estate Appraisers, and the American Society of Appraisers. Certifications available to appraisers are the Master Certified Appraiser from the Appraisal Institute and the Certified International Property Specialist.

Tips for Entry

1. Contact fee-based appraisal firms in your community and offer your assistance as a trainee while learning the appraisal business.
2. Contact banks and other financial institutions to determine if they hire appraisers or have any staff openings.
3. Read up on real estate trends in trade journals such as *Appraisal Today*.
4. Summer employment or part-time employment in a bank mortgage department or the investment department in an insurance company may also be helpful.

APPRAISER—COMMERCIAL REAL ESTATE

CAREER PROFILE

Duties: Estimates market value of commercial, industrial, office, and other income-producing properties

Alternate Title(s): Valuation Appraiser

Salary Range: $50,000 to $90,000 and up

Employment Prospects: Excellent

Advancement Prospects: Good

Prerequisites:

Education or Training—Some college courses required for licensing, four-year degree optional

Experience—One to two years' supervised experience

Special Skills and Personality Traits—Good analytical skills; strong communication skills; working

CAREER LADDER

Appraisal Manager

Commercial Appraiser

Commercial Appraiser Trainee

knowledge of Uniform Standards of Real Estate Professional Appraisal Procedures (USPAP)

Special Requirements—State license required in all 50 states

Position Description

Commercial Real Estate Appraisers give valuation estimates for all types of income-producing property. Some even appraise single-family residences, but the bulk of their work is commercial appraisals. Most commercial property appraisals are in the form of narrative reports, rather than the form reports commonly used in residential appraisals. The commercial property analysis emphasizes the financial benefits of ownership. Appraisers estimate a property's potential return on investment by performing a discounted cash flow analysis, a mathematical computation that reduces (or discounts) the expected future rental income stream to its present value, factoring in the investor's cost of borrowing.

Commercial appraisers work for independent appraisal firms, banks, and insurance companies. Independent appraisers, also known as fee appraisers because they are paid a percentage of the appraisal fee, perform appraisals for real estate management companies and real estate investors. Bank appraisers, sometimes known as staff appraisers, evaluate property to determine its collateral value when pledged as security for a bank loan. Insurance appraisers determine the replacement cost for commercial properties and their contents.

Appraisers also provide opinions in litigation cases, tax matters, and investment decisions. Very few appraisals by commercial appraisers are associated with property sales. About two-thirds are associated with loans, and the rest are done for litigation support, estates, tax issues, and inquiries from government agencies and a wide variety of other purposes.

Commercial property appraisers typically work a 40- to 50-hour workweek. They spend much of their time out of the office visiting and inspecting properties. This is a good career choice if you are analytical, are attentive to details, and like the challenge of handling complex projects and meeting production deadlines.

Salaries

Commercial appraisers generally work on a fee-split basis, much like residential appraisers. This fee split generally ranges between 30 percent and 50 percent, depending on the amount of support given by the senior appraiser or appraisal firm and the amount contributed by the junior appraiser. Potential earnings of commercial appraisers can vary widely and are determined by variables such as local competition, competency, areas of expertise, marketing expertise, and the amount of time and energy appraisers are willing to commit to their appraisal careers.

Commercial appraisers have higher earnings than residential appraisers, which compensates for their specialized skills. Annual earnings can range from $50,000 to $90,000 and up. At the high end of the earnings scale, commercial appraisers can potentially earn up to $150,000 in gross revenue per year.

Employment Prospects

There is a shortage of experienced Commercial Real Estate Appraisers, due partly to the education and extended on-the-job training requirements. While there is growing demand for qualified commercial property appraisers, getting that first job is the hardest part of becoming an appraiser. The U.S. Bureau of Labor Statistics estimates demand for appraisers will outpace market demand for all other occupations through 2014.

Market demand for commercial appraisers tends to follow the peaks and valleys of the real estate market. The cyclical nature of the real estate market has a strong influence on employment opportunities. Hiring of new appraisers may slow down during periods of slack economic activity, but experienced appraisers will have little trouble finding work.

Advancement Prospects

Commercial appraisers advance by taking positions of more responsibility, supervising a group of appraisers. Another advancement possibility is review appraising. Financial institutions or government agencies employ review appraisers to review the work of fee-paid appraisers. This function is considered an important part of risk management for the financial institution or agency. There are opportunities for review appraisers who have both commercial and residential appraisal backgrounds.

An appraisal background can also be helpful in related careers. Appraisers who become mortgage brokers, real estate lenders, and real estate brokers bring special expertise to these positions. Also, financial analysts with appraisal training who work in bank lending have a competitive advantage in the job market. Advancement usually requires earning an industry-recognized professional certification, such as Member—Appraisal Institute (MAI) or the Accredited Senior Appraiser designation.

Education and Training

Each state sets its own education and training requirements for property appraisers. These entry requirements typically include taking a certain number of college courses. Before 2008, there were minimal educational requirements to becoming an appraiser. Appraisers were required to do a certain number of appraisals during their first year of employment under the supervision of a more experienced appraiser. Most appraisers are compensated for training during this apprenticeship period. After January 2008, the educational requirement—the number of classroom hours—was increased by approximately 50 percent. Due to the more stringent education requirements, appraiser candidates will have to take more college-level courses to become certified property appraisers. The Appraisal Foundation's Web site (http://www.appraisalfoundation.org) has a searchable database of appraisal schools and colleges offering educational courses approved by the Appraisal Qualifications Board, an independent board of the Appraisal Foundation.

Special Requirements

State licensing is required in all 50 states. State regulations require 2000 hours of supervised employment and passing a licensing exam before becoming licensed.

Experience, Skills, and Personality Traits

Commercial appraisers rely on their experience and judgment to estimate fair market value of potential investment properties or their collateral value when pledged to secure a bank loan. Trainee appraisers typically gain this experience during their apprenticeship period which begins shortly after being hired.

Gathering and analyzing factual information, reading blueprints and architectural drawings, and performing mathematical calculations are important skills in appraisal work. Appraisers have to make valuation estimates and judgments based on previous real estate experience. Appraisers must also be alert to minor details, such as unusual activity or deterioration in maintenance that could adversely affect the resale value of property pledged as loan collateral.

Unions and Associations

Commercial Real Estate Appraisers can join one or more professional associations. Appraisers can become members of the American Institute of Real Estate Appraisers (the Appraisal Institute), the Society of Real Estate Appraisers, and the American Society of Appraisers. Certifications available to appraisers are the Master Certified Appraiser from the Appraisal Institute and the Certified International Property Specialist.

Tips for Entry

1. Finding an experienced appraiser willing to teach you the appraisal profession is an important part of the process of gaining entry. The Appraisal Institute is promoting a mentor program for individuals interested in a career in appraising. Check local AI chapters to find a mentor in your area.

2. Appraisal firms will often advertise trainee positions on trade association Web sites. The Appraisal Institute's job bank (www.appraisalinstitute.org) lists some current openings.

3. As with other real estate jobs, getting known by people who are in a position to help is crucial to landing that first job. Attend AI seminars and quarterly meetings of local chapters to meet experienced appraisers.

4. Consider working with your county assessor's office or state transportation department to gain experience in appraisal-related work and get through the supervised employment requirement.

ARCHITECT

Duties: Develops new designs and structures; oversees project design and space requirements; consults with project developer, construction contractor, and others

Alternate Title(s): Licensed Architect

Salary Range: $46,700 and $79,000

Employment Prospects: Good

Advancement Prospects: Good

Prerequisites:

 Education or Training—Five-year degree in architecture

 Experience—At least three years' apprenticeship training

 Special Skills and Personality Traits—Strong conceptual skills; effective verbal and written communication skills

 Special Requirements—Licensing required in all states and the District of Columbia

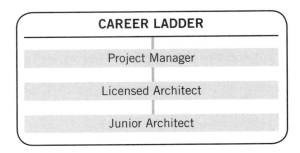

CAREER LADDER

Project Manager

Licensed Architect

Junior Architect

Position Description

Architects develop plans for development of new structures or dwelling units, and they create new designs for existing structures, using information provided by the client. Their duties require specific skills—designing, engineering, managing, supervising, and communicating with clients and builders. Architects design a wide variety of buildings, such as office and apartment buildings, schools, churches, factories, hospitals, houses, and airport terminals. They also design complexes such as urban centers, college campuses, industrial parks, and entire communities. They may advise on the selection of building sites, prepare cost analysis or land-use studies, and do long-range planning for land development.

An Architect typically begins a project with a client meeting to determine what components or spaces the client or project investors want in their project. Following this meeting, the Architect examines the building location, or in the case of an existing building, the Architect will take photographs and measurements of the building. The key to being a successful Architect is good planning and an understanding of what can and cannot be done because of environmental conditions, cost restrictions, budget limitations, or the expectations of the client.

Once the Architect has seen the physical space, he or she can begin developing proposals based on the information gathered. Written proposals are converted into architectural drawings or renderings, using computer assisted drafting software, and plans are reviewed with

the client. Many new computer programs actually allow creation of a three-dimensional model of the building or space to be created. The architect then facilitates obtaining of building codes and permits and works closely with the developer and construction supervisor to ensure the building is completed according to plan. Architects who own their own firms are more likely to be involved in total construction of the project than Architects who work for a large firm. Most Architects working in a large firm have minimal involvement in the actual construction phase after approval of the initial design.

Architects sometimes specialize in one phase of work. Some specialize in the design of one type of building—for example, hospitals, schools, or housing. Others focus on planning and pre-design services or construction management and do minimal design work.

Newly hired Architects can expect to spend much of their time researching zoning regulations, building codes, and legal filings and building models while supervised by a more experienced Architect. Successful Architects spend much of their day communicating their ideas to others; they must be able to communicate their unique vision persuasively.

Architects may be involved in all phases of development, from the initial discussion with the client through the entire construction process—obtaining construction bids, selecting contractors, and negotiating construction contracts. As construction proceeds, they may visit building sites to make sure that contractors follow the design, adhere to the schedule, use the specified materials, and meet work quality standards. The job is not complete until all construction is finished, required tests are conducted, and construction costs are paid. Sometimes, Architects also provide post-construction services, such as facilities management. They advise on energy efficiency measures, evaluate how well the building design adapts to the needs of occupants, and make necessary improvements.

Common work activities typically include:

- speaking with clients to determine their needs and requirements for a project
- traveling to various sites to conduct physical inspections and site surveys
- working with various computer programs to create floor plans and building designs
- meeting with clients to review proposals and make revisions as needed
- working with contractors and construction managers to obtain building permits and answer questions regarding the architectural plan
- finding solutions to construction problems when they arise, averting project delays

Architects work in an office setting, consulting with clients, developing reports and drawings. They periodically visit construction sites to review progress and consult with construction managers. While most Architects work a 40-hour week, they may have to work evenings and weekends to meet a contract delivery deadline.

Salaries

Practicing Architects earned between $46,690 and $79,230 in 2004, according to the U.S. Bureau of Labor Statistics. The top 10 percent of Architects earned more than $99,000 annually, and Architects well known in their field can earn in excess of $250,000 annually. Those just beginning their internship period can expect to earn salaries well below the industry average. Self-employed Architects set their fees based on several conditions, such as overhead expenses and local market competition.

Employment Prospects

The market for practicing Architects is competitive. New graduates will face competition if setting their sights on landing a job at a prestigious firm. Entry opportunities are best for individuals who have experience working for a firm while still in college and those who have specialized knowledge, such as computer-aided design and drafting. The U.S. Bureau of Labor

Statistics says employment opportunities for Architects will grow about as fast as job opportunities in all occupations through 2014.

Some job openings will come about as intermediate-level designers leave architectural firms to set up their own practices. Architects who have four to seven years' experience and the ability to step into intermediate or senior designer positions are likely to find work more easily.

Many architectural firms specialize in specific buildings, such as hospitals, retail shopping malls, and office buildings. Demand for new construction in these sectors can vary from one region to another, which will have an impact on job opportunities. Several fields in architecture are expected to gain stature over the next several years, offering above average job opportunities: interior architecture and space planning, building renovation and restoration, and low-cost multi-family housing.

Advancement Prospects

The typical line of advancement is from junior to intermediate designer, senior designer, or project director, and eventually to managing director or partner in the firm. Some senior architects prefer the challenges of creative design work, and opt to stay out of the management track. Many Architects choose to become self-employed, establishing their own practices. About one in four Architects in the United States is self-employed.

Education and Training

A four-year degree or five-year degree is the minimum educational background. There are several types of professional degrees in architecture, according to the National Architectural Accrediting Board. The primary degree programs are these three: a five-year Bachelor of Architecture program for students entering from high school or who have no architectural training; a two-year Master of Architecture program for those with college degrees in architecture or a related field (engineering, landscape architecture, etc.); and a three-year or four-year Master of Architecture program for students with a degree in another discipline.

New graduates typically spend the first three years of employment as intern architects under the supervision of a registered, practicing Architect. Architecture students who complete an internship program while still in school may have the option of counting some of that time toward the three-year training period.

Special Requirements

All states and the District of Columbia require individuals to be licensed before they may call themselves

Architects or provide architectural services for a fee. Licensing requirements generally include a professional degree in architecture from an accredited college or university, at least three years practical work experience, and passing all nine divisions of the Architect Registration Examination (ARE). Individuals who pass the ARE and meet all requirements of their state's licensing board become licensed to practice in that state. Also, most states require some form of continuing education to maintain an architectural license.

Experience, Skills, and Personality Traits

An ability to visually depict information is an essential job skill. Artistic and drawing ability are useful, but more important is knowing how to conceptualize ideas and spacial relationships. Because Architects spend much of their time selling their ideas to clients, effective written and verbal communication skills are important skills. Also useful are good computer skills and a working knowledge of computer-aided design.

Unions and Associations

The American Institute of Architects is the professional trade association for licensed Architects. The association sponsors numerous educational programs for continuing education and career advancement.

Tips for Entry

1. Use all possible resources to get employment: faculty references, school placement offices, campus job fairs, and direct contacts with employers.
2. Attend educational and networking meetings of the American Institute of Architects to make personal contacts with potential employers.
3. While in high school take courses in mathematics, drawing, drafting, and computer science.
4. Look into internship opportunities while still in college and compile a representative portfolio, including designs and sketches, of your recent work.

ASSESSOR

Duties: Determines taxable value of real estate; assesses taxes in accordance with prescribed schedules

Alternate Title(s): Tax Assessor

Salary Range: $31,000 to $60,000

Employment Prospects: Excellent

Advancement Prospects: Good

Prerequisites:

    Education or Training—Four-year degree in economics, finance, or real estate

    Experience—One to three years

    Special Skills and Personality Traits—Good analytical skills, good mathematical skills, computer

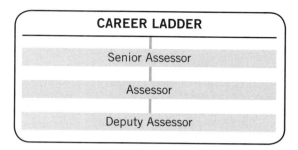

CAREER LADDER

Senior Assessor

Assessor

Deputy Assessor

skills, and research skills; facility with property appraisal software

    Special Requirements—State licensing (certification) required in most states

Position Description

Assessors of real estate estimate the value of real property to determine ad valorem property taxes payable to a municipality or local taxing authority. They may be asked to determine the value of any type of real estate, although they often specialize in valuing specific property types such as residential properties or commercial properties and office buildings.

Assessors work for local governments and have the duty of valuing properties so a tax formula can be used to assess property values. In most communities, the entire community must be re-valued periodically, usually once every 10 years, or more frequently if more frequent reassessments are required by state statutes.

Assessors employ valuation methods very similar to those used by property appraisers. Assessors take notice of any unique characteristics of the property, such as architectural style or the condition of the roof, and any recent renovations that may increase its estimated value for taxing purposes. They may take photographs to document certain features or visit the property and conduct a personal inspection. In determining the property's fair market value, Assessors take into consideration such things as comparable property sales, previous appraisals, and income potential.

Assessors write a detailed report of each property valuation, often using laptop computers and computer models. Assessors may employ a computer-programmed automated valuation model (AVM)

specifically developed for their assigned jurisdictions. Other computer-aided technologies impacting this occupation are electronic maps of a specific locality and its property distribution and digital cameras, which are frequently used to document specific features of a property. Assessors summarize their findings in a detailed report, stating the value of the property and the methodology used in determining that value.

Duties performed by Assessors typically include the following:

- inspecting properties and determining appraisal value, taking into account fair market value, location, and replacement cost
- identifying the ownership of each piece of taxable property
- issuing notices of assessments and taxes
- completing and maintaining assessment rolls that show the assessed values and status of all property located in a municipality
- determining taxability and values of property using various methods such as field inspection, market trend studies, income and expense analysis
- inspecting new construction and major improvements to existing structures to determine values
- explaining assessed values to property owners
- defending appealed assessments at public hearings
- preparing and maintaining current data on each property assessed, listing maps of boundaries, property characteristics, and any applicable exemptions

- conducting periodic reviews of properties within jurisdictions to determine changes in property due to construction or demolition
- reviewing information about transfers of property to ensure accuracy and making corrections as needed

Assessors usually work a standard 40-hour work-week. Their work schedule occasionally includes working evenings, as when presenting their findings of a property reassessment at a public hearing or answering taxpayer questions about their property's assessed value.

Salaries

Earnings vary according to experience and duties performed. Annual earnings of real estate Assessors ranged from $31,000 to $60,000 in 2006, according to the U.S. Bureau of Labor Statistics. Median annual earnings of Assessors employed by local governments were $38,940 in 2006. Assessors working in supervisory positions or in specialty occupations, such as commercial property assessments, typically earn higher salaries. Geographic location also has an impact on earnings; Assessors working in coastal and urban areas generally earn more than those employed in rural areas.

Employment Prospects

Employment opportunities for real estate Assessors are expected to rise faster then opportunities in all occupations through 2014. There is good demand for Assessors in most states. Assessors are impacted by fluctuations in the economy and real estate market to a lesser degree than other real estate occupations because qualified Assessors are needed in every municipality and taxing district for property tax purposes. While the field is still growing, experience requirements will limit the number of opportunities for recent college graduates. People entering the field directly from college will need to find a trainee position, where they can learn the profession under the supervision of a more experienced Assessor.

Advancement Prospects

Advancement is typically by gaining on-the-job experience and moving into more senior positions, such as assessor supervisor, or taking on more complex and challenging property valuations. Assessors who attain a passing grade on qualifying exams or earn an advanced certification can move into more senior, higher paying positions, such as senior assessor or personal property supervisor.

Education and Training

There are no formal education requirements to become an Assessor. Most applicants have four-year degrees in economics, finance, or real estate. Qualifications are set by state assessor boards, which determine the basic entry requirements. Assessors need to have the same education background as property appraisers, and they usually take the same college courses.

Assessors usually go through a training period of about a year under the supervision of a more experienced Assessor. Assessor candidates must also work a certain number of hours in a tax assessor's office and pass a written examination. Assessors are required to follow the Uniform Standards of Professional Appraisal (USPAP) standards in some states and are strongly encouraged to use these standards in most other states. Most Assessors also have a state appraisal license. On-the-job training is an essential part of becoming a fully qualified Assessor and is required for obtaining state licensing or certification.

Special Requirements

Most states require licensing by a state licensing or certification board that determines competency standards for property Assessors. Professional certification by a state board of assessors is often a condition of employment, ensuring that Assessors maintain certain competency standards. State laws in many states may require that a municipality's grand list of taxable properties be signed by a certified Assessor. Background checks may also be required, depending on the jurisdiction.

Most states have a voluntary certification program and continuing education (or recertification) for tax assessors. Assessors are required to complete a certain number of approved courses or workshops during the time period when their certifications are valid.

Certifications are typically valid for a five-year period. Individuals involved in the assessment field who have yet to complete the necessary education and experience requirements, or who do not intend to become state certified, can earn an Administrative Assessment Technician (AAT) designation in most states.

Experience, Skills, and Personality Traits

Assessors should have good analytical skills, good mathematical skills, computer skills, and research skills. It is also helpful to have some working knowledge of property appraisal software such as MicroSolve CAMA (Computer Assisted Mass Appraisal) and database application programs commonly used on property assessments. Some on-the-job experience with work done by Assessors is becoming a requirement.

Individuals can get qualifying experience by working in an Assessor's office, a property appraisal firm, or for a fee appraiser.

Unions and Associations

Many Assessors become members of a regionally or nationally recognized association and earn a professional designation. Designations are very useful in states where a license is not mandatory or a certificate program has not been established. The International Association of Assessing Officers (http://www.iaao.org) sponsors professional education programs for assessment officers. Earning a professional designation offers tangible and intangible benefits, which may include a salary increase or additional responsibilities. The association's professional development program has five professional designations: Assessment Administration Specialist (AA), Certified Assessment Evaluator (CAE), Cadastral Mapping Specialist (CMS), Personal Property Specialist (PPS), and Residential Evaluation Specialist (RES).

Tips for Entry

1. Get experience working in an Assessor's office as summer employee while in college.
2. The International Association of Assessor Officers (IAAO) has scholarship funding to help Assessors get to educational conferences and improve their job skills.
3. The IAAO annual conference and seminars provide platforms to discover best practices and learn from expert colleagues about the latest research in the field of property appraisal.

HOME INSPECTOR

Position Description

Home Inspectors make visual inspections of newly built or existing homes, reporting on the condition of a home's systems, components, and structure. A Home Inspector is charged with ensuring that homes in a local jurisdiction comply with all local building codes. Home Inspectors depend on referrals from real estate agents or building contractors for most of their business, which puts a premium on marketing to real estate agents in the local community. Home inspections can be done at any time, but are most often performed when a property is offered for sale.

A home inspection is a thorough analysis of any element of the home considered a permanent feature. An inspector may spend a few hours going through a home or the better part of the day, depending on the size of the home and its condition. Inspectors begin their work with a careful examination of the core structure of a house—the foundation and basement area—to look for cracks in the flooring, seepage indicating excessive ground water, presence of mold, or any weakened structural support.

Next, a Home Inspector surveys the condition of interior mechanical systems, including electrical, plumbing, heating, and air conditioning. Inspectors check for the presence of any code-required safety devices such as smoke detectors. Storage areas, including attics, windows, and ceilings are checked to make sure they are in good condition. Finally, the Home Inspector examines the exterior structure—roof, siding, and other areas—to look signs of wear. They look for proper roof flashing and drainage via gutters and down-spouts. They check the condition of any other buildings on the property such as garages or storage sheds.

Home Inspectors may be licensed to perform other inspections, including termite inspections, radon testing, and specialty inspections (pool, roof, well, and others). Home Inspectors use moisture meters, pressure meters, electrical meters, and other investigative tools and techniques to determine soundness and viability of a structure and its mechanical systems. Home Inspectors summarize their findings in a written report, usually a form report generated from a computer.

A home inspection helps buyers understand the condition of the property they are purchasing. The seller of a home might order an inspection to get an accurate assessment of its condition and head off any potential lawsuits from failure to disclose existing problems or defects prior to its sale.

Home Inspectors do much of their work on-site, as arranged with clients. They work flexible hours, usually working 35 to 40 hours a week. They may need to work evenings and weekends. During the height of the real estate season, the working day can be long—up to 14 hours. Generally, it takes three to four hours to complete a residential inspection. Inspectors may work independently as self-employed contractors or as employees of an inspection company.

Salaries

Home Inspectors are self-employed independent contractors, so earnings depend on how much work you do, how actively you market your services, and how much you charge for an inspection. Home Inspectors can earn between $30,000 and $42,000 after two to three years in business. In major markets, inspectors can earn $70,000 or more, the National Association of Home Inspectors estimates.

Home Inspectors may be paid a salary or a commission calculated as a percentage of the home inspection fee. Inspectors who are paid a percentage of the fee are paid only on inspections performed. Most inspectors are compensated on a commission basis. Home Inspectors working for a licensed home inspection company may also get paid vacations, company-paid health insurance, sick leave, and vacations.

Employment Prospects

The employment outlook is exceptionally good for Home Inspectors. The U.S. Department of Labor predicts that jobs for Home Inspectors will grow 14 percent by 2014, or faster than the growth rate for all occupations. Higher energy costs and home prices also play a role. There is steadily increasing market demand for Home Inspectors familiar with energy saving (or green design) heating and cooling systems. According to real estate industry experts, more than 90 percent of homes sold in major markets are professionally inspected, up from only 5 percent in 1980. The National Association of Realtors estimates the home inspection industry may top $1 billion within the next few years.

Home Inspectors can find employment opportunities with a licensed home inspection company doing business in their area. Franchise opportunities with a national home inspection company are also available.

Advancement Prospects

There are several advancement paths. After a few years' experience, Home Inspectors can open their own home inspection businesses and hire other inspectors. Home Inspectors who prefer to work independently can advance their careers by learning how to do inspections requiring specialized knowledge, such as inspections of multifamily properties or commercial property inspections.

Education and Training

Home Inspectors are always learning, regardless of how many years they have been in the business. A high school diploma is a foundation requirement, but having a diploma is only the first step. Home Inspectors have to constantly upgrade their knowledge to stay current with the latest innovations and techniques in home construction. Getting an industry certification from a professional association demonstrates profes-

sional competency and is a key step toward a successful career as a Home Inspector. Home Inspectors who have earned an industry certification must take a certain number of continuing education courses each year to maintain their skills.

Special Requirements

A state license is required in most states. After passing a written examination, inspectors can work for a licensed home inspection company or open their own businesses and hire other Home Inspectors. Inspectors must perform or participate in a specified number of home inspections (typically about 250 inspections) in most states before being certified. Check with your state's licensing board to learn more about specific requirements for Home Inspectors.

Experience, Skills, and Personality Traits

Home Inspectors have to be detail-oriented and have a working knowledge of electrical, plumbing, heating, and air conditioning systems commonly used in residential construction. You should have an interest in construction techniques, an ability to communicate well, and good time management skills. Managing your work schedule is important because earnings are largely determined by the number of reports an inspector can produce during the workweek.

Unions and Associations

Professional organizations have educational programs to help Home Inspectors maintain their skills, along with inspections standards and professional codes of conduct that will help inspectors entering the field become more professional.

Home inspectors can become members of several professional associations to maintain their job skills and stay current with trends in home construction. Among these are American Society of Home Inspectors, the National Association of Home Inspectors, and the National Association of Certified Home Inspectors. Most have local chapters that sponsor networking events. A list of available industry certifications can be found in Appendix III.

Tips for Entry

1. Take courses in business, mechanical drafting, and related subjects in high school.
2. Apply directly to home inspection companies in your area.
3. If you enjoy learning how things work and like working independently, home inspection can be the career for you.

LANDSCAPE ARCHITECT

CAREER PROFILE

Duties: Designs and plans outdoor spaces; prepares drawings and cost estimates; prepares environmental impact reports or statements

Alternate Title(s): None

Salary Range: $40,900 to $70,400

Employment Prospects: Excellent

Advancement Prospects: Good

Prerequisites:

    Education or Training—Four-year degree or master's degree in landscape architecture

    Experience—One to four years' experience required for state license

    Special Skills and Personality Traits—Strong conceptual skills or ability to visualize spatial rela-

tionships; good communication and marketing skills

    Special Requirements—State licensing required in 47 states

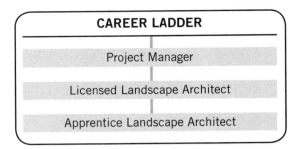

CAREER LADDER

Project Manager

Licensed Landscape Architect

Apprentice Landscape Architect

Position Description

Landscape Architects design and plan outdoor spaces. They plan the overall design for a wide range of outdoor projects, including industrial and office parks, residential subdivisions, parks, and recreational areas. Their work falls into the general categories of site design and planning, environmental planning, and land and natural resource management.

Landscape Architects work for many different types of organizations—from architectural and design firms to real estate development organizations. Architectural, engineering, and related professional services employ more Landscape Architects than any other group of industries.

Landscape Architects who design areas of land to protect the environment or to improve the landscape in an environmentally friendly way are known as environmental landscape architects. The landscaping may be completed for homeowners, companies, or government agencies. An environmental landscape architect researches the various soil types, animals, and birds that are in a designated environmentally sensitive area.

The work of the environmental landscape architect starts with meeting the various interested groups—local planning and zoning agencies, environmental groups, federal and state environmental protection agencies—and determining the best options for the project. A summary report of the environmental impact and potential benefits of the project is then written. A blueprint of

the proposed landscaping is developed based on the preliminary research. The Landscape Architect again meets with the various groups for project approval. Any revisions to the master plan are completed before the project is finalized. Working with diverse groups, organizing and chairing meetings, and communicating effectively are all requirements of the profession.

Among their duties, Landscape Architects may:

- create preliminary designs and site plans showing grading and drainage
- research various land types, animals, plants, and other living organisms in the area to be landscaped
- develop a landscape plan based on the requirements of the client, public, or private interest groups and the needs of animals and plants in the project site
- prepare models, sketches, diagrams, and other graphic aids
- meet with the interested parties to report on a landscaping plan and any environmental impact of the plan
- prepare working drawings and cost estimates
- observe construction and new planting so that work is completed according to design specifications
- prepare environmental impact statements or reports on projects that may significantly alter the environment
- provide written evaluations of various plan alternatives and make recommendations to the client

Many Landscape Architects do some residential work, but most practicing architects try to diversify their business to a mix of commercial and multi-unit residential projects. Landscape Architects who work for government agencies prepare environmental impact statements and studies on land use planning. Increasingly, Landscape Architects have been involved in environmental remediation projects, such as preservation and restoration of wetlands or abatement of storm water runoff in new developments. Historic preservation projects in older neighborhoods are another business opportunity for Landscape Architects.

Landscape Architects spend much of their time working in offices, preparing designs and cost estimates. The remainder of their time is spent on-site, verifying design plans or supervising construction. Salaried Landscape Architects usually work a 40-hour week, but they may work overtime to meet a project deadline. Hours of self-employed architects vary according to the demands of projects they are working on.

Salaries

Median annual earnings of Landscape Architects were $53,120 in 2004, according to the U.S. Bureau of Labor Statistics. The middle 50 percent earned between $40,930 and $70,400, while top earners—the highest 10 percent—earned more than $90,000. Because many Landscape Architects are self-employed, their fringe benefits are often less generous than benefits provided to workers in larger organizations.

Employment Prospects

Employment opportunities for Landscape Architects are expected to grow at a faster than average rate for all occupations through 2014. Public interest in improving quality of life, historic preservation, and conservation-oriented development will help keep Landscape Architects in demand. Landscape Architects can work on several different projects at the same time, which means they are buffered to some degree from the cyclical employment in the construction and real estate industries.

Employers generally prefer hiring entry-level Landscape Architects who have some internship experience, which significantly reduces the amount of on-the-job training required. New graduates may find the best opportunities are for Landscape Architects who have strong technical skills—such as computer design, good communication skills, and some knowledge of environmental codes and regulations.

Advancement Prospects

Landscape Architects begin their careers as junior designers or apprentice designers. The typical advancement path, after several years' experience, is to intermediate designer, senior designer, or project manager. Some Landscape Architects will become principals in the firms where they work. Others start their own landscape design and consulting firms. Nearly one in four Landscape Architects are self-employed.

Education and Training

A four-year degree or master's degree is usually required. According to the American Society of Landscape Architects, there are two types of undergraduate professional degrees: a Bachelor of Landscape Architecture (B.L.A.) and a Bachelor of Science in Landscape Architecture (B.S.L.A.). There are generally three types of graduate degree programs: a master's degree for those who have an undergraduate degree in landscape architecture or another field; a Master of Arts (M.A.) or master's of science (M.S.) degree for those who want to conduct research but do not want to become practicing architects. Individuals who have had training or prior experience in urban planning can increase their employment opportunities at architectural firms that specialize in site planning as well as landscape design.

Special Requirements

State licensing or registration is required in 47 states. Becoming licensed generally requires having a professional degree, passing a national licensing exam, and in some states, completing a period of supervised practice. Licensing requirements are not uniform, which means registration in one state may not be easily transferable to another. However, those who graduate from an accredited college, serve three years of internship supervised by a registered Landscape Architect, and attain a passing grade on the Landscape Architect Registration Examination, can meet the licensing requirements in most states.

Experience, Skills, and Personality Traits

Landscape Architects should be creative and analytical, able to visualize spatial relationships. Communication and marketing skills are important because they must sell or promote their services to win business from clients. Architects with excellent drafting and design skills, a good educational background, practical experience, and good marketing skills have the best opportunities for finding work.

Unions and Associations

The American Society of Landscape Architects (http://www.asla.org) is the organization representing professional Landscape Architects in the United States. The association sponsors conferences and online continuing education courses to help Landscape Architects stay abreast of developments in the field. (Most states require continuing education courses as a condition of maintaining state licensure.) Union membership is available to Landscape Architects who work for government agencies.

Tips for Entry

1. The career resources page on the American Society of Landscape Architects Web site is a good place to start your career search. The ASLA Web site lists accredited colleges and state licensing requirements, plus it has a searchable database of currently available positions.
2. Another career Web site, http://www.archcareers.com, is a good source of employment opportunities for architects.
3. Compile a well-organized portfolio of recent designs and drawings to present during job interviews.
4. Check yellow pages of directory listings for architectural firms in your area. Direct application to employers is one of the most effective job search methods.

REAL ESTATE ATTORNEY

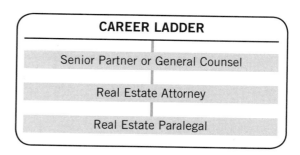
Position Description

Real Estate Attorneys handle all real estate–related legal issues, including transfers of titles and deeds, mortgages, and zoning. They provide legal advice to clients, business partners, and property owners. They prepare resolutions and legal documents. They represent clients in major legal actions.

In general, attorneys advise clients as to their legal rights and obligations, and they act as the client's advocate in a court of law or in negotiation proceedings. An attorney's duty to the client is to interpret case law (legal precedents) and the relevance of specific precedents to current issues. This requires researching previously applied laws handed down in judicial decisions called precedence. Attorneys also interpret statutes to business transactions such as a sale of property. Most attorneys starting their careers spend the greater part of their time researching case law and writing court briefs (official court documents). They may also interview clients in their office or at the client's home or office.

Some states permit Real Estate Attorneys to buy or sell property, acting as real estate agents or brokers. New York allows licensed attorneys to become real estate brokers without taking any exam. The use of a real estate broker is not a requirement for the sale of real estate or for obtaining a mortgage loan from a lender. However, once a broker is used, the settlement attorney or the party handling the closing will ensure that all parties involved be paid.

The normal workweek varies with an attorney's caseload. Attorneys frequently work more than a standard 40-hour workweek and may work evenings and weekends. Attorneys work under intense pressure to meet filing deadlines, as when preparing for a court case or working on a major project. Staying current with developments in the field adds to the workload. Attorneys must keep up with the latest court decisions and other developments in their field of practice.

Salaries

A number of factors can influence earnings of attorneys. Compensation varies with the size and reputation of law firms and small practices, location of employment, type of practice, and client base. Attorneys with private firms can start from $35,000 to $85,000 annually and earn more than $100,000 after five years. Salaries for lawyers employed in real estate work, as reported by Salary.com, ranged from $93,700 to $133,000 in 2007. Salaries can increase dramatically for associate lawyers selected for the partner track in their firm. Some law firm partners and those in private practice can earn upward of $400,000 annually. Attorneys who elect to go off on their own and set up their own independent practices can be well compensated for their work, but they also pay their own office rent, employee salaries, and other expenses. New attorneys starting their own practices may earn little more than their expenses during the first years or may not break even at all during the start-up years of their law practice.

Employment Prospects

There are fairly good employment opportunities for practicing real estate lawyers, although finding that first job after admission to the state bar can be challenging. Employment of lawyers is expected to grow 11 percent during the 2006-16 decade, about as fast as the average for all occupations. Competition is very strong for associate positions in prestigious law firms. Graduates of top-ranked law schools who rank high in their class will have the best opportunities for employment with a prestigious law firm. Many attorneys will work at a number of firms before finding a position matching their interest and area of specialization.

Advancement Prospects

Most lawyers specialize in one or more segments of law after three to five years. Many find it hard to switch specialization after five years. Partner track associates can spend most of their time at the office. Others will decide to pursue work at smaller law firms or work as in-house corporate counsel for real estate development firms, investment firms, and property management firms, where the opportunities for promotion are better. Corporate attorneys may not earn as much as those who stay with a law firm and reach partner status.

Attorneys typically report to top legal counsel or general counsel. Advancement possibilities include senior attorney. Attorneys may set up their own law practices and practice general law in addition to real estate–related work. A law degree can be a springboard to another profession. Many start careers in business, accounting, academia, or other areas. About 30 percent of those who receive law degrees are not regularly practicing law 10 years after graduation from law school.

Education and Training

The basic requirement is a four-year degree and graduation from a law school accredited by the American Bar Association. (In 2005 there were 191 ABA-accredited U.S. law schools.) Admission to law school is competitive, more so for the elite schools than law schools affiliated with a state university system. A high score on the Law School Admission Test (LSAT) is preferred, cou-pled with a high grade point average. An undergraduate degree in philosophy, English, business, accounting, political science, or history may provide an adequate background for studying law. The law school curriculum includes classes in torts, contracts, constitutional law, property law, trusts, and estates. A Juris Doctor (J.D.) degree or Bachelor of Laws (L.L.B.) degree is given after graduation from law school. After graduation, lawyers have to stay abreast of legal or nonlegal developments through continuing education. Forty states and jurisdictions have mandatory continuing legal education (CLE) programs, administered by law schools and state bar associations. Some law graduates will continue their education by earning a Master of Law degree in taxation or another specialty area.

Special Requirements

Real Estate Attorneys have to pass the bar exam and be admitted to the state bar in the state where they intend to practice law. Before an attorney can practice law, he or she must pass a state bar exam, a two-day or three-day written examination that tests their knowledge of specific laws in the state where they intend to practice. Most states and the District of Columbia use the six-hour Multistate Bar Exam as part of the overall bar exam. Law candidates also have to pass a "character and fitness" oral examination (Multistate Performance Testing) in most states, an exam given after the bar exam to test the practical skills of beginning lawyers.

Experience, Skills, and Personality Traits

The practice of law involves a great deal of responsibility. Individuals planning careers in law should like to work with people and be able to win the respect and confidence of their clients, associates, and the public. Real Estate Attorneys spend much of their day meeting with clients, either in person or by telephone. They should have excellent verbal and written communication skills. Perseverance, creativity, and reasoning ability also are essential to lawyers, who often analyze complex cases and handle new and unique legal problems.

Unions and Associations

Real Estate Attorneys can become members of the American Bar Association, the National Lawyers Guild, or the National Association of Real Estate Professionals for networking and career advancement opportunities at association-sponsored seminars and continuing education courses.

Tips for Entry

1. Pre-professional experience as a law intern or law clerk is strongly recommended because it can lead to a permanent job or provide valuable experience.
2. Law firms will often advertise career opportunities in law journals or post new vacancies on their Web sites.
3. Many jobs are obtained through old-fashioned networking at state bar association career events, seminars, and conferences.

REAL ESTATE PARALEGAL

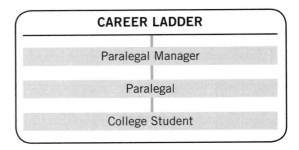

Special Skills and Personality Traits—Ability to read and comprehend legal documents; good written and verbal communication skills; good researching and organizational skills

Position Description

Paralegals do research on legal issues and perform other background work under the supervision of a lawyer. Paralegals (also known as legal assistants) are not licensed to practice law and cannot give legal advice, collect fees, or represent a client in court, but they help lawyers in their legal practice. According to the American Bar Association, a paralegal is a person qualified by education, training, or work experience who performs specifically designated substantive legal work for which a lawyer is responsible.

The legal assistant field dates to the late 1960s, when law firms and independent practice lawyers sought ways to deliver legal services at a lower effective cost. Other contributing factors were the consumer protection laws enacted over the last 40 years and direct marketing by law firms, which led to greater public awareness of litigation and other legal remedies to settle claims.

Working under the supervision of an attorney, a paralegal's work becomes part of the attorney's work output. A paralegal may perform any function performed by an attorney, including the following:

- conducting client interviews and maintaining general contact with clients
- locating and interviewing witnesses
- conducting investigations and documentary research
- conducting legal research
- drafting legal documents, correspondence, and pleadings
- summarizing depositions and testimony

- attending real estate closings, depositions, court hearings, and trials accompanied by an attorney
- managing the application process for various licenses and regulatory permits
- managing a portfolio of intellectual property, including trademarks and trade names
- assisting in collection of internal records for internal investigations and the resolution of disputes

Real Estate Paralegals perform functions related to property acquisitions and divestments, portfolio management, tax-free exchanges authorized by the Internal Revenue Code (1031 property exchanges), and other duties. They communicate with outside legal counsel, government agencies (including law enforcement), companies in the real estate industry, trade associations, and service organizations.

Paralegals assist in drafting loan closing documents, including loan agreements, notes, security deeds and mortgages, buy-sell agreements, guarantees, financing statements, affidavits, and lien waivers. They may also coordinate post-closing follow-up by recording documents, wiring funds, obtaining necessary cancellation documents, organizing and indexing files, and overseeing preparation of closing document binders.

Most paralegals are employed by law firms or law libraries, or by corporations with an in-house legal department. They use computers to research rules of law, statutes, and cases. Newly hired paralegals can expect to work beyond a standard 40-hour workweek—workloads of up to 90 hours a week are not unusual.

They normally work in an office setting and may travel occasionally to gather information and file documents.

Salaries

Paralegal earnings are determined by education, training, experience, and the type of employer. Paralegals who work for larger firms or live in metropolitan areas earn more than those who work in less populated areas. Nationally, paralegals can earn salaries of $39,000 to $49,000, according to the U.S. Bureau of Labor Statistics. The top 10 percent earn more than $61,000 annually.

Paralegals employed in a law firm bill their time allocated for substantive legal work (as distinct from clerical duties) in much the same manner as an attorney, but at a lower hourly rate. Overtime is normally paid for hours worked beyond the standard 40-hour workweek. Many law firms pay bonuses based on seniority or merit, or a combination of both.

Employment Prospects

Employment of paralegals is likely to increase as employers recognize that paralegals do many legal tasks for lower salaries than lawyers. The U.S. Bureau of Labor Statistics expects employment opportunities for paralegals to increase at a faster rate than opportunities in all occupations through 2014. Paralegals are usually hired after completing an American Bar Association–approved college or training program, or they are trained on the job. Individuals entering the paralegal field directly from college can expect plenty of competition, owing to the large number of graduates from paralegal educational programs. Competition for most entry-level positions is strong and healthy, and employers have their pick of qualified applicants. Many employers prefer those with at least three years' experience in a law office or a legal environment. Some job opportunities will come about from new positions created as the paralegal profession expands.

Advancement Prospects

Paralegals can advance to supervisory or management positions in their company or become trainers, although advancement opportunities are limited. Generally, only the largest companies offer management-level promotional opportunities. Some paralegals will enter law school after four or five years as a paralegal. Some will move to another employer for an increase in salary or open their own paralegal services firms; others will decide to make a career switch into another profession.

Education and Training

There are several ways to become a paralegal. Paralegal educational programs include two-year associate's degree programs, four-year bachelor's degree programs, and certificate programs that can take only a few months to complete. Most certificate programs provide intensive and, in some cases, specialized paralegal training for individuals who already hold college degrees, while associate's and bachelor's degree programs usually combine paralegal training with courses in other academic subjects. The current trend across the country, as reported by the National Federation of Paralegal Associations, is toward four-year degree programs as the basic educational requirement for paralegal employment. A four-year program at an American Bar Association–approved college or university—there are about 260 ABA-approved programs—will greatly enhance employment opportunities. Many paralegal training programs also offer an internship in which students gain practical experience by working for several months in a private law firm, a bank, a corporate legal department, a legal aid organization, or a government agency.

Currently, paralegals are not required to be certified. Obtaining voluntary certification has certain advantages, conveying competence in the field, and it may improve employment and advancement opportunities. A paralegal may take either the Certified Legal Assistant (CLA) exam, sponsored by the National Association of Legal Assistants (NALA), or the Paralegal Advanced Competency Exam (PACE), administered by the National Association for Paralegal Associations. The CLA exam is given several times a year at regional testing centers. College graduates with at least two years' experience are eligible to take the PACE exam; those who pass the exam may use the Registered Paralegal (RP) designation. Holders of the Certified Legal Assistant and Registered Paralegal designation need to meet continuing education requirements to maintain their certification.

Experience, Skills, and Personality Traits

Competence with office computer systems—word processing, Internet searching, e-mail, spreadsheet and database programs—is an essential job skill. Computer technology will continue to play an important role in the fact finding and document preparation stages in most legal cases. Paralegals frequently have access to highly sensitive information, which must be handled carefully to prevent unauthorized use or disclosure. Paralegals have a great deal of contact with clients, customers, and outside vendors, and they need to have effective written and verbal communication skills. Also important are good project management, research, and organizational skills.

Unions and Associations

Paralegals can become members of several professional associations: the National Association of Legal Assistants (http://www.nala.org), the National Federation of Paralegal Associations (http://www.paralegals.org), or their regional affiliates for networking and career advancement opportunities.

Tips for Entry

1. Experience gained in internships is an asset when one is seeking a job after graduation. Prospective students should examine the experiences of recent graduates before enrolling in a paralegal program.
2. Check classified ads in local newspapers, law journals, and college career centers for job leads in your area.
3. For general information on a career as a paralegal, visit the American Bar Association's paralegal Web site: http://www.abanet.org/legalservices/paralegals.

RELOCATION COUNSELOR

Duties: Administers employee relocation benefit programs for corporate clients for newly hired and transferring employees; will manage services contracted out to third-party servicers

Alternate Title(s): Relocation Agent, Relocation Consultant

Salary Range: $73,000 to $93,200

Employment Prospects: Good

Advancement Prospects: Good

Prerequisites:

> **Education or Training**—Four-year degree in business, social studies, or a related field of study
>
> **Experience**—Two to three years' real estate sales or customer service experience

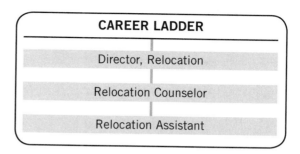

CAREER LADDER

Director, Relocation

Relocation Counselor

Relocation Assistant

Special Skills and Personality Traits—Good negotiating and organizational skills; good oral and written communication skills; attention to details

Position Description

Relocation Counselors help transferring or newly hired employees manage the move to another city or to another country if the employee is relocating internationally. Relocation Counselors, also called relocation agents, help smooth the transition to an unfamiliar city by attending to all the myriad details associated with selling a house, finding adequate housing, and getting acclimated in the destination city. In multinational companies operating around the world, the destination city very often is a city outside the United States.

Relocation companies assist companies with relocating employees by drafting a relocation policy appropriate to their annual volume of relocation activity. This policy addresses all aspects of employee relocation, from transportation of household goods to selling the employee's current home and selecting a new residence in the destination location. It outlines in detail all applicable policies and benefits offered to employees.

Typically, a Relocation Counselor is assigned to work one-on-one with each employee relocating to another destination. Establishing a rapport with the client's employees is an important part of the job. In larger relocation counseling firms, the Relocation Counselors may have experienced relocation themselves, and they can empathize with the employees going through the relocation process. Relocation Counselors begin with a needs assessment analysis with the transferring employee and will select an experienced real estate agent

to work with the transferee. The counselor remains in contact with the transferee throughout the home buying and relocation process and is available for consultation after working hours and on weekends.

Relocation Counselors assist transferring employees by providing customized relocation packets to each employee offered the opportunity to relocate. These information packets, often printed in glossy magazine or newsletter format, have detailed information about the area where the employee would be transferred, including information about public and private schools, recreation facilities and golf courses, colleges and universities, houses of worship, and area employers for the trailing spouse.

Relocation Counselors help their clients find housing by selecting an experienced real estate agent to assist in buying a new home, providing information about the area's real estate market, advising on the current home's salability, establishing the employee's price range in the new area, and helping to arrange mortgage finance prequalification.

If the relocating employee is married, relocation firms typically offer counseling services to the trailing spouse. Such services can include career counseling and tuition reimbursement for learning a new language and business or social contacts at the new destination.

Relocation companies may buy out an employee's house directly at a negotiated fair market price if no buyer can be found, allowing the transferring employee to concentrate on getting adjusted to the new job and the new community. Relocation services may also include educational consulting and special research on the new community.

Counselors assist their clients in other ways, by providing rental assistance or temporary housing until a new home has been purchased or providing marketing assistance to sell their current home. The counselor remains involved until the property is sold or closed. Counselors also arrange shipment of household goods by truck or other means of transportation to the destination city.

Assistance provided by relocation counselors may include any of the following:

- offering dual career job search assistance
- conducting orientation visits to a new city, accompanied by a trained counselor
- providing cross-cultural training and language training
- providing competitive market analysis to assist employees in selling a current home
- providing temporary hotel or apartment accommodations as needed
- providing repatriation support for employees nearing the end of their overseas service

Relocation Counselors work in a variety of settings. They may work for a company specializing in relocation services, for a real estate brokerage firm, or in the human resources department of a major corporation. Many large employers will contract out the entire relocation program to a relocation management company, which will in turn hire the household goods movers, real estate agencies, appraisers, and other service firms to do the actual work involved in relocation, as these services can often be provided at a lower cost by third-party servicers. Relocation Counselors work in an office setting and typically work a 40-hour week.

Salaries

The median salary for an employee relocation manager is $82,900, according to a salary survey by Salary.com. The middle 50 percent earned between $73,000 and $93,200. Pay scales can vary dramatically and are influenced by employer size, industry, years of experience, and geographic location. Other benefits typically include incentive bonuses based on performance, employer-sponsored pension or 401(k) plan, and medical and dental insurance coverage.

Employment Prospects

Employment opportunities in this field are relatively good. There is more competition worldwide for key employees, especially those with hard-to-find skills. Consequently, employers look to relocation professionals to help develop employee retention and workforce mobility strategies.

As countries become more interconnected economically and culturally, a growing number of U.S. companies see the value of having senior managers gain experience internationally, if only for a temporary assignment. Worldwide ERC, an association of relocation professionals, reports that fully half of the companies surveyed on relocation trends expect overseas assignments will increase by 50 percent over the next five years.

Advancement Prospects

With experience, Relocation Counselors can move into more senior positions in a relocation services firm with increased responsibility and an increase in compensation. Advancement to a senior position often requires attaining an industry certification such as Certified Relocation Professional, Senior Certified Relocation Professional, or Global Mobility Specialist. All are awarded by Worldwide ERC, a trade association for relocation professionals. Another option is taking a relocation management position in a company that routinely contracts its employee reassignments with a services firm specializing in corporate relocations.

Education and Training

Most employers prefer a four-year degree with college courses in business, management, real estate, social studies, or a related of study. A high school diploma or Graduate Equivalent Diploma is the minimum academic qualification. Further training is ordinarily provided on the job through employer-sponsored training for new employees and continuing education to maintain job skills.

Experience, Skills, and Personality Traits

Relocation Counselors should have good negotiating and organizational skills, very good oral and written communication skills, and good computer skills. They should have a working knowledge of the Microsoft Windows environment. They should be attentive to details and have an ability to handle multiple projects. Some experience in real estate sales, customer service, or mortgage processing is very useful background.

Unions and Associations

Relocation professionals can become members of Worldwide ERC (www.erc.org), a trade association formerly known as the Employee Relocation Council, or the International Relocation Association (www.tira.org), which represents relocation companies around the world.

Tips for Entry

1. The Worldwide ERC Web site (http://www.erc.org) has a career center with a searchable jobs database and job search tips for those entering the field.
2. Take college courses in business, management, or real estate for a solid academic foundation.
3. Contact relocation firms directly for job opportunities in your area.

SURVEYOR

CAREER PROFILE

Duties: Writes descriptions of land for deeds, leases, and other legal documents using specialized equipment

Alternate Title(s): Land Surveyor

Salary Range: $35,000 to $57,000

Employment Prospects: Good

Advancement Prospects: Good

Prerequisites:

Education or Training—Four-year degree or high school diploma plus on-the-job apprenticeship

Experience—Up to four years' experience required to become a Licensed Land Surveyor

Special Skills and Personality Traits—Good problem-solving skills; good math aptitude and facility with numbers; good research skills

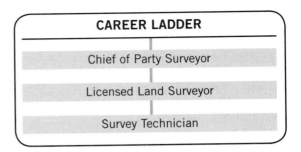

CAREER LADDER

Chief of Party Surveyor

Licensed Land Surveyor

Survey Technician

Special Requirements—The Licensed Surveyor position requires a state license in all states

Position Description

Surveyors determine official boundaries. They write descriptions of land for property deeds, leases, and other official documents. Surveyors use a variety of tools and calculations to make precise maps of rivers, properties, utility lines, and communities. They gather data that define the elevation or outline of land and land features. Their work establishes official land, airspace, and water boundaries. They take measurements for construction sites.

The work of Surveyors is typically done by a survey party, consisting of a party chief and several technicians. In the field they select known survey reference points and determine the precise location of important features in the survey area. These workers use survey tools to measure distances, directions, and angles between land points. They look for visual evidence of previous boundaries. From this information they prepare plots, maps, and reports. They record the results of the survey and verify that the data are accurate.

Surveyors examine legal records for evidence of previous boundaries and analyze the data to determine the location of boundary lines. Surveyors who establish boundaries must be licensed by the state in which they work. Surveyors are sometimes called to provide expert testimony in court cases in which survey data or boundary lines are contested.

Recent advances in technology have changed the nature of Surveyors' work. For large projects they use the Global Positioning System (GPS), a satellite system that precisely locates points on the earth by using radio signals. To use this system a receiver is mounted on a tripod at a desired point. Signals collected from several satellites can pinpoint a precise location of a boundary, river, or other land feature. Surveyors then interpret and check the results for accuracy.

A Surveyor's work typically includes the following:

- determining distances, angles, and elevations using specialized instruments
- checking construction plans and legal descriptions
- finding underground structures with electronic pipe locators and other equipment
- setting and marking stakes and other signals for electricians, road crews, and other professionals working on a construction site
- making calculations and assembling survey data

Surveyors usually work a 40-hour week and spend much of their time outdoors. They may work longer hours, as during the summer when weather and light conditions are most suitable for field work. Seasonal demands for construction-related work typically peak during the summer months.

Salaries

Surveyors can expect to earn salaries from $35,000 to $57,000, according to the U.S. Labor Department's Bureau of Labor Statistics. The median salary was $46,080 in 2004, and the top 10 percent of U.S. Surveyors earned more than $74,000. Salaries tend to increase as Surveyors gain experience and pass a series of qualifying exams demonstrating a mastery of the measurement techniques used by Surveyors in the field.

Employment Prospects

Employment opportunities for Surveyors are expected to grow about as fast as opportunities in all occupations through 2014, according to the Bureau of Labor Statistics. Advances in electronic distance measuring equipment and the Global Positioning System (GPS) will continue to improve the accuracy and productivity of these workers, potentially limiting future employment growth, the U.S. Bureau of Labor Statistics says. But new job openings will be created when Surveyors move into other occupations or reach retirement age. The best entry-level opportunities will be in architecture, engineering, and construction-related firms. Urban planning and redevelopment of core urban areas will add to employment opportunities for Surveyors over the next decade.

Advancement Prospects

A surveyor technician (or surveyor-in-training), the entry-level position, can advance to become chief of party surveyor, supervising a team of Surveyors, and eventually to licensed land surveyor by meeting the work experience and written exam requirements of state licensing boards. With additional on-the-job experience, Surveyors can advance to management positions. Some Surveyors will go into management positions, such as field engineers. Other may upgrade their skills by taking advanced courses and becoming civil engineers.

Education and Training

Surveyors who have a four-year degree and strong technical skills will find the best employment opportunities. Most people prepare for a career in surveying by combining college courses in surveying with on-the-job training. A four-year degree is becoming more necessary, due to the increasing use of sophisticated measuring technology in survey work. About 50 universities offer four-year programs leading to a bachelor's degree in surveying. Community colleges, technical institutes, and vocational schools offer one- to three-year education programs in surveying.

Newly hired Surveyors typically receive some on-the-job training. Training varies by employer but generally is from one to three months. Surveyors spend a certain amount of time each year learning about new hardware and software to keep up with advances in survey technology.

Special Requirements

State licensing is required in most states. Only one state, California, has a formal apprenticeship program for Surveyors in the construction industry. In most states, the route to licensure is four years of college followed by a state-administered exam. After passing the Fundamentals of Surveying Exam, most candidates work another four years under the supervision of an experienced Surveyor and then take the Principles and Practices of Surveyors exam to get their state license as a licensed Surveyor.

Experience, Skills, and Personality Traits

It takes two to four years of surveying experience in addition to a four-year degree to become a licensed Surveyor. (Without the college degree, it may require 10 to 12 years of experience to become licensed.) Entry-level Surveyors learn important job skills working under the supervision of a more experienced Surveyor for a two- to four-year period, which prepares them for state licensing exams.

Surveyors should have a competency working with numbers and making quick calculations. Other important skills are an ability to use survey equipment, Global Positioning System (GPS) mapping systems, Geographic Information System (GIS) software, and an ability to read and interpret topographical maps. Good office skills are essential because Surveyors must be able to research old deeds and other legal paperwork and prepare reports. Surveying is a cooperative operation, with an emphasis on being able to work as part of a team.

Unions and Associations

Several professional organizations are available to professional Surveyors for career advancement and networking opportunities. Among these are the American Congress on Surveying and Mapping (http://www.acsm.net) and the National Society of Professional Surveyors (http://www.nspsmo.org). The American Congress on Surveying and Mapping has partnered with the Federal Emergency Management Association to create the Certified Floodplain Surveyor program for licensed Surveyors. The National Society of Professional Surveyors sponsors the Certified Survey Technician program.

Tips for Entry

1. Get more information on career opportunities from the American Congress on Surveying and Mapping (ACSM) and the National Society of Professional Surveyors (http://www.nspsmo.org). The ACSM offers college scholarships to qualifying students.
2. Attend meetings of state affiliates of the National Society of Professional Surveyors to learn more about the field.
3. Take courses in algebra, computer science, drafting, and mechanical drawing if you are interested in surveying work as a career.
4. Check with a teacher or counselor to see if work-based learning opportunities are available in your school and community. These might include shadowing a licensed Surveyor, internship, or actual work experience.

TITLE INSURANCE REPRESENTATIVE

CAREER LADDER

Title Branch Manager

Title Insurance Representative

Title Insurance Sales Trainee

Position Description

Title Insurance Representatives sells title insurance policies to mortgage brokers, real estate agents, and mortgage lenders. They are sales agents for the title insurance underwriters—insurance companies that warrant the property's title is "good and marketable." Title insurance is sold by several national title insurance companies that operate across the country through a network of local offices.

There are two basic forms of title insurance: a lender's policy, which indemnifies the lender and is issued only to mortgage lenders, and an owner's policy, issued to homeowners. A separate policy covering construction loans is available in many states. Title insurance is sold in all states except Iowa, where it is illegal to sell title insurance. While title insurance is sold by private companies, the insurance forms are created by the American Land Title Association. The ALTA's standard insurance policy jackets (standard terms and conditions) are used almost universally, although modified in some states.

In a title insurance policy, the insurance company agrees to indemnify the lender (or the borrower if the borrower is the named beneficiary) against any financial losses resulting from title fraud and errors in the property title as recorded in public land records. Title Insurance Representatives prepare the documents and ensure the legality of transactions related to commercial and residential mortgages, easements, leases, and life estates.

Typically, the process begins when a realtor puts in a request to the title company to research the title to a specific piece of property. A real estate attorney then orders a lien certificate, a document listing any prior liens, legal actions, or housing code violations, from the municipality where the property is located. The title company, after receiving the title report from the attorney, takes the necessary steps to clear any title issues. In most jurisdictions, a title commitment indicating a clear title can be issued in 24 to 48 hours. After property closing and sale to a new owner, a new deed is recorded in public land records, and the title insurance policy is issued. This policy replaces the insurer's commitment issued at closing and remains in effect until the property is resold.

Title Insurance Representatives market title insurance in assigned sales territories. Title Insurance Representatives are responsible for developing their own sales leads or following through on sales leads provided by the underwriter. Representatives maintain contacts with local bank lenders, mortgage brokers, and others. They make sales presentations to prospective clients. They are responsible for completion of all duties associated with title insurance.

A career in title insurance sales offers the prospect of steady employment for those with a desire to succeed. This career may not be the best choice for entrepreneurs or risk takers because the rates for title insurance are set by state insurance departments. Title Insurance Representatives spend up to 50 percent of their time traveling to meet clients. They generally work a 40-hour week, making phone calls to prospects when not on the road. Some evening work or weekend work may be required to reach sales goals.

Salaries

Title Insurance Representatives are paid a base salary plus commissions. Earnings can range from $25,000 to $45,000 annually—more for top producing sales representatives. Compensation may also include full health benefits and a generous expense account. Other benefits typically offered are an employee stock purchase plan and employer matching on 401(k) savings plans.

Employment Prospects

Employment opportunities for Title Insurance Representatives are expected to decline moderately through 2014, according to the U.S. Bureau of Labor Statistics.

Employment opportunities are closely tied to the mortgage lending cycle and can become restricted during periods of declining home sales, resulting in fewer policies being written.

On the other hand, title underwriters are continually hiring new representatives to replace those leaving the field for other occupations. Most title representatives start as escrow assistants or sales trainees and work up from there, gaining knowledge and experience on the job.

Advancement Prospects

Advancement options are fairly limited. Some title representatives move up by taking on a bigger sales territory, increasing their earnings potential. Some will become title company managers and oversee the hiring, training, and supervision of title agents. Title company managers get involved in very complex title transfers. They usually have some experience in handling legal issues that come up in real estate sales. A state insurance license is not required for management positions. Working as a title representative for three to five years can be helpful background for moving to a related career selling other types of personal and business insurance.

Education and Training

A high school diploma is the basic entry level requirement. Some college courses are useful, although a college degree is generally not required; title companies train the title representative from the ground up. Title companies have a moderate on-the-job training program (up to three months) for newly hired employees. Title requirements vary from state to state, so most job skills are learned on the job rather than from taking a class or two.

The Land Title Institute, the educational subsidiary of the American Land Title Association, offers a full range of seminars, correspondence courses, and online courses for title agents, examiners, and other people involved in the title industry.

Special Requirements

Title insurance is regulated by state insurance departments in most states where it is sold. Some states require Title Insurance Representatives to get a state license to sell title insurance products. Check your state department of insurance's Web site for education and licensing requirements in your locality or the state where you plan to do business.

Experience, Skills, and Personality Traits

Most people who sell title insurance have some experience in mortgage lending, real estate sales, or working in a title office. Some employers are willing to hire individuals with no experience as trainee agents. More important than prior industry experience is a strong desire to succeed in a very competitive market.

This is a sales position, so you should be personable and outgoing and willing to invest time and energy in building relationships with mortgage brokers and realtors. Good communication skills and telephone skills are important. Some proficiency with e-mail and basic word processing are helpful.

Unions and Associations

The American Land Title Association and state title insurance associations sponsor continuing education programs for Title Insurance Representatives. Regularly scheduled seminars and conferences provide networking opportunities.

There are affiliated title associations in most states. State associations have annual conventions where title agents can meet other industry professionals and participate in educational and networking programs.

Tips for Entry

1. Ask a realtor friend for referrals to title insurance companies operating in your area.
2. Attend meetings of state title insurance associations. State associations hold regular meetings on title and closing issues.
3. Visit the local title insurance agency and talk to the office manager about work in the field.
4. The Title Insurance Career Center (http://www.titleboard.com) lists many job opportunities for title agents, closers, and processors.

ZONING OFFICER

CAREER PROFILE

Duties: Interprets and applies zoning regulations and municipal ordinances through the administration of zoning permit applications; investigates zoning violations

Alternate Title(s): Zoning Enforcement Officer

Salary Range: $50,000 to $65,000

Employment Prospects: Good

Advancement Prospects: Good

Prerequisites:

  Education or Training—Four-year degree in land planning, urban studies, public administration, or a related field; certification optional

  Experience—Two or more years' experience reviewing site development plans

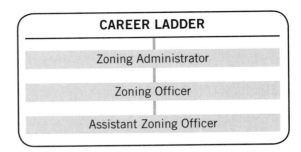

CAREER LADDER

Zoning Administrator

Zoning Officer

Assistant Zoning Officer

Special Skills and Personality Traits—Strong analytical skills; excellent verbal and written communication skills; good computer skills

Special Requirements—Valid driver's license

Position Description

The zoning enforcement officer is the key person in the enforcement of municipal zoning regulations. The Zoning Officer interprets and applies zoning regulations and municipal ordinances through the administration of zoning permit applications. The Zoning Officer investigates zoning violations. The Zoning Officer answers public inquiries about zoning regulations and provides information regarding applicable codes or regulations. The Zoning Officer serves as staff for the zoning board of appeals, which is typically an elected position.

Zoning is an essential act of city or town planning. Property may be zoned for commercial or industrial use, or for residential use. Sometimes, regions or subdivisions contain multiple zones, some for residential and some for commercial use. A property owner who wishes to change the terms of property use may need to go through the process of rezoning physical property, which may be simple or complex depending upon the demands and requirements of the city. The application for a zoning change or variance goes through the municipal zoning office.

The Zoning Officer directs the activities of the zoning department, including inspections of facilities, site plan reviews, complaint investigations, requests for zoning waivers or exceptions, zoning code enforcement, and other activities pertaining to zoning issues.

Other duties performed include the following:

- conferring with architects, engineers, developers, property owners, elected public officials, attorneys, and other organizations
- reviewing site plans submitted by property owners or developers
- conducting field inspections
- managing department employees and interviewing prospective employees
- conducting employee performance reviews
- approving employee training and administering disciplinary actions
- interpreting the zoning code and other related building codes or regulations
- advising elected municipal officials on proposed ordinances and amendments to existing ordinances
- acting as a liaison between the zoning department and community organizations, elected officials, and other government organizations
- providing staff support to the zoning board of appeals
- making zoning enforcement decisions and negotiating to resolve conflicts
- issuing certificates of occupancy
- initiating actions to prevent or correct violations of the zoning regulations
- maintaining complete, accurate, and well organized records of zoning orders to serve as a basis for future zoning regulations

Zoning Officers work in an office setting and normally work a 35- to 40-hour workweek. They are occasionally required to work longer hours, as when representing the department at public hearings on proposed changes or variances in zoning regulations submitted by a homeowner or by a developer. Zoning Officers spend part of their time inspecting proposed development sites. Some Zoning Officers may spend up to 25 percent of their working time traveling to inspect job sites.

Salaries

Salaries vary by department and on-the-job experience. In 2007, the annual salary of Zoning Officers ranged from $50,000 to $65,000. Zoning Officers in large metropolitan areas, where the entry requirements are generally higher than non-urban areas, generally earn higher salaries. Also, Zoning Officers with administrative or supervisory duties earn higher salaries than non-supervisory officers.

Zoning Officers also receive non-salary benefits including excellent health insurance, paid sick leave, and paid vacations. As salaried employees, they typically do not get overtime pay for hours worked beyond the standard 40-hour workweek. Many towns or municipalities provide zoning officials with a municipal car for use during working hours.

Employment Prospects

Job opportunities for zoning officials are expected to grow about as fast as all occupations through 2014. Over the last 10 years, municipalities have attempted to control property development by expanding their zoning regulations, or by hiring new staff—a trend that is expected to continue over the next 10 years and beyond.

The best entry route for college graduates is as an assistant zoning officer or zoning technician. Zoning technicians have the opportunity to learn more about the field under the supervision of a more experienced employee and prepare for their zoning certification exams.

Advancement Prospects

Zoning Officers can advance to become zoning administrators in larger offices, taking on staff supervision duties. Earning an advanced degree, usually a master's degree, is often a requirement for advancement in the field. Individuals who move into more senior positions usually have an industry certification—Certified Zoning Enforcement Officer. Earning a professional certification enhances the opportunities for advancement into higher paying, more responsible jobs. Zoning Officers in smaller municipalities advance their careers by taking positions in larger communities, where they have a larger budget and have overall administrative responsibility for a larger employee staff. Some Zoning Officers can also advance by furthering their education in related fields such as public administration.

Education and Training

Zoning enforcement, much like other code enforcement professions, requires special study, knowledge, and skills. Many jurisdictions now require a four-year degree or a master's degree in land planning, urban studies, public administration, or a related field as a minimum requirement. Continuing education to keep up with developments in the field and certification are also required.

Certification programs are administered by state associations of zoning enforcement officers. The Certified Zoning Enforcement Officer designation is designed for Zoning Officers employed by a local government or municipal planning and zoning commission. The program was established to raise the standards of the profession, to gain recognition by government officials as qualified, objective public employees, and to award a professional designation to zoning officials who meet all the requirements for certification. In most states, candidates for certification must have at least two to three years' job experience and pass a three-part written exam.

Special Requirements

A valid driver's license is normally required.

Experience, Skills, and Personality Traits

Employers look for individuals who have strong analytical skills, excellent verbal and written communication skills, and good computer skills. Candidates should have at least two years' experience in municipal land planning and subdivision, some experience reviewing site development plans, or an equivalent combination of education and experience.

Good verbal and written communication skills are important because Zoning Officers spend much of their time answering questions from the public and municipal staff. Other important skills include an ability to conduct site inspections in rough terrain and good computer skills, which are very useful in project tracking. Zoning officials occupy a highly visible position; they need to have good judgment and a sense of tact in dealing with the public.

Unions and Associations

Zoning enforcement officers can become members of state associations of zoning enforcement officers. These organizations sponsor continuing education programs to help Zoning Officers maintain their job skills and administer certification programs for zoning officials.

Tips for Entry

1. Take college courses in public administration, planning, and related subjects to learn the fundamentals of zoning and land use.

2. Learn more about the profession by contacting a state zoning officers association or visit a state association's Web site to learn more about certification requirements.

3. Contact a town zoning department in your area to learn specific job requirements.

4. Some state associations of zoning officials have searchable job banks on their Web sites.

APPENDIXES

I. Colleges and Universities
  A. Real Estate
  B. Planning
  C. Construction Management

II. Professional Associations and Organizations

III. Professional Certifications

IV. Professional Periodicals

V. Major Real Estate Management Firms

VI. Real Estate Licensing Agencies

VII. Real Estate Research Organizations

VIII. Planning Your Career in Real Estate

APPENDIX I
COLLEGES AND UNIVERSITIES

The preferred minimum educational requirement for the majority of positions discussed in this book is a four-year college degree. The colleges and universities in this appendix offer degree programs in real estate, planning, construction management, or related fields of study. This section contains the names, mailing addresses, and contact information for four- and two-year colleges and universities that offer degree programs, certificate programs, and continuing education unit (CEU) programs. Also included here are the names of business schools and universities offering postgraduate master's degrees and Master of Business Administration programs. Space limitations preclude the listing of all such colleges and universities.

Information about these and other colleges can be obtained by contacting them directly. You can get additional information about these and other colleges by talking to school and career counselors and industry professionals in your area. Other sources of information are college directories published by *Barron's*, *Peterson's*, *Princeton Review,* and others. College directories can be found in school or public libraries.

A. REAL ESTATE

FOUR-YEAR COLLEGES AND UNIVERSITIES

ALABAMA

The University of Alabama
P.O. Box 870132
203 Student Services Center
Tuscaloosa, AL 35487-0132
Phone: (800) 933-BAMA
Fax: (205) 348-9046
E-mail: admissions@ua.edu
http://www.ua.edu

ARIZONA

Arizona State University
P.O. Box 870112
Tempe, AZ 85287-0112
Phone: (480) 965-7788
Fax: (480) 965-3610
E-mail: ugradinq@asu.edu
http://www.east.asu.edu

Arizona State University
College of Business
P.O. Box 874011
Tempe, AZ 85287
Phone: (480) 965-5440
Fax: (480) 965-3610
E-mail: upgrading@asu.edu
http://www.asu.edu

Arizona State University
Student Recruitment
Arizona State University at the Polytechnic Campus
7001 East Williams Field Road #350
Mesa, AZ 85212
Phone: (480) 727-1165
Fax: (480) 727-1008
E-mail: asueast@asu.edu
http://www.asu.edu

Phoenix College
Director of Admissions, Registration and Records
1202 West Thomas Road
Phoenix, AZ 85013
Phone: (602) 285-7500
Fax: (602) 285-7813
E-mail: dl-pc-info@pcmail.maricopa.edu
http://www.pc.maricopa.edu

CALIFORNIA

California State Polytechnic University—Pomona
Office of Admissions
3801 West Temple Avenue
Pomona, CA 91768
Phone: (909) 869-3427

Fax: (909) 869-4529
E-mail: admissions@csupomona.edu
http://www.csupomona.edu

California State University, East Bay
Office of Admissions
25800 Carlos Bee Boulevard
Hayward, CA 94542-3035
Phone: (510) 885-3248
Fax: (510) 885-3816
E-mail: adminfo@csuhayward.edu
http://www.csuhayward.edu

California State University— Fresno
Office of Admissions
5150 North Maple Avenue, M/S JA 57
Fresno, CA 93740-8026
Phone: (559) 278-6115
Fax: (559) 278-4812
E-mail: vivian_franco@csufresno.edu
http://www.csufresno.edu

California State University— Fullerton
Office of Admissions

P.O. Box 6900
800 North State College Boulevard
Fullerton, CA 92834-2011
Phone: (714) 278-2350
http://www.fullerton.edu

California State University—Northridge

Department of Finance, Real Estate
& Insurance
18111 Nordhoff Street
Northridge, CA 91330-8207
Phone: (818) 677-3777
Fax: (818) 677-3766
E-mail: admissions.records@csun.edu
http://www.csun.edu

California State University—Sacramento

University Outreach Services
6000 J Street, Lassen Hall
Sacramento, CA 95819-6048
Phone: (916) 278-3901
Fax: (916) 278-5603
E-mail: admissions@csus.edu
http://www.csus.edu

California State University—San Bernardino

Office of Admissions
5500 University Parkway
University Hall, Room 107
San Bernardino, CA 92407-2397
Phone: (909) 537-5188
Fax: (909) 880-7034
E-mail: moreinfo@mail.csusb.edu
http://www.csub.edu

City College of San Francisco

Admissions and Records
50 Phelan Avenue
San Francisco, CA 94112-1821
Phone: (415) 239-3291
Fax: (415) 239-3936
http://www.ccsf.edu

College of the Desert

Registrar's Office
43-500 Monterey Avenue
Palm Desert, CA 92260-9305
Phone: (760) 346-8041
http://www.collegeofthedesert.edu

De Anza College

Records and Admissions
21250 Stevens Creek Boulevard
Cupertino, CA 95014
Phone: (408) 864-8292
Fax: (408) 864-8329
E-mail: webregda@fhda.edu
http://www.deanza.edu

El Camino College

Office of Admissions
16007 Crenshaw Boulevard
Torrance, CA 90506
Phone: (866) 352-2646
Fax: (310) 660-3818
http://www.elcamino.edu

Mt. San Antonio College

Admissions and Records
1100 North Grand Avenue
Walnut, CA 91789
Phone: (800) 672-2463 ext. 4415
E-mail: admissions@mtsac.edu
http://www.mtsac.edu

Mt. San Jacinto College

Enrollment Services
1499 North State Street
San Jacinto, CA 92583-2399
Phone: (800) 624-5561 Ext. 1410
Fax: (909) 654-6738
E-mail: egonzale@msjc.edu
http://www.msjc.edu

San Diego State University

SDSU College of Business
5500 Campanile Drive
San Diego, CA 92182-8236
Phone: (619) 594-5323
Fax: (619) 594-3272
E-mail: admissions@sdsu.edu
http://www.sdsu.edu

University of California at Berkeley

Undergraduate Admissions
University of California
Berkeley, CA 94720-6105
Phone: (510) 643-6105
Fax: (510) 643-7357
E-mail: creue@haas.berkeley.edu
http://www.berkeley.edu

University of San Diego

Admissions Office
5998 Alcala Park
San Diego, CA 92110
Phone: (800) 248-4873
Fax: (619) 260-6836
http://www.sandiego.edu

University of Southern California

Admissions Office
University Park Campus
Los Angeles, CA 90089
Phone: (213) 740-1111
Fax: (213) 740-6364
E-mail: admitusc.edu
http://www.usc.edu

University of Southern California

School of Policy, Planning, and Development
Ralph and Goldy Lewis Hall, Room 111
Los Angeles, CA 90089-0626
Phone: (213) 740-6842
Fax: (213) 740-7573
E-mail: marisolr@usc.edu
http://www.usc.edu/lusk

University of the Pacific

Office of Admissions
Eberhardt School of Business
3601 Pacific Avenue
Stockton, CA 95219
Phone: (209) 946-2637
http://web.pacific.edu

Ventura College

Registrar's Office
4667 Telegraph Road
Ventura, CA 93003-3899
Phone: (805) 654-6456
Fax: (805) 654-6466
E-mail: sbricker@server.vcccd.cc.ca.us
http://www.venturacollege.edu

COLORADO

Colorado State University

Admissions Office
Spruce Hall

Fort Collins, CO 80523-0015
Phone: (970) 491-6909
Fax: (970) 491-7799
http://www.admissions.colostate.edu

University of Colorado
Leeds School of Business
Campus P.O. Box 419
Boulder, CO 80309-0419
Phone: (303) 492-3643
E-mail: Katie.mrazik@colorado.edu
http://leeds.colorado.edu/realestate

University of Denver
2101 South University Boulevard, #380
Denver, CO 80208
Phone: (800) 525-9495
Fax: (303) 871-3301
E-mail: admission @du.edu
http://www.du.edu

CONNECTICUT

University of Connecticut
Center for Real Estate and Urban Economic Studies
School of Business, Room 402
2100 Hillside Road, Unit 1041RE
Storrs, CT 06269
Phone: (860) 486-3227
Fax: (860) 486-0349
E-mail: recenter@business.uconn.edu
http://www.business.uconn.edu/realestate

University of Hartford
Barney School of Business
2000 Bloomfield Avenue
West Hartford, CT 06117
Phone: (860) 768-4444
Fax: (860) 768-4821
http://barney.hartford.edu

DISTRICT OF COLUMBIA

The George Washington University
Office of Admissions
2121 I Street, NW
Suite 201
Washington, DC 20052

Phone: (800) 447-3765
Fax: (202) 944-0325
http://www.gwu.edu

Howard University
School of Business, Suite 500
2600 Sixth Street NW
Washington, DC 20059-0002
Phone: (202) 806-2700
Fax: (202) 806-4462
E-mail: admissions@howard.edu
http://www.howard.edu

FLORIDA

Florida Atlantic University
College of Business, LA 444
2912 College Avenue
Boca Raton, FL 33314
Phone: (800) 299-4FAU
Fax: (561) 297-2758
http://www.fau.edu/realestate

Florida International University
University Admissions
University Park
11200 South West Eighth Street
Miami, FL 33199
Phone: (305) 348-3675
Fax: (305) 348-3648
E-mail: admiss@fiu.edu
http://www.fiu.edu

Florida State University
University Admissions
Rovetta Business Building, Room 313
Department of Risk Management, Real Estate, and Business Law
Tallahassee, FL 32306-110
Phone: (850) 644-4070
Fax: (850) 644-0197
E-mail: dgatzla@fsu.edu
http://www.ree.fsu.edu

University of Florida
Bergstrom Center for Real Estate Studies
Warrington College of Business Administration
University of Florida
100 BRY
P.O. Box 117150

Gainesville, FL 32611-7150
Phone: (352) 392- 2397 ext. 1399
Fax: (352) 392-2086
E-mail: ufwcba@cba.ufl.edu
http://www.realestate.ufl.edu

University of North Florida
Department of Accounting and Finance
4567 St. Johns Bluff Road
Jacksonville, FL 32224
Phone: (904) 620-2630
E-mail: srosenbe@unf.edu
http://www.unf.edu/ccb

GEORGIA

Georgia State University
University Admissions
J. Mack Robinson College of Business
Department of Real Estate
1405 35 Broad Street
P.O. Box 4020
Atlanta, GA 30302
Phone: (404) 651-4614
E-mail: realestate@gsu.edu
http://www.robinson.gsu.edu/realestate

State University of West Georgia
University Admissions
1601 Maple Street
College of Business
Carrolton, GA 30118
Phone: (678) 839-5023
E-mail: jburton@westga.edu
http://www.westga.edu/~mktreal

University of Georgia
University Admissions
Terry College of Business, 206 Brooks Hall
Athens, GA 30602-6255
Phone: (706) 542-4290
E-mail: realestate@terry.uga.edu
http://www.terry.uga.edu/realestate

HAWAII

University of Hawaii at Manoa
Admissions and Records
2600 Campus Road

Honolulu, HI 96822
Phone: (800) 823-9771
Fax: (808) 956-4148
E-mail: ar-info@hawaii.edu
http://www.hawaii.edu

INDIANA

Indiana University
University Admissions
Kelley School of Business
1309 East 10th Street, Suite 738
Bloomington, IN 47405
Phone: (812) 855-7794
E-mail: fisher@indiana.edu
http://www.indiana.edu/~cres

IILLINOIS

DePaul University
Undergraduate Admissions
DePaul Center, Suite 6070
1 East Jackson Boulevard, Suite 9100
Chicago, IL 60604
Phone: (312) 362-8300
http://www.depaul.edu

University of Illinois at Chicago
Undergraduate Admissions
815 West Van Buren, Suite 220
Chicago, IL 60607-3525
Phone: (312) 996-4573
E-mail: mre@uic.edu
http://www.uic.edu/cba/lgradbiz

University of Illinois at Urbana-Champaign
University Admissions
901 West Illinois
Urbana, IL 61801
Phone: (217) 333-0302
E-mail: admissions@oar.uiuc.edu
http://www.uiuc.edu

IOWA

University of Northern Iowa
University Admissions
CBB 317 — Real Estate Education Program
Cedar Falls, IA 50614-0124
Phone: (800) 772-2037
Fax: (319) 273-2885

E-mail: admissions@uni.edu
http://www.uni.edu

KANSAS

Wichita State University
University Admissions
311A Clinton Hall Center for Real Estate
1845 Fairmount
Wichita, KS 67260-0077
Phone: (316) 978-7120
E-mail: realestate@wichita.edu
http://realestate.wichita.edu

KENTUCKY

Eastern Kentucky University
Admissions Office
SSB CPO 54, 521 Lancaster Avenue
Richmond, KY 40475-3102
Phone: (800) 465-9191
Fax: (859) 622-8024
E-mail: admissions@eku.edu
http://www.eku.edu

Morehead State University
Admissions Center
Combs Building, 212 UPO 703
150 University Drive
Morehead, KY 40351
Phone: (800) 585-6781
Fax: (606) 783-5038
E-mail: admissions@moreheadstate.edu
http://www.moreheadstate.edu/business

LOUISIANA

Louisiana State University
Admissions Office
Department of Finance
2164 CEBA Building
Baton Rouge, LA 70803
Phone: (225) 578-1175
Fax: (225) 578-4433
E-mail: admissions@lsu.edu
http://www.lsu.edu

Louisiana State University— Shreveport
University Admissions
One University Place, Finance Department

Shreveport, LA 71115-2399
Phone: (318) 707-5241
Fax: (318) 797-5204
E-mail: admissions@pilot.lsus.edu
http://www.lsus.edu

University of New Orleans
College of Business, Room 256
Lake Front Campus
New Orleans, LA 70148
Phone: (504) 280-6739
E-mail: wragas@uno.edu
http://www.uno.edu

MAINE

University of Southern Maine
Center for Real Estate Education
68 High Street
Portland, ME 04101
Phone: (800) 800-4876
Fax: (207) 228-8401
E-mail: lamont@usm.maine.edu
http://cree.usm.maine.edu

MASSACHUSETTS

Massachusetts Institute of Technology
Center for Real Estate
77 Massachusetts Avenue W31-310
Cambridge, MA 02139
Phone: (617) 253-4373
E-mail: mit-cre@mit.edu
http://www.mit.edu/cre

MICHIGAN

University of Michigan
Stephen M. Ross School of Business
701 Tappan Street, D4201
Ann Arbor, MI 48109-1234
Phone: (734) 764-1269
E-mail: capozza@umich.edu
http://www.umich.edu/~reecon/restate

MINNESOTA

College of St. Catherine
Admission and Financial Aid
2004 Randolph Avenue, F-02
St. Paul, MN 55105

Phone: (800) 656-5283
Fax: (651) 690-8824
E-mail: admissions@stkate.edu
http://www.stkate.edu

St. Cloud State University
G. R. Herberger College of Business
720 Fourth Avenue South
St. Cloud, MN 56321-4498
Phone: (320) 308-4986
Fax: (320) 308-3986
http://www.stcloudstate.edu/hcob

University of St. Thomas
Shenehon Center for Real Estate
  Education
1000 LaSalle Avenue, TMH 153
Minneapolis, MN 55403
Phone: (800) 328-6819
Fax: (651) 962-6930
E-mail: cob@stthomas.edu
http://www.stthomas.edu

MISSISSIPPI

Mississippi State University
Admissions
326 McCool Hall
P.O. Box 6305
Mississippi State, MS 39762
Phone: (662) 325-7478
Fax: (662) 325-7360
E-mail: admit@admissions.msstate.
  edu
http://www.cbi.msstate.edu

University of Mississippi
Admissions
145 Martindale Student Services
  Center
University, MS 38677
Phone: (800) 653-6477
Fax: (662) 915-5869
E-mail: admissions@olemiss.edu
http://www.olemiss.edu

MISSOURI

University of Missouri—
  Columbia
403 Cornell Hall
Columbia, MO 65211
Phone: (573) 882-6373

E-mail: westd@missouri.edu
http://business.missouri.edu

NEBRASKA

University of Nebraska at
  Omaha
RH 515 College of Business
  Administration
6001 Dodge Hall
Omaha, NE 68182-0048
Phone: (800) 858-8648
Fax: (402) 554-3472
E-mail: rsindt@mail.unomaha.edu
http://www.unomaha.edu

NEVADA

University of Nevada, Las Vegas
Beam Hall, Room 530
Lied Institute for Real Estate Studies
P.O. Box 456205
Las Vegas, NV 89154-4492
Phone: (702) 895-4492
E-mail: dmarch@ccmail.nevada.edu
http://liedinstitute.com

University of Nevada, Las Vegas
Undergraduate Recruitment
4505 Maryland Parkway, Box
  451021
Las Vegas, NV 89154-1021
Phone: (702) 774-8001
Fax: (702) 774-8008
E-mail: undergraduate.
  recruitment@ccmail.nevada.edu
http://www.unlv.edu

NEW JERSEY

Rutgers, The State University of
  New Jersey
Admissions Office
249 University Avenue
Newark, NJ 07102-1896
Phone: (973) 353-5205
Fax: (973) 353-1440
E-mail: admissions@ugadm.rutgers.
  edu
http://www.rutgers.edu

Thomas Edison State College
Admissions Services

101 West State Street
Trenton, NJ 08608-1176
Phone: (888) 442-8372
Fax: (609) 984-8447
E-mail: info@tesc.edu
http://www.tesc.edu

NEW MEXICO

University of New Mexico—
  Valencia Campus
Ms. Lucy Sanchez, Registrar
280 La Entrada
Los Lunas, NM 87031-7633
Phone: (505) 925-8580
Fax: (505) 925-8563
http://www.unm.edu/~unmvc

NEW YORK

Baruch College
Mr. James F. Murphy, Director of
  Undergraduate Admissions and
  Financial Aid
Bernard M. Baruch College of the
  City University of New York
Box H-0720
New York, NY 10010-5585
Phone: (212) 312-1400
http://www.baruch.cuny.edu

Cornell University
Undergraduate Admissions
410 Thurston Avenue
Ithaca, NY 14850
Phone: (607) 255-5241
Fax: (607) 255-0659
http://www.cornell.edu

New York University
School of Continuing and
  Professional Studies
Real Estate Institute
145 Fourth Avenue, Room 201
New York, NY 10003
Phone: (800) 998-7204
http://www.scps.nyu.edu/rei

NORTH CAROLINA

College of The Albemarle
Admissions
P.O. Box 2327

1208 North Road Street
Elizabeth City, NC 27909-2327
Phone: (252) 335-0821 ext. 2220
Fax: (252) 335-2011
E-mail: kkrentz@albemarle.edu
http://www.albemarle.edu

University of North Carolina at Chapel Hill
Campus Box # 2200, Jackson Hall
Chapel Hill, NC 27599-2200
Phone: (919) 966-3621
Fax: (919) 962-3045
E-mail: uadm@email.unc.edu
http://www.unc.edu

University of North Carolina at Charlotte
Center for Real Estate Studies
Belk College of Business
Friday Building
9201 University City Boulevard
Charlotte, NC 28223
Phone: (704) 687-2744
Fax: (704) 687-6987
E-mail: shott@email.uncc.edu
http://www.belkcollege.uncc.edu/
   Real_Estate/index.htm

OHIO

Cleveland State University
Undergraduate Admissions Office
Rhodes Tower West
Room 204, 1806 East 22nd Street
Cleveland, OH 44114
Phone: (888) CSU-OHIO
Fax: (216) 687-9210
E-mail: admissions@csuohio.edu
http://www.csuohio.edu

Ohio State University
Undergraduate Admissions
Enarson Hall, 154 West 12th Avenue
Columbus, OH 43210
Phone: (614) 247-6281
Fax: (614) 292-4818
E-mail: askabuckeye@osu.edu
http://www.osu.edu

Otterbein College
Admissions Office
One Otterbein College

Westerville, OH 43081-9924
Phone: (800) 488-8144
Fax: (614) 823-1200

The University of Akron
Admissions Office
Simone Hall, 277 East Buchtel
   Avenue
Akron, OH 44325-2001
Phone: (800) 655-4884
Fax: (330) 972-7022
E-mail: admissions@uakron.edu
http://www.uakron.edu

University of Cincinnati
Real Estate Program
403 Carl H. Lindner Hall College of
   Business
P.O. Box 210195
Cincinnati, OH 45221-0195
Phone: (513) 556-7193
E-mail: real.estate@uc.edu
http://www.uc.edu

University of Rio Grande
Admissions Office
P.O. Box 500
Rio Grande, OH 45674
Phone: (800) 282-7201
Fax: (740) 245-7260
E-mail: elambert@rio.edu
http://www.rio.edu

University of Toledo
Admissions Office
College of Business Administration
2801 West Bancroft
Toledo, OH 43606-3398
Phone: (800) 5TOLEDO
Fax: (419) 530-5872
E-mail: enroll@utnet.utoledo.edu
http://www.utoledo.edu

OKLAHOMA

University of Central Oklahoma
Office of Enrollment Services
100 North University Drive, Box
   151
Edmond, OK 73034-5209
Phone: (800) 254-4215
Fax: (405) 341-4964

E-mail: admituco@ucok.edu
http://www.ucok.edu

OREGON

Maryhurst University
212 Flavia Hall
17600 Pacific Highway—Highway 43
P.O. Box 261
Maryhurst, OR 97036-0261
Phone: (800) 634-9982
http://www.maryhurst.edu

PENNSYLVANIA

Lehigh University
Admissions Office
27 Memorial Drive West
Bethlehem, PA 18015
Phone: (610) 758-3100
Fax: (610) 758-4361
E-mail: admissions@lehigh.edu
http://www.lehigh.edu

Pennsylvania State University
The Mary Jean and Frank P. Smeal
   College of Business
409 Business Administration
   Building
University Park, PA 16802
Phone: (814) 865-4172
E-mail: jxc5@oas.psu.edu
http://www.smeal.psu.edu

Temple University
Enrollment Management
Fox School of Business &
   Management
1801 North Broad Street
Philadelphia, PA 19122
Phone: (215) 204-6675
Fax: (215) 204-5694
http://www.temple.edu

University of Pennsylvania
Pennsylvania School of Design
Joan Weston, Director
110 Meyerson Hall
Philadelphia, PA 19104-6311
Phone: (215) 898-6520
Fax: (215) 573-3927
E-mail: admissions@design.upenn.
   edu
http://www.design.upenn.edu

University of Pennsylvania

Wharton Real Estate Department
Steinberg-Dietrich Hall, Suite 1400
3620 Locust Walk
Philadelphia, PA 19104-6302
Phone: (215) 898-3824
Fax: (215) 573-2220
E-mail: lebermaj@wharton.upenn.
    edu
http://realestate.wharton.upenn.
    edu

SOUTH CAROLINA

University of South Carolina

Undergraduate Admissions
Columbia, SC 29208
Phone: (800) 868-5872
Fax: (803) 777-0101
E-mail: admissions@sc.edu
http://www.sc.edu

TEXAS

Angelo State University

University Admissions
2601 West Avenue North
San Angelo, TX 76909-1014
Phone: (800) 946-8627
Fax: (325) 942-2078
E-mail: admissions@angelo.edu
http://www.angelo.edu

Baylor University

Hankamer School of Business
One Bear Place #98001
Waco, TX 76798
Phone: (800) BAYLOR-U
Fax: (254) 710-3436
E-mail: admissions_office@baylor.
    edu
http://www.baylor.edu

Blinn College

Recruitment and Admissions
Blinn College
902 College Avenue
Brenham, TX 77833-4049
Phone: (979) 830-4152
Fax: (979) 830-4110
E-mail: recruit@blinn.edu
http://www.blinn.edu

College of the Mainland

Admissions Office
1200 Amburn Road
Texas City, TX 77591
Phone: (888) 258-8859 ext. 264
Fax: (409) 938-3126
E-mail: sem@com.edu

Grayson County College

Office of Admissions
Dr. David Petrash
6101 Grayson Drive
Denison, TX 75020-8299
Phone: (903) 465-6030
Fax: (903) 463-5284
http://www.grayson.edu

Midland College

Admissions Office
3600 North Garfield
Midland, TX 79705-6399
Phone: (432) 685-5502
Fax: (432) 685-6401
E-mail: twetendorf@midland.edu
http://www.midland.edu

Texas A&M University

Admissions Office
217 John J. Koldus Building
College Station, TX 77843-1265
Phone: (979) 845-3741
Fax: (979) 845-8737
E-mail: admissions@tamu.edu
http://www.tamu.edu

Texas Christian University

Freshman Admissions
TCU Box 297013
Fort Worth, TX 76129-0002
Phone: (800) 828-3764
Fax: (817) 257-7268
E-mail: frogmail@tcu.edu
http://www.tcu.edu
http://www.com.edu

Texas Tech University

Admissions Office
Rawls College of Business Area of
    Finance, MS 2101
Lubbock, TX 79409-2101
Phone: (806) 742-3339
E-mail: pgoebel@ba.tu.edu
http://www.tu.edu

University of North Texas

University Admissions
Box 311277
Denton, TX 76203-9988
Phone: (800) 868-8211
Fax: (940) 565-2408
E-mail: undergrad@unt.edu
http://www.unt.edu

University of Texas at Arlington

Admissions and Records
P.O. Box 19111
701 South Nedderman Drive
Room 110, Davis Hall
Arlington, TX 76019-0088
Phone: (817) 272-6287
Fax: (817) 272-3435
E-mail: admissions@uta.edu
http://www.uta.edu/realestate

The University of Texas at Austin

Office of Admissions
1 University Station B6600
Austin, TX 78712
Phone: (512) 232-7385
Fax: (512) 475-7475
http://cref.mccombs.utexas.edu

University of Texas at San Antonio

Department of Finance
One UTSA Circle 78249-1644
6900 North Loop, 1604 West
San Antonio, TX 78249-0637
Phone: (210) 458-4011
E-mail: CONMGT@utsa.edu
http://business.utsa.edu

VIRGINIA

Old Dominion University

University Admissions
108 Rollins Hall
Norfolk, VA 23529-0050
Phone: (800) 348-7926
Fax: (757) 683-3255
E-mail: admit@od.edu
http://www.odu.edu

Virginia Commonwealth University

Business Building—5174

1015 Floyd Avenue
P.O. Box 844000
Richmond, VA 23284-4000
Phone: (804) 828-1721
E-mail: dhdowns@vcu.edu
http://realestate.bus.vcu.edu

**Virginia Polytechnic Institute
and State University**
University Admisisons, 201 Burruss
Hall
Blacksburg, VA 24061
Phone: (540) 231-6267
Fax: (540) 231-3242
E-mail: vtadmiss@vt.edu
http://www.vt.edu

WASHINGTON

Washington State University
University Admissions
P.O. Box 641067
Pullman, WA 99164-1067
Phone: (888) 468-6978
Fax: (509) 335-4902
E-mail: admiss2@wsu.edu
http://www.wsu.edu

WEST VIRGINIA

**American Public University
System**
111 West Congress Street
Charles Town, WV 25414
Phone: (877) 468-6268
Fax: (304) 724-3780
E-mail: info@apus.edu
http://www.apus.edu

Marshall University
University Admissions
1 John Marshall Drive
Huntington, WV 25755
Phone: (800) 642-3499
Fax: (304) 696-3135
E-mail: admissions@marshall.edu
http://www.marshall.edu

WISCONSIN

Marquette University
Undergraduate Admissions
P.O. Box 1881

Milwaukee, WI 53201-1881
Phone: (800) 222-6544
Fax: (414) 288-3764
E-mail: admissions@marquette.edu
http://www.marquette.edu

University of Wisconsin
Department of Real Estate and
Urban Land Economics
5262 Grainger Hall
975 University Avenue
Madison, WI 53706-1323
Phone: (608) 262-9816
Fax: (608) 262-7706
E-mail: onwisconsin@admissions.
wisc.edu
http://www.bus.wisc.edu/realestate

WYOMING

University of Wyoming
University Admissions
1000 East University Avenue
Laramie, WY 82071
Phone: (307) 766-2363
Fax: (307) 766-4042
E-mail: real-est@uwyo.edu
http://www.uwyo.edu

CANADA

**Université du Québec à
Montréal**
University Admissions
R-3770 Case postale 8888
Montreal, Québec
Canada
Phone: (514) 987-3000 ext. 4436
E-mail: ozdilek.unsal@uqam.ca
http://www.uqam.ca

University of British Columbia
University Admissions
Sauder School of Business
2053 Main Mall
Vancouver, BC V6T 1Z2
Canada
Phone: (604) 822-8343
Fax: (604) 822-9888
E-mail: trsur.somerville@sauder.
ubc.ca
http://sauder.ubc.ca

University of Guelph
Admissions Coordinator
L-3 University Centre
Guelph, Ontario N1G 2W1
Canada
Phone: (519) 824-4120 ext. 56066
E-mail: jlonderv@uoguelph.ca

TWO-YEAR COLLEGES

ALABAMA

Calhoun Community College
P.O. Box 2216
6250 Highway 31 North
Decatur, AL 35609-2216
Phone: (800) 626-3628 ext. 2594
Fax: (256) 306-2941
E-mail: pml@calhoun.edu
http://www.calhoun.edu

**Chattahoochee Valley
Community College**
P.O. Box 1000
Phenix City, AL 36869
Phone: (800) 842-2822
Fax: (334) 291-4994
E-mail: information@cv.edu
http://www.cv.edu

**Jefferson State Community
College**
2601 Carson Road
Birmingham, AL 35215-3098
Phone: (800) 239-5900
Fax: (205) 856-6070
http://www.jeffstateonline.com

**Northeast Alabama
Community College**
P.O. Box 159
Rainsville, AL 35986
Phone: (256) 228-6001
http://www.nacc.edu

**Wallace State Community
College**
P.O. Box 2000
Hanceville, AL 35077-2000
Phone: (256) 352-8278
Fax: (256) 352-8228
http://www.wallacestate.edu

ARIZONA

Coconino Community College

3000 North Fourth Street
Flagstaff, AZ 86003
Phone: (800) 350-7122
Fax: (520) 526-1821
E-mail: smiller@coco.cc.az.us
http://www.coco.cc.az.us

Glendale Community College

6000 West Olive Avenue
Glendale, AZ 85302
Phone: (623) 845-3000
Fax: (623) 845-3303
E-mail: info@gc.maricopa.edu
http://www.gc.maricopa.edu

Mohave Community College

1971 Jagerson Avenue
Kingman, AZ 86401
Phone: (888) 664-2832
Fax: (928) 757-0808
E-mail: thinkmcc@mohave.edu
http://www.mohave.edu

Pima Community College

4905B East Broadway Boulevard
Tucson, AZ 85709-1120
Phone: (520) 206-4640
Fax: (520) 206-4790
http://www.pima.edu

Scottsdale Community College

9000 East Chaparral Road
Scottsdale, AZ 85256
Phone: (602) 423-6133
Fax: (480) 423-6200
E-mail: fran.watkins@sccmail.
maricopa.edu
http://www.scottsdalecc.edu

CALIFORNIA

American River College

4700 College Oak Drive
Sacramento, CA 95841-4286
Phone: (916) 484-8171
E-mail: recadmiss@mail.arc.losrios.
cc.ca.us
http://www. www.arc.losrios.edu

Antelope Valley College

3041 West Avenue K
Lancaster, CA 93536-5426
Phone: (661) 722-6300
E-mail: info@avc.edu
http://www.avc.edu

Bakersfield College

Enrollment Services
1801 Panorama Drive
Bakersfield, CA 93305-1299
Phone: (661) 395-4301
E-mail: svaughn@bc.cc.ca.us
http://www.bakersfieldcollege.edu

Barstow College

2700 Barstow Road
Barstow, CA 92311-6699
Phone: (760) 252-2411
Fax: (760) 252-1875
http://www.barstow.edu

Butte College

3536 Butte Campus Drive
Oroville, CA 95965
Phone: (530) 895-2361
E-mail: admissions@butte.cc.ca.us
http://www.butte.edu

Cabrillo College

6500 Soquel Drive
Aptos, CA 95003
Phone: (831) 479-6201
Fax: (831) 479-5782
E-mail: ar-mail@cabrillo.edu
http://www.cabrillo.edu

Cerritos College

11110 Alondra Boulevard
Norwalk, CA 90650-6298
Phone: (562) 860-2451
E-mail: rbell@cerritos.edu
http://www.cerritos.edu

Chabot College

25555 Hesperian Boulevard
Hayward, CA 94545
Phone: (510) 723-6700
Fax: (510) 723-7510
http://www.chabotcollege.edu

Chaffey College

5885 Haven Avenue

Rancho Cucamonga, CA 91737-
3002
Phone: (909) 941-2631
http://www.chaffey.edu

Coastline Community College

11460 Warner Avenue
Fountain Valley, CA 92708
Phone: (714) 241-6163
Fax: (714) 241-6288
http://www.coastline.edu

College of the Canyons

26455 Rockwell Canyon Road
Santa Clara, CA 91355
Phone: (888) 206-7827
Fax: (661) 254-7996
http://www.canyons.edu

College of the Desert

Admissions Office
43-500 Monterey Avenue
Palm Desert, CA 92260-9305
Phone: (760) 773-2516
http://www.collegeofthedesert.edu

College of the Redwoods

7351 Tompkins Hill Road
Eureka, CA 95501-9300
Phone: (800) 641-0400
Fax: (707) 476-4406
E-mail: admissions@redwoods.edu

College of San Mateo

1700 West Hillsdale Boulevard
San Mateo, CA 94402-3784
Phone: (650) 574-6594
E-mail: csmadmission@smcccd.
cc.ca.us
http://www.collegeofsanmateo.edu

College of the Sequoias

915 South Mooney Boulevard
Visalia, CA 93277-2234
Phone: (559) 737-4844
Fax: (559) 737-4820
http://www.cos.edu

Contra Costa College

2600 Mission Bell Drive
San Pablo, CA 94806-3195
Phone: (510) 235-7800
http://www.contracosta.cc.ca.us

Cosumnes River College
8401 Center Parkway
Sacramento, CA 95823-5799
Phone: (916) 688-7423
Fax: (916) 688-7467
http://www.crc.losrios.edu

College of the Siskiyous
800 College Avenue
Weed, CA 96094
Phone: (888) 397-4339 ext. 5847
Fax: (530) 938-5367
E-mail: info@siskiyous.edu
http://www.siskiyous.edu

Cuesta College
P.O. Box 8106, Highway 1
San Luis Obispo, CA 93403-8106
Phone: (805) 546-3140
Fax: (805) 546-3975
E-mail: admit@cuesta.edu
http://www.cuesta.edu

Diablo Valley College
Admissions and Records
321 Golf Club Road
Pleasant Hill, CA 94523-1529
Phone: (925) 685-1230 ext. 2561
http://www.dvc.edu

East Los Angeles College
Admissions Office
1301 Avenida Cesar Chavez
Monterey Park, CA 91754-6001
Phone: (323) 265-8801
Fax: (323) 265-8688
http://www.elac.edu

Foothill College
Admissions and Records
12345 El Monte Road
Los Altos Hills, CA 94022
Phone: (650) 949-7326
Fax: (650) 949-7375
http:// www.foothill.fhda.edu

Fullerton College
Admissions and Records
321 East Chapman Avenue
Fullerton, CA 92832-2095
Phone: (714) 992-7582
E-mail: pfong@fullcoll.edu
http://www.fullcoll.edu

Glendale Community College
1500 North Verdugo Road
Glendale, CA 91208
Phone: (818) 551-5115
Fax: (818) 551-5255
E-mail: info@glendale.edu
http://www.glendale.edu

Golden West College
Enrollment Services
15744 Golden West Street
Huntington Beach, CA 92647
Phone: (714) 892-7711 ext. 58196
http://www.gwc.info

Hartnell College
Office Admissions
156 Homestead Avenue
Salinas, CA 93901-1697
Phone: (831) 755-6711
Fax: (831) 759-6014
http://www.hartnell.edu

Imperial Valley College
Office of Admisisons
P.O. Box 158
Imperial, CA 92251
Phone: (760) 352-8320 ext. 200
http://www.imperial.edu

Irvine Valley College
5500 Irvine Center Drive
Irvine, CA 92618
Phone: (949) 451-5416
http://www.ivc.edu

Lake Tahoe Community College
Admissions and Records
One College Drive
South Lake Tahoe, CA 96150-4524
Phone: (530) 541-4660 ext. 211
Fax: (530) 541-7852
http://www.ltcc.edu

Las Positas College
Admissions and Records
3033 Collier Canyon Road
Livermore, CA 94551-7650
Phone: (925) 373-4942
Fax: (925) 443-0742
http://www.laspositas.edu

Lassen Community College District
Highway 139
P.O. Box 3000
Susanville, CA 96130
Phone: (530) 257-6181 ext. 132
http://www.lassencollege.edu

Long Beach City College
4901 East Carson Boulevard
Long Beach, CA 90808
Phone: (562) 938-4130
Fax: (562) 938-4858
http://www.lbcc.edu

Los Angeles City College
855 North Vermont Avenue
Los Angeles, CA 90029
Phone: (323) 953-4340
Fax: (323) 953-4536
http://www.lacitycollege.edu

Los Angeles Harbor College
Admissions and Records
1111 Figueroa Place
Wilmington, CA 90744-2397
Phone: (310) 233-4091
Fax: (310) 834-1882
http://www.lahc.edu

Los Angeles Mission College
Office of Admissions
13356 Eldridge Avenue
Sylmar, CA 91342-3245
Phone: (818) 364-7658
http://www.lamission.edu

Los Angeles Southwest College
Student Services
1600 West Imperial Highway
Los Angeles, CA 90047-4810
Phone: (323) 241-5279
http://www.lasc.edu

Los Angeles Trade-Technical College
400 West Washington Boulevard
Los Angeles, CA 90015
Phone: (213) 763-5301
http://www.lattc.edu

Los Angeles Valley College
5800 Fulton Avenue

Valley Glen, CA 91401
Phone: (818) 947-2353
Fax: (818) 947-2501
http://www.lavc.edu

Los Medanos College
2700 East Leland Road
Pittsburg, CA 94565-5197
Phone: (925) 439-2181 ext. 7500
http://www.losmedanos.edu

Mendocino College
1000 Hensley Creek Road
Ukiah, CA 95482-0300
Phone: (707) 468-3103
Fax: (707) 468-3430
E-mail: ktaylor@mendocino.cc.ca.us
http://www. mendocino.cc.ca.us

Merritt College
Admissions Officer
12500 Campus Drive
Oakland, CA 94619-3196
Phone: (510) 466-7369
E-mail: hperdue@peralta.cc.ca.us
http://www.merritt.edu

MiraCosta College
One Barnard Drive
Oceanside, CA 92056
Phone: (888) 201-8480
Fax: (760) 795-6626
http://www.miracosta.edu

Modesto Junior College
435 College Avenue
Modesto, CA 95350
Phone: (209) 575-6470
Fax: (209) 575-6859
E-mail: mjcadmissions@mail.
    yosemite.cc.ca.us
http://www.gomjc.org

Monterey Peninsula College
980 Fremont Street
Monterey, CA 93940
Phone: (831) 646-4007
Fax: (831) 646-4015
E-mail: rmontori@mpc.edu
http://www.mpc.edu

Napa Valley College
Student Services

2277 Napa-Vallejo Highway
Napa, CA 94558-6236
Phone: (800) 826-1077
Fax: (707) 253-3064
E-mail: snelson@admin.nvc.cc.ca.us
http://www.napavalley.edu

Ohlone College
Registrar
43600 Mission Boulevard
Fremont, CA 94539-5884
Phone: (510) 659-6165
http://www.ohlone.cc.ca.us

Oxnard College
Registrar's Office
4000 South Rose Avenue
Oxnard, CA 93033-6699
Phone: (805) 986-5843
Fax: (805) 986-5943
http://www.oxnard.cc.ca.us

Pasadena City College
1570 East Colorado Boulevard
Pasadena, CA 91106
Phone: (626) 585-7397
Fax: (626) 585-7915
http://www.pasadena.edu

Saddleback College
Admissions Office
28000 Marguerite Parkway
Mission Viejo, CA 92692-3635
Phone: (949) 582-4555
E-mail: earaiza@saddleback.cc.ca.us
http://www.saddleback.edu

San Diego City College
1313 12th Avenue
San Diego, CA 92101-4787
Phone: (619) 388-3474
Fax: (619) 388-3135
E-mail: lhumphr@sdccd.edu
http://www.sdcity.edu

San Diego Mesa College
Admissions and Records
7250 Mesa College Drive
San Diego, CA 92111
Phone: (619) 388-2686
Fax: (619) 388-3960
E-mail: ialvarez@sdccd.cc.ca.us
http:// www.sdmesa.sdccd.cc.ca.us

San Joaquin Delta College
Registrar
5151 Pacific Avenue
Stockton, CA 95207
Phone: (209) 954-5635
Fax: (209) 954-5769
E-mail: admissions@deltacollege.edu
http://www.deltacollege.edu

San Jose City College
2100 Moorpark Avenue
San Jose, CA 95128-2799
Phone: (408) 288-3707
http://www.sjcc.edu

Santa Ana College
Office of Admissions
1530 West 17th Street
Santa Ana, CA 92704
Phone: (714) 564-6053
Fax: (714) 564-4379
http://www.sac.edu

Santa Monica College
Enrollment Services
1900 Pico Boulevard
Santa Monica, CA 90405-1628
Phone: (310) 434-4880 ext. 4774
http://www.smc.edu

Shasta College
Admissions and Records
P.O. Box 496006
Redding, CA 96049-6006
Phone: (530) 225-4841
http://www.shastacollege.edu

Solano Community College
4000 Suisun Valley Road
Fairfield, CA 94534
Phone: (707) 864-7113
Fax: (707) 864-7175
E-mail: admissions@solano.cc.ca.us
http://www. solano.cc.ca.us

Southwestern College
Admissions and Records
900 Otay Lakes Road
Chula Vista, CA 91910
Phone: (619) 482-6550
http://www.swccd.edu

Victor Valley College
Admissions and Records

18422 Bear Valley Road
Victorville, CA 92392
Phone: (760) 245-4271
Fax: (760) 245-9745
E-mail: millenb@vvc.edu
http://www.vvc.edu

COLORADO

Aims Community College
P.O. Box 69
Greeley, CO 80632-0069
Phone: (970) 330-8008 ext. 6624
Fax: (970) 339-6682
E-mail: wgreen@aims.edu
http://www.aims.edu

Community College of Aurora
16000 East CentreTech Parkway
Aurora, CO 80011-9036
Phone: (303) 360-4700
Fax: (303) 361-7432
E-mail: connie.simpson@ccaurora.
edu
http://www.ccaurora.edu

Pikes Peak Community College
5675 South Academy Boulevard
Colorado Springs, CO 80906-5498
Phone: (866) 411-7722
Fax: (719) 540-7092
E-mail: admissions@ppcc.edu
http://www.ppcc.edu

CONNECTICUT

Manchester Community College
P.O. Box 1046
MS #12
Manchester, CT 06045-1046
Phone: (860) 512-3210
Fax: (860) 512-3221
http:// www.mcc.commnet.edu

FLORIDA

Brevard Community College
1519 Clearlake Road
Cocoa, FL 32922-6597
Phone: (321) 433-7271
Fax: (321) 433-7172
http:// www.brevard.cc.fl.us

Broward Community College
225 East Las Olas Boulevard
Fort Lauderdale, FL 33301-2298
Phone: (954) 761-7465
http://www.broward.edu

Edison Community College
Office of Admissions
P.O. Box 60210
Fort Myers, FL 33906-6210
Phone: (800) 749-2ECC
Fax: (941) 489-9094

Florida Community College at Jacksonville
Enrollment Services
501 West State Street
Jacksonville, FL 32202
Phone: (904) 632-3131
Fax: (904) 632-5105
E-mail: admissions@fccj.edu
http://www.fccj.edu

Miami Dade College
11011 SW 104th Street
Miami, FL 33176
Phone: (305) 237-0633
Fax: (305) 237-2964
http://www.mdc.edu

Okaloosa-Walton College
100 College Boulevard
Niceville, FL 32578
Phone: (850) 729-5373
Fax: (850) 729-5323
E-mail: registrar@owcc.net
http:// www.owcc.cc.fl.us

IDAHO

College of Southern Idaho
P.O. Box 1238
315 Falls Avenue
Twin Falls, ID 83303
Phone: (800) 680-0274
Fax: (208) 736-3014
http://www.csi.edu

ILLINOIS

City Colleges of Chicago, Harold Washington College
30 East Lake Street
Admissions Office

Chicago, IL 60601-2449
Phone: (312) 553-6006
Fax: (312) 553-6077
http://hwashington.ccc.edu

City Colleges of Chicago, Kennedy-King College
6800 South Wentworth Avenue
Chicago, IL 60621
Phone: (773) 602-5000 ext. 5055
Fax: (773) 602-5247
E-mail: w.murphy@ccc.edu
http://kennedyking.ccc.edu

College of DuPage
SRC 2046, 425 Fawell Boulevard
Glen Ellyn, IL 60137-6599
Phone: (630) 942-2442
Fax: (630) 790-2686
E-mail: protis@cdnet.cod.edu
http://www.cod.edu

College of Lake County
19351 West Washington Street
Grayslake, IL 60030-1198
Phone: (847) 543-2383
Fax: (847) 543-3061
E-mail: mallen@clcillinois.edu
http://www.clcillinois.edu

Illinois Central College
Office of Admissions
One College Drive
East Peoria, IL 61635-0001
Phone: (800) 422-2293
Fax: (309) 694-5450
http://www.icc.edu

Joliet Junior College
1215 Houbolt Road
Joliet, IL 60431
Phone: (815) 280-2493
http://www.jjc.cc.il.us

Kankakee Community College
P.O. Box 888
Kankakee, IL 60901
Phone: (815) 802-8520
http:// www.kcc.cc.il.us

Kishwaukee College
Admissions Office
21193 Malta Road

Malta, IL 60150-9699
Phone: (815) 825-2086 ext. 400
Fax: (815) 825-2306
http://www.kishwaukeecollege.edu

Lewis and Clark Community College
Enrollment Center, 5800 Godfrey Road
Godfrey, IL 62035
Phone: (800) 500-LCCC
Fax: (618) 467-2310
http://www.lc.cc.il.us

Lincoln Land Community College
Admissions and Records
5250 Shepherd Road
P.O. Box 19256
Springfield, IL 62794-9256
Phone: (800) 727-4161 ext. 298
Fax: (217) 786-2492
E-mail: ron.gregoire@llcc.edu
http://www.llcc.edu

McHenry County College
8900 U.S. Highway 14
Crystal Lake, IL 60012
Phone: (815) 455-8530
E-mail: admissions@mchenry.edu
http://www.mchenry.edu

Oakton Community College
1600 East Golf Road
Des Plaines, IL 60016
Phone: (847) 635-1703
Fax: (847) 635-1890
E-mail: admiss@oakton.edu
http://www.oakton.edu

Prairie State College
Enrollment and Career Development Services
202 South Halsted Street
Chicago Heights, IL 60411
Phone: (708) 709-3516
E-mail: webmaster@prairiestate.edu
http://www.prairiestate.edu

Sauk Valley Community College
Director of Admissions
173 Illinois Route 2
Dixon, IL 61021

Phone: (815) 288-5511 ext. 310
Fax: (815) 288-3190
E-mail: skyhawk@svcc.edu
http://www.svcc.edu

Triton College
Student Services
2000 Fifth Avenue
River Grove, IL 60171
Phone: (800) 942-7404
E-mail: gfuller@triton.cc.il.us
http://www.triton.edu

Waubonsee Community College
Office of Recruitment and Retention
Route 47 at Waubonsee Drive
Sugar Grove, IL 60554
Phone: (630) 466-7900 ext. 2938
Fax: (630) 466-4964
E-mail: recruitment@waubonsee.edu
http://www.waubonsee.edu

KANSAS

Butler County Community College
Director of Enrollment Management
901 South Haverhill Road
El Dorado, KS 67042
Phone: (316) 321-2222 ext. 3255
E-mail: admissions@butlercc.edu
http://www.butlercc.edu

Dodge City Community College
Director of Admissions
2501 North 14th Avenue
Dodge City, KS 67801-2399
Phone: (800) 742-9519
Fax: (316) 225-0918
E-mail: admin@dccc.dodge-city.cc.ks.us
http://www. dccc.dodge-city.cc.ks.us

Independence Community College
Director of Admissions
P.O. Box 708
Independence, KS 67301

Phone: (800) 842-6063
Fax: (620) 331-5344
E-mail: admissions@indycc.edu
http://www.indycc.edu

KENTUCKY

Elizabethtown Community and Technical College
Office of Admissions
600 College Street Road
Elizabethtown, KY 42701
Phone: (877) 246-2322
Fax: (270) 769-0736
http://www.elizabethtown.kctcs.edu

Jefferson Community and Technical College
Admissions Coordinator
109 East Broadway
Louisville, KY 40202
Phone: (502) 213-4000
Fax: (502) 213-2540
http://www.jefferson.kctcs.edu

Madisonville Community College
Registrar
2000 College Drive
Madisonville, KY 42431
Phone: (270) 821-2250
Fax: (502) 821-1555
E-mail: dmcox@pop.uky.edu
http://www.madisonville.kctcs.edu

MARYLAND

The Community College of Baltimore County
Director of Admissions
800 South Rolling Road
Baltimore, MD 21228-5381
Phone: (410) 455-4392
http://www.ccbcmd.edu

MASSACHUSETTS

Bristol Community College
Director of Admissions
777 Elsbree Street, Hudnall Administration Building
Fall River, MA 02720
Phone: (508) 678-2811 ext. 2177

Fax: (508) 730-3265
E-mail: rclark@bristol.mass.edu
http://www.bristol.mass.edu

Greenfield Community College
Director of Admission
1 College Drive
Greenfield, MA 01301-9739
Phone: (413) 775-1000
E-mail: admission@gcc.mass.edu
http://www. gcc.mass.edu

Massachusetts Bay Community College
Director of Admissions
50 Oakland Street
Wellesley Hills, MA 02481
Phone: (781) 239-2500
Fax: (781) 239-1047
http://massbay.edu

MICHIGAN

Delta College
Office of Admissions
1961 Delta Road
University Center, MI 48710
Phone: (800) 285-1705
Fax: (989) 667-2202
E-mail: admit@delta.edu
http://www.delta.edu

Lansing Community College
Director of Admissions/Registrar
P.O. Box 40010
Lansing, MI 48901-7210
Phone: (800) 644-4LCC
Fax: (517) 483-9668
E-mail: jhearns@lcc.edu
http://www.lcc.edu

Macomb Community College
Coordinator of Admissions and
  Assessment
G312
14500 East 12 Mile Road
Warren, MI 48088-3896
Phone: (866) 622-6624
Fax: (586) 445-7140
http://www.macomb.edu

Oakland Community College
Director of Enrollment Services

METC Building, 2900 Featherstone
  Road
Auburn Hills, MI 48304-2845
Phone: (248) 341-2186
http://www.oaklandcc.edu

Wayne County Community College District
Office of Enrollment Management
  and Student Services
801 West Fort Street
Detroit, MI 48226-2539
Phone: (313) 496-2600
Fax: (313) 961-2791
E-mail: caafjh@wccc.edu
http://www.wccc.edu

MINNESOTA

Dakota County Technical College
Office of Admissions
1300 145th Street East
Rosemount, MN 55068
Phone: (877) YES-DCTC ext. 302
Fax: (651) 423-8775
E-mail: admissions@dctc.mnscu.edu
http://www. dctc.mnscu.edu

MISSISSIPPI

Hinds Community College
Director of Admissions and Records
P.O. Box 1100
Raymond, MS 39154-1100
Phone: (800) HINDSCC
Fax: (601) 857-3539
http://www.hindscc.edu

MISSOURI

St. Louis Community College at Meramec
Coordinator of Admissions
11333 Big Bend Boulevard
Kirkwood, MO 63122-5720
Phone: (314) 984-7608
Fax: (314) 984-7051
http://www.stlcc.edu

NEBRASKA

Northeast Community College
Dean of Enrollment Management

P.O.Box 469
Norfolk, NE 68702-0469
Phone: (800) 348-9033 ext. 7260
Fax: (402) 844-7400
E-mail: admission@
  northeastcollege.com
http://www.northeastcollege.com

NEVADA

Community College of Southern Nevada
Admissions and Records
3200 East Cheyenne Avenue
North Las Vegas, NV 89030-4296
Phone: (800) 492-5728
Fax: (702) 643-1474
E-mail: stops@ccsn.nevada.edu
http://www.ccsn.nevada.edu

Truckee Meadows Community College
Admissions and Records
Mail Station #15
7000 Dandini Boulevard, MS
  RDMT 319
Reno, NV 89512-3901
Phone: (775) 674-7623
http://www.tmcc.edu

Western Nevada Community College
Admissions and Records
2201 West College Parkway
Carson City, NV 89703-7399
Phone: (775) 445-2377
Fax: (775) 445-3147
E-mail: wncc_aro@wncc.edu
http://www.wncc.edu

NEW HAMPSHIRE

New Hampshire Community Technical College
Office of Admissions
020 Riverside Drive
Berlin, NH 03570-3717
http://www.nashua.nhctc.edu

White Mountains Community College
Office of Admissions
2020 Riverside Drive

Berlin, NH 03570-3717
Phone: (800) 445-4525
Fax: (603) 752-6335
E-mail: berlin4u@nhctc.edu
http://www.berlin.nhctc.edu

NEW JERSEY

Bergen Community College
Director of Admissions and
    Recruitment
400 Paramus Road
Paramus, NJ 07652-1595
Phone: (201) 447-7193
Fax: (201) 670-7973
E-mail: admsoffice@bergen.edu
http://www.bergen.edu

Gloucester County College
Admissions and Recruitment
1400 Tanyard Road
Sewell, NJ 08080
Phone: (856) 468-5000
Fax: (856) 468-8498
E-mail: hsimmons@gccnj.edu
http://www.gccnj.edu

Ocean County College
Director of Admissions and Records
College Drive, P.O. Box 2001
Toms River, NJ 08754-2001
Phone: (732) 255-0304 ext. 2423
http://www.ocean.edu

Raritan Valley Community
College
Registrar—Enrollment Services
P.O. Box 3300
Somerville, NJ 08876-1265
Phone: (908) 526-1200 ext. 8206
Fax: (908) 704-3442
http://www.raritanval.edu

NEW MEXICO

Clovis Community College
Admissions and Records
417 Schepps Boulevard
Clovis, NM 88101-8381
Phone: (505) 769-4962
Fax: (505) 769-4190
E-mail: admissions@clovis.edu
http://www.clovis.edu

San Juan College
Office of Admissions
4601 College Boulevard
Farmington, NM 87402
Phone: (505) 566-3318
Fax: (505) 566-3500
http://www.sjc.cc.nm.us

Santa Fe Community College
Office of Admissions
6401 Richards Avenue
Santa Fe, NM 87505
Phone: (505) 428-1406
Fax: (505) 428-1237
http://www.sfccnm.edu

NEW YORK

Nassau Community College
Enrollment Management
One Education Drive
Garden City, NY 11530
Phone: (516) 572-7345
E-mail: admissions@sunynassau.edu
http://wwwsunynassau.edu

Rockland Community College
Admissions Office
145 College Road
Suffern, NY 10901-3699
Phone: (800) 722-7666
Fax: (845) 574-4433
E-mail: info@sunyrockland.edu
http://www.sunyrockland.edu

Sullivan County Community
College
Admissions and Registration
    Services
112 College Road
Loch Sheldrake, NY 12759
Phone: (800) 577-5243
Fax: (914) 434-4806
E-mail: dbrown@sullivan.suny.edu
http://www.sullivan.suny.edu

NORTH CAROLINA

Alamance Community College
Admissions
Jimmy Kerr Road
Graham, NC 27253-8000
Phone: (336) 506-4120

Fax: (336) 578-1987
E-mail: admissions@alamance.
    cc.nc.us
http://www.alamance.cc.nc.us

Asheville-Buncombe Technical
Community College
Director, Admissions
340 Victoria Road
Asheville, NC 28801
Phone: (828) 254-1921 ext. 202
Fax: (828) 251-6718
E-mail: admissions@abtech.edu
http://www.abtech.edu

Beaufort County Community
College
Director of Admissions
P.O. Box 1069, 5337 U.S. Highway
    264 East
Washington, NC 27889-1069
Phone: (252) 940-6233
Fax: (252) 940-6393
E-mail: garyb@email.beaufort.
    cc.nc.us
http://www. beaufort.cc.nc.us

Blue Ridge Community
College
Registrar
180 West Campus Drive
Flat Rock, NC 28731
Phone: (828) 694-1810
E-mail: sarahj@blueridge.edu
http://www.blueridge.edu

Caldwell Community College
and Technical Institute
Enrollment Management Services
2855 Hickory Boulevard
Hudson, NC 28638
Phone: (828) 726-2703
Fax: (828) 726-2709
http://www.ccti.edu

Cape Fear Community College
Enrollment Management
411 North Front Street
Wilmington, NC 28401-3993
Phone: (910) 362-7557
Fax: (910) 362-7080
E-mail: admissions@cfcc.edu
http://www.cfcc.edu

Catawba Valley Community College

Director of Admissions and Records
2550 Highway 70 SE
Hickory, NC 28602-9699
Phone: (828) 327-7000 ext. 4218
Fax: (828) 327-7000 ext. 4224
E-mail: cfarmer@cvcc.cc.nc.us
http://www.cvcc.cc.nc.us

Central Piedmont Community College

Office of Admissions
P.O. Box 35009
Charlotte, NC 28235-5009
Phone: (704) 330-6784
http:// www1.cpcc.edu

Forsyth Technical Community College

Enrollment Services
2100 Silas Creek Parkway
Winston-Salem, NC 27103-5197
Phone: (336) 734-7331
Fax: (336) 761-2098
E-mail: admissions@forsythtech.edu
http://www.forsythtech.edu

Guilford Technical Community College

Admissions Office
P.O. Box 309
Jamestown, NC 27282
Phone: (336) 334-4822 ext. 2396
E-mail: knighte@gtcc.cc.nc.us
http://www. gtcc.cc.nc.us

Haywood Community College

Coordinator of Admissions
185 Freedlander Drive
Clyde, NC 28721-9453
Phone: (828) 627-4505
Fax: (828) 627-4513
E-mail: drowland@haywood.cc.nc.us
http://www. haywood.cc.nc.us

James Sprunt Community College

Registrar
Highway 11 South, 133 James
  Sprunt Drive
Kenansville, NC 28349
Phone: (910) 296-2500

Fax: (910) 296-1222
E-mail: rbrown@jscc.cc.nc.us
http://www. jscc.cc.nc.us

McDowell Technical Community College

Admissions Office
Route 1
Box 170
Marion, NC 28752-9724
Phone: (828) 652-6024
Fax: (828) 652-1014
http://www.mcdowelltech.cc.nc.us

Pitt Community College

Office of Admissions
P.O. Drawer 7007
1986 Pitt Tech Road
Greenville, NC 27835-7007
Phone: (252) 321-4217
Fax: (252) 321-4612
E-mail: pittadm@pcc.pitt.cc.nc.us
http://www. pcc.pitt.cc.nc.us

Randolph Community College

Director of Admissions and Registrar
P.O. Box 1009
Asheboro, NC 27204-1009
Phone: (336) 633-0213
Fax: (336) 629-4695
E-mail: info@randolph.edu
http://www.randolph.edu

Rockingham Community College

Enrollment Services
P.O. Box 38
Wentworth, NC 27375-0038
Phone: (336) 342-4261 ext. 2333
http://www.rcc.cc.nc.us

Southwestern Community College

Admissions and Planning
447 College Drive
Sylva, NC 28779
Phone: (800) 447-4091
Fax: (828) 586-3129
E-mail: pweast@southwest.cc.nc.us
http://www. southwest.cc.nc.us

Wake Technical Community College

Director of Admissions

9101 Fayetteville Road
Raleigh, NC 27603-5696
Phone: (919) 662-3357
Fax: (919) 662-3529
E-mail: srbloomf@waketech.edu
http://www.waketech.edu

Western Piedmont Community College

Admissions Office
1001 Burkemont Avenue
Morganton, NC 28655-4511
Phone: (828) 438-6051
http://www.wp.cc.nc.us

Wilson Technical Community College

Admissions Office
P.O. Box 4305
Wilson, NC 27893-0305
Phone: (252) 246-1275
Fax: (252) 246-1285
E-mail: bpage@wilsontech.edu
http://www.wilsontech.edu

OHIO

Cincinnati State Technical and Community College

Director of Admission
3520 Central Parkway
Cincinnati, OH 45223-2690
Phone: (513) 569-1550
Fax: (513) 569-1562
E-mail: adm@cincinnatistate.edu
http://www.cincinnatistate.edu

Columbus State Community College

Director of Admissions
550 East Spring Street, Madison
  Hall
Columbus, OH 43215
Phone: (800) 621-6407 ext. 2669
Fax: (614) 287-6019
http://www.cscc.edu

Cuyahoga Community College

Director of Admissions and Records
2900 Community College Avenue
Cleveland, OH 44115
Phone: (800) 954-8742
Fax: (216) 696-2567
http://www.tri-c.edu

Hondros College
Office of Admissions
4140 Executive Parkway
Westerville, OH 43081
Phone: (800) 783-0095
Fax: (614) 508-7279
E-mail: hondras@hondras.com
http://www.hondras.edu

Jefferson Community College
Director of Admissions
4000 Sunset Boulevard
Steubenville, OH 43952
Phone: (800) 68-COLLEGE ext. 142
Fax: (740) 266-2944
http://ns3.jcc.edu/jcc/directions.asp

Lorain County Community College
Director of Enrollment Services
1005 Abbe Road, North
Elyria, OH 44035
Phone: (800) 995-5222 ext. 4032
Fax: (440) 365-6519
http://www.loraincc.edu

Northwest State Community College
Admissions Office
22600 State Route 34
Archbold, OH 43502-9542
Phone: (419) 267-1213
Fax: (419) 267-5604
E-mail: admissions@northweststate.edu
http://www.northweststate.edu

Sinclair Community College
Office of Admissions
444 West Third Street
Dayton, OH 45402-1460
Phone: (800) 315-3000
Fax: (937) 512-2393
http://www.sinclair.edu

Southern State Community College
Director of Admissions
100 Hobart Drive
Hillsboro, OH 45133
Phone: (800) 628-7722
Fax: (937) 393-6682
E-mail: info@sscc.edu
http://www.sscc.edu

Terra State Community College
Associate Dean of Student Services
2830 Napoleon Road
Fremont, OH 43420
Phone: (800) 334-3886
Fax: (419) 334-9035
http://www.terra.edu

University of Cincinnati Raymond Walters College
Admissions Office
9555 Plainfield Road
Cincinnati, OH 45236-1007
Phone: (513) 745-5700
Fax: (513) 745-5768
E-mail: colrel@ucrwcu.rwc.uc.edu
http://www.rwc.uc.edu

OKLAHOMA

Oklahoma City Community College
Dean of Admissions/Registrar
7777 South May Avenue
Oklahoma City, OK 73159
Phone: (405) 682-7515
E-mail: sedwards@okccc.edu
http://www.okccc.edu

OREGON

Chemeketa Community College
Admissions Contact Enrollment Center
4000 Lancaster Drive, NE
Salem, OR 97305-7070
Phone: (503) 399-5001
Fax: (503) 399-3918
E-mail: broc@chemeketa.edu
http://www.chemketa.edu

Clackamas Community College
Registrar
19600 South Molalla Avenue
Oregon City, OR 97045
Phone: (503) 657-6958 ext. 2742
Fax: (503) 650-6654
E-mail: pattyw@clackamas.edu
http://www.clackamas.edu

Lane Community College
Director of Admissions/Registrar

4000 East 30th Avenue
Eugene, OR 97405-0640
Phone: (541) 747-4501 ext. 2686
E-mail: williamss@lanecc.edu
http://www.lanecc.edu

Portland Community College
Director of Admissions
P.O. Box 19000
Portland, OR 97280
Phone: (503) 977-4519
Fax: (503) 977-4740
E-mail: admissions@pcc.edu
http://www.pcc.edu

Southwestern Oregon Community College
Office of Admissions
Student First Stop, 1988 Newmark Avenue
Coos Bay, OR 97420
Phone: (800) 962-2838
E-mail: lwells@socc.edu
http://www.socc.edu

PENNSYLVANIA

Community College of Philadelphia
Office of Admissions
1700 Spring Garden Street
Philadelphia, PA 19130-3991
Phone: (215) 751-8010
E-mail: admissions@ccp.edu
http://www.ccp.edu

Harrisburg Area Community College
Office of Admissions
1 HACC Drive
Harrisburg, PA 17110
Phone: (800) ABC-HACC
E-mail: admit@hacc.edu
http://www.hacc.edu

Lehigh Carbon Community College
Associate Dean of Admissions
4525 Education Park Drive
Schnecksville, PA 18078-2598
Phone: (610) 799-1575
Fax: (610) 799-1527
E-mail: tellme@lccc.edu
http://www.lccc.edu

Luzerne County Community College

Director of Admissions
1333 South Prospect Street
Nanticoke, PA 18634
Phone: (800) 377-5222 ext. 337
Fax: (570) 740-0238
E-mail: admissions@luzerne.edu
http://www.luzerne.edu

Montgomery County Community College

Director of Admissions and
  Recruitment
Office of Admissions and Records
Blue Bell, PA 19422
Phone: (215) 641-6551
Fax: (215) 619-7188
E-mail: admrec@admin.mc3.edu
http://www.mc3.edu

Northampton County Area Community College

Director of Admissions
3835 Green Pond Road
Bethlehem, PA 18020-7599
Phone: (610) 861-5506
Fax: (610) 861-5551
E-mail: adminfo@northampton.edu
http://www.northampton.edu

RHODE ISLAND

Community College of Rhode Island

Admissions Office
400 East Avenue
Warwick, RI 02886
Phone: (401) 333-7302
Fax: (401) 825-2394
E-mail: webadmission@ccri.cc.ri.us
http://www.ccri.cc.ri.us

TENNESSEE

North Central Institute

Student Services
168 Jack Miller Boulevard
Clarksville, TN 37042
Phone: (931) 431-9700 ext. 247
Fax: (931) 431-9771
E-mail: admissions@nci.edu
http://www.nci.edu

Pellissippi State Technical Community College

Director of Admissions and
  Records
P.O. Box 22990
Knoxville, TN 37933-0990
Phone: (865) 694-6681
E-mail: latouzeau@pstcc.cc.tn.us
http://www.pstcc.cc.tn.us

TEXAS

Amarillo College

Student Services
P.O. Box 447
Amarillo, TX 79178-0001
Phone: (806) 371-5000
Fax: (806) 371-5066
E-mail: austin-rc@actx.edu
http://www.actx.edu

Angelina College

Registrar — Enrollment Director
P.O. Box 1768
Lufkin, TX 75902-1768
Phone: (936) 639-1301 ext. 213
Fax: (936) 639-4299
http://www.angelina.edu

Austin Community College

Admissions and Records
5930 Middle Fiskville Road
Austin, TX 78752-4390
Phone: (512) 223-7766
Fax: (512) 223-7665
E-mail: outreach@austincc.edu
http://www.austincc.edu

Central Texas College

Admissions Office
P.O. Box 1800
Killeen, TX 76540-1800
Phone: (800) 792-3348 ext. 1696
Fax: (254) 526-1545
E-mail: admrec@ctcd.edu
http://www.ctcd.edu

Cisco Junior College

Dean of Admissions/Registrar
101 College Heights
Cisco, TX 76437-9321
Phone: (254) 442-2567 ext. 130
http://www.cisco.cc.tx.us

Coastal Bend College

Office of Admissions/Registrar
3800 Charco Road
Beeville, TX 78102-2197
Phone: (361) 354-2245
Fax: (361) 354-2254
E-mail: register@coastalbend.edu
http://www.coastalbend.edu

College of the Mainland

Registrar/Director of Admissions
1200 Amburn Road
Texas City, TX 77591
Phone: (888) 258-8859 ext. 264
Fax: (409) 938-3126
E-mail: sem@com.edu
http://www.com.edu

Collin County Community College District

Registrar
2200 West University Drive
McKinney, TX 75070-8001
Phone: (972) 881-5174
Fax: (972) 881-5175
E-mail: smeinhardt@ccccd.edu
http://www.ccccd.edu

Del Mar College

Enrollment Services
101 Baldwin Boulevard
Corpus Christi, TX 78404-3897
Phone: (800) 652-3357
http://www.delmar.edu

El Paso Community College

Director of Admissions
P.O. Box 20500
El Paso, TX 79998-0500
Phone: (915) 831-2580
http://epcc.edu

Houston Community College System

Registrar
3100 Main Street
P.O. Box 667517
Houston, TX 77266-7517
Phone: (713) 718-8500
Fax: (713) 718-2111
http://www.hccs.cc.tx.us

Howard College

Office of Admission

1001 Birdwell Lane
Big Spring, TX 79720-3702
Phone: (866) HC-HAWKS
E-mail: rvillanueva@howardcollege.edu
http://www.howardcollege.edu

Lamar Institute of Technology
P.O. Box 10043
Beaumont, TX 77710
Phone: (800) 950-8321
http://www.lit.edu

Laredo Community College
Office of Admissions & Records
West End Washington Street
Laredo, TX 78040-4395
Phone: (956) 721-5177
Fax: (956) 721-5493
http://www.laredo.cc.tx.us

Northeast Texas Community College
Director of Admissions
P.O. Box 1307
1735 Farm to Market Road
Mount Pleasant, TX 75456-1307
Phone: (903) 572-1911 ext. 263
Fax: (903) 572-6712
E-mail: skeys@ntcc.edu
http://www.ntcc.edu

North Harris College
Office of Admissions
2700 W.W. Thorne Drive
Houston, TX 77073
Phone: (281) 618-5794
Fax: (281) 618-7141
E-mail: nhc.startcollege@nhmccd.edu
http://northharris.lonestar.edu

Paris Junior College
Director of Admissions
2400 Clarksville Street
Paris, TX 75460-6298
Phone: (800) 232-5804
http://www.parisjc.edu

San Antonio College
Admissions and Records
1300 San Pedro Avenue
San Antonio, TX 78212-4299

Phone: (800) 944-7575
http://www.accd.edu

South Plains College
Admissions and Records
1401 College Avenue
Levelland, TX 78336
Phone: (806) 894-9611 ext. 2370
Fax: (806) 897-3167
E-mail: arangel@southplainscollege.edu
http://www.southplainscollege.edu

Tarrant County College District
Admissions and Records
1500 Houston Street
Fort Worth, TX 76102-6599
Phone: (817) 515-5291
http://www.tccd.edu

Temple College
Admissions and Records
2600 South First Street
Temple, TX 76504-7435
Phone: (800) 460-4636
Fax: (254) 298-8288
E-mail: angela.balch@templejc.edu
http://www.templejc.edu

Texarkana College
Director of Admissions
2500 North Robison Road
Texarkana, TX 75599
Phone: (903) 838-4541 ext. 3358
Fax: (903) 832-5030
E-mail: vmiller@texarkanacollege.edu
http://www.texarkanacollege.edu

Texas Southmost College
Admissions Office
80 Fort Brown
Brownsville, TX 78520-4991
Phone: (956) 544-8992
E-mail: admissions@utb.edu
http://www.utb.edu

Trinity Valley Community College
Dean of Enrollment Management
and Registrar

100 Cardinal Drive
Athens, TX 75751
Phone: (903) 675-6209 ext. 209
http://www.tvcc.edu

UTAH

Salt Lake Community College
Student Orientation
P.O. Box 30808
Salt Lake City, UT 84130
Phone: (801) 957-4433
Fax: (801) 957-4958
http://www.slcc.edu

VIRGINIA

Eastern Shore Community College
Dean of Student Services
29300 Lankford Highway
Melfa, VA 23410
Phone: (877) 871-8455
Fax: (757) 787-5984
http://www.es.cc.va.us

Lord Fairfax Community College
Office of Admissions
173 Skirmisher Lane
Middletown, VA 22645
Phone: (800) 906-5322 ext. 7107
Fax: (540) 868-7005
E-mail: lfsmitt@lfcc.edu
http://www.lfcc.edu

Northern Virginia Community College
Dean of Academic and Student Services
4001 Wakefield Chapel Road
Annandale, VA 22003-3796
Phone: (703) 323-3195
http://www.nvcc.edu

Piedmont Virginia Community College
Dean of Student Services
501 College Drive
Charlottesville, VA 22902-7589
Phone: (434) 961-6540
Fax: (434) 961-5425
http://www.pvcc.edu

Rappahannock Community College

Admissions and Records Officer
Glenns Campus, 12745 College
  Drive
Glenns, VA 23149-2616
Phone: (804) 758-6742
Fax: (804) 758-3852
http://www.rappahannock.edu

Virginia Highlands Community College

Director of Admissions
Records, and Financial Aid
P.O. Box 828
Abingdon, VA 24212-0828
Phone: (877) 207-6115
Fax: (540) 676-5591
http://vhcc.edu

WASHINGTON

Columbia Basin Community College

Enrollment Management
2600 North 20th Avenue
Pasco, WA 99301
Phone: (509) 547-0511 ext. 2250
Fax: (509) 546-0401
http://www.columbiabasin.edu

North Seattle Community College

Registrar
9600 College Way North
Seattle, WA 98103-3599
Phone: (206) 527-3663
Fax: (206) 527-3671
E-mail: babts@sccd.ctc.edu
http://www.sccd.ctc.edu

Spokane Falls Community College

Student Services
3410 West Fort George Wright Drive
Spokane, WA 99224-5288
Phone: (888) 509-7944
http://www.spokanefalls.edu

Yakima Valley Community College

Office of Admissions
P.O. Box 22520

Yakima, WA 98907-2520
Phone: (509) 574-4713
Fax: (509) 574-6860
E-mail: admis@yvcc.edu
http://www.yvcc.edu

WISCONSIN

Madison Area Technical College

Office of Admissions
3550 Anderson Street
Madison, WI 53704-2599
Phone: (608) 246-6212
http://www.matcmadison.edu

Waukesha County Technical College

Director of Student Development
800 Main Street
Pewaukee, WI 53072-4601
Phone: (888) 892-WCTC
http://www.wctc.edu

Wisconsin Indianhead Technical College

Dean—Student Services
505 Pine Ridge Drive
Shell Lake, WI 54871
Phone: (800) 243-9482
Fax: (715) 468-2819
http://www.witc.edu

GRADUATE AND MBA PROGRAMS

ALABAMA

University of Alabama

149 Bidgood Hall
Tuscaloosa, AL 35487
Phone: (205) 348-4117
E-mail: rerec@cba.ua.edu
http://www.cba.ua.edu

CALIFORNIA

University of California at Berkeley

Haas School of Business
545 Student Services #1900
Berkeley, CA 94720-1900

Phone: (510) 642-1405
http://www.haas.berkeley.edu/mba

University of San Diego

Olin Hall 108, 5998 Alcala Park
San Diego, CA 92110
Phone: (619) 260-4150
E-mail: lchambers@sandiego.edu
http://www.usdrealestate.com

University of Southern California

Lusk Center for Real Estate
650 Childs Way, Suite 331
Los Angeles, CA 90089-0626
Phone: (213) 740-5000
Fax: (213) 740-6170
E-mail: sonia@usc.edu
http://www.usc.edu/lusk

University of Southern California

School of Policy, Planning, and
  Development
Ralph and Goldy Lewis Hall,
  Room 111
Los Angeles, CA 90089-0626
Phone: (213) 740-6842
Fax: (213) 740-7573
E-mail: marisolr@usc.edu
http://www.usc.edu/sppd

COLORADO

University of Colorado

Leeds School of Business
Room 251 Real Estate Center
Campus P.O. Box 419
Boulder, CO 80309-0419
Phone: (303) 492-3643
E-mail: Katie.mrazik@colorado.
  edu
http://leeds.colorado.edu/
  realestate

University of Denver

Daniels College of Business
2101 South University Boulevard,
  #380
Denver, CO 80208
Phone: (303) 871-3432
E-mail: mlevine@du.edu
http://daniels.du.edu/burns

CONNECTICUT

University of Connecticut
School of Business Administration
368 Fairfield Road, U-41RE
Storrs, CT 06269
Phone: (860) 486-3227
E-mail: recenter@sba.uconn.edu
http://www.business.uconn.edu/
realestate

DISTRICT OF COLUMBIA

American University
Kogod School of Business
4400 Massachusetts Avenue NW
Washington, DC 20016
Phone: (202) 885-1951
E-mail: chinloy@american.edu
http://www.kogod.american.edu

FLORIDA

Florida Atlantic University
College of Business, LA 444
2912 College Avenue
Boca Raton, FL 33314
Phone: (561) 297-3684
http://www.fau.edu/realestate

Florida Gulf Coast University
College of Business
10501 FGCU Boulevard South
Ft. Myers, FL 33965-6565
Phone: (239) 590-7373
E-mail: sweeks@fgcu.edu
http://cps.fgcu.edu

Florida State University
Rovetta Business Building, Room
313
Department of Risk Management,
Real Estate and Business Law
Tallahassee, FL 32306-1110
Phone: (850) 644-4070
E-mail: dgatzla@fsu.edu
http://www.ree.fsu.edu

University of Florida
Stutzin Hall 301— Center for Real
Estate Studies
Warrington College of Business
Administration

P.O. Box 117168
Gainesville, FL 32611-7168
Phone: (352) 392-9307
E-mail: ling@dale.cba.ufl.edu
http://www.realestate.ufl.edu

GEORGIA

Georgia State University
J. Mack Robinson College of
Business
Department of Real Estate
P.O. Box 4020
Atlanta, GA 30302
Phone: (404) 651-2760
E-mail: realestate@gsu.edu
http://www.gsu.edu

University of Georgia
Terry College of Business, 206
Brooks Hall
Athens, GA 30602-6255
Phone: (706) 542-4290
E-mail: realestate@terry.uga.edu
http://www.terry.uga.edu/realestate

University of West Georgia
State University of West Georgia
1601 Maple Street
College of Business, 170
Carrolton, GA 30118
Phone: (678) 839-5023
E-mail: jburton@westga.edu
http://www.westga.edu/~mktreal

ILLINOIS

DePaul University
The Real Estate Center
DePaul Center, Suite 6070
1 East Jackson
Chicago, IL 60604
Phone: (312) 362-5906
E-mail: realestate@depaul.edu
http://www.realestate.depaul.edu

Kellogg School of Management
6214 Jacobs Hall
Northwestern University
2001 Sheridan Road
Evanston, IL 60208-2001
Phone: (847) 491-3564

E-mail: tsm@kellogg.northwestern.
edu
http://www.kellogg.northwestern.
edu/realestate

Roosevelt University
430 South Michigan Avenue
Chicago, IL 60605
Phone: (312) 281-3355
E-mail: sdermisi@roosevelt.edu
http://www.roosevelt.edu/
realestate

**University of Illinois at
Chicago**
815 West Van Buren, Suite 220
Chicago, IL 60607-3525
Phone: (312) 996-4573
E-mail: mre@uic.edu
http://www.uic.edu/cba/lgradbiz

INDIANA

Indiana University
Center for Real Estate Studies
Kelley School of Business
1309 East 10th Street, Suite 738
Bloomington, IN 47405
Phone: (812) 855-7794
E-mail: fisher@indiana.edu
http://www.indiana.edu/~cres

MARYLAND

Johns Hopkins University
100 North Charles Street SPSBE,
Seventh floor
Baltimore, MD 21201
Phone: (410) 516-0772
E-mail: mcmoineau@jhu.edu
http:www.spsbe.jhu.edu

MASSACHUSETTS

**Harvard Graduate School of
Design**
Gund Hall
48 Quincy Street
Cambridge, MA 01238
Phone: (617) 495-2337
E-mail: rbrincke@gsd.harvard.edu
http://www.gsd.harvard.edu

Massachusetts Institute of Technology
Center for Real Estate
77 Massachusetts Avenue W31-310
Cambridge, MA 02139
Phone: (617) 253-8308
E-mail: mit-cre@mit.edu
http://www.mit.edu/cre

Massachusetts Institute of Technology
Sloan School of Management
50 Memorial Drive
Cambridge, MA 02142
Phone: (617) 253-2659
http://www.mitsloan.mit.edu

MICHIGAN

Stephen M. Ross School of Business
701 Tappan Street, D4201
Ann Arbor, MI 48109-1234
Phone: (734) 764-1269
E-mail: capozza@umich.edu
http://www.umich.edu/~reecon/
  restate

MINNESOTA

St. Cloud State University
G.R. Herberger College of Business
720 Fourth Avenue South
St. Cloud, MN 56320-4498
Phone: (320) 308-4986
E-mail: moon@stcloudstate.edu
http://www. stcloudstate.edu/hcob

University of St. Thomas
Shenehon Center for Real Estate
  Education
1000 LaSalle Avenue, TMH 153
Minneapolis, MN 55403
Phone: (651) 962-5551
Fax: (651) 962-6930
E-mail: cob@stthomas.edu
http://www.stthomas.edu/realestate/
  degrees/default.htm

NEW YORK

Columbia Business School
325A 3022 Broadway, Uris Hall
New York, NY 10027
Phone: (212) 854-8556
E-mail: cc2263@columbia.edu
http://www2.gsb.columbia.edu/
  departments/realestate

Cornell University
Program in Real Estate
114 West Sibley
Ithaca, NY 14853
Phone: (607) 255-7110
E-mail: jc347@cornell.edu
http://www.realestate.cornell.edu

New York University
Real Estate Institute
School of Continuing and
  Professional Studies
11 West 42nd Street, Suite 509
New York, NY 10036
Phone: (800) 998-7204
E-mail: Marcie.burros@nyu.edu
http://www.scps.nyu.edu/rei

OHIO

Cleveland State University
UR223 Levin College Urban Affairs
Cleveland, OH 44115
Phone: (216) 687-5258
E-mail: roby@urban.csuohio.edu
http://urban.csuohio.edu

Ohio State University
Fisher College of Business
Graduate Programs Office
100 Gerlach Hall
2108 Neil Avenue
Columbus, OH 43210-1144
Phone: (614) 292-8511
E-mail: fishergrad@cob.osu.edu
http://www.cob.ohio-state.edu

University of Cincinnati
Real Estate Program
403 Carl H. Lindner Hall College of
  Business
P.O. Box 210195
Cincinnati, OH 45221-0195
Phone: (513) 556-7193
E-mail: real.estate@uc.edu
http://www.business.uc.edu/
  realestate

PENNSYLVANIA

Pennsylvania State University
The Mary Jean and Frank P. Smeal
  College of Business
409 Business Administration
  Building
University Park, PA 16802
Phone: (814) 865-4172
E-mail: jxc5@oas.psu.edu
http://www.smeal.psu.edu

University of Pennsylvania
Samuel Zell and Robert Lurie Real
  Estate Center
The Wharton School
256 South 37th Street
Philadelphia, PA 19104
Phone: (215) 898-9687
E-mail: lebermaj@wharton.upenn.
  edu
http://realestate.wharton.upenn.
  edu

SOUTH CAROLINA

Clemson University
121 Lee Hall
Clemson, SC 29634
Phone: (864) 656-3903
E-mail: jfaris@clemson.edu
http://www.clemson.edu/caah/pla/
  mred/index.htm

University of South Carolina
The Darla Moore School of
  Business
Columbia, SC 29205
Phone: (803) 777-5960
E-mail: rrogers@moore.sc.edu
http://mooreschool.sc.edu/moore/
  sccre

TEXAS

University of Texas at Austin
McCombs School of Business
1 University Station B6600
Austin, TX 78712-1179
Phone: (512) 232-7385
E-mail: angela.dorsey@mccombs.
  utexas.edu.
http://cref.mccombs.utexas.edu

VIRGINIA

Virginia Commonwealth University
Business Building— 5714
1015 Floyd Avenue
P.O. Box 844000
Richmond, VA 23284-4000
Phone: (804) 828-1721
E-mail: dhdowns@vcu.edu
http://realestate.bus.vcu.edu

WASHINGTON

University of Washington
3949 15th Avenue NE
P.O. Box 355740
Seattle, WA 98195
Phone: (206) 616-2090
E-mail: jdelisle@u.washington.edu
http://reuw.washington.edu

WISCONSIN

University of Wisconsin
Department of Real Estate and
Urban Land Economics
5262 Grainger Hall
975 University Avenue
Madison, WI 53706-1323
Phone: (608) 262-9816
E-mail: smalpezzi@bus.wisc.edu
http://www.bus.wisc.edu/realestate

CANADA

Université du Québec à Montréal
University Admissions
R-3770 Case postale 8888
Montreal, Québec
Canada
Phone: (514) 987-3000 ext. 4436

E-mail: ozdilek.unsal@uqam.ca
http://www.uqam.ca

University of British Columbia
Sauder School of Business
Henry Angus 2053 Main Mall
Vancouver, British Columbia
Canada
Phone: (604) 822-8343
E-mail: tsur.somerville@sauder.ubc.ca
http://sauder.ubc.ca

York University
Schulich School of Business
4700 Keele Street
Toronto, Ontario
Canada
Phone: (416) 736-5967
E-mail: jmcjkellar@schulich.yorku.ca
http://www.schulich.yorku.ca

B. PLANNING

FOUR-YEAR COLLEGES AND UNIVERSITIES

ALABAMA

Alabama A&M University
School of Agriculture &
Environmental Sciences
Department of Community
Planning & Urban Studies
308 Dawson Building
Normal, AL 35762
Phone: (256) 372-5425
Fax: (256) 372-5906
E-mail: chukudi.izeogu@aamu.edu
http://www.aamu.edu

ARIZONA

Arizona State University
College of Design
School of Planning
P.O. Box 872005
Tempe, AZ 85286-2005
Phone: (480) 965-7167
Fax: (480) 965-9656
E-mail: hemelata.dandekar@asu.edu
http://design.asu.edu

CALIFORNIA

California Polytechnic State University—San Luis Obispo
College of Architecture &
Environmental Design
City & Regional Planning
Department
1 Grand Avenue
San Luis Obispo, CA 93407
Phone: (805) 756-1315
Fax: (805) 756-1340
E-mail: wsiembie@calpoly.edu
http://www.planning.calpoly.edu/~crp/

California State Polytechnic University—Pomona
College of Environmental Design
Department of Urban and Regional
Planning
3801 West Temple Avenue
Pomona, CA 91768-4048
Phone: (909) 869-2688
Fax: (909) 869-4688
E-mail: rwwillson@csupomona.edu
http://www.csupomona.edu

California State University—Northridge
College of Social and Behavioral
Sciences
Department of Urban Studies and
Planning
18111 Nordhoff Street
Northridge, CA 91330-8259
Phone: (818) 677-2904
Fax: (818) 677-5850
E-mail: tdagodag@csun.edu
http://www.csun.edu/~hfoao078

ILLINOIS

University of Illinois at Urbana-Champaign
College of Fine & Applied Arts
Department of Urban and Regional
Planning
111 Temple Buell Hall
611 Taft Drive
Champaign, IL 61820
Phone: (217) 333-3890
Fax: (217) 244-1717
E-mail: robo@uiuc.edu
http://www.urban.uiuc.edu

INDIANA

Ball State University

College of Architecture and
   Planning
Department of Urban Planning
Architecture Building 327
Muncie, IN 47306-0315
Phone: (765) 285-1963
Fax: (765) 285-2648
E-mail: ekelly@bsu.edu
http://www.bsu.edu/urban

IOWA

Iowa State University

College of Design
Department of Community and
   Regional Planning
126 College of Design
Ames, IA 50011-2035
Phone: (515) 294-8958
Fax: (515) 294-2348
E-mail: tkeller@iastate.edu
http://www.public.iastate.edu/
   ~design/crp/crp.html

MICHIGAN

Eastern Michigan University

Department of Geography and
   Geology
Urban and Regional Planning
   Program
205 Strong Hall
Ypsilanti, MI 48197-2219
Phone: (734) 487-7656
Fax: (734) 487-6979
E-mail: ntyler@emich.edu
http://planning.emich.edu

Michigan State University

Department of Geography
Urban and Regional Planning
   Program
101 UPLA Building
East Lansing, MI 48824-1221
Phone: (517) 353-9054
Fax: (517) 355-7697
E-mail: wilsonmm@msu.edu
http://spdc.msu.edu/urp

MISSOURI

Missouri State University

College of Natural and Applied
   Sciences
Department of Geography, Geology
   and Planning
901 South National
Springfield, IL 65897
Phone: (417) 836-5800
Fax: (417) 836-6006
E-mail: paulrillinson@
   missouristate.edu
http://www.geosciences.
   missouristate.edu

NORTH CAROLINA

East Carolina University

Thomas Harriot College of Arts and
   Sciences
Department of Geography
Urban and Regional Planning
   Program
Rawl Annex 139
Greenville, NC 27858
Phone: (252) 328-6565
Fax: (252) 328-1269
E-mail: wubnehm@mail.ecu.edu
http://www.ecu.edu/plan/

OHIO

University of Cincinnati

College of Design, Architecture, Art
   and Planning
School of Planning
6210 DAAP Building
2624 Clifton Avenue
Cincinnati, OH 45221-0016
Phone: (513) 556-4943
Fax: (513) 556-1274
E-mail: david.edelman@uc.edu
http://ucplanning.uc.edu

VIRGINIA

University of Virginia

School of Architecture
Department of Urban and
   Environmental Planning
Campbell Hall
P.O. Box 400122

Charlottesville, VA 22904-4122
Phone: (434) 924-1339
Fax: (434) 982-2678
E-mail: spain@virginia.edu
http://www.arch.virginia.edu/
   planning/

WASHINGTON

Eastern Washington
University

College of Business & Public
   Administration
Department of Urban Planning,
   Public Health Administration
668 North Riverpoint Boulevard,
   Suite A
Spokane, WA 99202-1660
Phone: (509) 358-2230
Fax: (509) 358-2267
E-mail: fhurand@mail.ewu.edu
http://www.ewu.edu

CANADA

Université de Montréal

Faculty of Environmental Design
Institut d'Urbanisme
C.P. 6128, succ. Centre-ville
Montréal
Quebéc, Canada H3C 3J7
Phone: (514) 343-5699
Fax: (514) 343-2338
E-mail: Gerard.beaudet@
   umontreal.ca
http://www.urb.umontreal.ca

GRADUATE PROGRAMS

ALABAMA

Alabama A&M University

School of Agriculture &
   Environmental Sciences
Department of Community
   Planning & Urban Studies
308 Dawson Building
Normal, AL 35762
Phone: (256) 372-5425
Fax: (256) 372-5906
E-mail: chukudi.izeogu@aamu.edu
http://www.aamu.edu

Auburn University
School of Architecture
Graduate Program in Community
    Planning
104 Dudley Hall
Auburn, AL 36849
Phone: (334) 844-4516
Fax: (334) 844-5419
E-mail: pittajj@auburn.edu
http://www.cadc.auburn.edu

ARIZONA

Arizona State University
College of Design
School of Planning
P.O. Box 872005
Tempe, AZ 85286-2005
Phone: (480) 965-7167
Fax: (480) 965-9656
E-mail: hemelata.dandekar@asu.
    edu
http://design.asu.edu

University of Arizona
College of Social and Behavioral
    Sciences
Planning Degree Program
1103 East Second Street
Harvill Building, Room 341
Tucson, AZ 85721-0076
Phone: (520) 621-9597
Fax: (520) 621-9820
E-mail: bbecker@u.arizona.edu
http://www.planning.arizona.edu

CALIFORNIA

**California Polytechnic State
University—San Luis
Obispo**
College of Architecture &
    Environmental Design
City & Regional Planning
    Department
1 Grand Avenue
San Luis Obispo, CA 93407
Phone: (805) 756-1315
Fax: (805) 756-1340
E-mail: wsiembie@calpoly.edu
http://www.planning.calpoly.
    edu/~crp/

**California State Polytechnic
University—Pomona**
College of Environmental Design
Department of Urban and Regional
    Planning
3801 West Temple Avenue
Pomona, CA 91768-4048
Phone: (909) 869-2688
Fax: (909) 869-4688
E-mail: rwwillson@csupomona.edu
http://www.csupomona.edu

San Jose State University
College of Social Sciences
Urban and Regional Planning
    Department
One Washington Square
San Jose, CA 95192-0185
Phone: (408) 924-5882
Fax: (408) 924-5872
E-mail: jmp@pogodzinski.net
http://www.sjsu.edu/
    urbanplanning/

**University of California—
Berkeley**
College of Environmental Design
Department of City and Regional
    Planning
228 Wurster Hall, #1850
Berkeley, CA 94720-1850
Phone: (510) 642-3256
Fax: (510) 642-1641
E-mail: robertc@berkeley.edu
http://www.dcrp.ced.berkeley.edu

**University of California—
Irvine**
School of Social Ecology
Department of Planning, Policy and
    Design
202 Social Ecology I Building
Irvine, CA 92697-7075
Phone: (949) 824-3480
Fax: (949) 824-8566
E-mail: chew@uci.edu
http://www.seweb.uci.edu./ppd/

**University of California—Los
Angeles**
School of Public Policy and Social
    Research
Department of Urban Planning

3250 Public Policy Building
Los Angeles, CA 90095-1656
Phone: (310) 825-4025
Fax: (310) 206-5566
E-mail: sideris@ucla.edu
http://www.spa.ucla.edu

**University of Southern
California**
School of Policy, Planning and
    Development
Urban and Regional Planning
    Program
Ralph and Goldy Lewis Hall
    —Room 108
Los Angeles, CA 90089-0626
Phone: (213) 740-6842
Fax: (213) 740-7573
E-mail: dsloane@usc.edu
http://www.usc.edu/sppd/mpl

COLORADO

**University of Colorado at
Denver**
College of Architecture and
    Planning
Campus Box 126
P.O. Box 173364
Denver, CO 80217-3364
Phone: (303) 556-4866
Fax: (303) 556-3687
E-mail: sancar@colorado.edu
http://www.colorado.edu

FLORIDA

Florida Atlantic University
College of Architecture, Urban and
    Public Affairs
Department of Urban and Regional
    Planning
111 East Las Olas Boulevard
Fort Lauderdale, FL 33301
Phone: (954) 764-5652
Fax: (964) 762-5673
E-mail: jvos@fau.edu
http://www.fau.edu/durp

Florida State University
College of Social Science
Department of Urban and Regional
    Planning

330 Bellamy Building
Tallahassee, FL 32306-2280
Phone: (850) 644-4510
Fax: (850) 645-4841
E-mail: cconerl@garnet.acns.fsu.edu
http://www.fsu.edu/durp

University of Florida

College of Design, Construction &
    Planning
Department of Urban and Regional
    Planning
P.O. Box 115706
Gainesville, FL 32611-5706
Phone: (352) 392-0997
Fax: (352) 392-3308
E-mail: paul@geoplan.ufl.edu
http://web.dcp.ufl.edu/urp/

GEORGIA

Georgia Institute of Technology

College of Architecture
City and Regional Planning
    Program
245 Fourth Street NW, Room 204
Atlanta, GA 30332-0155
Phone: (404) 894-2350
Fax: (404) 894-1628
E-mail: michael.elliott@coa.gatech.
    edu
http://www.coa.gatech.edu/crp/

HAWAII

University of Hawaii at Manoa

College of Social Science
Department of Urban and Regional
    Planning
2424 Maile Way, Room 107
Honolulu, HI 96822
Phone: (808) 956-7381
Fax: (808) 956-6870
E-mail: karlk@hawaii.edu
http://www.durp.hawaii.edu

ILLINOIS

University of Illinois at Chicago

College of Urban Planning and
    Public Affairs
Urban Planning and Policy
    Program

412 South Peoria Street, Suite 215
Chicago, IL 60617-7065
Phone: (312) 996-5240
Fax: (312) 413-2314
E-mail: mjaffe@uic.edu
http://www.uic.edu/cuppa/upp

University of Illinois at
Urbana-Champaign

College of Fine & Applied Arts
Department of Urban and Regional
    Planning
111 Temple Buell Hall
611 Taft Drive
Champaign, IL 61820
Phone: (217) 333-3890
Fax: (217) 244-1717
E-mail: robo@uiuc.edu
http://www.urban.uiuc.edu

INDIANA

Ball State University

College of Architecture and
    Planning
Department of Urban Planning
Architecture Building 327
Muncie, IN 47306-0315
Phone: (765) 285-1963
Fax: (765) 285-2648
E-mail: ekelly@bsu.edu
http://www.bsu.edu/urban

IOWA

Iowa State University

College of Design
Department of Community and
    Regional Planning
126 College of Design
Ames, IA 50011-2035
Phone: (515) 294-8958
Fax: (515) 294-2348
E-mail: tkeller@iastate.edu
http://www.public.iastate.edu/
    ~design/crp/crp.html

University of Iowa

Graduate College
Graduate Program in Urban and
    Regional Planning
338 Jessup Hall
Iowa City, IA 52242-1316

Phone: (319) 335-0032
Fax: (319) 335-3330
E-mail: alan-peters@uiowa.edu
http://www.urban.uiowa.edu

KANSAS

Kansas State University

College of Architecture, Planning
    and Design
Department of Landscape
    Architecture, Regional and
    Community Planning
302 Seaton Hall
Manhattan, KS 66506-2909
Phone: (785) 532-5961
Fax: (785) 532-6722
E-mail: cak@ksu.edu
http://larcp.arch.ksu.edu/larcp

University of Kansas

School of Architecture and Urban
    Design
Graduate Program in Urban
    Planning
317 Marvin Hall
1465 Jayhawk Building
Lawrence, KS 66045-7614
Phone: (785) 864-4184
Fax: (785) 864-5301
E-mail: jimmayo@ku.edu
http://www.sau.ku.edu/Academic/
    UBPL.shtml

LOUISIANA

University of New Orleans

Department of Planning and Urban
    Studies
308 Mathematics Building
New Orleans, LA 70148-2910
Phone: (504) 280-6277
Fax: (504) 280-6272
E-mail: jsbrooks@uno.edu
http://cupa.uno.edu/murp.html

MARYLAND

Morgan State University

Institute of Architecture and
    Planning
Graduate Program in City and
    Regional Planning

1700 East Cold Spring Lane &
   Hillen Road
Baltimore, MD 21251
Phone: (443) 885-3255
Fax: (443) 885-8233
E-mail: ssen@morgan.edu
http://www.morgan.edu/academics/
   IAP/index.html

University of Maryland at College Park

School of Architecture, Planning
   and Preservation
Urban Studies and Planning Program
1200 School of Architecture
College Park, MD 20742
Phone: (301) 405-6789
Fax: (301) 314-9583
E-mail: jimcohen@umd.edu
http://www.umd.edu.ursp

MASSACHUSETTS

Harvard University

Graduate School of Design
Department of Urban Planning and
   Design
48 Quincy Street, Room 312
Cambridge, MA 02138
Phone: (617) 495-2521
Fax: (617) 496-1292
E-mail: jkayden@gsd.harvard.edu
http://www.gsd.harvard.edu/
   academic/upd/

Massachusetts Institute of Technology

School of Architecture and Planning
Department of Urban Studies &
   Planning
77 Massachusetts Avenue, Building
   7—No. 337
Cambridge, MA 02139
Phone: (617) 253-1907
Fax: (617) 253-2654
E-mail: ljvale@mit.edu
http://dusp.mit.edu

Tufts University

Graduate School of Arts and Sciences
Department of Urban and
   Environmental Policy and
   Planning
97 Talbot Avenue

Medford, MA 02155
Phone: (617) 627-3394
Fax: (617) 627-3377
E-mail: Rachel.bratt@tufts.edu
http://ase.tufts.edu/uep/

University of Massachusetts at Amherst

College of Natural Resources and
   the Environment
Department of Landscape
   Architecture and Regional
   Planning
109 Hills North
Amherst, MA 01003-9328
Phone: (413) 545-2255
Fax: (413) 545-1772
E-mail: mhamim@larp.umass.edu
http://umass.edu/larp/

MICHIGAN

Michigan State University

Department of Geography
Urban and Regional Planning
   Program
101 UPLA Building
East Lansing, MI 48824-1221
Phone: (517) 353-9054
Fax: (517) 355-7697
E-mail: wilsonmm@msu.edu
http://spdc.msu.edu/urp/

Wayne State University

Department of Geography and
   Urban Planning
College of Liberal Arts and Sciences
3198 Faculty/Administration
   Building
Detroit, MI 48202
Phone: (313) 577-2701
Fax: (313) 577-0022
E-mail: r.boyle@wayne.edu
http://www.clas.wayne.edu/GUP

MINNESOTA

University of Minnesota

Humphrey Institute of Public Affairs
Urban and Regional Planning
   Program
301 19th Avenue South
Minneapolis, MN 55455

Phone: (612) 626-1074
Fax: (612) 625-6351
E-mail: egoetz@hhh.umn.edu
http://www.hhh.umn.edu

NEBRASKA

University of Nebraska— Lincoln

College of Architecture
Community & Regional Planning
   Program
302 Architecture Hall
Lincoln, NE 68558-0105
Phone: (402) 472-9280
Fax: (402) 472-3806
E-mail: gscholzl@unl.edu
http://www.unl.edu/archcoll/crp/
   index.html

NEW JERSEY

Rutgers—The State University of New Jersey

Edward J. Bloustein School of
   Planning and Urban Policy
Urban Planning and Policy
   Development Program
33 Livingston Avenue, Suite 302
New Brunswick, NJ 08901-1987
Phone: (732) 932-3822
Fax: (732) 932-2253
E-mail: cja1@rci.rutgers.edu
http://www.policy.rutgers.edu/
   uppd/index.html

NEW MEXICO

University of New Mexico

School of Architecture and Planning
Community and Regional Planning
   Program
2414 Central Avenue SE 277-0076
Albequerque, NM 87106
Phone: (505) 277-5050
Fax: (505) 277-0076
E-mail: cymro@unm.edu
http://www.unm.edu/~crp/

NEW YORK

Columbia University

Graduate School of Architecture,
   Planning and Preservation

Urban Planning Program
1172 Amsterdam Avenue—Avery
    Hall 413
New York, NY 10027
Phone: (212) 854-3513
Fax: (212) 854-9092
E-mail: eds2@columbia.edu
http://www.arch.columbia.edu/UP

Cornell University

College of Architecture, Art and
    Planning
Department of City and Regional
    Planning
109 West Sibley Hall
Ithaca, NY 14853
Phone: (607) 255-6848
Fax: (607) 255-1971
E-mail: kmr22@cornell.edu
http://www.dcrp.cornell.edu

Hunter College, City University of New York

School of Arts and Sciences
Graduate Program in Urban
    Planning
695 Park Avenue
New York, NY 10021
Phone: (212) 772-5518
Fax: (212) 772-5593
E-mail: lmccormi@hunter.cuny.
    edu
http://www.maxweber.hunter.cuny.
    edu/urban

New York University

Wagner Graduate School of Public
    Service
Urban Planning Program
295 Lafayette Street
New York, NY 10012
Phone: (212) 998-7400
Fax: (212) 995-3890
E-mail: rae.zimmerman@nyu.edu
http://www.nyu.edu/wagner/urban.
    planning

Pratt Institute

School of Architecture
Graduate Center for Planning and
    the Environment
200 Willoughby Avenue
Brooklyn, NY 11205

Phone: (718) 399-4314
Fax: (718) 399-4379
E-mail: lwolfpow@pratt.edu
http://prat.edu/arch/gcpe

University at Albany—State University of New York

College of Arts and Sciences
Graduate Planning Program
Arts & Sciences 218
Albany, NY 12222
Phone: (518) 442-4770
Fax: (518) 442-4742
E-mail: lawsonc@albany.edu
http://www.albany.edu/gp/

University at Buffalo, State University of New York

School of Architecture and
    Planning
Department of Urban and Regional
    Planning
3435 Main Street—116 Hayes Hall
Buffalo, NY 14214-3087
Phone: (716) 829-2133
Fax: (716) 829-3256
E-mail: nverma@ap.buffalo.edu
http://ap.buffalo.edu/planning

NORTH CAROLINA

The University of North Carolina at Chapel Hill

College of Arts and Sciences
Department of City and Regional
    Planning
New East Building—CB #3140
Chapel Hill, NC 25799-3140
Phone: (919) 962-3983
Fax: (919) 962-5206
E-mail: malizia@email.unc.edu
http://planning.unc.edu

OHIO

Cleveland State University

Levin College of Urban Affairs
Urban Planning, Design and
    Development Program
1717 Euclid Avenue—Room UR
    316
Cleveland, OH 44115
Phone: (216) 687-2136

Fax: (216) 687-9342
E-mail: wendy@urban.csuohio.edu
http://urban.csuohio.edu

Ohio State University

Knowlton School of Architecture
City and Regional Planning
    Program
275 West Woodruff Avenue
Columbus, OH 43210-1135
Phone: (614) 292-1012
Fax: (614) 292-7016
E-mail: pearlman1@osu.edu
http://knowlton.osu.edu

University of Cincinnati

College of Design, Architecture, Art
    and Planning
School of Planning
6210 DAAP Building
2624 Clifton Avenue
Cincinnati, OH 45221-0016
Phone: (513) 556-4943
Fax: (513) 556-1274
E-mail: david.edelman@uc.edu
http://ucplanning.uc.edu

OKLAHOMA

University of Oklahoma

College of Architecture
Division of City and Regional
    Planning
Room 204 Carnegie Building
Norman, OK 73019-6141
Phone: (405) 325-2444
Fax: (405) 325-7558
E-mail: guoquiangs@ou.edu
http://rcp.ou.edu

OREGON

Portland State University

College of Urban and Public
    Affairs
Nohad A. Toulan School of Urban
    Studies and Planning
P.O. Box 751-USP
Portland, OR 97207-0751
Phone: (503) 725-4045
Fax: (503) 725-8770
E-mail: seltzere@pdx.edu
http://www.pdx.edu/usp/

University of Oregon

Department of Planning, Public
    Policy & Management
Graduate Program in Community
    and Regional Planning
134 Hendricks Hall
Eugene, OR 97403-1209
Phone: (541) 346-3635
Fax: (541) 346-2040
E-mail: rdm@uoregon.edu
http://pppm.uoregon.edu

PENNSYLVANIA

University of Pennsylvania

School of Design
Department of City and Regional
    Planning
127 Meyerson Hall
Philadelphia, PA 19104-631
Phone: (215) 898-8330
Fax: (215) 898-5731
E-mail: elbirch@design.upenn.edu
http://www.design.upenn.edu/new/
    cplan/index.php

SOUTH CAROLINA

Clemson University

College of Architecture, Arts and
    Humanities
Department of Planning and
    Landscape Architecture
121 Lee Hall, Box 34051
Clemson, SC 29634-0511
Phone: (864) 656-3926
Fax: (864) 656-7519
E-mail: london1@clemson.edu
http://www.clemson.edu/caah/pla/

TENNESSEE

University of Memphis

School of Urban Affairs and Public
    Policy
Graduate Program in City and
    Regional Planning
208 McCord Hall
Memphis, TN 38152
Phone: (901) 678-2161
Fax: (901) 678-4162
E-mail: gpearson@memphis.edu
http://planning.memphis.edu

TEXAS

Texas A&M University

College of Architecture
Department of Landscape
    Architecture & Urban Planning
MS 3137
College Station, TX 77843-3137
Phone: (979) 845-1019
Fax: (979) 862-1784
E-mail: ebright@tamu.edu/LAUP
http://archone.tamu.edu/LAUP

Texas Southern University

Barbara Jordan-Mickey Leland
    School of Public Affairs
Department of Urban Planning and
    Environmental Policy
3100 Cleburne Street
Houston, TX 77004
Phone: (713) 313-7011
Fax: (713) 313-7447
E-mail: sullivanal@tsu.edu
http://www.tsu.edu/academics/
    public/programs/index.asp

University of Texas at Arlington

School of Urban and Public Affairs
City and Regional Planning
    Program
601 South Nedderman Drive—501
    University Hall
Arlington, TX 76010
Phone: (817) 272-3340
Fax: (817) 272-5008
E-mail: enid@uta.edu
http://uta.edu/supa/cirp

University of Texas at Austin

School of Architecture
Graduate Program in Community
    and Regional Planning
Goldsmith Hall 2.308
Austin, TX 78712-1160
Phone: (512) 471-1922
Fax: (512) 471-0716
E-mail: kbutler@mail.utexas.edu
http://soa.utexas.edu/crp

VIRGINIA

University of Virginia

School of Architecture

Department of Urban and
    Environmental Planning
Campbell Hall
P.O. Box 400122
Charlottesville, VA 22904-4122
Phone: (434) 924-1339
Fax: (434) 982-2678
E-mail: spain@virginia.edu
http://www.arch.virginia.edu/
    planning/

Virginia Commonwealth University

L. Douglas Wilder School of
    Government and Public Affairs
Master of Urban and Regional
    Planning Program
923 West Franklin Street, # 517
Richmond, VA 23284-2028
Phone: (804) 828-2292
Fax: (804) 827-1275
E-mail: jaccordi@vcu.edu
http://www.has.vcu.edu/gov/
    Programs/murp.html

Virginia Polytechnic Institute & State University

College of Architecture and Urban
    Studies
Urban Affairs and Planning
    Program
201 Architecture Annex
Blacksburg, VA 24061-0451
Phone: (540) 231-5485
Fax: (540) 231-3367
E-mail: tkoebel@vt.edu
http://www.uap.vt.edu

WASHINGTON

Eastern Washington University

College of Business & Public
    Administration
Department of Urban Planning,
    Public Health Administration
668 North Riverpoint Boulevard,
    Suite A
Spokane, WA 99202-1660
Phone: (509) 358-2230
Fax: (509) 358-2267
E-mail: fhurand@mail.ewu.edu
http://www.ewu.edu

University of Washington
College of Architecture and Urban
  Planning
Department of Urban Design and
  Planning
410 Gould Hall—Box 355740
Seattle, WA 98195-5740
Phone: (206) 543-4190
Fax: (206) 685-9597
E-mail: hblanco@u.washington.edu
http://www.caup.washington.edu/
  html/urbdp/

WISCONSIN

**University of Wisconsin—
  Madison**
College of Letters & Science and
  College of Agriculture & Life
  Sciences
Department of Urban and Regional
  Planning
925 Bascom Mall / 110 Music Hall
Madison, WI 53706-1317
Phone: (608) 262-1004
Fax: (608) 262-9307
E-mail: jalagro@wisc.edu
http://www.wisc.edu/urpl

**University of Wisconsin—
  Milwaukee**
School of Architecture and Urban
  Planning
Department of Urban Planning
P.O. Box 413
Milwaukee, WI 53210-0413
Phone: (414) 229-5563
Fax: (414) 229-6976
E-mail: frankn@uwm.edu
http://urbanplanning.uwm.edu

CANADA

Université de Montréal
Faculty of Environmental Design
Institut d'Urbanisme
C.P. 6128, succ. Centre-ville
Montréal
Québec, Canada H3C 3J7
Phone: (514) 343-5699
Fax: (514) 343-2338
E-mail: Gerard.beaudet@
  umontreal.ca
http://www.urb.umontreal.ca

University of British Columbia
Faculty of Graduate Studies

School of Community and Regional
  Planning
433-6333 Memorial Road
Vancouver
British Columbia, Canada V6T 1Z2
Phone: (604) 822-3276
Fax: (604) 822-3787
E-mail: leonies@interchange.ubc.ca
http://www.scarp.ubc.ca

PUERTO RICO

University of Puerto Rico
Graduate School of Planning
Rio Piedras Campus
P.O. Box 23500
San Juan, PR 00931-3500
Phone: (787) 764-0000 ext. 3182
Fax: (787) 763-5375
E-mail: eliasgutierrez@yahoo.com
http://egp.rrp.upr.edu

C. CONSTRUCTION MANAGEMENT

FOUR-YEAR COLLEGES AND UNIVERSITIES

ALABAMA

Auburn University
Department of Building Science
College of Architecture, Design &
  Construction
108 Mary Martin Hall
Auburn, AL 36849-5315
Phone: (334) 844-4080
Fax: (334) 844-6179
http://www.auburn.edu

ARIZONA

Arizona State University
Del E. Webb School of
  Construction
Ira A. Fulton School of Engineering

Tempe, AZ 85287
Phone: (480) 965-5440
Fax: (480) 965-3610
E-mail: upgrading@asu.edu
http://www.asu.edu

Northern Arizona University
Construction Management Program
College of Engineering & Natural
  Sciences
P.O. Box 4084
Flagstaff, AZ 86011-4084
Phone: (928) 523-5511
Fax: (928) 523-0226
http:// www.nau.edu

ARKANSAS

John Brown University
Construction Management Program

Division of Engineering &
  Construction Management
2000 West University Street
Siloam Springs, AR 72761
Phone: (877) 528-4636
Fax: (479) 524-4196
http://www.jbu.edu

**University of Arkansas—Little
  Rock**
Construction Management
  Program
Donaghey College of
  Information, Science &
  Systems Engineering
2801 South University Avenue
Little Rock, AR 72204
Phone: (501) 569-3127
Fax: (501) 569-8915
http://www.ualr.edu

CALIFORNIA

California Polytechnic State University

College of Architecture & Environmental Design
San Luis Obispo, CA 93407
Phone: (805) 756-2311
Fax: (805) 756-5400
http://www.calpoly.edu

California State University— Chico

Department of Construction Management
College of Engineering, Computer Science & Construction Management
400 West First Street
Chico, CA 95929-0722
Phone: (530) 898-4428
Fax: (530) 898-6456
http://www.csuchico.edu

California State University— Fresno

College of Engineering
5150 North Maple Avenue M/S JA 57
Fresno, CA 93740-8026
Phone: (559) 278-2261
Fax: (559) 278-4812
http://www.csufresno.edu

California State University— Sacramento

Construction Management Program
Department of Civil Engineering
6000 J Street, Lassen Hall
Sacramento, CA 95819-6048
Phone: (916) 278-3901
Fax: (916) 278-5603
E-mail: admissions@csus.edu
http://www.csus.edu

COLORADO

Colorado State University

Department of Construction Management
Spruce Hall
Fort Collins, CO 80523-8020
Phone: (970) 491-6909

Fax: (970) 491-7799
http://www.welcome.colostate.edu

CONNECTICUT

Central Connecticut State University

Department of Manufacturing & Construction Management
School of Technology
New Britain
1615 Stanley Street
New Britain, CT 06050
Phone: (860) 832-2278
Fax: (862) 832-2295
http:// www.ccsu.edu

FLORIDA

Florida International University

College of Engineering & Computing
University Park
11200 South West Eighth Street
Miami, FL 33199
Phone: (305) 348-3675
Fax: (305) 348-3648
E-mail: admiss@fiu.edu
http://www.fiu.edu

University of Florida

M. E. Rinker, Sr. School of Building Construction
College of Design, Construction & Planning
P.O. Box 117150
Gainesville, FL 32611-7150
Phone: (352) 392- 2397 ext.1399
Fax: (352) 392-2086
E-mail: ufwcba @ cba.ufl.edu
http://www.realestate.ufl.edu

University of North Florida

Department of Building Construction Management
College of Computing, Engineering & Construction
4567 Saint Johns Bluff Road South
Jacksonville, FL 32224
Phone: (904) 620-2630
E-mail: srosenbe@unf.edu
http://www.unf.edu/ccb

GEORGIA

Georgia Institute of Technology

College of Architecture
Georgia Institute of Technology
Atlanta, GA 30332-0320
Phone: (404) 894-4154
Fax: (404) 894-9511
http://www.gatech.edu

Georgia Southern University

Building Construction & Contracting
Allen E. Paulson College of Science & Technology
P.O. Box 8024
Statesboro, GA 30460-8047
Phone: (912) 681-5391
Fax: (912) 486-7240
http://www.georgiasouthern.edu

Southern Polytechnic State University

Construction Management Department
School of Architecture, Civil Engineering Technology & Construction
1100 South Marietta Parkway
Marietta, GA 30060-2896
Phone: (678) 915-4188
Fax: (678) 915-7292
http://www.spsu.edu

IDAHO

Boise State University

Construction Management Program
Department of Construction Management
1910 University Drive
Boise, ID 83725
Phone: (208) 426-1156
Fax: (208) 426-3765
http://www.boisestate.edu

ILLINOIS

Bradley University

Department of Civil Engineering & Construction
College of Engineering & Technology

1501 West Bradley Avenue
Peoria, IL 61625
Phone: (309) 677-1000
Fax: (309) 677-2797
http://www.bradley.edu

Illinois State University
Construction Management Program
Department of Technology
Campus Box 2200
Normal, IL 61790-2200
Phone: (309) 438-2181
Fax: (309) 438-3932
http:// www.ilstu.edu

**Southern Illinois University—
Edwardsville**
Construction Management
Program
Department of Construction
P.O. Box 1600
Edwardsville, IL 62026-1080
Phone: (618) 650-3705
Fax: (618) 650-5013
http://www.siue.edu

INDIANA

Ball State University
Construction Management Program
2000 University Avenue
Muncie, IN 47306
Phone: (765) 285-8300
Fax: (765) 285-1632
http://www.bsu.edu

Indiana State University
Construction Management
Program
Department of Technology
Management
Tirey Hall 134
Terra Haute, IN 47809
Phone: (812) 237-2121
Fax: (812) 237-8023
http:// www.indstate.edu

Purdue University
Building Construction Management
College of Technology
1080 Schleman Hall
West Lafayette, IN 47907
Phone: (765) 494-1776

Fax: (765) 494-0544
http:// www.purdue.edu

KANSAS

Kansas State University
Construction & Science Management
119 Anderson Hall
Manhattan, KS 66506
Phone: (785) 532-6250
Fax: (785) 532-6393
http://www.k-state.edu

KENTUCKY

Eastern Kentucky University
Construction Technology Program
Department of Technology
SB CPO 54
521 Lancaster Avenue
Richmond, KY 40475
Phone: (859) 622-2106
Fax: (859) 622-8024
http://www.eku.edu

Northern Kentucky University
Construction Management
Program
Department of Construction
Management
Administrative Center
401 Nunn Drive
Highland Heights, KY 41099
Phone: (859) 572-5220
Fax: (859) 572-6665
http://www.nku.edu

Western Kentucky University
Construction Management Program
Architectural & Manufacturing
Science Department
Potter Hall
1171906 College Heights Boulevard
Bowling Green, KY 42101-1020
Phone: (270) 745-2551
Fax: (270) 745-6133
http://www. www.wku.edu

LOUISIANA

Louisiana State University
Construction Management &
Industrial Engineering

College of Engineering
Baton Rouge
2164 CEBA Building
Baton Rouge, LA 70803
Phone: (225) 578-1175
Fax: (225) 578-4433
E-mail: admissions@lsu.edu
http://www.lsu.edu

**University of Louisiana at
Monroe**
College of Engineering
Construction Management Program
700 University Avenue
Monroe, LA 71209-0100
Phone: (318) 342-1100
Fax: (318) 342-1101
http://www.ele.ulm.edu

MARYLAND

**University of Maryland—
Eastern Shore**
Construction Management
Technology
1 Backbone Road
Princess Anne, MD 21853
Phone: (410) 651-2200
http://www.umes.edu

MASSACHUSETTS

**Wentworth Institute of
Technology**
Department of Civil, Construction
& Environment
550 Huntington Avenue
Boston, MA 02115-5998
Phone: (617) 989-4000
Fax: (617) 989-4010
http://www.wit.edu

MICHIGAN

Eastern Michigan University
Construction Management
Program
School of Engineering Technology
400 Pierce Hall
Ypsilanti, MI 48197
Phone: (734) 487-3060
Fax: (734) 487-1484
http://www.emich.edu

Ferris State University
Department of Construction
Technology & Management
College of Technology
1201 South State Street
Big Rapids, MI 49307-2292
Phone: (231) 591-2100
Fax: (231) 591-3944
http://www.ferris.edu

Michigan State University
Construction Management
Program
School of Planning, Design &
Construction
250 Administration Building
East Lansing, MI 48824-1046
Phone: (517) 355-8332
Fax: (517) 353-1647
http:// www.msu.edu

MINNESOTA

**Minnesota State University—
Moorhead**
Construction Management
Department of Technology
Owens Hall
Moorhead, MN 56563
Phone: (218) 477-2161
Fax: (218) 477-4374
http://www.mnstate.edu

MISSISSIPPI

**University of Southern
Mississippi**
School of Construction
College of Science & Technology
118 College Drive #5166
Hattiesburg, MS 39406
Phone: (601) 266-5000
Fax: (601) 266-5148
http://www.usm.edu

MISSOURI

Missouri State University
Construction Management
Program
Department of Industrial
Management
901 South National

Springfield, MO 65897
Phone: (417) 836-5517
Fax: (417) 836-6334
http://www.missouristate.edu

University of Central Missouri
Construction Management
Program
Department of Technology
WDE 1400
Warrensburg, MO 64093
Phone: (660) 543-4290
Fax: (660) 543-8517
http:// www.cmsu.edu

NEBRASKA

University of Nebraska
Construction Management Program
College of Engineering &
Technology
1100 Seaton Hall
P.O. Box 880619
Lincoln, NE 68588-0619
Phone: (402) 472-2878
Fax: (402) 472-0589
http://www.unl.edu

NEVADA

**University of Nevada—Las
Vegas**
Construction Management
Program
Howard R. Hughes College of
Engineering
4505 Maryland Parkway
P.O. Box 451021
Las Vegas, NV 89154-1021
Phone: (702) 774-8658
Fax: (702) 774-8008
http://www.unlv.edu

NEW MEXICO

University of New Mexico
Construction Management
Department of Civil Engineering
P.O. Box 4895
Albuquerque, NM 87196-4895
Phone: (505) 277-2446
Fax: (505) 277-6686
http://www.unm.edu

NEW YORK

Alfred State College
Construction Management
Technology
Department of Civil Engineering
Technology
Huntington Administration
Building
Alfred, NY 14802
Phone: (607) 587-4215
Fax: (607) 587-4299
http://www.alfredstate.edu

NORTH CAROLINA

East Carolina University
Department of Construction
Management
College of Technology & Computer
Science
106 Whichard Building
Greenville, NC 27858-4353
Phone: (252) 328-6640
Fax: (252) 328-6945
http://www.ecu.edu

**North Carolina A&T State
University**
Construction Management &
Occupational Safety and Health
Department
1601 East Market Street
Greensboro, NC 27411
Phone: (336) 334-7946
Fax: (336) 334-7478
http://www.ncat.edu

Western Carolina University
Construction Management Program
Kimmel School of Construction
Management, Engineering &
Technology
242 HFR Administration
Cullowhee, NC 28723
Phone: (828) 227-7317
Fax: (828) 227-7319
http:// www.wcu.edu

NORTH DAKOTA

North Dakota State University
Construction Management
Program

Department of Construction
Management & Engineering
P.O. Box 5454
Fargo, ND 58105
Phone: (701) 231-8643
Fax: (701) 231-8802
http://www.ndsu.edu

OHIO

Bowling Green State University
Construction Management &
Technology
Department of Technology Systems
110 McFall Center
Bowling Green, OH 43403-0301
Phone: (419) 372-2478
Fax: (419) 372-6955
http://www.bgsu.edu

Ohio State University
Construction Management
Program
College of Food, Agriculture and
Environmental Sciences
110 Enarson Hall
Columbus, OH 43210
154 West 12th Avenue
Phone: (614) 292-3980
Fax: (614) 292-4818
http://www.osu.edu

University of Cincinnati
Department of Construction
Science
College of Applied Science
P.O. Box 210091
Cincinnati, OH 45206
Phone: (513) 556-1100
Fax: (513) 556-1105
http:// www.uc.edu

OKLAHOMA

University of Oklahoma
Construction Science Program
College of Architecture
660 Parrington Oval
Norman, OK 73019-0390
Phone: (800) 234-6868
E-mail: ou-pss@ou.edu
http://go2.ou.edu

OREGON

Oregon State University
Construction Engineering
Management Program
Department of Civil and
Construction Engineering
104 Kerr Administration Building
Corvallis, OR 97331-2302
Phone: (541) 737-4411
Fax: (541) 737-2482
http://www.oregonstate.edu

PENNSYLVANIA

Drexel University
Construction Management
Program
Richard C. Goodwin College of
Professional Studies
3141 Chestnut Street
Philadelphia, PA 19104
Phone: (215) 895-2400
Fax: (215) 895-5939
http://www.drexel.edu

Pennsylvania College of Technology
Construction Management Program
Building Construction Department
One College Avenue
Williamsport, PA 17701-5799
Phone: (570) 327-4761
Fax: (570) 321-5551
http://www.pct.edu/princeton/

RHODE ISLAND

Roger Williams University
Construction Management
Program
School of Engineering, Computing,
& Construction Management
One Old Ferry Road
Bristol, RI 02809-2921
Phone: (401) 254-3500
Fax: (401) 254-3557
http://www.rwu.edu

SOUTH CAROLINA

Clemson University
Department of Construction
Science & Management

School of Design and Building
105 Sikes Hall
Box 345124
Clemson, SC 29634-0507
Phone: (864) 656-2287
Fax: (864) 656-2464
http:// www.clemson.edu

SOUTH DAKOTA

South Dakota State University
Construction Management
Program
Engineering Technology &
Management
P.O. Box 2201
Brookings, SD 57007
Phone: (605) 688-4121
Fax: (605) 688-6891
http://www3.sdstate.edu

TEXAS

Texas A & M University
Department of Construction
Science
College of Architecture
College Station, TX 77843-3137
Phone: (979) 845-3741
Fax: (979) 847-8737
http://www.tamu.edu

Texas State University
Construction Management
Department of Technology
601 University Drive
San Marcos, TX 78666
Phone: (512) 245-2364
Fax: (512) 245-9020
http://www.txstate.edu

University of Houston
Construction Management
Technology
Department of Engineering
Technology
One Main Street
Houston, TX 77204
Phone: (713) 221-8522
Fax: (713) 221-5220
http://www.uh.edu

UTAH

Brigham Young University
Construction Management
School of Technology
A-153 ASB
Provo, UT 84602
Phone: (801) 422-2507
Fax: (801) 422-0005
http://www.byu.edu

Weber State University
Parson Construction Management
   Technology
College of Applied Science &
   Technology
1137 University Circle
Ogden, UT 84408-1802
Phone: (801) 626-6744
Fax: (801) 626-6747
http://weber.edu

VIRGINIA

**Virginia Polytechnic Institute
   & State University**
Department of Building
   Construction College of
   Architecture & Urban Studies
201 Burruss Hall
Blacksburg, VA 24061-0156
Phone: (540) 231-6267
Fax: (540) 231-3242
http://www.vt.edu

WASHINGTON

Central Washington University
Construction Management
   Program
Department of Industrial &
   Engineering Technology
400 East University Way
Ellensburg, WA 98926-7584
Phone: (509) 963-1211
Fax: (509) 963-3022
http://www.cwu.edu

University of Washington
Department of Construction
   Management
College of Architecture & Urban
   Planning
UW Box 355852

Seattle, WA 98195-1610
Phone: (206) 543-9686
Fax: (206) 685-3655
http://www.washington.edu

Washington State University
Construction Management Program
School of Architecture and
   Construction Management
College of Engineering &
   Architecture
P.O. Box 641067
Pullman, WA 99164-2220
Phone: (509) 335-5586
Fax: (509) 335-4902
http://www.wsu.edu

WISCONSIN

**Milwaukee School of
   Engineering**
Construction Management
   Program
Department of Architectural
   Engineering & Building
   Construction
1025 North Broadway
Milwaukee, WI 53202-3109
Phone: (414) 277-6763
Fax: (414) 277-7475
http://www.msoe.edu

University of Wisconsin—Stout
Stout Construction Program
College of Technology, Engineering
   & Management
Menomonie, WI 54751
Phone: (715) 232-1411
Fax: (715) 232-1667
http:// www.uwstout.edu

CANADA

**Saskatchewan Institute
   of Applied Science
   & Technology**
Palliser Institute
Saskatchewan Street and Sixth
   Avenue NW
P.O. Box 1420
Moose Jaw, Saskatchewan S6H 4R4
Phone: (866) goSIAST [467-4278]
http://www.siast.sk.ca

TWO-YEAR COLLEGES

ALABAMA

**Jefferson State Community
   College**
Construction Management
Department of Building Science
   Technology
601 Carson Road
Birmingham, AL 35215-3098
Phone: (205) 853-1200
Fax: (205) 815-8499
http://www.jeffstateonline.com

FLORIDA

Santa Fe Community College
Building Construction Program
   Department of Industrial
   Technology
3000 N.W. 83rd Street
Gainesville, FL 32602-6200
Phone: (352) 395-5000
Fax: (352) 395-5581
http://www.santafe.cc.fl.us

ILLINOIS

College of Lake County
Construction Management
   Technology
19351 West Washington Street
Grayslake, IL 60030
Phone: (847) 223-6601
Fax: (847) 543-3061
http://www.clc.cc.il.us

John A. Logan College
Construction Management
   Technology
Department of Applied
   Technologies
700 Logan College Road
Carterville, IL 62918
Phone: (618) 985-3741
Fax: (618) 985-2248
http://www.jal.cc.il.us

Triton College
Construction Program
School of Technology
2000 Fifth Avenue
River Grove, IL 60171-1995

Phone: (708) 456-0300
E-mail: triton@triton.edu
http://www.triton.edu

MISSOURI

State Fair Community College
Construction Management
    Program Department of Applied
    Science & Technology
3201 West 16th Street
Sedalia, MO 65301-2199
Phone: (660) 530-5800
Fax: (660) 530-5820
http://sfcc.cc.mo.us

NEW MEXICO

Central New Mexico
    Community College
Construction Management
    Technology
525 Buena Vista Drive SE
Albuquerque, NM 87106
Phone: (505) 224-3000
http://www.cnm.edu

NEW YORK

New York City Technical College
Construction Management &
    Civil Engineering Technology
    Department

Construction Management
    Technology Program
300 Jay Street
Brooklyn, NY 11201-2983
Phone: (718) 260-5500
Fax: (718) 260-5504
http://www.citytech.cuny.edu

State University of New York
College of Technology at Delhi
Construction Technology Program
    Technology Division
2 Main Street
Delhi, NY 13753
Phone: (800) 96-DELHI
http://www.delhi.edu

OHIO

Cincinnati State Technical &
    Community College
Construction Management
    Program
Engineering Technologies Division
3520 Central Parkway
Cincinnati, OH 45223
Phone: (513) 569-1500
http://www.cincinnatistate.edu

Columbus State Community
    College
Construction Management
    Program

Construction Sciences Department
550 East Spring Street
Columbus, OH 43215
Phone: (614) 287-2408
http://www.cscc.edu

TEXAS

North Lake College
Construction Management &
    Technology
Technology Division
5001 North MacArthur Boulevard
Irving, TX 75038
Phone: (972) 273-3000
http://www.dcccd.edu
http://www.northlakecollege.edu

WASHINGTON

Edmonds Community College
Construction Management
    Department
20000 68th Avenue
West Lynwood, WA 98036
Phone: (425) 640-1459
http://www.edcc.edu

APPENDIX II
PROFESSIONAL ASSOCIATIONS
AND ORGANIZATIONS

The associations listed here are all closely related to the careers discussed in this book. Those that are mentioned in the position descriptions are included as well as others that are of importance in banking, finance, and insurance. This section includes the name and address of each organization, plus contact information such as telephone numbers, Internet addresses, and e-mail addresses.

You can contact these groups or visit their Web sites on the Internet to learn about career opportunities,

professional certification, conferences, and seminars. An organization's Web site is the first place to look to get more information about its activities and contact association executives. A number of the organizations listed here have state or local affiliate chapters. To learn about any professional associations that may be in your area, talk with local professionals or look for that information at an association's Web site.

Accredited Review Appraisers Council
303 West Cypress Street
San Antonio, TX 78212
Phone: (800) 486-3676
http://arac.lincoln-grad.org

Affordable Housing Tax Credit Coalition
1900 K Street, NW, Suite 1200
Washington, DC 20006-1109
Phone: (202) 419-2025
Fax: (202) 828-3738
E-mail: info@taxcreditcoalition.org
http://www. taxcreditcoalition.org

Alliance of Tenant Representatives
1146 19th Street NW
Washington, DC 20036
Phone: (703) 779-4778
Fax: (202) 467-0556
E-mail: info@alltenrep.com
http://www.alltenrep.com

American College of Real Estate Lawyers
One Central Plaza
11300 Rockville Pike, Suite 903
Rockville, MD 20852
Phone: (301) 816-9811
Fax: (301) 816-9786
http://acrel.org

American Construction Inspectors Association
530 South Lake Avenue
Suite 431
Pasadena, CA 91101
Phone: (888) 867-ACIA [2242]
Fax: (626) 797-2214
E-mail: office@acia.com
http://www.acia.com

American Escrow Association
211 North Union Street, Suite 100
Alexandria, VA 22314
Phone: (703) 519-1240
http://www.a-e-a.org

American Homeowners Foundation
6776 Little Falls Road
Arlington, VA 22213-1213
Phone: (800) 489-7776
Fax: (703) 536-7079
http://www.americanhomeowners
.org

American Hotel & Lodging Association
1201 New York Avenue NW
Washington, DC 20005-3931
Phone: (202) 289-3100
Fax: (202) 289-3199
http://www.ahla.com

American Industrial Real Estate Association
800 West Sixth Street, Suite 800
Los Angeles, CA 90017
Phone: (213) 687-8777
http://www.airea.com

American Institute of Architects
1735 New York Avenue, NW
Washington, DC 20006-5292
Phone: (800) AIA-3837
Fax: (202) 626-7547
E-mail: infocentral@aia.org
http://www.aia.org

American Land Title Association
1828 L Street NW
Suite 705
Washington, DC 20036
Phone: (800) 787-ALTA
E-mail: service@alta.org
http://www.alta.org

American Planning Association
1776 Massachusetts Avenue NW
Washington, DC 20036-1904
Phone: (202) 872-0611
E-mail: customerservice@planning
.org
http://www.planning.org

**The American Real Estate &
Urban Economics Society**
P.O. Box 9958
Richmond, VA 23228
Phone: (866) 273-8321
E-mail: areuea@areuea.org
http://www.areuea.org

American Real Estate Society
Florida Atlantic University College
of Business
5353 Parkside Drive
Jupiter, FL 33458
Phone: (561) 779-8594
E-mail: dcooper@fau.edu
http://www.aresnet.org

**American Resort Development
Association**
1201 15th Street NW
Suite 400
Washington, DC 20005-2842
Phone: (202) 371-6700
Fax: (202) 289-8544
http://www.arda.org

**American Seniors Housing
Association**
5100 Wisconsin Avenue NW, Suite
307
Washington, DC 20016
Phone: (202) 237-0900
Fax: (202) 237-1616
http://www.seniorshousing.org

American Society of Appraisers
555 Herndon Parkway, Suite 125
Herndon, VA 20170
Phone: (703) 478-2228
Fax: (703) 742-8471
http://www.appraisers.org

**American Society of Farm
Managers and Rural
Appraisers**
950 South Cherry Street, Suite 508
Denver, CO 80246-2664
Phone: (303) 758-3513
Fax: (303) 758-0190
http://www.asfmra.org

**American Society of Home
Inspectors**
932 Lee Street, Suite 101

Des Plaines, IL 60016
Phone: (800) 743-2744
E-mail: webmaster@ashi.org
http://www.ashi.org

Appraisal Institute
550 West Van Buren Street
Suite 1000
Chicago, IL 60607
Phone: (312) 335-4100
E-mail: wwoodburn@
    appraisalinstitute.org
http://appraisalinstitute.org

Appraisal Institute of Canada
203-150 Isabella Street
Ottawa, Canada KIS 1V7
Phone: (613) 234-6533
http://www.aicanada.ca

**Asian Real Estate Association
of America**
5740 Fleet Street Suite 155
Carlsbad, CA 92008
Phone: (760) 918-9162
Fax: (760) 918-6924
E-mail: contact@areaa.org
http://www.areaa.org

**Associated Builders and
Contractors**
4250 North Fairfax Drive, Ninth
    Floor
Arlington, VA 22203-1607
Phone: (703) 812-2000
E-mail: gotquestions@abc.org
http://www.abc.org

**Associated General
Contractors of America**
2300 Wilson Boulevard, Suite 400
Arlington, VA 22201
Phone: (800) 242-1767
Fax: (703) 548-319
E-mail: info@agc.org
http://www.agc.org

**Association of Foreign
Investors in Real Estate**
Ronald Reagan Building
1300 Pennsylvania Avenue NW
Washington, DC 20004
Phone: (202) 312-1400

Fax: (202) 312-1401
http://www.afire.org

**Association of Higher
Education Facilities Officers**
1643 Prince Street
Alexandria, VA 22314-2818
Phone: (703) 684-1446
Fax: (703) 549-2772
http://www.appa.org

**Association of Real Estate Law
License Officials**
7900 East Union Street
Suite 1009A
Denver, CO 80237
Phone: (303) 217-7069
Fax: (303) 217-7556
E-mail: mailbox@arello.org
http://wwwarello.org

**Association of Real Estate
Women**
322 Eighth Avenue, Suite 501
New York, NY 10001
Phone: (212) 599-6181
Fax: (212) 645-1147
http://www.arew.org

**Association of University Real
Estate Officials**
c/o North Carolina State University
P.O. Box 7230
Raleigh, NC 27695-7230
Phone: (540) 231-8430
Fax: (303) 894-7478
http://www.aureo.org

**Building Owners & Managers
Institute**
1521 Ritchie Highway
Arnold, MD 21012
Phone: (800) 235-BOMI
Fax: (410) 974-0544
E-mail: service@bomi-edu.org
http://www.bomi-edu.org

California Escrow Association
2520 Venture Oaks Way, Suite 150
Sacramento, CA 95833
Phone: (916) 239-4075
Fax: (916) 924-7323
E-mail: cea@camgmt.com
http://www.ceaescrow.org

CCIM Institute
430 North Michigan Avenue, Suite
800
Chicago, IL 60611-4092
Phone: (312) 321-4460
E-mail: info@ccim.com
http://www.ccim.com

**Commercial Mortgage
Securities Association**
30 Broad Street, 28th Floor
New York, NY 10004-2304
Phone: (212) 509-1844
Fax: (212) 509-1895
http://www.cmbs.org

Commercial Real Estate Women
1201 Wakarusa Drive, Suite C3
Lawrence, KS 66049
Phone: (785) 832-1808
E-mail: lindah@crewnetwork.org
http://www.crewnetwork.org

**Community Associations
Institute**
225 Reinekers Lane
Suite 300
Alexandria, VA 22314
Phone: (888) 224-4321
Fax: (703) 684-1581
http://www.caionline.org

Community Economics
538 Ninth Street, Suite 200
Oakland, CA 94607
Phone: (510) 832-8300
Fax: (510) 832-2227
E-mail: info@communityeconomics
.org
http://www.communityeconomics
.org

**Construction Financial
Management Association**
29 Emmons Drive, Suite F-50
Princeton, NJ 08540
Phone: (609) 452-8000
Fax: (609) 452-0474
E-mail: info@cfma.org
http://www.cfma.org

**Construction Management
Association of America**
7926 Jones Branch Drive, Suite 800

McLean, VA 22102
Phone: (703) 356-2622
Fax: (703) 356-6388
E-mail: info@cmaanet.org
http://www.cmaanet.org

CoreNet Global
260 Peachtree Street, Suite 1500
Atlanta, GA 30303
Phone: (800) 726-8111
http://www.corenetglobal.com

CoStar Group
2 Bethesda Metro Center, 10th
Floor
Bethesda, MD 20814-5388
Phone: (800) 204-5960
E-mail: info@costar.com
http://www.costar.com

**Council of Real Estate
Brokerage Managers**
430 North Michigan Avenue
Chicago, IL 60611
Phone: (800) 621-8738
Fax: (312) 329-8882
E-mail: info@crb.com
http://www.crb.com

**Council of Residential
Specialists**
430 North Michigan Avenue
Chicago, IL 60611
Phone: (800) 462-8841
Fax: (312) 329-8882
http://www.crs.com

The Counselors of Real Estate
430 North Michigan Avenue
Chicago, IL 60611-4089
Phone: (312) 329-8427
E-mail: info@cre.org
http://www.cre.org

**Electronic Financial Services
Council**
1250 24th Street, NW, Suite 700
Washington, DC 20037
Phone: (202) 349-8067
Fax: (202) 349-8080
E-mail: info@spers.org
http://www.efscouncil.org

**Environmental Assessment
Association**
1224 North Nokomis NE
Alexandria, MN 56308
Phone: (320) 763-4320
Fax: (320) 763-9290
E-mail: eaa@iami.org
http://iami.org/eaa.htm

**FIABCI—International Real
Estate Federation**
2000 North 15th Street
Alexandria, VA 22201
Phone: (703) 524-4279
E-mail: info@fiabci-usa.com
http://wwwfiabci-usa.com

**Foundation of Real Estate
Appraisers**
4907 Morena Boulevard, Suite 1415
San Diego, CA 92117
Phone: (800) 882-4410
Fax: (858) 273-8026
E-mail: info@frea.com
http://www.frea.com

Hotel Brokers International
1420 NW Vivion Road, Suite 111
Kansas City, MO 64118
Phone: (816) 505-4315
Fax: (816) 505-4319
E-mail: info@hbihotels.com
http://www.hbihotels.com

Housing Inspection Foundation
1224 North Nokomis NE
Alexandria, MN 56308
Phone: (320) 763-6350
E-mail: hif@iami.org
http://iami.org/hif.htm

**Institute for Professionals in
Taxation**
600 Northpark Town Center
1200 Abernathy Road, Suite L-2
Atlanta, GA 30328-1040
Phone: (404) 240-2300
http://www.ipt.org

**Institute for Responsible
Housing Preservation**
401 Ninth Street NW
Suite 900

Washington, DC 20004
Phone: (202) 585-8739
Fax: (202) 585-8080
E-mail: info@HousingPreservation
.org
http://www.housingpreservation.org

Institute of Real Estate Management

430 North Michigan Avenue
Chicago, IL 60611
Phone: (800) 837-0706
Fax: (800) 338-4736
E-mail: custserv@irem.org
http://www.irem.org

International Association of Assessing Officers

314 West 10th Street
Kansas City, MO 64105-1616
Phone: (800) 616-4226
http://www.iaao.org

International Council of Shopping Centers

1221 Avenue of the Americas, 41st
Floor
New York, NY 10020-1099
Phone: (646) 728-3800
Fax: (732) 694-1755
E-mail: icsc@icsc.org
http://www.icsc.org

International Facility Management Association

1 East Greenway Plaza
Suite 1100
Houston, TX 77046-0194
Phone: (713) 623-4362
Fax: (713) 623-6124
http://www.ifma.org

International Real Estate Institute

1224 North Nokomis NE
Alexandria, MN 56308
Phone: (320) 763-4648
Fax: (320) 763-9290
http://www.iami.org/

International Right of Way Association

19750 South Vermont Avenue, Suite
220

Torrance, CA 90502-1144
Phone: (310) 538-0233
Fax: (310) 538-1471
E-mail: info@irwaonline.org
http://www.irwaonline.org

The Luxury Home Council

1224 NE Walnut Suite 324
Roseburg, OR 97470
Phone: (866) 465-6183
Fax: (866) 495-6078
E-mail: support@
luxuryhomecouncil.com
http://www.luxuryhomecouncil
.com

Mortgage Bankers Association of America

1919 Pennsylvania Avenue NW
Washington, DC 20006-3404
Phone: (202) 557-2700
http://www.mbaa.org

National Affordable Housing Management Association

400 North Columbus Street,
Suite 203
Alexandria, VA 22314
Phone: (703) 683-8630
Fax: (703) 683-8634
http://www.nahma.org

National Apartment Association

4300 Wilson Boulevard, Suite 400
Arlington, VA 22203
Phone: (703) 518-6141
Fax: (703) 248-9440
http://www.naahq.org

National Association of Certified Home Inspectors

1750 30th Street
Boulder, CO 80301
Phone: (650) 429-2057
Fax: (650) 429-2057
E-mail: fastreply@nachi.org
http://www.nachi.org

National Association of Counselors

303 West Cypress Street

San Antonio, TX
Phone: (800) 486-3676
http://nac.lincoln-grad.org

National Association of Development Organizations

400 North Capitol Street NW, Suite
390
Washington, DC 20001
Phone: (202) 624-7806
Fax: (202) 624-8813
E-mail: info@nado.org
http://nado.org

National Association of Exclusive Buyer Agents

929 South 20th Street
Arlington VA 22202
Phone: (888) 623-2299
Fax: (703) 920-9101
E-mail: naeba@naeba.info
http://www.naeba.org

National Association of Hispanic Real Estate Professionals

1150 17th Street NW
Suite 504
Washington, DC 20036
Phone: (800) 964-5373
Fax: (202) 955-1066
http://www.nahrep.org

National Association of Home Builders

1201 15th Street NW
Washington, DC 20005
Phone: (800) 368-5242
Fax: (202) 266-8400
http://www.nahb.org

National Association of Home Inspectors

4248 Park Glen Road
Minneapolis, MN 55416
Phone: (800) 448-3942
Fax: (952) 929-1318
E-mail: info@nahi.org
http://www.nahi.org

**National Association
of Housing and
Redevelopment Officials**
630 I Street NW
Washington, DC 20001
Phone: (877) 866-2476
Fax: (202) 289-8181
E-mail: nahro@nahro.org
http://nahro.org

**National Association
of Independent Fee
Appraisers**
401 North Michigan Avenue, Suite
2200
Chicago, IL 60611
Phone: (312) 321-6830
Fax: (312) 673-6652
E-mail: info@naifa.com
http://www.naifa.com

**National Association of
Industrial and Office
Properties**
2201 Cooperative Way, Third
Floor
Herndon, VA 20171-3034
Phone: (703) 904-7100
Fax: (703) 904-7942
http://www.naiop.org

**National Association of Master
Appraisers**
303 West Cypress Street
San Antonio, TX 78212
Phone: (800) 229-6262
Fax: (210) 225-8450
http://www.masterappraisers.org

**National Association of
Mortgage Brokers**
7900 Westpark Drive, Suite T309
McLean, VA 22102
Phone: (703) 342-5900
Fax: (703) 342-5905
http://www.namb.org

**National Association of
Professional Mortgage
Women**
P.O. Box 140218
Irving, TX 75014-0218

Phone: (800) 827-3034
Fax: (469) 524-5121
E-mail: info@napmw.org
http://www.napmw.org

**National Association of Real
Estate Appraisers**
1224 North Nokomis NE
Alexandria, MN 56308
Phone: (320) 763-7626
Fax: (320) 763-9290
http://www.iami.org/NAREA

**National Association of
Real Estate Investment
Fiduciaries**
Two Prudential Plaza
180 North Stetson Avenue
Suite 2515
Chicago, IL 60601
Phone: (312) 819-5890
Fax: (312) 819-5891
http://www.ncreif.com

**National Association of
Real Estate Investment
Managers**
11755 Wilshire Boulevard, Suite
1380
Los Angeles, CA 90025-1539
Phone: (310) 479-2219
http://www.nareim.org

**National Association of Real
Estate Investment Trusts**
1875 I Street, Suite 600
Washington, DC 20006
Phone: (202) 739-9400
Fax: (202) 739-9401
E-mail: info@nareit.com
http://www.nareit.org

**National Association of
Realtors**
430 North Michigan Avenue
Chicago, IL 60611-4087
Phone: (800) 874-6500
http://www.realtor.org

**National Association of
Residential Property
Managers**
638 Independence Parkway

Suite 100
Chesapeake, VA 23320
Phone: (800) 782-3452
Fax: (866) 466-2776
E-mail: info@narpm.org
http://www.naprm.org

**National Auctioneers
Association**
8880 Ballentine
Overland Park, KS 66214
Phone: (913) 541-8084
Fax: (913) 894-5281
http://www.auctioneers.org

**National Council of
Exchangors**
P.O. Box 668
Morro Bay, CA 93443-0668
Phone: (800) 324-1031
E-mail: nce@infoville.com
http://www.nce.org

**National Council of State
Housing Agencies**
444 North Capitol Street NW
Suite 438
Washington, DC 20001
Phone: (202) 624-7710
Fax: (202) 624-5899
http://www.ncsha.org

**National Housing Conference
and the Center for Housing
Policy**
1801 K Street NW
Suite M-100
Washington, DC 20006-1301
Phone: (202) 466-2121
Fax: (202) 466-2122
http://www.nhc.org

**National Leased Housing
Association**
1900 L Street NW, Suite 300
Washington, DC 20036
Phone: (202) 785-8888
Fax: (202) 785-2008
E-mail: info@hudnlha.com
http://www.hudnlha.com

National Multi-Housing Council
1850 M Street NW
Suite 540
Washington, DC 20036-5803
Phone: (202) 974-2300
Fax: (202) 775-0112
http://www.nmhc.org

National Property Management Association
28100 U.S. Highway 19 North
Suite 400
Clearwater, FL 33761
Phone: (727) 736-3788
Fax: (727) 736-6707
E-mail: hq@npma.org
http://www.npma.org

National Real Estate Investors Association
525 West Fifth Street, Suite 230
Covington, KY 41011
Phone: (888) 762-7342
Fax: (859) 581-5993
http://www.nationalreia.com

National Residential Appraisers Institute
2001 Cooper Foster Park Road
Amherst, OH 44001
Phone: (440) 282-7925
Fax: (440) 282-7925
E-mail: questions@nraiappraisers
.com
http://www.nraiappraisers.com

National Society of Environmental Consultants
303 West Cypress Street
San Antonio, TX 78212
Phone: (800) 486-3676
http://www.nsec.lincoln-grad.org

National Society of Real Estate Appraisers
2700 North State Road 7
Hollywood, FL 33021
Phone: (320) 763-7626
Fax: (320) 763-9290
E-mail: narea@iami.org
http://www.narea.org

Pension Real Estate Association
100 Pearl Street, 13th Floor
Hartford, CT 06103
Phone: (860) 692-6341
Fax: (860) 692-6351
E-mail: prea@prea.org
http://www.prea.org

Property Records Industry Association
2501 Aerial Center Parkway, Suite 103
Morrisville, NC 27560
Phone: (919) 459-2081
Fax: (919) 459-2081
http://www.pria.us

Real Estate Buyer's Agent Council
430 North Michigan Avenue
Chicago, IL 60611
Phone: (800) 648-6224
Fax: (312) 329-8632
E-mail: rebac@realtors.org
http://www.rebac.net

Real Estate CyberSpace Society
Four Longfellow Place, Suite 2003
Boston, MA 02114
Phone: (617) 523-4440
Fax: (617) 523-4736
E-mail: bostonjack@earthlink.net
http://www.REcyber.com

The Real Estate Educators Association
19 Mantua Road
Mt. Royal, NJ 08061
Phone: (856) 423-3215
Fax: (856) 423-3420
E-mail: info@reea.org
http://www.reea.org

Real Estate Information Professionals Association
c/o IMI Association Executives
P.O. Box 3159
Durham, NC 27715-3159
Phone: (919) 383-0044
Fax: (919) 383-0035
E-mail: mikeb@reipa.org
http://www.reipa.org

Real Estate Investment Advisory Council
800 South Pacific Coast Highway, Suite 8-338
Redondo Beach, CA 90277-4778
Phone: (310) 375-5750
Fax: (310) 375-3017
http://www.reiac.org

Real Estate Professionals Society
8 Argonaut, Suite 100
Aliso Viejo, CA 92656
Tel: (949) 600-7179
Fax: (949) 349-9392
E-mail: info@repsociety.com
http://www.realestateprofessional
society.com

The Real Estate Roundtable
801 Pennsylvania Avenue NW
Suite 720
Washington, DC 20004
Phone: (202) 639-8400
Fax: (202) 639-8442
E-mail: info@rer.org
http://www.rer.org

Real Estate Services Providers Council, Inc.
2000 L Street NW
Washington, DC 20036
Phone: (202) 862-2051
Fax: (202) 862-2052
http://www.respro.org

Realtors Land Institute
430 North Michigan Avenue
Chicago, IL 60611
Phone: (800) 441-5263
Fax: (312) 329-8633
E-mail: rli@realtors.org
http://www.rliland.com

Seller Agency Council
8 Argonaut, Suite 100
Aliso Viejo, CA 92656
Phone: (949) 600-7190
Fax: (949) 349-9392
E-mail: info@selleragency.com
http://www.selleragency.com

Senior Advantage Real Estate Council
430 North Michigan Avenue
Chicago, IL 60611
Phone: (800) 500-4564
Fax: (312) 329-8232
E-mail: SRES@realtors.org
http://realtors.org

Society of Industrial and Office Realtors
1201 New York Avenue, Suite 350
Washington, DC 20005-6126
Phone: (202) 449-8200
Fax: (202) 216-9325
E-mail: admin@sior.com
http://www.sior.com

United States Green Building Council
1800 Massachusetts Avenue NW
Suite 300
Washington, DC 20036
Phone: (800) 795-1747
Fax: (202) 828-5110
http://www.usbgc.org

Urban Land Institute
1025 Thomas Jefferson Street NW
Suite 500 West
Washington, DC 20007
Phone: (800) 321-5011
Fax: (202) 624-7140
E-mail: customerservice@uli.org
http://www.uli.org

Vacation Rental Managers Association
P.O. Box 1202
Santa Cruz, CA 95061-1202
Phone: (831) 426-8762
Fax: (831) 458-3637

E-mail: info@vrma.com
http://www.vrma.com

Women's Council of Realtors
430 North Michigan Avenue
Chicago, IL 60611
Phone: (800) 874-6500
E-mail: info@wcr.org
http://www.wcr.org

CANADA

Real Estate Institute of Canada
5407 Eglinton Avenue West
Suite 208
Toronto, ON M9C 5K6
Phone: (800) 542-REIC (7342)
Fax: (416) 695-7230
http://www.reic.ca

APPENDIX III
PROFESSIONAL CERTIFICATIONS

Professional certifications and credentials indicate that an individual has met educational, experience, and ethical qualifications and has achieved a level of professional competence. Many organizations are continuing to enhance their existing qualification standards while adding new certifications. Many real estate professionals have earned one or more professional certifications in their careers. Some have served as officers of local, regional, or national associations.

This section provides information about some of the more common professional certifications in banking, finance, and insurance. You can get more information about available certifications by going to these organizations' Web sites or by contacting the organizations directly. Remember that attaining professional certification often takes two to three years, or longer, to achieve. Talk to industry professionals in your field of interest about professional certification and ask them how certification can help advance your career or employability before committing your time and resources to an industry-sponsored certification program.

Accredited Review Appraisers Council
303 West Cypress Street
San Antonio, TX 78212
Phone: (800) 486-3676
http://arac.lincoln-grad.org
Certifications: Accredited Review Appraiser

American Association of Certified Appraisers
3129 Perlett Drive
Cameron Park, CA 95672
Phone: (530) 676-0391
Fax: (530) 676-0391
http://www.appraisal-professionals.net
Certifications: Certified Appraiser—Residential; Certified Appraiser—Senior; Certified Appraiser—Consultant

American Construction Inspectors Association
530 South Lake Avenue
Suite 431
Pasadena, CA 91101
Phone: (888) 867-ACIA (2242)
Fax: (626) 797-2214
E-mail: office@acia.com
http://www.acia.com
Certifications: Certified Code Specialist; Registered Construction Inspector

American Institute of Certified Public Accountants for CPA
1211 Avenue of the Americas
New York, NY 10036
Phone: (212) 596-6200
Fax: (212) 596-6213
http://aicpa.org

American Society of Appraisers
555 Herndon Parkway, Suite 125
Herndon, VA 20170
Phone: (703) 478-2228
Fax: (703) 742-8471
http://www.appraisers.org
Certifications: Accredited Member; Accredited Senior Appraiser

Appraisal Institute
550 West Van Buren Street
Suite 1000
Chicago, IL 60607
Phone: (312) 335-4100
E-mail: wwoodburn@ appraisalinstitute.org
http://www.appraisalinstitute.org
Certifications: Member— Appraisal Institute; Senior Residential Appraiser; Senior Real Property Appraiser

Association of Higher Education Facilities Officers
1643 Prince Street
Alexandria, VA 22314-2818
Phone: (703) 684-1446
Fax: (703) 549-2772
http://www.appa.org
Certifications: Education Facilities Professional; Certified Education Facilities Professional

Building Owners & Managers Institute
1521 Ritchie Highway
Arnold, MD 21012
Phone: (800) 235-BOMI
Fax: (410) 974-0544
E-mail: service@bomi-edu.org
http://www.bomi-edu.org
Certifications: Real Property Administrator; Facilities Management Administrator; Systems Maintenance Administrator; Systems Maintenance Technician

CCIM Institute
430 North Michigan Avenue, Suite 800
Chicago, IL 60611-4092
Phone: (312) 321-4460

E-mail: info@ccim.com
http://www.ccim.com
Certifications: Certified
Commercial Investment
Member

Community Associations Institute
225 Reinekers Lane
Suite 300
Alexandria, VA 22314
Phone: (888) 224-4321
Fax: (703) 684-1581
http://www.caionline.org
Certifications: Accredited
Association Company Manager;
Association Management
Specialist; College of Community
Association Lawyers;
Community Insurance and Risk
Management Specialist; Large
Scale Manager; Professional
Community Association
Manager; Reserve Specialist

Construction Financial Management Association
29 Emmons Drive, Suite F-50
Princeton, NJ 08540
Phone: (609) 452-8000
Fax: (609) 452-0474
E-mail: info@cfma.org
http://www.cfma.org
Certifications: Certified
Construction Industry Financial
Professional

Construction Management Association of America
7926 Jones Branch Drive, Suite 800
McLean, VA 22102
Phone: (703) 356-2622
Fax: (703) 356-6388
E-mail: info@cmaanet.org
http://www.cmaanet.org
Certifications: Construction
Manager in Training; Certified
Construction Manager

Council of Residential Specialists
430 North Michigan Avenue
Chicago, IL 60611
Phone: (800) 462-8841
Fax: (312) 329-8882
http://www.crs.com
Certifications: Certified
Residential Specialist

Council of Real Estate Brokerage Managers
430 North Michigan Avenue
Chicago, IL 60611
Phone: (800) 621-8738
Fax: (312) 329-8882
E-mail: info@crb.com
http://www.crb.com
Certifications: Certified Real Estate
Brokerage Manager

The Counselors of Real Estate
430 North Michigan Avenue
Chicago, IL 60611-4089
Phone: (312) 329-8427
E-mail: info@cre.org
http://www.cre.org
Certifications: Counselor of Real
Estate

Employee Relocation Council
Worldwide ERC
4401 Wilson Boulevard, Suite 510
Arlington, VA 22203
Phone: (703) 842-3400
Fax: (703) 527-1552
http://www.erc.org
Certifications: Certified Relocation
Professional

Environmental Assessment Association
1224 North Nokomis NE
Alexandria, MN 56308
Phone: (320) 763-4320
Fax: (320) 763-9290
E-mail: eaa@iami.org
http://iami.org/eaa.htm
Certifications: Certified
Environmental Inspector;
Certified Testing Specialist;
Certified Remediation
Specialist; Certified
Environmental Specialist;
Certified Environmental
Manager; Certified Mold
Specialist

Hotel Brokers International
1420 NW Vivion Road, Suite 111
Kansas City, MO 64118
Phone: (816) 505-4315
Fax: (816) 505-4319
E-mail: info@hbihotels.com
http://www.hbihotels.com
Certifications: Certified Hotel
Broker

Institute for Professionals in Taxation
600 Northpark Town Center
1200 Abernathy Road, Suite L-2
Atlanta, GA 30328-1040
Phone: (404) 240-2300
http://www.ipt.org
Certifications: Certified Member
of the Institute

Institute of Real Estate Management
430 North Michigan Avenue
Chicago, IL 60611
Phone: (800) 837-0706
Fax: (800) 338-4736
E-mail: custserv@irem.org
http://www.irem.org
Certifications: Certified
Property Manager; Accredited
Resident Manager; Accredited
Management Organization

International Association of Assessing Officers
314 West 10th Street
Kansas City, MO 64105-1616
Phone: (800) 616-4226
http://www.iaao.org
Certifications: Assessment
Administration Specialist;
Certified Assessment Evaluator;
Cadastral Mapping Specialist;
Personal Property Specialist;
Residential Evaluation
Specialist

International Council of Shopping Centers
1221 Avenue of the Americas, 41st
Floor
New York, NY 10020-1099
Phone: (646) 728-3800

Fax: (732) 694-1755
E-mail: icsc@icsc.org
http://www.icsc.org
Certifications: Certified Leasing
Specialist; Certified Shopping
Center Manager; Certified
Marketing Director

International Facility Management Association
1 East Greenway Plaza
Suite 1100
Houston, TX 77046-0194
Phone: (713) 623-4362
Fax: (713) 623-6124
http://www.ifma.org
Certifications: Certified Facility
Manager

International Right of Way Association
19750 South Vermont Avenue, Suite
220
Torrance, CA 90502-1144
Phone: (310) 538-0233
Fax: (310) 538-1471
E-mail: info@irwaonline.org
http://www.irwaonline.org
Certifications: Senior Member,
International Right of Way
Association

Mortgage Bankers Association of America
1919 Pennsylvania Avenue NW
Washington, DC 20006-3404
Phone: (202) 557-2700
http://www.mbaa.org
Certifications: Certified Mortgage
Banker; Accredited Mortgage
Professional; Certified Mortgage
Servicer; Certified Mortgage
Technologist; Certified Quality
Assurance Professional; Certified
Residential Originator; Certified
Residential Underwriter

National Affordable Housing Management Association
400 North Columbus Street, Suite
203
Alexandria, VA 22314
Phone: (703) 683-8630

Fax: (703) 683-8634
http://www.nahma.org
Certifications: National Affordable
Housing Professional;
Certified Professional of
Occupancy; Specialist in
Housing Credit Management;
National Affordable Housing
Maintenance Technician;
National Affordable Housing
Maintenance Supervisor

National Apartment Association
4300 Wilson Boulevard, Suite 400
Arlington, VA 22203
Phone: (703) 518-6141
Fax: (703) 248-9440
http://www.naahq.org
Certifications: Certified Apartment
Manager; Certified Apartment
Maintenance Technician;
Certified Apartment Property
Supervisor; Certified Apartment
Supplier; National Apartment
Leasing Professional; Certified
Professional of Occupancy;
Specialist in Housing Credit
Management

National Association of Certified Home Inspectors
1750 30th Street
Boulder, CO 80301
Phone: (650) 429-2057
Fax: (650) 429-2057
E-mail: fastreply@nachi.org
http://www.nachi.org
Certifications: Certified Master
Inspector

National Association of Counselors
303 West Cypress Street
San Antonio, TX 78212
Phone: (800) 486-3676
http://nac.lincoln-grad.org
Certifications: Senior Real Estate
Counselor

National Association of Home Builders
1201 15th Street NW

Washington, DC 20005
Phone: (800) 368-5242
Fax: (202) 266-8400
http://www.nahb.org
Certifications: Certified Active
Adult Specialist in Housing;
Certified In-Place Aging
Specialist; Certified Graduate
Associate; Certified Graduate
Remodeler; Certified New
Home Marketing Professional;
Graduate Master Builder;
Housing Credit Certified
Professional; Member, Institute
of Residential Marketing;
Certified Green Professional;
Master Certified New Home
Sales Professional; Registered
in Apartment Management;
Residential Construction
Superintendent

National Association of Home Inspectors
4248 Park Glen Road
Minneapolis, MN 55416
Phone: (800) 448-3942
Fax: (952) 929-1318
E-mail: info@nahi.org
http://www.nahi.org
Certifications: Certified Real Estate
Inspector

National Association of Independent Fee Appraisers
401 North Michigan Avenue, Suite
2200
Chicago, IL 60611
Phone: (312) 321-6830
Fax: (312) 673-6652
E-mail: info@naifa.com
http://www.naifa.com
Certifications: Certified Appraisal
Reviewer; Certified Mortgage
Appraisal Reviewer

National Association of Master Appraisers
303 West Cypress Street
San Antonio, TX 78212
Phone: (800) 229-6262
Fax: (210) 225-8450
http://www.masterappraisers.org

Certifications: Master Residential Appraiser; Master Farm & Land Appraiser; Master Senior Appraiser

National Association of Mortgage Brokers
7900 Westpark Drive, Suite T309
McLean, VA 22102
Phone: (703) 342-5900
Fax: (703) 342-5905
http://www.namb.org
Certifications: Certified Mortgage Consultant; Certified Residential Mortgage Specialist; General Mortgage Associate

National Association of Real Estate Appraisers
1224 North Nokomis NE
Alexandria, MN 56308
Phone: (320) 763-7626
Fax: (320) 763-9290
http://www.iami.org/NAREA
Certifications: Certified Real Estate Appraiser; Certified Commercial Real Estate Appraiser; Registered Trainee Appraiser; Registered Professional Member

National Association of Realtors
430 North Michigan Avenue
Chicago, IL 60611-4087
Phone: (800) 874-6500
http://www.realtor.org
Certifications: Accredited Buyer Representative; Accredited Buyer Representative Manager; Certified International Property Specialist; Certified Real Estate Brokerage Manager; Certified Residential Specialist; Graduate Realtor Institute; Realtor Association Certified Executive; Residential Accredited Appraiser; Senior Real Estate Specialist; At Home with Diversity Certification; Real Estate Professional Assistant; Resorts & Second-Home Markets Certification; Transnational Referral

Certification; REALTOR Association Certified Executive

National Association of Residential Property Managers
638 Independence Parkway
Suite 100
Chesapeake, VA 23320
Phone: (800) 782-3452
Fax: (866) 466-2776
E-mail: info@narpm.org
http://www.naprm.org
Certifications: Residential Management Professional; Master Property Manager; Certified Support Specialist; Certified Residential Management Company

National Auctioneers Association
8880 Ballentine
Overland Park, KS 66214
Phone: (913) 541-8084
Fax: (913) 894-5281
http://www.auctioneers.org
Certifications: Auction Technology Specialist; Accredited Auctioneer Real Estate; Benefit Auctioneer Specialist; Certified Estate Specialist; Graduate Personal Property Appraiser; Graduate Personal Property Appraiser—Master

National Board of Certification for Community Association Managers
225 Reinekers Lane, Suite 310
Alexandria, VA 22314
Phone: (703) 836-6902
Fax: (703) 837-9490
E-mail: info@nbccam.org
http://www.nbccam.org
Certifications: Certified Manager of Community Associations

National Property Management Association
28100 U.S. Highway 19 North
Suite 400
Clearwater, FL 33761

Phone: (727) 736-3788
Fax: (727) 736-6707
E-mail: hq@npma.org
http://www.npma.org
Certifications: Certified Professional Property Specialist; Certified Professional Property Administrator; Certified Professional Property Manager

National Residential Appraisers Institute
2001 Cooper Foster Park Road
Amherst, OH 44001
Phone: (440) 282-7925
Fax: (440) 282-7925
http://www.nraiappraisers.com
Certifications: Certified Market Data Analyst; Graduate Senior Appraiser; State Certified Appraiser; Senior Licensed Appraiser

Real Estate CyberSpace Society
Four Longfellow Place, Suite 2003
Boston, MA 02114
Phone: (617) 523-4440
Fax: (617) 523-4736
E-mail: bostonjack@earthlink.net
http://www.REcyber.com
Certifications: Real Estate CyberSpace Specialist

Real Estate Educators Association
19 Mantua Road
Mt. Royal, NJ 08061
Phone: (856) 423-3215
Fax: (856) 423-3420
E-mail: info@reea.org
http://www.reea.org
Certifications: Distinguished Real Estate Instructor

Real Estate Professionals Society
8 Argonaut, Suite 100
Aliso Viejo, CA 92656
Phone: (949) 600-7179
Fax: (949) 349-9392
E-mail: info@repsociety.com
http://www.realestateprofessional
society.com

Certifications: Accredited Real Estate Professional; Career Management Real Estate Professional; e-Business Real Estate Professional; Referral Real Estate Professional; Commercial Real Estate Professional; Mortgage Real Estate Professional; Appraisal Real Estate Professional

Realtors Land Institute

430 North Michigan Avenue
Chicago, IL 60611
Phone: (800) 441-5263

Fax: (312) 329-8633
E-mail: rli@realtors.org
http://www.rliland.com
Certifications: Accredited Land Consultant

Sellers Agency Council

8 Argonaut, Suite 100
Aliso Viejo, CA 92656
Phone: (949) 600-7190
Fax: (949) 349-9392
E-mail: info@selleragency.com
http://www.selleragency.com
Certifications: Accredited Seller Representative

Urban Land Institute

1025 Thomas Jefferson Street NW
Suite 500 West
Washington, DC 20007
Phone: (800) 321-5011
Fax: (202) 624-7140
E-mail: customerservice@uli.org
http://www.uli.org
Certifications: Real Estate Development Certificate; Real Estate Development Finance Certificate

APPENDIX IV
PROFESSIONAL PERIODICALS

This section contains a list of professional journals, magazines, newsletters, and other real estate publications. Some report on news and events in one segment of the real estate industry sector, such as apartment buildings, multi-family housing, or shopping centers. Many others report more broadly on business trends and financial issues affecting the broad spectrum of real estate in North America.

The name, publisher, and contact information for each publication is included below. Readers can obtain more information, including subscription prices, from the publisher's Web address. Please note that this list comprises a core group of real estate publications. There are many more publications, including Weblogs (blogs) and online newsletters, available to interested readers who want to follow the latest developments in the North American real estate market.

Affordable Housing Finance
111 Sutter Street, Suite 975
San Francisco, CA 94104
Phone: (415) 315-1241
Fax: (415) 315-1248
http://www.housingfinance.com

Apartment Finance Today
P.O. Box 3567
Northbrook, IL 60065-3567
Phone: (888) 269-8410
Fax: (847) 291-4816
http://www.housingfinance.com/aft

The Appraisal Journal
Appraisal Institute
550 West Van Buren Street
Suite 1000
Chicago, IL 60607
Phone: (312) 335-4100
http://www.appraisalinstitute.org

Appraisal Today
Real Estate Communication
 Resources
2015 Clement Avenue
Alameda, CA 94501
Phone: (510) 865-8041
E-mail: info@appraisaltoday.com.
http://www.appraisaltoday.com

Area Development
400 Post Avenue
Westbury, NY 11590
Phone: (800) 7352732
Fax: (516) 338-0100
E-mail: areadev@areadevelopment
 .com
http://www.areadevelopment.com

Black's Guide
444 North Frederick Avenue
Gaithersburg, MD 20877-2432
Phone: (800) 500-2450
Fax: (301) 258-9237
http://blacksguide.com

BOMA Magazine
Building Owners and Managers
 Association International
1101 15th Street NW
Suite 800
Washington, DC 20005
Phone: (202) 408-2662
Fax: (202) 326-6377
E-mail: info@boma.org
http://www.boma.org

Brownfield News
5440 North Cumberland
Chicago, IL 60650
Phone: (773) 714-0407
Fax: (773) 714-0989
http://www.brownfieldcentral.com

Builder
One Thomas Circle NW
Suite 600
Washington, DC 20005
Phone: (202) 452-0800
Fax: (202) 785-1974
http://www.builderonline.com

*Building Design &
 Construction*
Reed Business Information
2000 Clearwater Drive
Oak Brook, IL 60523
Phone: (630) 288-8000
http://www.bdcnetwork.com

*Building Operating
 Management*
2100 West Florist Avenue
Milwaukee, WI 53209
Phone: (800) 727-7995
Fax: (414) 228-1134
E-mail: info@tradepress.com
http://www.tradepress.com

Buildings
Stamats Business Media, Inc.
615 Fifth Street SE
Cedar Rapids, IA 52401
Phone: (319) 364-6167
Fax: (319) 364-4278
http://www.buildings.com

Business Facilities
44 Apple Street, Suite 3
Tinton Falls, NJ 07724
Phone: (800) 524-0337

Fax: (732) 758-6634
http://www.businessfacilities.com

California Real Estate
California Association of Realtors
525 South Virgil
Los Angeles, CA 90020
Phone: (213) 739-8200
Fax: (213) 480-7724
http://www.car.org

Commercial Builder Magazine
National Association of Home
   Builders
1201 15th Street NW
Washington, DC 20005
Phone: (800) 368-5242
Fax: (202) 266-8400
E-mail: aflank@nahb.com
http://www.nahb.org

**Commercial Investment Real
Estate Journal**
CCIM Institute
430 North Michigan Avenue, Suite
   800
Chicago, IL 60611-4092
Phone: (312) 321-4460
Fax: (312) 321-4530
http://www.ccim.com/journal

Commercial Mortgage Alert
5 Marine View Plaza, Suite 400
Hoboken, NJ 07030-5795
Phone: (201) 659-1700
Fax: (201) 659-4141
E-mail: info@hspnews.com
http://www.hspnews.com

Commercial Mortgage Insight
P.O. Box 2180
Waterbury, CT 06722
Phone: (800) 325-6745
Fax: (203) 262-4680
E-mail: info@cmi-online.com
http://www.cmi-online.com

Commercial Property News
770 Broadway
New York, NY 10003-9595
Phone: (646) 654-5380
Fax: (646) 654-4598
http:// www.cpnrenet.com

The Commercial Record
Warren Group
280 Summer Street
Boston, MA 02210
Phone: (617) 428-5100
Fax: (617) 428-5118
http://www.thewarrengroup.com

Community Development Report
CD Publications
8204 Fenton Street
Silver Spring, MD 20910
Phone: (800) 666-6380
Fax: (301) 588-6385
E-mail: info@cdpublications.com
http://www.cppublications.com

Creative Real Estate Magazine
9191 Towne Centre Drive, Suite 180
San Diego, CA 92122
Phone: (800) 839-4607
Fax: (858) 435-4374
http://www.cremag.com

Corporate Real Estate Leader
CoreNet Global
260 Peachtree Street, Suite 1500
Atlanta, GA 30303
Phone: (800) 726-8111
E-mail: leader@corenetglobal.org
http://www.corenetglobal.com

Design-Build
Cygnus Business Media
1233 Janesville Avenue
Fort Atkinson, WI 53538
Phone: (800) 547-7347
Fax: (920) 563-1797
http://www.dbbonline.com

Development Magazine
National Association of Industrial
   and Office Properties
2201 Cooperative Way, Third Floor
Herndon, VA 20171-3034
Phone: (703) 904-7100
Fax: (703) 904-7942
http://www.naiop.org

Facility Management Journal
One East Greenway Plaza
Suite 1100
Houston, TX 77046-0194

Phone: (713) 623-4262
Fax: (713) 623-6142
http://www.ifma.org

Facilities Manager
Association of Higher Education
   Facilities Officers
1643 Prince Street
Alexandria, VA 22314
Phone: (703) 684-1446
Fax: (703) 549-2772
http://www.appa.org

Habitat Magazine
928 Broadway, Suite 1105
New York, NY 10010
Phone: (212) 505-2030
Fax: (212) 254-6795
http://www.habitatmag.com

Hotel & Motel Management
7500 Old Oak Boulevard
Cleveland, OH 44130
Phone: (216) 243-8100
http://www.hmmonline.com

Hotel Journal
45 Research Way, Suite 106
East Setauket, NY 11733
Phone: (631) 246-9300
Fax: (631) 246-9496
E-mail: info@hoteljournal.com
http://hoteljournal.com

Housing Market Report
CD Publications
8204 Fenton Street
Silver Spring, MD 20910
Phone: (800) 666-6380
Fax: (301) 588-6385
E-mail: info@cdpublications.com
http://www.cdpublications.com

Inman Real Estate News
1480 64th Street, Suite 100
Emeryville, CA 94608
Phone: (800) 775-4662
Fax: (510) 658-9317
http://www.inman.com

Inside Mortgage Finance
Inside Mortgage Finance
   Publications

7910 Woodmont Avenue, Suite
1000
Bethesda, MD 20814
Phone: (301) 951-1240
Fax: (301) 656-1709
http://www.imfpubs.com

The Institutional Real Estate Letter
Institutional Real Estate, Inc.
2274 Camino Ramon
San Ramon, CA 94583
Phone: (925) 244-0500
Fax: (925) 244-0520
http://www.irei.com

Journal of Housing and Community Development
National Association of Housing
and Redevelopment Officials
630 I Street NW
Washington DC 20001
Phone: (877) 866-2476
Fax: (202) 289-8181
E-mail: nahro@nahro.org
http://www.nahro.org

Journal of Property Management
Institute of Real Estate Management
P.O. Box 109025
Chicago, IL 60610-9025
Phone: (312) 329-6000
http:// www.irem.org

Journal of Real Estate Literature
American Real Estate Society
P.O. Box 41323
Clemson, SC 29634-1323
Phone: (864) 656-1373
Fax: (864) 656-3748
http://www.business.fullerton.edu/
finance/jrel

Journal of Real Estate Research
American Real Estate Society
Clemson University
P.O. Box 341323
Clemson, SC 29634-1323
Phone: (864) 656-1373
Fax: (864) 656-3748
http://www.business.fullerton.edu/
finance/jrer

Land Development Magazine
National Association of Home
Builders
1201 15th Street NW
Washington, DC 20005
Phone: (800) 368-5242
Fax: (202) 266-8400
http://www.nahb.org

Maintenance Solutions
2100 West Florist Avenue
Milwaukee, WI 53209
Phone: (414) 228-7701
Fax: (414) 228-1134
http://www.facilitiesnet.com

Mortgage Banking
Mortgage Bankers Association of
America
1919 Pennsylvania Avenue NW
Washington, DC 20006-3404
Phone: (202) 557-2700
http://www.mbaa.org

Multifamily Executive
One Thomas Circle NW
Suite 600
Washington, DC 20005
Phone: (202) 452-0800
Fax: (202) 785-1974
http://www.multifamilyexecutive
.com

Multi-Housing News
770 Broadway
New York, NY 10003-9595
Phone: (646) 654-5000
http://www.multi-housingnews.com

National Hotel Executive Magazine
1230 Market Street, Suite 500
San Francisco, CA 94102
Phone: (415) 830-3940
E-mail: online@hotelexecutive.com
http://www.hotelexecutive.com

National Mortgage News
One State Street Plaza, 26th Floor
New York, NY 10004
Phone: (800) 221-1809
Fax: (212) 843-9649
http://www.nationalmortgagenews
.com

National Real Estate Investor
6151 Powers Ferry Boulevard NW
Atlanta, GA 30339-2941
Phone: (770) 955-2500
Fax: (770) 955-0400
http://www.nreonline.com

Pensions & Investments
711 Third Avenue
New York, NY 10017
Phone: (212) 210-0100
Fax: (212) 210-0117
http://www.pionline.com

Professional Builder
Reed Business Information
2000 Clearwater Drive
Oak Brook, IL 60523
Phone: (630) 320-7000
Fax: (630) 288-8145
http://www.housingzone.com/
probuilder

Real Estate Alert
5 Marine View Plaza, #400
Hoboken, NJ 07030-5795
Phone: (201) 659-1700
Fax: (201) 659-4141
E-mail: info@hspnews.com
http://www.hspnews.com

Real Estate Economics
8961 Research Drive, Suite 200
Irvine, CA 92618
Phone: (888) 820-5123
http://www.realestateeconomics.com

Real Estate Finance
488 Madison Avenue
New York, NY 10022
Phone: (212) 224-3300
Fax: (212) 224-3527
http://www.iirealestate.com

Real Estate Forum
111 Eighth Avenue, Suite 151
New York, NY 10018-5201
Phone: (212) 929-6900
Fax: (212) 929-7124
http://www.reforum.com

Real Estate Issues
The Counselors of Real Estate

430 North Michigan Avenue
Chicago, IL 60611-4089
Phone: (312) 329-8427
E-mail: info@cre.org
http://www.cre.org

Real Estate Journal
Dow Jones & Co.
P.O. Box 300
Princeton, NJ 08543-0300
Phone: (609) 520-4000
http://www.realestatejournal.com

Real Estate Magazine
69 East Avenue
Norwalk, CT 06851
Phone: (800) 724-6000
E-mail: online@rismedia.com
http://www.rismedia.com

Real Estate News
3550 West Peterson Avenue #100
Chicago, IL 60659
Phone: (888) 641-3169
Fax: (773) 866-9881
E-mail: Bonnie@
    RealEstateNewsUSA.com
http://www.RealEstateNewsUSA
    .com

Real Estate Portfolio
National Association of Real Estate
    Investment Trusts
1875 I Street, Suite 600
Washington, DC 20006
Phone: (202) 739-9400
Fax: (202) 739-9401
E-mail: info@nareit.com
http://www.nareit.org

Realtor Magazine
National Association of Realtors
430 North Michigan Avenue
Chicago, IL 60611-4087

Phone: (800) 874-6500
E-mail: narpubs@realtors.org
http://www.realtor.org

Realty Times
5949 Sherry Lane, Suite 700
Dallas, TX 75225
Phone: (214) 353-6980
Fax: (214) 368-0699
http://www.realtytimes.com

Shopping Centers Today
International Council of Shopping
    Centers
1221 Avenue of the Americas, 41st
    Floor
New York, NY 10020-1099
Phone: (646) 728-3800
Fax: (732) 694-1755
E-mail: icsc@icsc.org
http://www.icsc.org

Site Selection Magazine
6625 The Corners Parkway, Suite 200
Norcross, GA 30092-2901
Phone: (770) 446-6996
Fax: (770) 263-8825
http://www.sitenet.com

The Slatin Report
156 West 56th Street, Suite 1101
New York, NY 10019
Phone: (212) 265-0500
Fax: (212) 586-7302
E-mail: pslatin@theslatinreport.com
http://www.theslatinreport.com

Today's Facility Manager
44 Apple Street, Suite 3
Tinton Falls, NJ 07724
Phone: (732) 842-7433
Fax: (732) 758-6634
http://www.todaysfacilitymanager
    .com

Today's Realtor
National Association of Realtors
430 North Michigan Avenue
Chicago, IL 60611-4087
Phone: (800) 874-6500
E-mail: narpubs@realtor.org
http://www.realtor.org

Units Magazine
National Apartment Association
4300 Wilson Boulevard, Suite 400
Arlington, VA 22203
Phone: (703) 518-6141
Fax: (703) 248-9440
http://www.naahq.org

Urban Land Magazine
Urban Land Institute
1025 Thomas Jefferson Street NW
Suite 500 West
Washington, DC 20007
Phone: (800) 321-5011
Fax: (202) 624-7140
http://www.uli.org

Vacation Industry Review
Interval Publications
6262 Sunset Drive
Miami, FL 33143
Phone: (305) 666-1861
http://www.resortdeveloper.com

Valuation Insight & Perspective
Appraisal Institute
550 West Van Buren Street
Suite 1000
Chicago, IL 60607
Phone: (312) 335-4478
Fax: (312) 335-4474
E-mail: wwoodburn@
    appraisalinstitute.org
http://appraisalinstitute.org

APPENDIX V
MAJOR REAL ESTATE MANAGEMENT FIRMS

The following list shows the largest property management companies operating in the United States in 2007, as compiled by *Commercial Property News*. Many of these are full-service real estate companies and are active in real estate brokerage and property development, in addition to property management.

CALIFORNIA

Burnham Real Estate
4435 Eastgate Mall, Suite 200
San Diego, CA 92121
Phone: (858) 452-6500
Fax: (858) 452-3206
http://www.burnhamrealestate.com

C.B. Richard Ellis Inc.
11150 Santa Monica Boulevard,
  Suite 1600
Los Angeles, CA 90025
http://www.cbre.com

Charles Dunn Co.
800 West Sixth Street, Suite 600
Los Angeles, CA 90017
Phone: (213) 683-0500
Fax: (213) 683-1551
http://www.charlesdunn.com

The Conam Group of Companies
3990 Ruffin Road, Suite 100
San Diego, CA 92123
Phone: (858) 614-7200
Fax: (858) 614-7525
http://www.conam.com

Donohue Schriber
200 East Baker Street, Suite 100
Costa Mesa, CA 92626
Phone: (714) 545-1400
Fax: (714) 545-4222
http://www.donohueschriber.com

Eugene Burger Management Corp.
6600 Hunter Drive

Rohnert Park, CA 94928
Phone: (707) 584-5123
Fax: (707) 584-5124
http://www.ebmc.com

Grubb & Ellis Co.
1551 North Tustin Avenue, Suite 200
Santa Ana, CA 92705
Phone: (800) 877-9066
http://www.grubb-ellis.com

Legacy Partners Commercial, Inc.
4000 East Third Avenue, Suite 600
Foster City, CA 94404
Phone: (650) 571-2200
Fax: (650) 571-2224
http://www.legacypartners.com

Shea Properties
130 Vantis, Suite 200
Aliso Viejo, CA 92656
Phone: (949) 389-7000
Fax: (949) 389-7466
http://www.sheaproperties.com

Shorenstein Properties LLC
555 California Street, 49th Floor
San Francisco, CA 94104
Phone: (415) 772-7000
Fax: (415) 772-7030
http://www.shorenstein.com

Western National Property Management
Eight Executive Circle
Irvine, CA 92614
Phone: (949) 862-6200

Fax: (949) 862-6494
http://www.wng.com

Westfield LLC
11601 Wilshire Boulevard, 11th
  Floor
Los Angeles, CA 90025
Phone: (310) 478-4456
http://www.westfield.com

COLORADO

Archstone-Smith
9200 East Panorama Circle,
  Suite 400
Englewood, CO 80112
Phone: (303) 708-5959
http://www.archstonesmith.com

PROLOGIS
4545 Airport Way
Denver, CO 80239
Phone: (303) 567-5000
Fax: (303) 567-5605
http://www.prologis.com

DISTRICT OF COLUMBIA

Akridge
601 13th Street NW, Suite 300 N
Washington, DC 20005
Phone: (202) 638-3000
Fax: (202) 347-8043
http://www.akridge.com

FLORIDA

Corfac International
1930 Harrison Street, Suite 101

Hollywood, FL 33020
Phone: (954) 923-6160
Fax: (954) 925-7170
http://www.corfac.com

GEORGIA

CARTER
171 17th Street, Suite 1200
Atlanta, GA 30363
Phone: (404) 888-3000
Fax: (404) 888-3001
http://www.carterusa.com

GVA Advantis
3445 Peachtree Road, Suite 300
Atlanta, GA 30326
Phone: (404) 949-6132
Fax: (404) 262-1083
http://www.gvaadvantis.com

IDI Services Group, Inc.
Monarch Tower, Suite 1500
3424 Peachtree Road NE
Atlanta, GA 30326
Phone: (404) 479-4000
Fax: (404) 479-4115
http://www.idisg.com

INDIANA

Duke Realty Corp.
600 East 96th Street, Suite 100
Indianapolis, IN 46240
Phone: (317) 808-6000
Fax: (317) 808-6770
http://www.dukerealty.com

ILLINOIS

Equity Residential
Two North Riverside Plaza
Chicago, IL 60606
Phone: (312) 474-1300
Fax: (312) 454-8703
http://www.equityapartments.com

First Industrial Realty Trust, Inc.
311 South Wacker Drive, Suite 4000
Chicago, IL 60606
Phone: (312) 344-4300
http://www.firstindustrial.com

GVA Worldwide
1569 Sherman Avenue, Suite 201C
Evanston, IL 60201
Phone: (847) 733-0883
Fax: (847) 733-0887
http://www.gvaworldwide.com

The Inland Real Estate Group of Companies
2901 Butterfield Road
Oak Brook, Illinois 60523
Phone: (630) 218-8000
Fax: (630) 218-8039
http://www.inlandgroup.com

Jones Lang Lasalle, Inc.
200 East Randolph Drive
Chicago, IL 60601
Phone: (312) 782-5800
Fax: (312) 782-4339
http://www.joneslanglasalle.com

MB Real Estate Services, LLC
181 West Madison Street, Suite 3900
Chicago, Illinios 60601
Phone: (312) 726-1700
Fax: (312) 807-3853
http://www.mbres.com

Mid-America Asset Management, Inc.
One Parkview Plaza, Ninth Floor
Oakbrook Terrace, Ilinois 60181
Phone: (630) 954-7300
Fax: (630) 954-7306
http://www.midamericagrp.com

Oakwood Development Corp.
414 Plaza Drive, Suite 302
Westmont, IL 60559
Phone: (630) 430-5635
http://www.oakwood-development.com

U.S. Equities Realty/ Oncor International
20 North Michigan Avenue, Suite 400
Chicago, Ilinois 60602
Phone: (312) 456-7000
Fax: (312) 456-0056
http://www.usequities.com

LOUISIANA

Sterling Properties Inc.
109 Northpark Boulevard, Suite 300
Covington, LA 70433
Phone: (985) 898-2022
Fax: (985) 898-2077
http://www.stirlingproperties.com

MARYLAND

Washington Real Estate Investment Trust
6110 Executive Boulevard, Suite 800
Rockville, MD 20852
Phone: (301) 984-9400
Fax: (301) 984-9610
http://www.writ.com

MASSACHUSETTS

Boston Properties, Inc.
800 Boylston Street
Boston, MA 02199
Phone: (617) 236-3300
Fax: (617) 236-3311
http://www.bostonproperties.com

Colliers International
50 Milk Street
Boston, MA 02109
Phone: (617) 722-0221
Fax: (617) 722-0224
http://www.colliers.com

Colliers Meredith & Grew
160 Federal Street
Boston, MA 02110
Phone: (617) 330-8000
Fax: (617) 330-8127
http://www.m-g.com

NPV/Direct Invest
211 Congress Street, Eighth Floor
Boston, MA 02110
Phone: (866) 678-1031
Fax: (617) 820-5005
http://www.npvllc.com

MICHIGAN

Edward Rose Building Enterprise
P.O. Box 9070

Farmington Hills, MI 48333
Phone: (248) 539-2255
Fax: (248) 539-2125
http://www.edwardrose.com

Finsilver/Friedman Management Group
37975 West Twelve Mile Road, Suite 100
Farmington Hills, MI 48331
Phone: (248) 324-2030
Fax: (248) 848-3506
http://www.freg.com

NAI Farbman
28400 Northwestern Highway, Fourth Floor
Southfield, MI 48034
Phone: (248) 353-0500
Fax: (248) 353-0501
http://www.naifarbman.com

Taubman Centers, Inc.
200 East Long Lake Road, P.O. Box 300
Bloomfield Hills, MI 48303
Phone: (248) 258-6800
Fax: (248) 258-7596
http://www.taubman.com

Village Green Companies
30833 Northwestern Highway, Suite 300
Farmington Hills, MI 48334
Phone: (248) 851-9600
Fax: (248) 851-6161
http://www.villagegreen.com

MINNESOTA

Meritex Enterprises, Inc.
2285 Walnut Street
Roseville, MN 55113
Phone: (651) 855-9700
Fax: (651) 855-9701
http://www.meritex.com

Opus Group
10350 Bren Road, West
Minnetonka, MN 55343
Phone: (952) 656-4444
Fax: (952) 656-4529
http://www.opuscorp.com

United Properties
3500 West American Boulevard, Suite 200
Bloomington, MN 55431
Phone: (952) 831-1000
http://www.uproperties.com

MISSOURI

Block & Company, Inc., Realtors
700 West 47th Street, Suite 200
Kansas City, MO 64112
Phone: (816) 756-1400
Fax: (816) 932-5598
http://www.blockandco.com

Colliers Turley Martin Tucker
7701 Forsyth Boulevard, Suite 500
St. Louis, MO 63105
Phone: (314) 862-7100
Fax: (314) 862-1648
http://www.ctmt.com

Solon Gershman Inc. / Oncor International
Seven North Bemiston
Clayton, MO 63105
Phone: (314) 862-9400
Fax: (314) 889-0611
http://www.gershmancommercial.com

THF Realty, Inc.
2127 Innerbelt Business Center Drive, Suite 200
St. Louis, MO 63114
Phone: (314) 429-0900
Fax: (314) 429-0999
http://www.thfrealty.com

NEW JERSEY

Lamar Companies
365 South Street
Morristown, NJ 07960
Phone: (973) 285-0660
Fax: (973) 285-9236
http://www.lamarcompanies.com

Levin Management Corp.
893 Route 22 West
North Plainfield, NJ 07060
Phone: (908) 226-5267

Fax: (908) 756-6757
http://www.levinmgt.com

Linque Management Co.
301 Route 17 N
Rutherford, NJ 07070
Phone: (201) 460-3440
Fax: (201) 460-1848
http://www.lincolnequities.com

Mack-Cali Realty Corp.
343 Thornall Street
Edison, NJ 08837
Phone: (732) 590-1000
Fax: (732) 205-8237
http://www.mack-cali.com

Sheldon Gross Realty, Inc.
80 Main Street
West Orange, NJ 07052
Phone: (973) 325-6200
Fax: (973) 325-9090
http://www.sheldongrossrealty.com

NEW YORK

Home Properties, Inc.
850 Clinton Square
Rochester, NY 14604
Phone: (585) 546-4900
Fax: (585) 546-5433
http://www.homeproperties.com

ING Clarion Partners
230 Park Avenue, 12th Floor
New York, NY 10169
Phone: (212) 883-2500
Fax: (212) 883-2700
http://www.ingclarion.com

Kimco Realty Corp.
3333 New Hyde Park Road
New Hyde Park, NY 11042
Phone: (516) 869-9000
Fax: (516) 869-9001
http://www.kimcorealty.com

The Lightstone Group, LLC
460 Park Avenue, 13th Floor
New York, NY 10022
Phone: (212) 755-4600

Fax: (201) 831-0601
http://www.lightstonegroup.com

Newmark Knight Frank
125 Park Avenue
New York, NY 10017
Phone: (212) 372-2000
Fax: (212) 372-2424
http://www.newmarkkf.com

Rockefeller Group Development Corp.
1221 Avenue of the Americas
New York, NY 10020
Phone: (212) 282-2000
Fax: (212) 282-2179
http://www.rockgroupdevelopment
.com

RREEF
280 Park Avenue, 23rd Floor
New York, NY 10017
Phone: (212) 454-3908
Fax: (212) 454-6606
http://www.rreef.com

Sentinel Real Estate Corp.
1251 Avenue of the Americas, 35th
Floor
New York, NY 10020
Phone: (212) 408-5000
Fax: (212) 603-4964
http://www.sentinelcorp.com

Tarragon Corp.
423 West 55th Street, 12th Floor
New York, NY 10019
Phone: (212) 949-5000
Fax: (212) 949-8001
http://www.tarragoncorp.com

Tishman Speyer Properties
45 Rockefeller Plaza
New York, NY 10111
Phone: (212) 715-0300
Fax: (212) 319-1745
http://www.tishmanspeyer.com

Vornado Realty Trust
888 Seventh Avenue
New York, NY 10019
Phone: (212) 894-7000
Fax: (212) 894-7070
http://www.vno.com

NORTH CAROLINA

Crosland
227 West Trade Street, Suite 800
Charlotte, NC 28202
Phone: (704) 529-1166
Fax: (704) 523-7110
http://www.crosland.com

Highwoods Properties, Inc.
3100 Smoketree Court
Raleigh, NC 27604
Phone: (919) 872-4924
Fax: (919) 431-1439
http://www.highwoods.com

NORCOM Properties, Inc.
1512 East Fourth Street
Charlotte, NC 28204
Phone: (704) 332-4146
Fax: (704) 332-9348
http://www.norcomproperties.com

OHIO

Associated Estates Realty Corp.
One AEC Parkway
Richmond Heights, OH 44143
Phone: (216) 261-5000
Fax: (216) 289-9600
http://www.aecrealty.com

Developers Diversified Realty Corp.
3300 Enterprise Parkway
Beachwood, OH 44122
Phone: (216) 755-5500
Fax: (216) 755-1500
http://www.ddr.com

Glimcher Realty Trust
180 East Broad Street
Columbus, OH 43215
Phone: (614) 621-9000
Fax: (614) 621-2018
http://www.glimcher.com

PENNSYLVANIA

The Flynn Co.
1621 Wood Street
Philadelphia, PA 19103
Phone: (215) 561-6565

Fax: (215) 561-5025
http://www.flynnco.com

Liberty Property Trust
500 Chesterfield Parkway
Malvern, PA 19355
Phone: (610) 648-1700
Fax: (610) 644-4129
http://www.libertyproperty.com

Pennsylvania Real Estate Investment Trust
200 South Broad Street
Philadelphia, PA 19102
Phone: (215) 875-0700
Fax: (215) 546-7311
http://www.preit.com

RHODE ISLAND

Picerne Real Estate Group
75 Lambert Lind Highway
Warwick, RI 02886
Phone: (401) 732-3700
Fax: (401) 738-6452
http://www.picerne.com

TENNESSEE

ALCO Management, Inc.
35 Union Avenue, Suite 200
Memphis, TN 38103
Phone: (901) 544-1705
Fax: (901) 544-1744
http://www.alcomgt.com

CBL & Associates Properties, Inc.
CBL Center, 2030 Hamilton Place
Boulevard, Suite 500
Chattanooga, TN 37421
Phone: (423) 855-0001
Fax: (423) 490-8390
http://www.cblproperties.com

Freeman Webb, Inc.
555 Great Circle Road, Suite 100
Nashville, TN 37228
Phone: (615) 271-2700
Fax: (615) 726-1937
http://www.freemanwebb.com

TEXAS

Bradford Companies
9400 North Central Expressway, Suite 500
Dallas, TX 75231
Phone: (972) 776-7000
Fax: (972) 776-7083
http://www.bradford.com

Camden Property Trust
Three East Greenway Plaza, Suite 1300
Houston, TX 77046
Phone: (713) 354-2500
Fax: (713) 354-2700
http://www.camdenliving.com

Cencor Realty Services
3102 Maple Avenue, Suite 500
Dallas, TX 75201
Phone: (214) 954-0300
Fax: (214) 953-0860
http://www.cencorrealty.com

Crimson Services, LLC
1980 Post Oak Boulevard, Suite 1600
Houston, TX 77056
Phone: (713) 840-2700
Fax: (713) 840-2705
http://www.crimsoncorp.com

Hillwood
5430 LBJ Freeway, Eighth Floor
Dallas, TX 75240
Phone: (972) 201-2800
Fax: (972) 201-2829
http://www.hillwood.com

Hines
2800 Post Oak Boulevard
Houston, TX 77056
Phone: (713) 966-8000
Fax: (713) 966-7886
http://www.hines.com

JPI
600 East Las Colinas Boulevard, Suite 2100
Irving, TX 75039
Phone: (972) 556-1700
Fax: (972) 444-2102
http://www.jpi.com

Lincoln Property Co.
3300 Lincoln Plaza, 500 North Akard Street
Dallas, TX 75201
Phone: (214) 740-3300
Fax: (214) 740-3441
http://www.lincolnproperty.com

MILESTONE MANAGEMENT
5429 LBJ Freeway, Suite 800
Dallas, TX 75240
Phone: (214) 561-1200
Fax: (214) 561-1381
http://www.milestone-mgt.com

TCN Worldwide
400 Chisholm Place, Suite 104
Plano, TX 75075
Phone: (972) 769-8701
Fax: (972) 769-8401
http://www.tcnworldwide.com

Transwestern
1900 West Loop, South, Suite 1300
Houston, TX 77027
Phone: (713) 270-7700
Fax: (713) 270-6285
http://www.transwestern.net

Weingarten Realty Investors
2600 Citadel Plaza Drive
Houston, TX 77008
Phone: (713) 866-6000
Fax: (713) 866-6072
http://www.weingarten.com

Westdale Asset Management Ltd.
3300 Commerce Street
Dallas, TX 75226
Phone: (214) 515-7000
Fax: (214) 887-0998
http://www.westdale.com

VIRGINIA

Divaris Property Management Corp.
One Columbus Center, Suite 700
Virginia Beach, VA 23462
Phone: (757) 497-2113
Fax: (757) 497-1338
http://www.divaris.com

Harbor Group International
999 Waterside Drive, Suite 2300
Norfolk, VA 23510
Phone: (757) 640-0800
Fax: (757) 640-0817
http://www.harborgroupint.com

S.L. Nusbaum Realty Co.
1000 Bank of America Center
Norfolk, VA 23510
Phone: (757) 627-8611
Fax: (757) 640-2281
http://www.slnusbaum.com

Thalhimer/Cushman & Wakefield
1313 East Main Street
Richmond, VA 23219
Phone: (804) 648-5881
Fax: (804) 697-3479
http://www.thalhimer.com

WASHINGTON

GVA Kidder Mathews
601 Union Street
Seattle, WA 98101
Phone: (206) 296-9606
Fax: (206) 296-9629
http://www.gvakm.com

APPENDIX VI
REAL ESTATE LICENSING AGENCIES

Real estate brokers and sales agents must obtain state licenses in every state and the District of Columbia. These licensing statutes form the framework for state regulation and oversight by setting the requirements for licensing and requirements regarding business practices and professional conduct. There are certain minimum licensing requirements, such as age, education, and experience. State commissions, frequently composed of real estate brokers, oversee the drafting and compliance with these laws and regulations.

In most states and licensing jurisdictions the licensing requirements are the same. Prospective brokers and agents must pass a written examination. The examination—more comprehensive for brokers than for agents—includes questions on basic real estate transactions and laws affecting the sale of property. Most states require candidates for the general sales license to complete between 30 and 90 hours of classroom instruction. To get a broker's license, an individual needs between 60 and 90 hours of formal training and a specific amount of experience selling real estate, usually one to three years. Some states waive the experience requirements for the broker's license for applicants who have a bachelor's degree in real estate.

State licenses typically must be renewed every one or two years; usually, no examination is needed. However, many states require continuing education for license renewals. Prospective agents and brokers should contact the real estate licensing commission of the state in which they wish to work to verify the exact licensing requirements.

Most states have similar course requirements, including hours of required classroom instruction, to become a licensed real estate sales agent or broker. Typically, applicants must provide satisfactory evidence of successfully completing the following education: Principles of Real Estate, Real Estate Law, Real Estate Contracts, and real estate related courses. In most states there are three options for taking real estate licensing courses: 1) approved educational institutions such as real estate schools or community colleges offering real estate courses; 2) real estate courses offered by professional trade associations; 3) correspondence courses and alternative delivery instruction such as self-paced, online courses. Contact any of these schools and organizations for dates and locations of specific course offerings. Sales agents and brokers renewing their real estate licenses must take a certain number of hours of approved instruction, as required by their state real estate licensing board, and pass a continuing education exam.

Following is a list of real estate licensing agencies in all 50 states, U.S. territories, and Canadian provinces. Contact these agencies or commissions to verify your state's requirements for real estate education, obtain information on how to become a real estate agent, or get information on real estate continuing education. State licensing agencies or real estate licensing boards will also provide a list of approved educational institutions offering continuing education classroom courses and online instruction qualifying for real estate license renewals.

Alabama Real Estate Commission
1201 Carmichael Way
Montgomery, AL 38106
Phone: (334) 242-5544
Fax: (334) 270-9118
E-mail: arec@arec.alabama.gov
http://www.alabama.gov

Alaska Real Estate Commission
Division of Occupational Licensing
Robert B. Atwood Building

550 West Seventh Avenue, Suite 1500
Anchorage, AK 99501
Phone: (907) 269-8197
Fax: (907) 269-8156
E-mail: sharon.walsh@alaska.gov
http://www.dced.state.ak.us/OCC/prec.htm

Arizona Department of Real Estate
2910 North 44th Street
Phoenix, AZ 85018
Phone: (602) 468-1414

Fax: (602) 468-0562
E-mail: info@azre.gov
http://www.re.state.az.us

Arkansas Real Estate Commission
612 South Summit Street
Little Rock, AR 72201-4740
Phone: (501) 683-8010
Fax: (501) 683-8020
http://www.arkansas.gov/arec/arecweb.html

California Department of Real Estate
2201 Broadway
Sacramento, CA 95818
Phone: (916) 227-0782
Fax: (916) 227-0925
http://www.dre.cahwnet.gov

Colorado Division of Real Estate
Department of Regulatory Agencies
1900 Grant Street, Suite 600
Denver, CO 80203
Phone: (303) 894-2166
Fax: (303) 894-2683
E-mail: real-estate@dora.state.co.us
http://www.dora.state.co.us

Connecticut Real Estate Division
Department of Consumer Protection
165 Capital Avenue, Room G-B
Hartford, CT 06106
Phone: (860) 713-6150
Fax: (860) 713-7243
http://www.ct.gov/dcp

Delaware Real Estate Commission
P.O. Box 1401
Dover, DE 19901
861 Silver Lake Boulevard, Suite 203
Dover, DE 19904
Phone: (302) 744-4519
Fax: (302) 729-2711
E-mail: melissa.wheatley@state.de.us
http://www.dpr.delaware.gov/
boards/realestate

District of Columbia Department of Consumer & Regulatory Affairs
614 H Street NW, Room 821
P.O. Box 37200
Washington, DC 20013-7200
Phone: (202) 727-7450
Fax: (202) 442-4528
http://dcra.dc.gov/dcra

Florida Real Estate Commission
Department of Business & Professional Regulation

400 West Robinson Street, N801
Orlando, FL 32801
Phone: (850) 487-1395
Fax: (407) 317-7245
E-mail: call.center@dbpr.state.fl.us
http://www.myflorida.com/dbpr/re/
frec.html

Georgia Real Estate Commission
Suite 1000—Cain Tower
229 Peachtree Street NW
Atlanta, GA 30303-1605
Phone: (404) 656-3916
Fax: (404) 656-6650
E-mail: grecmail@grec.state.ga.us
http://www.grec.state.ga.us

Hawaii Real Estate Branch
Department of Commerce & Consumer Affairs
King Kalakaua Building
335 Merchant Street, Room 333
Honolulu, HI 96813
Phone: (808) 586-3000
E-mail: hirec@dcca.hawaii.gov
http://www.hawaii.gov

Idaho Real Estate Commission
P.O. Box 83720
633 North Fourth Street
Boise, ID 83720-0077
Phone: (208) 334-3285
Fax: (208) 334-2050
E-mail: irec@irec.state.id.us
http://www.irec.state.id.us

Illinois Bureau of Real Estate Professions
Department of Professional Regulation
320 West Washington Street
Springfield, IL 82788
Phone: (217) 785-0800
Fax: (217) 782-7545
http://www.idfpr.com

Indiana Real Estate Commission
Professional Licensing Agency
402 West Washington Street, Room W072
Indianapolis, IN 46204-2700
Phone: (317) 234-3009

E-mail: pla9@pla.in.gov
http://www.in.gov/pla

Iowa Real Estate Division
Professional Licensing & Regulation Division
1918 Southeast Hulsizer Avenue
Ankeny, IA 50021
Phone: (515) 281-7393
Fax: (515) 281-7411
E-mail: roger.hansen@iowa.gov
http://www.state.ia.us/government/
com/prof

Kansas Real Estate Commission
Three Townsite Plaza, Suite 200
120 Southeast Sixth Avenue
Topeka, KS 66603-3511
Phone: (785) 296-3411
Fax: (785) 296-1771
E-mail: krec@krec.state.ks.us

Kentucky Real Estate Commission
10200 Linn Station Road, Suite 201
Louisville, KY 40223
Phone: (502) 429-7250
Fax: (502) 429-7246
http://www.krec.ky.gov

Louisiana Real Estate Commission
P.O. Box 14785
Baton Rouge, LA 70898-4785
Phone: (225) 765-0191
Fax: (225) 765-0637
E-mail: info@lrec.state.la.us
http://www.lrec.state.la.us

Maine Real Estate Commission
Department of Financial and Professional Regulation
35 State House Station
Augusta, ME 04333
Phone: (207) 624-8515
Fax: (207) 624-8637
E-mail: carol.j.leighton@maine
.gov
http://maine.gov/pfr/
professionallicensing/
professions/real_estate

Maryland Real Estate Commission
Division of Occupational &
Professional Licensing
500 North Calvert Street
Baltimore, MD 21202-3651
Phone: (410) 230-6230
Fax: (410) 333-0023
E-mail: mrec@dllr.state.md.us
http://www.dllr.state.md.us/
occprof/recomm.html

Massachusetts Board of Registration of Real Estate Brokers & Salespeople
Division of Professional Licensure
239 Causeway Street
Boston, MA 02114
Phone: (617) 727-3074
Fax: (617) 727-1944
E-mail: neal.fenochietti@state.ma.us
http://www.mass.gov/dpl

Michigan State Board of Real Estate Brokers and Salespersons
Department of Consumer &
Industry Services
P.O. Box 30243
611 West Ottawa
Lansing, MI 48909
Phone: (517) 241-9265
Fax: (517) 373-1044
E-mail: bcslic@michigan.gov
http://michigan.gov/dleg/realestate

Minnesota Department of Commerce
85 East Seventh Place
St. Paul, MN 55101
Phone: (651) 296-4026
Fax: (651) 297-1959
E-mail: general.commerce@state
.mn.us
http://www.commerce.state.mn.us

Mississippi Real Estate Commission
P.O. Box 12685
Jackson, MS 39216-5087
P.O. Box 12685
Jackson, MS 39236
Phone: (601) 932-6770

Fax: (601) 932-2990
E-mail: info@mrec.state.ms.us
http://www.mrec.state.ms.us

Missouri Real Estate Commission
Division of Professional Registration
3605 Missouri Boulevard
P.O. Box 1339
Jefferson City, MO 65102
Phone: (573) 751-2628
Fax: (573) 751-2777
E-mail: realestate@pr.mo.gov
http://pr.mo.gov/realestate.asp

Montana Board of Realty Regulation
301 South Park, Fourth Floor
Helena, MT 59620
Phone: (406) 444-2961
Fax: (406) 841-2323
E-mail: dlibsdrre@mt.gov
http://mt.gov/dli/rre

Nebraska Real Estate Commission
1200 N Street, Suite 402
Lincoln, NE 68508
Phone: (402) 471-2004
Fax: (402) 471-4492
E-mail: infotech@nrec.state.ne.us
http://www.nrec.state.ne.us

Nevada Real Estate Division
2501 East Sahara Avenue, Suite 102
Las Vegas, NV 89104-4137
Phone: (702) 486-4033
Fax: (702) 486-4275
E-mail: realest@red.state.nv.us
http://www.red.state.nv.us

New Hampshire Real Estate Commission
State House Annex, Room 437
25 Capital Street
Concord, NH 03301
Phone: (603) 271-2701
E-mail: nhrec@nhrec.state.nh.us
http://www. nhrec.state.nh.us

New Jersey Real Estate Commission
20 West State Street

CN-328
P.O. Box 328
Trenton, NJ 08625
Phone: (609) 292-8300
Fax: (609) 292-0944
E-mail: realestate@dobi.sate.nj.us
http://www. dobi.sate.nj.us

New Mexico Real Estate Commission
5200 Oakland Avenue NE, Suite B
Albuquerque, NM 87113
Phone: (800) 801-7505
Fax: (505) 222-9886
E-mail: andrea.armijo@state.nm.us
http://rld.state.nm.us/Real_Estate_
Commission

New York State Department of State
Division of Licensing Services
84 Holland Avenue
Albany, NY 12208
Phone: (518) 474-4429
Fax: (518) 473-6648
E-mail: licensing@dos.state.ny.us
http://www.dos.state.ny.us

North Carolina Real Estate Commission
P.O. Box 17100
Raleigh, NC 27619-7100
Phone: (919) 875-3700
Fax: (919) 877-4217
E-mail: admin@ncrec.state.nc.us
http://www.nrec.state.nc.us

North Dakota Real Estate Commission
P.O. Box 727
200 East Main Street, Suite 204
Bismarck, ND 58502-0727
Phone: (701) 328-9749
Fax: (701) 328-9750
E-mail: ndrealestatecom@nd.gov
http://www.realestatend.org

Ohio Division of Real Estate
77 South High Street, 20th Floor
Columbus, OH 43266-0547
Phone: (614) 466-4100
Fax: (614) 644-0584
E-mail: repld@com.state.oh.us
http://www.com.state.oh.us

Oklahoma Real Estate Commission
2401 NW 23rd, Suite 18
Oklahoma City, OK 73107
Phone: (405) 521-3387
Fax: (405) 521-2189
E-mail: orec.help@orec.ok.gov
http://www.orec.ok.gov

Oregon Real Estate Agency
1177 Center Street NE
Salem, OR 97310-2503
Phone: (503) 378-4170
Fax: (503) 378-2491
E-mail: orea.info@state.or.us
http://www.oregon.gov/REA

Pennsylvania Real Estate Commission
P.O. Box 2649
Harrisburg, PA 17105-2649
Phone: (717) 783-3658
Fax: (717) 787-0250
E-mail: st-realestate@state.pa.us
http://www.dos.state.pa.us

Rhode Island Division of Commercial Licensing & Regulation
Department of Business Regulation
233 Richmond Street
Providence, RI 02903
Phone: (401) 222-2246
Fax: (401) 222-6098
E-mail: asmith@dbr.state.ri.us
http://www.dbr.ri.gov/divisions/
commlicensing/realestate.php

South Carolina Real Estate Commission
Department of Labor Licensing & Regulation
110 Centerview Drive, Suite 201
Columbia, SC 29201
Phone: (803) 896-4400
Fax: (803) 896-4404
E-mail: parrisa@llr.sc.gov
http://www.llr.state.sc.us

South Dakota Real Estate Commission
221 West Capitol, Suite 101

P.O. Box 490
Pierre, SD 57501-0490
Phone: (605) 773-3600
Fax: (605) 773-4356
E-mail: drr.realestate@state.sd.us
http://www.state.sd.us/sdrec

Tennessee Real Estate Commission
500 James Robertson Parkway
Suite 180, Volunteer Plaza
Nashville, TN 37243-1151
Phone: (615) 741-2273
Fax: (615) 741-0313
E-mail: info@state.tn.us
http://www.tennessee.gov/
commerce/boards/trec

Texas Real Estate Commission
1101 Camino La Costa
P.O. Box 12188
Austin, TX 78711-2188
Phone: (512) 459-6544
Fax: (512) 465-3998
E-mail: admin@trec.state.tx.us
http://www.trec.state.tx.us

Utah Division of Real Estate
Department of Commerce
Heber M. Wells Building
160 East 300 South Second Street
P.O. Box 45806
Salt Lake City, UT 84114-6711
Phone: (801) 530-6747
Fax: (801) 530-6749
E-mail: realestate@utah.gov
http://realestate.utah.gov/

Vermont Real Estate Commission
Heritage Building
81 River Street
Montpelier, VT 05609-1106
Phone: (802) 828-3228
E-mail: jgriffen@sec.state.vt.us
http://vtprofessionals.org/opr1/
real_estate/

Virginia Department of Professional & Occupational Registration
3600 West Broad Street

Richmond, VA 23230-4917
Phone: (804) 367-8500
Fax: (804) 367-2475
E-mail: dpor@dpor.virginia.gov
http://www.dpor.virginia.gov/
dporweb

Washington State Department of Licensing
Professional Licensing Services
Real Estate Program
P.O. Box 2445
Olympia, Washington 98507-9015
Phone: (360) 664-6115
Fax: (360) 570-4941
E-mail: realestate@dol.wa.gov
http://www.dol.wa.gov

West Virginia Real Estate Commission
300 Capitol Street, Suite 400
Charleston, WV 25301-2315
Phone: (304) 558-3555
Fax: (304) 558-6442
E-mail: wvrec@wvrec.org
http://www.wvrec.org/

Wisconsin Real Estate Commission
P.O. Box 8934
Madison, WI 53708-8935
Phone: (608) 266-2112
E-mail: web@drl.state.wi.us
http://drl.wi.gov

Wyoming Real Estate Commission
2020 Carey Avenue, Suite 100
Cheyenne, WY 82002
Phone: (307) 777-7141
E-mail: bblake@state.wy.us
http://realestate.state.wy.us/

U.S. TERRITORIES AND POSSESSIONS

Guam Real Estate Division
Department of Revenue & Taxation
278 Chalan San Antonio
Tamuning, GU 96911
Phone: (671) 477-5198
https://www.guamtax.com

Virgin Islands Department of Licensing & Consumer Affairs
Bldg. #1 Subbase
Property & Procurement Building, Room 205
St. Thomas, VI 00802
Phone: (809) 774-3130
http://www.dlca.gov.vi/

CANADA

Real Estate Council of Alberta
Suite 350, 4954 Richard Road SW
Calgary, Alberta T3E 6L1
Phone: (403) 228-2954
Fax: (403) 228-3065
E-mail: info@reca.ca
http://www.reca.ca

Real Estate Council of British Columbia
900–750 West Pender Street
Vancouver, British Columbia V6C 2T8
Phone: (604) 683-9664
Fax: (604) 683-9017
E-mail: info@recbc.bc.ca
http://www.recbc.ca/

Manitoba Securities Commission
500–400 St. Mary Avenue Winnipeg

Manitoba, Canada R3C 4K5
Phone: (204) 945-2548
Fax: (204) 945-0330
E-mail: securities@gov.mb.ca
http://www.gov.mb.ca

Goverment of New Brunswick
P.O. Box 6000
Fredericton, New Brunswick E3B 1P8
Phone: (506) 453-2240
Fax: (506) 453-5329
http://www.gnb.ca

Northwest Territories Municipal & Community Affairs
Northwest Tower, Sixth Floor
Yellowknife, Northwest Territories
Phone: (867) 873-7125
Fax: (867) 873-0609
E-mail: michael_gagnon@gov.nt.ca
http://www.gov.nt.ca

Nova Scotia Real Estate Commission
7 Scarfe Court
Dartmouth, Nova Scotia B3B 1W4
Phone: (902) 468-3511
Fax: (902) 468-1016
E-mail: info@nsrec.ns.ca
http://www.nsrec.ns.ca

Real Estate Council of Ontario
3250 Bloor Street West, Suite 600
East Tower
Toronto, Ontario M8X 2X9
Phone: (416) 207-4800
Fax: (416) 207-4820
E-mail: communications@reco.on.ca
http://www.reco.on.ca

Association des courtiers et agents immobiliers du Quebec
6300 Auteuil, Suite 300
Brossard, Québec J4Z 3P2
Phone: (540) 676-4800
Fax: (450) 676-7801
E-mail: info@acaiq.com
http://www.acaiq.com

Saskachewan Real Estate Commission
237 Robin Crescent Saskatoon
Saskatechewan S7L 6M8
Phone: (306) 374-5233
Fax: (306) 373-2295
E-mail: info@srec.ca
http://www.srec.ca

APPENDIX VII
REAL ESTATE RESEARCH ORGANIZATIONS

The following colleges and universities have established programs dedicated to research and education in areas related to real estate development, property management, urban planning, and investing in real estate.

ALABAMA

Alabama Real Estate Research and Education Center
Culverhouse College of Business and Commerce
University of Alabama
127 Bidgood Hall, Box 870221
Tuscaloosa, AL 35487-0221
Phone: (205) 348-4117
Fax: (205) 348-4125
E-mail: bevans@cba.ua.edu
http://arerec.cba.us.edu

ARIZONA

Arizona Real Estate Center
Arizona State University—
Polytechnic Campus
7001 East Williams Field Road
Sutton 301C
Mesa, AZ 85212
Phone: (480) 727-1688
Fax: (480) 727-1407
E-mail: lambrakis@asu.edu
http://www.poly.asu.edu/realty

CALIFORNIA

Center for Real Estate
California State University—
Northridge
College of Business Administration
and Economics
1811 Nordhoff Street
Northridge, CA 91330
Phone: (818) 677-2410
Fax: (818) 677-6079
E-mail: cre@csun.edu
http://wwwcsun.edu/cre

Fisher Center for Real Estate and Urban Economics
Haas School of Business
University of California at Berkeley
Berkeley, CA 94720-6105
Phone: (510) 643-6105
Fax: (510) 643-7357
E-mail: creue@haas.berkeley.edu
http://haas.berkeley.edu

Lusk Center for Real Estate Development
University of Southern California
331 Ralph and Goldy Lewis Hall
Los Angeles, CA 90089-0626
Phone: (213) 740-5000
Fax: (213) 740-6170
http://www.usc.edu/schools/spd/lusk/index.php

COLORADO

Real Estate Center
University of Colorado at Boulder
Leeds School of Business, Room 251
419 UCB
Boulder, CO 80309-0419
Phone: (303) 492-3643
Fax: (303) 492-5507
http://leeds.colorado.edu/realestate

CONNECTICUT

Center for Real Estate and Urban Economic Studies
University of Connecticut
School of Business
368 Fairfield Road, U-41RE
Storrs, CT 06269
Phone: (860) 486-3227
Fax: (860) 486-0349

E-mail: recenter@business.uconn.edu
http://www.business.uconn.edu

FLORIDA

Bergstrom Center for Real Estate Studies
University of Florida
Warrington College of Business Administration
100 BRY
P.O. Box 117150
Gainesville, FL 32611-7150
Phone: (352) 392-2397
Fax: (352) 392-2086
E-mail: ufwcba@cba.ufl.edu
http://wwwcba.ufl.edu

Haas Center for Business Research and Economic Development
University of West Florida
College of Business
Building 53, Room 240
11000 University Parkway
Pensacola, FL 32514
Phone: (850) 474-2657
Fax: (850) 474-3174
E-mail: haasinfo@ufw.edu
http://www.haas.ufw.edu

Homer Hoyt Advanced Studies Institute
The Hoyt Center
760 U.S. Highway One, Suite 300
North Palm Beach, FL 33408
Phone: (561) 694-7621
Fax: (561) 694-7629
E-mail: info@hoyt.org
http://www.hoyt.org

GEORGIA

Real Estate Research Center

Georgia State University
J. Mack Robinson College of
   Business
35 Broad Street NW
Atlanta, GA 30303
Phone: (404) 651-2600
http://www.robinson.edu/realestate/
   rerc

ILLINOIS

Center for Real Estate Law

The John Marshall Law School
315 South Plymouth Court
Chicago, IL 60604
Phone: (312) 427-2737 ext. 500
http://wwwjmls.edu

Center for Real Estate Research

Northwestern University
Kellogg Graduate School of
   Management
Jacobs Center Room 6214
2001 Sheridan Road
Evanston, IL 60208
Phone: (847) 491-3564
Fax: (847) 467-6459
E-mail: tsm@kellogg.northwestern
   .edu
http://www.kellogg.northwestern
   .edu/academic/realestate

INDIANA

Benecki Center for Real Estate Studies

Indiana University
Kelley School of Business
1309 East 10th Street, Suite 746
Bloomington, IN 47405-1701
Phone: (812) 855-7794
Fax: (812) 855-9006
E-mail: fisher@indiana.edu
http://www.indiana.edu/~cres/
   realestate

LOUISIANA

Real Estate Market Data Center

University of New Orleans

College of Business Administration
Lake Front Campus
New Orleans, LA 70148
Phone: (504) 280-6241
Fax: (504) 280-6693
E-mail: wragas@uno.edu
http://business.uno.edu/remdc

Real Estate Research Institute

E. J. Ourso College of Business
Louisiana State University
3304 CEBA Building
Baton Rouge, LA 70803
Phone: (225) 578-3211
Fax: (225) 578-5256
E-mail: kpace@lsu.edu
http://www.bus.lsu.edu

MAINE

Center for Real Estate Education

University of Southern Maine
68 High Street
Portland, ME 04101
Phone: (800) 800-4876
Fax: (207) 228-8401
E-mail: cree@usm.maine.edu
http://cree.maine.edu

MASSACHUSETTS

Center for Real Estate

Massachusetts Institute of
   Technology
77 Massachusetts Avenue
W31-310
Cambridge, MA 02139
Phone: (617) 253-4373
Fax: (617) 258-6991
E-mail: mit-cre@mit.edu
http://web.mit.edu/cre

Joint Center for Housing Studies

Harvard University
1033 Massachusetts Avenue, Fifth
   Floor
Cambridge, MA 02138
Phone: (617) 495-7908
Fax: (617) 496-9957
http://www.jchs.harvard.edu

NEW JERSEY

Center for Urban Policy Research

Edward J. Bloustein School of
   Planning and Public Policy
Rutgers University
33 Livingston Avenue
Civic Square, Suite 400
New Brunswick, NJ 08901-1982
Phone: (732) 932-3133
Fax: (732) 932-2363
E-mail: glickman@rci.rutgers.edu
http://www.policy.rutgers.edu/cupr

NEW YORK

The Real Estate Institute

School of Continuing and
   Professional Studies
New York University
145 East Fourth Avenue
Room 201
New York, NY 10003
Phone: (888) 998-7204
http://www.scps.nyu.edu

NORTH CAROLINA

Urban Investment Strategies Center

Frank Hawkins Kenan Institute of
   Private Enterprise
University of North Carolina at
   Chapel Hill
Campus Box 3440, The Kenan
   Center
Chapel Hill, NC 25799-3440
Phone: (919) 962-1535
Fax: (919) 962-8202
E-mail: jim_johnson@unc.edu
http://www.kenan-flagler.unc.edu/
   KI/urbaninvestment

OHIO

Center for Real Estate Education and Research

Fisher College of Business
Ohio State University
218 Fisher Hall
2100 Neil Avenue
Columbus, OH 43210-1144
Phone: (614) 292-7312

Fax: (614) 292-0562
E-mail: pavlickr@cob.ohio-state.
edu
http://fisher.osu.edu/realestate

Real Estate Program & Center
College of Business
University of Cincinnati
Carl H. Lindner Hall
2925 Campus Green Drive
P.O. Box 210195
Cincinnati, OH 45221-0195
Phone: (513) 556-7193
Fax: (513) 556-4891
E-mail: real.estate@uc.edu
http://www.business.uc.edu/
realestate

PENNSYLVANIA

Institute for Real Estate Studies
Smeal College of Business
The Pennsylvania State University
355 Business Building
University Park, PA 16802
Phone: (814) 865-4172
Fax: (814) 865-6284
E-mail: ires@smeal.psu.edu
http://www.smeal.psu.edu/ires

Murray H. Goodman Center for Real Estate Studies
Rauch Business Center, Room 302
Lehigh University
621 Taylor Street
Bethlehem, PA 18015
Phone: (610) 758-4557
E-mail: inrev@lehigh.edu
http://www.lehigh.edu

The Samuel Zell and Robert Lurie Real Estate Center
The Wharton School
University of Pennsylvania
Suite 1400, Steinberg Hall-Dietrich
Hall, 3620 Locust Walk
Philadelphia, PA 19104-6302
Phone: (215) 898-9687

Fax: (215) 573-2220
E-mail: wrec@wharton.upenn.edu
http://realestate.wharton.upenn.edu

SOUTH CAROLINA

Center for Applied Real Estate Education and Research
The Darla Moore School of
Business
University of South Carolina
1705 College Street
Columbia, SC 29208
Phone: (803) 777-5984
E-mail: rrogers@darla.badm.sc.edu
http://mooreschool.sc.edu

TEXAS

Center for Research in Real Estate and Land Use Economics
Edwin L. Cox School of Business
Southern Methodist University
6212 Bishop Boulevard
P.O. Box 750333
Dallas, TX 75275-0333
Phone: (214) 768-3548
E-mail: wbruegge@mail.cox.smu.
edu
http://www.cox.smu.edu

Real Estate Center
Texas A&M University
Lowery Mays College & Graduate
School of Business
215 TAMU
College Station, TX 77843-2115
Phone: (979) 845-2031
Fax: (979) 845-0460
E-mail: info@recenter.tamu.edu
http://recenter.tamu.edu

VIRGINIA

Center for Housing Research
Virginia Polytechnic Institute and
State University

Blacksburg, VA 24061
Phone: (540) 231-3993
Fax: (540) 231-7331
E-mail: tkoebel@vt.edu
http://vchr.vt.edu

WASHINGTON

Washington Center for Real Estate Research
Washington State University
P.O. Box 644844
Pullman, Washington 99164-4844
Phone: (800) 835-9683
E-mail: wcrer@wsu.edu
http://www.cbe.wsu.edu/~wcrer

WISCONSIN

Center for Urban Land Economics Research
University of Wisconsin—Madison
School of Business
975 University Avenue
Madison, WI 53706
Phone: (608) 262-5800
E-mail: kvandell@bus.wisc.edu
http://www.bus.wisc.edu/centers/
culer.htm

CANADA

Centre for Real Estate and Urban Land Economics
Sauder School of Business
University of British Columbia
2053 Main Mall
Vancouver, British Columbia V6T
1Z2
Phone: (604) 822-8500
Fax: (604) 822-8468
E-mail: heleho@commerce.ubc.ca
http:www.sauder.ubc.ca

APPENDIX VIII
PLANNING YOUR CAREER IN REAL ESTATE

The Internet is changing the way people manage their careers. With so much information available on the World Wide Web—the network of linked pages we look at when we surf the Internet—career planning has changed completely. Colleges and universities offer useful information about courses offered and career opportunities by field of study. Job seekers post their resumes on Internet job banks or e-mail them directly to employers. There are Internet sites offering career counseling—free of charge—to individuals considering careers in a specific field. A vast amount of education and employment-related information is only a mouse click away, if you know where to look.

What follows are suggestions for making the best use of the Internet while gathering information about education and employment opportunities. Remember that the Internet is a constantly changing set of data sources, so some of the Internet addresses listed below may have changed by the time you are reading this page. Use the search techniques listed below to collect more information about employers, industry trends, and current opportunities. In most cases, a combination of traditional and online techniques is the best approach to landing that first job or moving on in your career.

1. GENERAL INFORMATION

These Web sites can give you more information about various careers:

2008–09 Occupational Outlook Handbook
Bureau of Labor Statistics
http://www.stats.bls.gov/ocohome.htm

The U.S. Department of Labor's Occupational Outlook Handbook is the most comprehensive guide to careers and employment trends. State labor departments and state universities often have Web sites with state-specific information on career opportunities. Here are three examples:

California Occupational Guides
http://www.labormarketinfo.edd.ca.gov/cgi/career

Indiana Career and Postsecondary Advancement Center
http://www.learnmoreindiana.org/careers/exploring/Pages/CareerProfiles.aspx

Virginia's Career Information System
http://www.doe.virginia.gov/VDOE/Instruction/CTE/careerclusters/

2. INTERNET SEARCH ENGINES AND DIRECTORIES

There are two general tools for researching anything on the World Wide Web. Directory services such as Yahoo! (http://www.yahoo.com) compile lists of information categorized by topic. Then there are search engines such as Alta Vista or Google that search for information based on keywords you type in. Search engines allow you to cast the widest net in your research. Typing the search term "real estate + careers" yields a long list of Internet job banks or companies with available positions.

Some search engines, including Google, have directory services for more targeted searches. For example, you can search for employment opportunities in specific industries, such as banking or insurance.

Use these and other sources to add to your collection of bookmarks.

3. FINDING COLLEGES AND UNIVERSITIES

There are more than 3,000 colleges offering business administration majors. Several hundred educational institutions have four-year degree programs in banking, finance, and related fields of study. The complete list is too extensive to list in an appendix, but here are some suggestions for locating a college matching your career interest.

Published Guides. Printed guides such as *Peterson's Guide to Colleges* or *The Princeton Review Complete Guide to Colleges* have extensive databases on a large number of educational institutions. Starting your search with a published directory is still the most efficient way to collect background information about colleges and universities. Then you can look up a college's Web site for up-to-date information about courses offered, academic schedules, tuition, and financial aid.

Web Guides. Web sites such as Peterson's (http://www.petersons.com) or Princeton Review (http://www.princetonreview.com) have search engines that will match your keywords to college majors and programs. These Web sites have fairly comprehensive databases. A search on one of these sites can yield names of several dozen colleges or more than 1,000 institutions if you're doing a nationwide search.

You might want to check your search results with college accrediting agencies to see whether your selections are accredited educational institutions. The Association to Advance Collegiate Schools of Business (http://www.aacsb.edu) is the premier accrediting agency for bachelor's, master's, and doctoral degree programs in business administration and accounting. The Accrediting Commission for Community and Junior Colleges (http://www.accjc.org) performs similar evaluations on community colleges. Names of accredited institutions can be found by visiting their Web sites.

Web Directories. Another way to find the name of a specific college is searching on a Web directory such as Yahoo! or Google Web Directory (http://directory.google.com). Both have organized listings of colleges by state so you can easily find schools matching your interest in your region.

Evaluating Educational Programs. On-campus interviews are always recommended when evaluating colleges. If possible, arrange interviews at several colleges that look to be good possibilities. Ask about internship programs, work-study programs, or other opportunities to gain practical experience before graduation. Try to compare the printed catalog of courses offered against the job requirements in help-wanted advertisements or the position descriptions in this book.

If you can, get recommendations from people working in your intended career field. If you don't know anyone, don't worry. You will have plenty of opportunities to make connections while in college. Consider the range of academic courses offered by colleges on your selection list. While many of the positions described in this book require some academic background in accounting, finance, or business administration, a liberal and diverse education is an asset in financial services today. Strong verbal and written communication skills are as important in many positions as technical knowledge.

Continuing Education. Education does not end with entry into the workforce. Employers are investing large sums of money in continuing education and training programs for employees at all levels of the organization. These programs help employees maintain or upgrade key job-related skills, thereby avoiding skills obsolescence, and are given in a variety of formats. A growing number of organizations offer distance learning courses (called e-learning or online learning if delivered over the Internet) in addition to conventional classroom instructor-led courses. Distance learning courses are offered by accredited colleges and professional associations. If your eventual aim is a college degree, it is important to check with state accrediting agencies or a professional accrediting organization before enrolling.

Classroom instruction is still preferred for executive education programs, where group discussion and interaction are important parts of the learning experience. Professional education and training programs can be anywhere from one-day workshops to one-week seminars presented on a college campus or conference center.

4. SEARCHING FOR JOB OPENINGS.

After obtaining the necessary academic credentials plus some work experience, it's time to enter the job market. There are many sources of job listings, including the traditional sources—newspaper classified advertisements, trade journals, job fairs, state employment agencies, and college employment centers. Executive recruiting agencies, also known as search firms, are an important source of job leads for professional and management positions. Executive recruiters are paid a fee by employers to fill position vacancies. They place advertisements of current vacancies in professional journals, newspapers, and on the Internet. You can use recruiters to locate opportunities you wouldn't think of yourself and also to weed out the unattractive positions.

Search firms active in real estate executive placements include the following:

Christopher Group Executive Search
12 Hawk View Drive
Asheville, NC 28804
Phone: (828) 225-4348
Fax: (828) 225-4349
E-mail: chrisgroup@bellsouth.net
http://christophergroup.net

The Emlin Group
373 Crestview Drive
Fort Washington, PA 19034
Phone: (215) 654-9299
Fax: (215) 654-1495

E-mail: Linda@emlingroup.com
http://www.emlingroup.com

Equinox Partners
675 Third Avenue, 20th Floor
New York, NY 10017
Phone: (212) 661-2000
Fax: (212) 661-0505
E-mail: alopinto@equinoxsearch.com
http://equinoxsearch.com

Executive Quest
7251 Lake Drive
Fort Myers, FL 33908
Phone: (239) 454-1100
Fax: (239) 432-9531
E-mail: keith@execq.com
http://www.execq.com

Executive Search for California
611 South Palm Canyon Drive, Suite 7571
Palm Springs, CA 92264
Fax: (760) 327-1076
E-mail: rita@californiarecruiter.com
http://www.californiarecruiter.com

Failoa Associates
212 Third Avenue North
Suite 354
Minneapolis, MN 55401
Phone: (612) 659-7800
E-mail: info@failoaassociates.com
http://www.failoaassociates.com

Huntington Partners Executive Search
Oakbrook Commons
400 Oakbrook Drive, Suite 2102
Greensburg, PA 15601-9700
Phone: (724) 864-1600
Fax: (724) 864-0818
E-mail: info@huntingtonpartners.com
http://www.huntingtonpartners.com

JCR Executive Search
4501 Magnolia Cove Drive, Suite 201
Kingwood, TX 77345
Phone: (281) 359-2107
Fax: (281) 359-0067
E-mail: bulick@jcrexecutivesearch.net
http://www.jcrexecutivesearch.net

John Morrow & Associates, Inc.
320 Main Street

Irwin, PA 15642
Phone: (724) 864-9512
Fax: (724) 864-9654
http://www.morrowassociates.com

Klein, Mejia & Associates
P.O. Box 3042
Orange, CA 92857
Phone: (714) 632-8585
Fax: (413) 647-8291
E-mail: dmejia@kmsearch.com
http://www.kmsearch.com

MacInnis, Ward & Associates, Inc.
551 Fifth Avenue
New York, NY 10176
Phone: (212) 808-8080
Fax: (212) 808-8088
http://www.macinnisward.com

Real Estate Executive Search, Inc.
306 SE Fourth Street
Dania Beach, FL 33004
Phone: (954) 927-6000
Fax: (954) 927-6003
E-mail: REESearch954@aol.com
http://reesearchinc.com/

Roberta Rea & Company, Inc.
4510 Executive Drive, Plaza 4
San Diego, CA 92121
Phone: (858) 457-3566
Fax: (858) 457-4409
http://www.robertareaco.com

Specialty Consultants Inc.
2710 Gateway Towers
Pittsburgh, PA 15222-1189
Phone: (412) 355-8200
Fax: (412) 355-0498
E-mail: info@specialtyconsultants.com
http://www.specon.com

Stewart Search, Inc.
(561) 818-1007
222 Lakeview Avenue, Suite 160-708
West Palm Beach, FL 33401
Phone: (561) 818-1007
http://www.stewartsearchinc.com

Synergy One
244 Fifth Avenue, Suite D 279
New York NY 10001
Phone: (212) 655-5411

Fax: (866) 483-6972
E-mail: info@synergy1ny.com
http://www.synergyonerecruiting.com

Searching on the Internet. There are a variety of Internet sites specializing in job listings. Many compile listings submitted by employers or from other sources such as newsgroups. Many of these sites are free to any users and have unrestricted access; some are limited to association members, requiring a member log-in to access a job board for employment opportunities.

Here are some examples of popular real estate job sites on the Internet. There are many career help and job search Web sites listing real estate and construction industry jobs. The Web sites listed here are a representative sample of what's available on the Internet. Remember that these career sites are updated constantly and new sites added, so be sure to check back often.

CoreNet Global Career Resources Center:
http://www2.corenetglobal.org/career_services/index.vsp

Commercial Real Estate Women's San Francisco chapter lists job leads for association members: http://www.crewsf.org

Commercial real estate employment opportunities: http://www.realestatejobs.com

Employment opportunities in construction:
http://www.constructionwork.com
http://www.ihireconstruction.com
http://www.constructionexecutive.com

Employment opportunities for appraisal, development, leasing, corporate real estate, site analysis, mortgage lending, and construction:
http://www.real-jobs.com

National Association of Industrial and Office Properties career planning site:
http://www.naiop.org/careers/index.cfm

Select Leaders Real Estate Job Network—jointly sponsored by several real estate professional associations: http://www.selectleaders.com

General career search Web sites:
Career OneStop (http://www.jobbankinfo.org) lists jobs posted from more than 2,000 state employment offices.

HotJobs (http://www.hotjobs.com) has company profiles and resume writing tips.

Job Search Engine (http://www.job-search-engine.com) has a searchable database allowing searches by job title, industry, geographic location, or keyword.

The Monster Board (http://www.monster.com) has postings for more than one million jobs, company profiles, and offers job search tips.

5. GETTING SALARY INFORMATION

Information about salaries isn't hard to get if you know where to look. To prepare yourself for a reasonable salary demand or to evaluate an employer's offer, it's a good idea to check surveys of salaries in the financial services field.

The Riley Guide (http://www.rileyguide.com) has a collection of links to Web sites with salary information in various occupations. CareerJournal (http://careers.wsj.com) has occupational profiles and salary charts from the National Business Employment Weekly. Another source of information is the federal government's Bureau of Labor Statistics (http://stats.bls.gov/blshome.htm), which has government surveys on employment and wages.

Remember that salaries can vary quite a bit, depending on qualifications, experience, and where you happen to live. Employers in high cost-of-living areas on the East Coast or West Coast pay higher starting salaries than in other regions, the Midwest for instance, because they have to in order to attract qualified candidates.

Some career Web sites such as CareerBuilder (http://www.careerbuilder.com) have online salary calculators to help manage the cost of living issue. CareerBuilder's Salary Wizard is searchable by postal zip code, and it can be used to figure out salary ranges in many U.S. and foreign cities. Online salary calculators are useful, but they usually disclose salary information on only a small number of positions. If the position you are seeking isn't listed, the guide might have data on similar positions, which is still very useful information in a job search.

6. OTHER SOURCES OF INFORMATION

Company-based Web sites contain a wealth of information about the company as well as current job opportunities. Company Web sites often have job profiles or interviews with recent college graduates, which offer additional information about career opportunities. It's always a good idea to study a company's products and services, its position in the field, and what employees say about their jobs before going out on a job interview. That's the real value of the Internet as a research tool during a job search. You can find much of the information you need by going to an employer's home page or by doing a Web search using the company name as a keyword.

Public documents such as the annual 10K or quarterly 10Q filings with the Securities and Exchange Commission yield plenty of information about a company and its officers. You can search SEC documents on Free Edgar (http://www.freeedgar.com).

Other sites worth checking are Yahoo Finance (http://finance.yahoo.com) and Hoover's (http://www.hoovers.com). Both have extensive directories with links to analyst research reports on both public and private companies.

Professional association Web sites and career-oriented Web sites are excellent places to gather information about specific careers, including advancement opportunities and job entry tips. You can find this information by going to the Career Center page, which is usually prominently displayed on the association's homepage.

GLOSSARY

The following is a list of frequently used terms that you may find useful as you learn about the real estate industry. These are terms you should be familiar with as you contact employers and arrange interviews. Important terms from this list are used in the position descriptions in this book.

absorption   Inventory of commercial property occupied during specified time period, usually a year, typically reported as the absorption rate

annual percentage rate (APR)   cost of a loan or other financing as an annual rate. The APR includes the interest rate, points, broker fees, and certain other credit charges a borrower is required to pay.

appraisal   A professional analysis used to estimate the value of the property, including examples of sales of similar properties.

appraiser   A professional who conducts an analysis of the property, including examples of sales of similar properties, in order to develop an estimate of the value of the property. The analysis is called an *appraisal*.

appreciation   An increase in the market value of a property due to changing market conditions and/or improvements.

application fee   The fee that a mortgage lender or broker charges to apply for a mortgage to cover processing costs.

arbitration   A process where disputes are settled by referring them to a fair and neutral third party (arbitrator). The disputing parties agree in advance to agree with the decision of the arbitrator. There is a hearing where both parties have an opportunity to be heard, after which the arbitrator makes a decision.

assessed value   Typically the value placed on property for the purpose of taxation.

assessor   A public official who establishes the value of a property for taxation purposes.

asset   Anything of monetary value that is owned by a person or company. Assets include real property, personal property, stocks, mutual funds, etc.

assignment of mortgage   A document evidencing the transfer of ownership of a mortgage from one person to another.

automated underwriting   An automated process performed by a technology application that streamlines the processing of loan applications and provides a recommendation to the lender to approve the loan or refer it for manual underwriting.

balance sheet   A financial statement that shows assets, liabilities, and net worth as of a specific date.

balloon mortgage   A mortgage with monthly payments often based on a 30-year amortization schedule, with the unpaid balance due in a lump sum payment at the end of a specific period of time (usually 5 or 7 years). The mortgage may contain an option to accelerate the interest rate to the current market rate and to extend the due date if certain conditions are met.

balloon payment   A final lump sum payment that is due, often at the maturity date of a *balloon mortgage.*

base rent   Minimum rent due a landlord, typically a fixed amount; the annual base rent is the amount on which rent escalations are calculated.

before-tax income   Income before taxes are deducted. Also known as *gross income.*

bridge loan   A short-term loan secured by the borrower's current home (which is usually for sale) that allows the proceeds to be used for building or closing on a new house before the current home is sold. Also known as a *swing loan.*

break-even point   Stage at which an income-producing property generates enough income to cover recurring expenses, or when gross income is equal to normal operating expenses.

broker   An individual or firm that acts as an agent between providers and users of products or services, such as a mortgage broker or real estate broker.

building code   Local regulations that set forth the standards and requirements for the construction, maintenance, and occupancy of buildings. The codes are designed to provide for the safety, health, and welfare of the public.

buydown   An arrangement whereby the property developer or another third party provides an interest subsidy to reduce the borrower's monthly payments, typically in the early years of the loan.

capitalization rate   Comparison of the value of an income-producing property to its future income, expressed as net operating income divided by purchase price. The capitalization rate (also called the cap rate) measures how fast an investment property will pay for itself.

chain of title The history of all of the documents that have transferred title to a parcel of real property, starting with the earliest existing document and ending with the most recent.

change orders A change in the original construction plans ordered by the property owner or general contractor.

clear title Ownership that is free of liens, defects, or other legal encumbrances.

closing The process of completing a financial transaction. For mortgage loans, the process of signing mortgage documents, disbursing funds, and, if applicable, transferring ownership of the property. In some jurisdictions, closing is referred to as escrow, a process by which a buyer and seller deliver legal documents to a third party who completes the transaction in accordance with their instructions.

closing agent The person or entity that coordinates the various closing activities, including the preparation and recordation of closing documents and the disbursement of funds. (May be referred to as an escrow agent or settlement agent in some jurisdictions.) Typically, the closing is conducted by title companies, escrow companies, or attorneys.

closing costs The upfront fees charged in connection with a mortgage loan transaction. Money paid by a buyer (and/or seller or other third party, if applicable) to effect the closing of a mortgage loan, generally including, but not limited to a loan origination fee, title examination and insurance, survey, attorney's fee, and prepaid items, such as escrow deposits for taxes and insurance.

closing date The date on which the sale of a property is to be finalized and a loan transaction completed. Often, a real estate sales professional coordinates the setting of this date with the buyer, the seller, the closing agent, and the lender.

co-borrower Any borrower other than the first borrower whose name appears on the application and mortgage note, even when that person owns the property jointly with the first borrower and shares liability for the note.

collateral An asset that is pledged as security for a loan. The borrower risks losing the asset if the loan is not repaid according to the terms of the loan agreement. In the case of a mortgage, the collateral would be the house and real property.

commission The fee charged for services performed, usually based on a percentage of the price of the items sold (such as the fee a real estate agent earns on the sale of a house).

commitment letter A binding offer from a lender that includes the amount of the mortgage, the interest rate, and repayment terms.

common area maintenance (CAM) Fees paid by tenants for the upkeep of areas designated as available for use by all tenants, such as lobbies, hallways, parking lots, or swimming pools and other recreational facilities in a residential community.

comparables An abbreviation for comparable properties, which are used as a comparison in determining the current value of a property that is being appraised.

concession Something given up or agreed to in negotiating the sale of a property. For example, the sellers may agree to help pay for closing costs.

construction loan A loan for financing the cost of construction or improvements to a property; the lender disburses payments to the builder at periodic intervals during construction.

contingency A condition that must be met before a contract is legally binding. For example, home purchasers often include a home inspection contingency; the sales contract is not binding unless and until the purchaser has the property inspected.

conventional mortgage A mortgage loan that is not insured or guaranteed by the federal government or one of its agencies, such as the Federal Housing Administration (FHA), the U.S. Department of Veterans Affairs (VA), or the Rural Housing Service (RHS). Contrast with *government mortgage.*

cost of funds index (COFI) An index that is used to determine interest rate changes for certain adjustable-rate mortgage (ARM) loans. It is based on the weighted monthly average cost of deposits, advances, and other borrowings of members of the Federal Home Loan Bank of San Francisco.

cost of occupancy Expenses required to assume and maintain occupancy, such as rent or mortgage payments, real estate taxes, and building repairs.

counter-offer An offer made in response to a previous offer. For example, after the buyer presents a first offer, the seller may make a counter-offer with a slightly higher sale price.

credit The ability of a person to borrow money or buy goods by paying over time. Credit is extended based on a lender's opinion of the personal financial situation and reliability, among other factors.

credit bureau A company that gathers information on consumers who use credit. These companies sell that information to lenders and other businesses in the form of a credit report.

credit history   Information in the files of a credit bureau, primarily comprised of a list of individual consumer debts and a record of whether or not these debts were paid back on time or as agreed. A credit history is called a credit report when provided by a *credit bureau* to a lender or other business.

credit report information   Provided by a *credit bureau* that allows a lender or other business to examine an individual's use of credit. It provides information on money borrowed from credit institutions and payment history.

credit score   A numerical value that ranks a borrower's credit risk at a given point in time based on a statistical evaluation of information in the individual's credit history that has been proven to be predictive of loan performance.

deed   The legal document transferring ownership or title to a property.

deed-in-lieu of foreclosure   The transfer of title from a borrower to the lender to satisfy the mortgage debt and avoid foreclosure. Also called a voluntary conveyance.

deed of trust   A legal document in which the borrower transfers the title to a third party (trustee) to hold as security for the lender. When the loan is paid in full, the trustee transfers title back to the borrower. If the borrower defaults on the loan, the trustee will sell the property and pay the lender the mortgage debt.

default   Failure to fulfill a legal obligation. A default includes failure to pay on a financial obligation but also may be a failure to perform some action or service that is non-monetary.

delinquency   Failure to make a payment when it is due. The condition of a loan when a scheduled payment has not been received by the due date, but generally used to refer to a loan for which payment is 30 or more days past due.

discount point   A fee paid by the borrower at closing to reduce the interest rate. A point equals 1 percent of the loan amount.

due diligence   Careful examination of a property, related documents, and procedures conducted by the potential lender or purchaser to ensure that consistent standards are applied and also to reduce risks.

due-on-sale clause   A provision in a mortgage that allows the lender to demand repayment in full of the outstanding balance if the property securing the mortgage is sold.

encumbrance   Any claim on a property, such as a *lien*, mortgage, or easement.

escrow   An item of value, money, or documents deposited with a third party to be delivered upon the fulfillment of a condition. For example, the deposit by a borrower with the lender of funds to pay taxes and insurance premiums when they become due, or the deposit of funds or documents with an attorney or escrow agent to be disbursed upon the closing of a sale of real estate.

escrow account   An account that a mortgage servicer establishes on behalf of a borrower to pay taxes, insurance premiums, or other charges when they are due. Sometimes referred to as an impound or reserve account.

escrow analysis   The accounting that a mortgage servicer performs to determine the appropriate balances for the escrow account, compute the borrower's monthly escrow payments, and determine whether any shortages, surpluses, or deficiencies exist in the account.

exchange   Tax-deferred trade of a like-kind property or business held as an investment, authorized under Section 1031 of the Internal Revenue Code. Capital gains taxes are deferred until the newly acquired property is disposed of in a taxable transaction.

exclusive right-to-sell listing   The traditional kind of listing agreement under which the property owner appoints a real estate broker (known as the listing broker) as exclusive agent to sell the property on the owner's stated terms and agrees to pay the listing broker a commission when the property is sold, regardless of whether the buyer is found by the broker, the owner, or another broker. This is the kind of listing agreement that is commonly used by a listing broker to provide the traditional full range of real estate brokerage services. If a second real estate broker (known as a selling broker) finds the buyer for the property, then some commission will be paid to the selling broker.

exclusive agency listing   A listing agreement under which a real estate broker (known as the listing broker) acts as an exclusive agent to sell the property for the property owner but may be paid a reduced or no commission when the property is sold if, for example, the property owner rather than the listing broker finds the buyer. This kind of listing agreement can be used to provide the owner a limited range of real estate brokerage services rather than the traditional full range. As with other kinds of listing agreements, if a second real estate broker (known as a selling broker) finds the buyer for the property, then some commission will be paid to the selling broker.

fair market value   The price at which property would be transferred between a willing buyer and willing seller, each of whom has a reasonable knowledge of all pertinent facts and is not under any compulsion to buy or sell.

fixed-period adjustable-rate mortgage   An adjustable-rate mortgage (ARM) that offers a fixed rate for an initial period, typically three to 10 years, and then adjusts every six months, annually, or at another specified period, for the remainder of the term. Also known as a *hybrid loan.*

fixed-rate mortgage   A mortgage with an interest rate that does not change during the entire term of the loan.

foreclosure   A legal action that ends all ownership rights in a home when the home buyer fails to make the mortgage payments or is otherwise in default under the terms of the mortgage.

forfeiture   The loss of money, property, rights, or privileges due to a breach of a legal obligation.

fully amortized mortgage   A mortgage in which the monthly payments are designed to retire the obligation at the end of the mortgage term.

general contractor   A person who oversees a home improvement or construction project and handles various aspects such as scheduling workers and ordering supplies.

good-faith estimate   A form required by the Real Estate Settlement Procedures Act (RESPA) that discloses an estimate of the amount or range of charges for specific settlement services the borrower is likely to incur in connection with the mortgage transaction.

government mortgage   A mortgage loan that is insured or guaranteed by a federal government entity such as the Federal Housing Administration (FHA), the U.S. Department of Veterans Affairs (VA), or the Rural Housing Service (RHS).

gross leasable area   Total floor area designated for tenant occupancy, including basements, mezzanines, and upper floors—the income-producing area in an investment property.

gross monthly income   The income earned in a month before taxes and other deductions. It may include rental income, self-employment income, income from alimony, child support, public assistance payments, and retirement benefits.

highest and best use   Reasonably probable and legal use for vacant land or improved property, resulting in the highest value.

home inspection   A professional inspection of a home to determine the condition of the property. The inspection should include an evaluation of the plumbing, heating, and cooling systems, roof, wiring, foundation, and pest inspection.

homeowner's insurance   A policy that protects a mortgage borrower and the lender from fire or flood that damages the structure of the house; a liability, such as an injury to a visitor to your home; or damage to personal property, such as furniture, clothes, or appliances.

homeowners' association   An organization of homeowners residing within a particular area whose principal purpose is to ensure the provision and maintenance of community facilities and services for the common benefit of the residents.

HUD-1 settlement statement   A final listing of the closing costs of the mortgage transaction. It provides the sales price and down payment, as well as the total settlement costs required from the buyer and seller.

hybrid loan   An adjustable-rate mortgage (ARM) that offers a fixed rate for an initial period, typically three to 10 years, and then adjusts every six months, annually, or at another specified period, for the remainder of the term.

income property   Real estate developed or purchased to produce income, such as a rental unit.

index   A number used to compute the interest rate for an adjustable-rate mortgage (ARM). The index is generally a published number or percentage, such as the average interest rate or yield on U.S. Treasury bills. A *margin* is added to the index to determine the interest rate that will be charged on the ARM. This interest rate is subject to any caps on the maximum or minimum interest rate that may be charged on the mortgage, stated in the note.

initial interest rate   The original interest rate for an adjustable-rate mortgage (ARM). Sometimes known as the start rate.

investment property   A property purchased to generate rental income, tax benefits, or profitable resale rather than to serve as the borrower's primary residence.

judgment lien   A *lien* on the property of a debtor resulting from the decree of a court.

jumbo loan   A loan that exceeds the mortgage amount eligible for purchase by Fannie Mae or Freddie Mac. Also called non-conforming loan.

junior mortgage A loan that is subordinate to the primary loan or first-lien mortgage loan, such as a *second* or third *mortgage.*

lease-purchase option An option sometimes used by sellers to rent a property to a consumer, who has the option to buy the home within a specified period of time. Typically, part of each rental payment is put aside for the purpose of accumulating funds to pay the down payment and closing costs.

LIBOR-index An index used to determine interest rate changes for certain adjustable-rate mortgage (ARM) plans, based on the average interest rate at which international banks lend to or borrow funds from the London Interbank Market.

lien A claim or charge on property for payment of a debt.

liquid asset A cash asset or an asset that is easily converted into cash.

loan origination The process by which a loan is made, which may include taking a loan application, processing and underwriting the application, and closing the loan.

loan origination fees Fees paid to a mortgage lender or broker for processing the mortgage application. This fee is usually in the form of points. One point equals 1 percent of the mortgage amount.

loan-to-value (LTV) ratio The relationship between the loan amount and the value of the property (the lower of appraised value or sales price), expressed as a percentage of the property's value. For example, a $100,000 home with an $80,000 mortgage has an LTV of 80 percent.

margin A percentage added to the index for an adjustable-rate mortgage (ARM) to establish the interest rate on each adjustment date.

market value The current value of a property home based on what a purchaser would pay. An appraisal is sometimes used to determine market value.

maturity date The date on which a mortgage loan is scheduled to be paid in full, as stated in the note.

merged credit report A credit report issued by a credit reporting company that combines information from two or three major credit bureaus.

modification Any change to the terms of a mortgage loan, including changes to the interest rate, loan balance, or loan term.

mortgage A loan using a home or property as collateral. In some states the term mortgage is also used to describe the document signed to grant the lender a *lien*. It also may be used to indicate the amount of money borrowed, with interest.

mortgage broker An individual or firm that brings borrowers and lenders together for the purpose of *loan origination*. A mortgage broker typically takes loan applications and may process loans. A mortgage broker also may close the loan.

mortgage insurance (MI) Insurance that protects lenders against losses caused by a borrower's default on a mortgage loan. MI typically is required if the borrower's down payment is less than 20 percent of the purchase price.

mortgage insurance premium (MIP) The amount paid by a borrower for *mortgage insurance,* either to a government agency such as the Federal Housing Administration (FHA) or to a private mortgage insurance (PMI) company.

mortgage lender The lender providing funds for a *mortgage.* Lenders also manage the credit and financial information review, the property and the loan application process through closing.

multiple listing service (MLS) A clearinghouse through which member real estate brokerage firms regularly and systematically exchange information on listings of real estate properties and share commissions with members who locate purchasers. The MLS for an area is usually operated by the local, private real estate association as a joint venture among its members designed to foster real estate brokerage services.

negative amortization An increase in the balance of a loan caused by adding unpaid interest to the loan balance; this occurs when the payment does not cover the interest due.

net worth The value of a company or individual's assets, including cash, less total liabilities.

offer A formal bid from the buyer to the seller to purchase a home or property.

original principal balance The total amount of principal owed on a *mortgage* before any payments are made.

owner financing A transaction in which the property seller provides all or part of the financing for the buyer's purchase of the property.

owner-occupied property A property that serves as the borrower's primary residence.

planned unit development (PUD) A real estate project in which individuals hold title to a residential lot and home while the common facilities are owned and maintained by a *homeowners' association* for the benefit and use of the individual PUD unit owners.

pre-approval A process by which a lender provides a prospective borrower with an indication of how much money he or she will be eligible to borrow when applying for a mortgage loan. This process typically includes a review of the applicant's credit history and may involve the review and verification of income and assets to close.

pre-qualification   A preliminary assessment by a lender of the amount it will lend to a potential home buyer. The process of determining how much money a prospective home buyer may be eligible to borrow before he or she applies for a loan.

prepayment penalty   A fee that a borrower may be required to pay to the lender, in the early years of a mortgage loan, for repaying the loan in full or prepaying a substantial amount to reduce the unpaid *principal* balance.

principal   The amount of money borrowed or the amount of the loan that has not yet been repaid to the lender.

property type   Classification of commercial real estate by its primary use: retail, industrial, office, or multifamily residential.

purchase and sale agreement   A document that details the price and conditions for a transaction. In connection with the sale of a residential property, the agreement typically would include: information about the property to be sold, sale price, down payment, earnest money deposit, financing, closing date, occupancy date, length of time the offer is valid, and any special contingencies.

qualifying ratios   Calculations that are used in determining the loan amount that a borrower qualifies for, typically a comparison of the borrower's total monthly income to monthly debt payments and other recurring monthly obligations.

quality control   A system of safeguards to ensure that loans are originated, underwritten, and serviced according to the lender's standards and, if applicable, the standards of the investor, governmental agency, or mortgage document.

real estate professional   An individual who provides services in buying and selling homes. The real estate professional is paid a percentage of the home sale price by the seller. Unless specifically contracted as a buyer's agent, the real estate professional represents the interest of the seller.

real estate investment   Trust investment vehicle in which investors purchase shares of ownership in a trust, which in turn invests in real property and distributes any profits to investors.

recorder   The public official who keeps records of transactions that affect real property in the area. Sometimes known as a Registrar of Deeds or County Clerk.

rescission   The cancellation or annulment of a transaction or contract by operation of law or by mutual consent. Borrowers have a right to cancel certain mortgage refinance and home equity transactions within three business days after closing, or for up to three years in certain instances.

rentable area   Computed area of a building as defined by guidelines of the Building Owners and Managers Association; typically measured in square feet—the actual square footage for which tenants pay rent.

right of first refusal   A provision in an agreement that requires the owner of a property to give another party the first opportunity to purchase or lease the property before he or she offers it for sale or lease to others.

sale-leaseback   A transaction in which the buyer leases the property back to the seller for a specified period of time.

sales comparison value   Estimate of a property's value by comparing the property being appraised to similar properties recently sold.

second mortgage   A *mortgage* that has a *lien* position subordinate to the first mortgage.

secondary mortgage market   The market in which mortgage loan and mortgage-backed securities are bought and sold.

servicing   The tasks a lender performs to protect the mortgage investment, including the collection of mortgage payments, escrow administration, and delinquency management.

settlement   The process of completing a loan transaction, at which time the mortgage documents are signed and then recorded, funds are disbursed, and the property is transferred to the buyer (if applicable). Also called *closing* or *escrow* in different jurisdictions.

single-family properties   One- to four-unit properties including detached homes, townhouses, condominiums, and cooperatives, and manufactured homes attached to a permanent foundation and classified as real property under applicable state law.

subordinate financing   Any *mortgage* or other *lien* with lower priority than the first mortgage.

survey   A precise measurement of a property by a licensed surveyor, showing legal boundaries of a property and the dimensions and location of improvements.

title   The right to, and the ownership of, property. A title or deed is sometimes used as proof of ownership of land.

title insurance Insurance that protects lenders and homeowners against legal problems with the title.

title search A check of the public records to ensure that the seller is the legal owner of the property and to identify any *liens* or claims against the property.

two- to four-family property A residential property that provides living space (dwelling units) for two to four families, although ownership of the structure is evidenced by a single deed; a loan secured by such a property is considered to be a single-family mortgage.

underwriting The process used to determine loan approval. It involves evaluating the property and the borrower's credit and ability to pay the *mortgage*.

useable area Rentable area, less common areas available to all tenants in an office building, such as corridors, storage facilities, or bathrooms—the area available for exclusive use of tenants.

walk-through A common clause in a sales contract that allows the buyer to examine the property being purchased at a specified time immediately before the closing, for example, within the 24 hours before closing.

zoning Designation of specific areas by a local planning authority for legally defined land use.

BIBLIOGRAPHY

There are many books about job searching. The following titles focus on careers in real estate, the job search strategy, resume writing, and how to effectively use the Internet for career research and job hunting. The following list is a representative sampling of currently available resources for individuals considering a career in real estate, or anyone who has recently started a career as a real estate sales agent or broker.

Allan, Jennifer. *Sell with Soul: The New Agent's Guide to an Extraordinary Career in Real Estate.* Bloomington, Ind.: AuthorHouse, 2007.

Bolles, Richard Nelson. *Job-Hunting on the Internet.* 4th Ed. Berkeley, Calif.: Ten Speed Press, 2005.

Cook, Frank. *21 Things I Wish My Broker Had Told Me: Practical Advice for New Real Estate Professionals.* Chicago: Dearborn Financial Publishing Inc., 2002.

Criscito, Pat, and Dee Funkhouser. *Interview Answers in a Flash.* Hauppauge, N.Y.: Barron's Educational Series, 2006.

Dawson, Roger. *Secrets of Power Negotiating.* 2nd Ed. Franklin Lakes, N.J.; Career Press, 2006.

Dikel, Margaret Riley, and Frances E. Roehm. *Guide to Internet Job Searching, 2008–2009.* New York: McGraw-Hill, 2006.

Edwards, Kenneth W. *Your Successful Real Estate Career.* New York: AMACOM—a division of American Management Association, 2007.

Fournier, Myra, and Jeff Spin. *Encyclopedia of Job-Winning Resumes.* Franklin Lakes, N.J.: Career Press, 2006.

Keim, Loren K. *The Fundamentals of Listing and Selling Commercial Real Estate.* West Conshohocken, Pa.: Infinity Publishing, 2007.

Kessler, Robin. *Competency-Based Interviews.* Franklin Lakes, N.J.: Career Press, 2006.

Miller, Norm, and Margot Weinstein. *Commercial Real Estate Career Education and Resource Guide.* North Palm Beach, Fla.: The Hoyt Institute of Real Estate, 2006.

Mintzner, Rich. *Start Your Career in Real Estate.* Newburgh, N.Y.: Entrepreneurial Media Inc., 2006.

Myers, Henry D. *The First Steps to Becoming a Real Estate Agent: An Insight to the Initial Costs of a Career in Real Estate.* I-Universe, 2008.

Oldman, Mark, and Samuel Hamadah. *The Internship Bible.* 10th ed. New York: Princeton Review, 2005.

Ross, Stan, and James Carberry. *The Insider's Guide to Careers in Real Estate.* Washington, D.C.: Urban Land Institute, 2006.

Russell, Dameon. *The ABC's of Prospecting: The Ultimate System for Every Real Estate Sales Professional.*

Zeller, Dirk. *The Champion Real Estate Agent.* New York: McGraw Hill, 2006.

INDEX